Tomruk engages the reader in a narrative that is contextually rich, guiding the audience through a journey, signposted by the lived experiences of couturiers that have shaped global culture. As a Practising couturier, I find her investigation as captivating, questioning the copyright laws which underpin the definition of artistic work, in consideration of Couture. The analysis compels a progressive unsettling, questioning the challenges of a closed list to a craft which at the highest level, produces artefacts. These visual timestamps mark the evolution of fashion history. The collective contribution of the design process, crafts people, and hand production give birth to a living breathing organism, a Couture garment. When married with innovation, it is a critique, reflection and response to society and a vision into the future.

Joshua Masih, *Senior Lecturer, UAL, London College of Fashion*

Couture Fashion Law

This book provides an insight into the legal workings of the most ostentatious fashion sector, Couture, whilst simultaneously advocating for stronger legal protection in this industry.

Offering an interdisciplinary approach, including art theory from Tolstoy and Rand amongst others, the book examines where Couture fashion sits within the law. Most significantly the book considers the couturier as an 'artist' and Couture as 'art' in relation to how this art form may be protected legally by copyright. Reflecting on contemporary issues, it analyses recent legal cases together with legislation, to provide awareness on the current position, and considers implications for the future by suggesting legal frameworks in pursuit of improvements. Using U.K. law as a case study, the book also comparatively assesses global fashion law, analysing the legal workings in the E.U. and the U.S.

The book will be of interest to researchers in the field of fashion law, copyright law, art, and intellectual property.

Tomruk Űstűnkaya is Associate Lecturer at the University of Surrey. Her academic pursuits over several years continue to cover core law subjects, in addition to intellectual property law. Tomruk has published a range of articles in peer-reviewed law journals, examining topics such as fashion law, law and technology (specifically 3D printing), and cultural property. This book is a fusion of her arts/fashion and legal background, culminating in a study which explores the relationship between the two.

Routledge Research in Fashion Law

Protecting Creativity in Fashion Design
US Laws, EU Design Rights, and Other Dimensions of Protection
Susanna Monseau

Artificial Intelligence, Design Law and Fashion
Hasan Kadir Yılmaztekin

Couture Fashion Law
Copyright and Artistic Works
Tomruk Űstűnkaya

For more information about this series, please visit *Routledge Research in Fashion Law – Book Series – Routledge & CRC Press*

Couture Fashion Law

Copyright and Artistic Works

Tomruk Űstűnkaya

Routledge
Taylor & Francis Group
LONDON AND NEW YORK

First published 2025
by Routledge
4 Park Square, Milton Park, Abingdon, Oxon OX14 4RN

and by Routledge
605 Third Avenue, New York, NY 10158

Routledge is an imprint of the Taylor & Francis Group, an informa business

British Library Cataloguing-in-Publication Data
A catalogue record for this book is available from the British Library

ISBN: 978-1-032-97508-5 (hbk)
ISBN: 978-1-032-98581-7 (pbk)
ISBN: 978-1-003-59945-6 (ebk)

DOI: 10.4324/9781003599456

Typeset in Times New Roman
by Apex CoVantage, LLC

This work is dedicated to my most beloved Yılmaz and Ece – eternally.

Contents

Illustrations

During 2021–2023 whilst compiling my research for this study, I felt as part of the process, it was important to visually study/examine Couture garments. Within this book, I include a collection of my illustrations as an additional feature of the research, accordingly.

Tables

Table of Cases

U.K.

Abraham Moon and Sons v Thornber [2012] E.W.P.C.C. 37
Alan Kenneth McKenzie v Associated Newspapers [1998] R.P.C. 261
Chiron v Murex (No 12) [1996] R.P.C. 535, 607
Creation Records Ltd v News Group Newspapers [1997] E.M.L.R. 444
Designers Guild Ltd v Russel Williams (Textiles) Ltd [1998] F.R. 803
George Hensher Ltd v Restawhile [1976] A.C. 64
Green v Broadcasting Corp, of New Zealand [1989] [1989] R.P.C. 700 Privy Council New Zealand
Green Lane Products Ltd v PMS International Group Ltd [2007] E.W.H.C. 1712
Harrods Ltd v Harrodian School Ltd [1996] R.P.C. 697
Hong Kong Fir Shipping Ltd v Kisen Kaisha Ltd (1962) E.W.C.A. Civ 7
Human Genome Sciences v Eli Lilly [2011] U.K.SC 51, [107]
Interlego v Tyco Industries [1987] F.S.R. 409
IRC v Muller and Co's Margarine [1901] A.C. 217
J Choo (Jersey) Ltd v Towerstone Ltd [2008] E.W.H.C. 346
Ladbroke v William Hill [1964] 1 All E.R. 465, 469
Lucasfilm Limited and others (Appellants) v Ainsworth and another (Respondents), [2011] U.K.SC 39
Magmatic Ltd v PMS International Ltd [2016] U.K.SC 12; [2016] 4 All E.R. 1027; [2016] 3 WLU.K. 280 (SC)
Neutrogena Corporation and Another [1996] R.P.C. 473
Norowzian v Arks [2000] F.S.R. 363
Pioneer Electronics Capital Inc v Warner Music Manufacturing Europe GmbH [1995] R.P.C. 487; [1995] 1 WLU.K. 464 (Ch D (Patents Ct))
Proctor & Gamble C v Reckitt Benckiser (U.K.) Ltd [2007] E.W.C.A. Civ 936; [2008] Bus.
Radley Gowns v Costas Syprou [1975] F.S.R. 455
Reckitt & Colman Products Ltd v Borden Inc (No.3) [1990] 1 W.L.R. 491; [1990] R.P.C. 341 HL
Redwood Music v Chappell [1982] R.P.C. 109, 120

Response Clothing Ltd v Edinburgh Woollen Mill Ltd [2020] E.W.H.C. 148 (IPE.Z.L.RC)
Schenck v Universal Balancing [2012] E.W.H.C. 1920, [86]
Shirin Guild v Eskandar [2001] (38) F.S.R. 645
Signature Realty Ltd v Fortis Developments Ltd and another [2016] E.W.H.C. 3583 (Ch)
Smith v Dryden & Ors [2021] E.W.H.C. 2277 (IPEC)
Temple Island Collection v New English Teas Ltd [2011] E.W.P.C.C. 19; [2012] F.S.R.
United Biscuits (U.K.) Ltd v Asda Stores Ltd [1997] R.P.C. 513

E.U.

Austretherm v Termo Organika, Case R 998/2013-3
Bezpečnostni softwarová asociace Case C-393/09 [2011] ECR I-13,971, [49]
Brompton Bicycle Ltd v Chedech/Get2Get (C-833/18)
Cofemel v G-Star Raw CV (C-683/17)
DOCERAM (C-395/16), E.U:C:2017:779
Eva-Maria Painer v Standard Verlags GmbH and Others Case C-145/10
Flashing Badge Co Ltd v Groves [2007] E.W.H.C. 1372
Flos SpA v Semeraro Casa e Famiglia SpA Case C-168/09
Football Association Premier League v QC Leisure and Karen Murphy v Media Protection Services, Joined cases C-403/08 and C-429/08 [2011] ECR I-9083 (ECJ, Grand Chamber)
Infopaq International A/S v Danske Dagblades Forening Case C-5/08
Komesoroff [1988] R.P.C.
KWS Saat AG v OHIM, Case 447/02P [2004] ECR I-10107
Libertel Groep BV v Benelux-Merkenbureau (C-104/01) E.U:C:2003:244; [2005] 2 CMLR. 45
Lindner (R-690/2007-3), 22 October 2009 at [42]
Louboutin v Van Haren Schoenen BV Case C-163/16
Max-Planck/BDPI phosphatase, T870/04 [2006] EPOR 14[6],[7], [21] Zymogenetics/Hematopoietic cytokine receptor, T 898/05 [2007] EPOR 2, [4]
Nichols v Registrar, Case C-404/02 [2004] ECRI-8499, [43]
Painer v Standard Verlags GmbH E.U:C:2011:798; [2012] E.C.D.R. 6
Peek & Cloppenburg v OHIM [2006] E.T.M.R. 35
Philips v Remington [2002] ECR Case C-299/99
SAS Institute Inc v World Programming Ltd, Case C-406/10 [2012] 3 CMLR. (4) 55,68, [AG44] (AG Bot)
SAS Institute Inc v World Programming Ltd, Case C-406/10 [2012] 3 CMLR. (4) 55,68, [AG44] (AG Bot)
Westwood v Knight [2010] E.W.P.C.C. 16
Windsurfing International v Taylor Marine (1985) R.P.C. 59 (CA)
Windsurfing v Chiemsee [1999] ECR at para 25 Cases 108/97
Winward Industries, Radio Watch Co Ltd, Joined cases C-53/01, C-54/01C-55/01 [2003] ECRI-3161

Italy

Casucci spa v Unipol Sai Assicurazione unreported 29 May 2020 (It Cass (I))

U.S.

Baker v Selden, 101 U.S. 99, 102 (1879)
Burke v Margot Burke Ltd. v Spicers Dress Designs Ltd. [1936] Ch.D. 400
Central District of California, Case No. CV 21–4402-MWF (SHK) [2022] at 1011
Christian Louboutin v Yves Saint Laurent AM Holding Inc., No. 11–3303 (2d Cir. 2013)
Corinna Warm and Studio Warm LLC v Innermost Ltd. et al, United States District Court
Louboutin v Yves Saint Laurent 696 F. 3d 206 (5 September 2012)
Merchandising Corporation of America Inc v Harpbond Ltd [1983] F.S.R. 32
Qualitex Co v Jacobson Products Co 514 U.S. 159 at 162; 115 S. Ct 1300; 131 L. Ed. 2d 248 (1995)
Star Athletica v Varsity Brands Inc 799 F.3d 468 (2015) (6th Cir (US))
Veeck v Southern Blg. Code Cong. Int'l, Inc. 293 F 3rd 791, 793 (5th Circuit 2002)

Preface

Background and Problem

The purpose of this thesis is to determine whether Couture should be included within s.4 of the CDPA 1988 as an artistic work, since the CDPA operates as a closed list system.[1] Currently, there is a limited list of types of artistic works in the U.K. copyright legislation (s.4 of the CDPA 1988). This comprises of graphic work, photograph, sculpture or collage, a work of architecture being a building or a model for a building or a work of artistic craftsmanship.[2] Further, the extent to which Couture can be described as a work of artistic craftmanship shall be deliberated throughout the study. The thesis aims to examine the extent to which Couture can be defined as such, for the purpose of being regarded as an artistic work.[3] Couture garments acknowledge the interlink between 'artistic' and 'technicality' particularly within an industrial contextualisation; it is therefore observed that both components are integral to Couture and exist in unison.[4] The process for creativity of Couture must include and integrate technical features to enable the functionality for the garment. On this basis, it is argued that copyright legislation must be extended to include Couture garments specifically (the end-product) for the purpose of protecting Couture as an artistic work within s.4 of the CDPA 1988. This is due to Couture being derived from art and artistic processes. It is observed that Couture garments fall outside of the scope of an artistic work, according to the apparent closed list system the U.K. adheres to, and copyright is regarded as 'restrictive' on this basis.[5] In a wider context, the U.K. is a signatory to the Berne Convention whereby Article 2 protects literary and artistic works, although this point will be examined regarding the extent to which Couture is considered as an artistic work in law within the thesis.[6]

The overriding legal issue for the study is that *fashion* as subject matter has neither acquired adequate *nor* specific acknowledgement within the existing IP

1 Rosie Burbridge, *European Fashion Law* (Edward Elgar 2019) 58
2 S.4 CDPA 1988
3 S.4 CDPA 1988, artistic works are categorised into a graphic work, photograph, sculpture or collage, a work of architecture being a building or a model for a building and a work of artistic craftsmanship
4 Marco Pedroni and Paolo Volanté, 'Art Seen From Outside: Non-Artistic Legitimation Within the Field of Fashion Design' (2014) 43 Poetics 102–19
5 Rosie Burbridge, *European Fashion Law* (Edward Elgar 2019) 58
6 The Berne Convention for the Protection of Literary and Artistic Works 1886, Article 2 (1)

framework, although more pertinent to this study is the absence of legal protection within the closed list of artistic works under s.4 of the CDPA 1988 for Couture fashion. The study focuses on Couture specifically, and not mass-produced fashion generally. This study identifies Couture as the most significant category of fashion as it relates to the market level, due to Couture having a substantial influence on the market levels below it, such as high street brands. These high street brands interpret the Couture designs to influence production of cost-efficient derivatives.[7] It is for these reasons that the study raises concerns for Couture being excluded from the closed list copyright system.[8] A derivative issue lies directly within the concept of labour (exerted by the author of the work), and therefore the incorporeal relationship between the creator (author) and the creation, and the extent to which this relationship is acknowledged and valued within the U.K. legal provisions.

The quest for restraints on the expansion of copyright protected works raises arguments echoing a sentiment that copyright may 'stifle the creativity that law is designed to foster.'[9] Without any specific legal provisions available to protect Couture in U.K. law, the view from this study is that any further limitations placed on the expansion of copyright may leave couturiers and their creations vulnerable to exploitation. For this reason, the perspective of this thesis is based on the theoretical approach to the process of creation (from the conceptual idea through to the end-product), holding value, and therefore artistic works should be protected and rewarded based on the intellectual creative expression and labour exerted by the author. This argument is supported historically through Locke's property theory related to labour:

> [y]et every man has a property in his own person . . . the labour of his body, and the work of his hands, we may say, are properly his.[10]

In application of Locke's theory to this study, it appears that property, as a concept, never truly departs from the author. In contrast to Locke's labour theory, it is suggested that labour and the products derived from it are not necessarily owned by the person, as 'labour is an abstract entity or process.'[11] This is of significance in understanding the incorporeal relationship between the creator, the creation (the end-product), and further, in consideration of a third party wishing to use or

7 Fashion Addicted, 'Does Haute Couture Affect High Street Style?' (*Fashion Addicted*, 13 January 2014) https://duncanozann.wordpress.com/2014/01/13/does-haute-couture-affect-high-street-style/ accessed 26 March 2022

8 Rosie Burbridge, *European Fashion Law* (Edward Elgar 2019) 58

9 Rebecca Tushnet, 'Brief of Copyright Scholars as Amici Curiae in Support of the Petitioner' (*SSRN*, 14 January 2020) https://ssrn.com/abstract=3519378> or <http://dx.doi.org/10.2139/ssrn.3519378> referring to *Campbell v Acuff–Rose Music, Inc.*, 510 U.S. 569, 577 (1994)

10 Laurence Houlgate, *Understanding John Locke: The Smart Student's Guide to Locke's Second Treatise of Government* (Houlgate Books 2017) 66

11 Roger T Simonds, *Rational Individualism: The Perennial Philosophy of Legal Interpretation* (Brill 1995) 215

acquire some aspect of the original creation for his own advantage.[12] The analysis for this study, therefore, requires the balancing of the undeniable limitations related to monopoly considerations against the extent copyright may, and should, protect Couture.

Research Questions

Primary Questions

Should copyright legislation widen the criterion of 'artistic works' in s.4 of the Copyright Designs and Patents Act 1988 (CDPA) to include Couture fashion garments, which may be defined as inherently technical and as a conceptual work of art simultaneously?[13]

Secondary research questions: To what extent is Couture defined as art, in law?

a. Are the limitations in copyright justified in Couture, as for other subject matter, in consideration of the exclusion of Couture from s.4 of the CDPA 1988?
b. Should the limitations of copyright to technical features be prevented from encroaching upon the artistic components of Couture, in consideration of the extent that protection is affected?
c. To what degree does the doctrine of functionality apply to Couture, and what are the implications?

Objectives and Arguments

The thesis aims to recognise the extent of the problem, and further intends to outline a balanced approach to Couture in copyright law for the future. Currently, whilst scholarly work in fashion law exists, this study provides for an original contribution by focusing on Couture specifically. This is achieved by examining two major themes which are firstly, the evaluation of Couture in determining and defining it as art, in law. This aspect particularly aims to highlight the disparity between industry definitions and the law. Secondly, the work is original to the extent that it furthers existing discussions in 'fashion law,' although in addition, it adds generally to the existing body of work regarding the impact of technical limitations in copyright law. This is significant not only to unearth the implications for Couture, but it may also widen future scholarly discussions pertaining to other subject matter in copyright.

The intersection between design rights and copyright is examined to understand the relationship between the two intellectual property (IP) rights, but moreover to provide clarity in distinction between the two. This is of notable importance

12 Laurence Houlgate, *Understanding John Locke: The Smart student's Guide to Locke's Second Treatise of Government* (Houlgate Books 2017) 66

13 S.4 Copyright Designs and Patents Act 1988 (CDPA 1988)

for the study as it provides a justification for the study being primarily concerned with the problem in copyright and not design rights. Design rights are concerned with the appearance and shape of a product, whereas s.4 of the CDPA 1988 considers an artistic work.[14]

Copyright law has developed a set of requirements, one of which is that works must be original; however, to satisfy this, functionality must be considered in relation to the extent of creative contribution to the work. It is for this reason that the doctrine of functionality is examined to determine the extent to which this impacts the possibility of acquiring copyright protection for Couture garments and whether the reason for the application of the doctrine is justified. E.U. case law particularly illustrates the implications of functionality within the case of *Bezpečnostni Softwarová Asociace* (*BSA*), which concerned the technical workings of the 'graphic user interface.'[15] The Court of Justice of the European Union (CJEU) held that originality was absent when the technical function dictated the expression.[16] It is hereby observed that the principle for copyright law is that a work must be original, technical components shall render the work functional, and therefore the work may potentially be regarded as being absent in originality, in law. As expressed earlier, Couture works comprise of technical features for the purposes of enabling functionality for the garment, and therefore examination of the disparity between the doctrine of functionality and legal requirements for the grant of copyright is a major part of the study and the original argument in the thesis.

Contemporary Issues, Questions, and Developments

The case of *Cofemel* is an instrumental feature of the study and has been analysed to clarify the E.U. position on copyright in relation to the author's intellectual creation. Moreover, it was essential to consider 'artistic' for the purposes of copyright; a dispute of copyright infringement over the design of clothing was at issue.[17] This is significant in relation to the thesis question for this book, as it echoes the aim of the research in striking a balance between the application of copyright, the limitations as they relate to technical features, and the justifications rooted in competition concerns for those limitations. More recently, in 2020 the case of *Brompton Bicycle Ltd* concerned the design of a bicycle, whose shape is necessary to obtain a technical

14 The focus of a design right on the other hand, is the appearance and shape of a product. Firstly, if Couture is to be defined as an artistic work, it is effectively more than a product, and moreover the appearance and shape (which a design right is concerned with) is an element of the art, not the entire art form. The study, at the heart of the thesis (Chapter 4) shall consider the definition of art and the relationship between Couture and copyright

15 *Bezpečnostni Softwarová Asociace* Case C-393/09 [2011] ECR I-13971 [49]

16 L Bentley and others, *Intellectual Property Law* (6th edn, Oxford University Press 2022) 108 referring to *Bezpečnostni Softwarová Asociace*, Case C-393/09 [2011] ECR I-13,971, [49]

17 *Cofemel v G-Star Raw CV* (C-683/17) AG3

function; this was held to be capable of attracting copyright.[18] Therefore, although copyright issues are mainly deliberated in law pertaining to two key aspects, technical function and artistry, both are reliant on more complex issues when considering the grant of copyright protection. For instance, technical function is dependent upon competition concerns as they relate to monopolies within the market; artistry is dependent upon the originality qualification, although it is argued that within fashion, both functional and artistic attributes co-exist as an intrinsic form. The thesis argues on both counts for Couture, to suggest possible developments and remedies for the reform of the CDPA 1988. The approach to artistic works is considered throughout the study by a comparative analysis between the E.U., U.K., France, the U.S., and Tűrkiye. A summary of the different approaches to copyright is noted.

Methodological Framework and Approach

A mixed method approach is followed to enrich the study in understanding the problems raised, specifically by evaluating the results and validating inferences gained.[19] The thesis engages in research from both primary and secondary legal sources. Primary research is conducted using legislative provisions and case law, while secondary research provides information from scholarly text, journal articles, books, and reports. International legislation such as the Berne Convention and the Agreement on Trade-Related Aspects of Intellectual Property Rights (TRIPS) are used to illustrate and provide the reader with an understanding of the wider legislative considerations on an international basis. Both primary and secondary sources of information in combination provide for an invaluable insight into the legal position regarding copyright protection for Couture. The study uses doctrinal, empirical, and comparative law research methods, and these are discussed next.

Doctrinal Research

The doctrinal research methodology within this thesis is implemented through a thorough textual analysis of statute and case law. The doctrinal research method has been defined as '[t]he research process used to identify, analyse and synthesise the content of law.'[20] Further, it is established that the term 'doctrinal' refers to the 'quality' of legal rules due to their consistency, slow and organic evolution[21] and function of ascertaining what the law is.[22] In relation to how the doctrinal process is

18 *Brompton Bicycle Ltd v Chedech/Get2Get* (C-833/18) Opinion of Advocate General M. Campos Sánchez-Bordona, E.U:C:2020:79

19 Jose F Molina-Azorin, 'Mixed Methods Research: An Opportunity to Improve Our Studies and Our Research Skills' (2016) 25(2) European Journal of Management and Business Economics 37–8

20 Terry Hutchinson, Dawn Watkins and Mandy Burton, *Research Methods in Law* (2nd edn, Routledge 2018) 384

21 Terry Hutchinson, Dawn Watkins and Mandy Burton, *Research Methods in Law* (2nd edn, Routledge 2018) 384 referring to

22 Martin Dixon, 'A Doctrinal Approach to Property Law Scholarship: Who Cares and Why' (2014) 3 Property Law Review 160

affected, the system necessitates the evaluation of legislative processes, provisions, and case law.[23] This is for the purpose of amalgamating the pertinent components to determine the account of law within a specific contextual framework.[24] Although this research method attempts to provide a precise statement of the law, legal reasoning considers judgements relating to appeals, setting and overriding precedent.[25] It is suggested that legislation and regulatory provisions can seldom establish the outcome of legal problems.[26]

This method analyses the written principles of the law, and the focus, therefore, is to lessen the emphasis on the application or effect of the law, but to state and illustrate the position as it is. The thesis attempts to analyse and synthesise U.K. copyright law and examine the changes in the law to accommodate intellectual creative expression for Couture. The examination of the CDPA 1988 is analysed in depth throughout the study but most specifically in chapters 4 and 5. The doctrinal approach is consistently used when examining the legislative provisions of the E.U., France, Tűrkiye, and the U.S.

The emphasis shifts in chapter 5 to the issue of the functionality doctrine by considering technical features within creative works. This supports the use of the doctrinal approach through the analysis of statute and case law. This is for the purpose of ascertaining the reasoning for the application of the legal rule and principle of the functionality doctrine.[27] As expressed earlier, as the doctrinal approach can rarely determine the outcome of a legal problem, case law will inevitably accompany the body of research.

Empirical Research

Empirical law is defined as determining how the law operates.[28] Although there are subdivisions in empirical legal research such as empirically orientated law, economics, and judicial behaviour/politics, the research contained within this study uses the socio legal methodology.[29] Whilst this type of empirical research engages in the legal discipline, in essence, it is multi-disciplinary in nature with strong ties to sociological components.[30] Empirical methodology is significant for the study as the

23 Terry Hutchinson, Dawn Watkins and Mandy Burton, *Research Methods in Law* (2nd edn, Routledge 2018) 393

24 Terry Hutchinson, Dawn Watkins and Mandy Burton, *Research Methods in Law* (2nd edn, Routledge 2018) 393

25 Please see Terry Hutchinson, Dawn Watkins and Mandy Burton, *Research Methods in Law* (2nd edn, Routledge 2018) 513 referring to Hofheinz

26 Terry Hutchinson, Dawn Watkins and Mandy Burton, *Research Methods in Law* (2nd edn, Routledge 2018) 521

27 Amrit Kharel, 'Doctrinal Legal Research', 10.2139/ssrn.3130525

28 Peter Cane and Herbert M Kritzer, *The Oxford Handbook on Empirical Legal Research* (Oxford University Press 2010)

29 Peter Cane and Herbert M Kritzer, *The Oxford Handbook on Empirical Legal Research* (Oxford University Press 2010)

30 Peter Cane and Herbert M Kritzer, *The Oxford Handbook on Empirical Legal Research* (Oxford University Press 2010) 323

cultural and social context of fashion must be understood, appreciated, and identified as a valuable part of the creative process, if the law is to be applied adequately.

How the law operates is analysed through establishing an understanding of the workings of the law, in both the U.K. and the jurisdictions previously mentioned. Various sources are examined, including information through the British Fashion Council for the U.K. and for France, the Fédération de la Haute Couture et de la Mode.[31] The main legal sources are dependent upon the U.K. CDPA 1988, the US Copyright Act 1976, Article L.112–2.73 of the French Code de la propriété intellectuelle,[32] and the Tűrkiye *Fikir ve Sanat Eserleri Kanunu 5486* (the code).[33] On this basis, the study aims to generate new contextual information pertaining to copyright protection of Couture, specifically.[34]

Comparative Law

A comparative law examination is applied in this thesis, as it examines the differences of law in different jurisdictions.[35] Comparative law is not restricted by specific legal text pertaining to a particular issue; instead the 'realities of law' as it operates within the country in question are examined. The findings from the analysis will then provide the information as it pertains to the similarities and differences.[36] Although the viewpoint of this thesis comes from the U.K. perspective, due to the recent Brexit implementation, the study examines other jurisdictional approaches to fashion to ascertain the current position for the U.K. in copyright and further consider possible developments for the near future. This is achieved through a global appreciation approach for laws in other jurisdictions such as France, Tűrkiye, and the U.S. (both Tűrkiye and the U.S. are outside of the E.U. and therefore provide insight for the U.K.'s newfound independent position, when examined from the viewpoint of Brexit). Further, whilst interest in Tűrkiye for the study originally derives from the industrial manufacturing aspect, as it is regarded as a 'hub for fashion manufacture,'[37] the study has developed the appreciation for the Turkish legal system regarding fashion creation.

31 Federation de la haute Couture et de la mode, 'Federation' *(Federation de la haute Couture et de la mode,* 2021) <https://www.fhcm.paris/en> accessed 8 May 2021

32 Article L112-2 - Code de la propriété intellectuelle

33 Turkish legislation: Fikir ve Sanat Eserleri Kanunu 5486. Please also see Gurulkan Çakir, 'Copyright Protection' (*Gurulkan Çakir*, 2021) <https://www.gurulkan.com/doing-business-in-Tűrkiye/copyright-protection> accessed 31 December 2021

34 Emily Hudson and Andrew Kenyon, *Intellectual Property Law and Empirical Research From Part III: Across Disciplines* (Cambridge University Press Online 27 March 2020)

35 Uwe Kischel, *Comparative Law* (Oxford University Press 2019)

36 Uwe Kischel, *Comparative Law* (Oxford University Press 2019)

37 Please see: Fashion United, 'Fashion Statistics Turkey' (*Fashion United*, 2016) <https://fashionunited.com/statistics/turkey> accessed 17 October 2024 and in 2021, the value of exported textiles from Tűrkiye is estimated to be USD 15.2 billion, please see: Zeynep Dierks, 'Value of Textile Exports From Turkey 2000–2022' (*Statista*, 2024) <https://www.statista.com/statistics/880470/textile-trade-exports-turkey/> accessed 17 October 2024

The approach to *haute Couture* in France (as a member of the E.U.) shall be examined for the purposes of examining the cultural value it places on fashion and specifically, supported by Article L.112–2.73 of the Code de la propriété intellectuelle. Aside, the law of Tűrkiye shall be examined for the purposes of analysing the approach to the concept of fashion; the *Fikir ve Sanat Eserleri Kanunu* shall form the basis for the position of Tűrkiye.[38] Finally, the position of the U.S. shall be examined due to the vast scholarly literature available on the subject and the seminal decision in *Star Athletica LLC v Varsity Brands Inc.*[39] This case introduced the aspect of 'separability,' which granted the images on cheerleader uniforms copyright protection, although not the uniform *per se* due to the utilitarian (use) nature it possesses. The concept of separability shall be analysed in consideration of the current position in copyright in the U.K., with inferences drawn for Couture.

The prevalence of a qualitative research methodology is integral to this study, supported by the view of 'qualitative methods, which are methodically more in keeping with legal doctrinal scholarship and more amenable to a complex, multi-layered world view.'[40] The study is not only multi-disciplinary, but also requires a multi-layered view of the issues involved to achieve unearthing of the relevant information to satisfy both the primary and secondary research questions.

Addressing the Criticisms of the Methodology

Legal systems must be amalgamated within the behavioural forms of the society for the purposes of establishing an effective process for law.[41] The complications relating to the current study specifically arise through ascertaining the societal characteristics as it relates to the culture of Couture, and as to how this may impact the success of the legal system within the individual jurisdiction. Most significantly, the issue of measuring the success of the law is imperative in determining the position for each country being examined in relation to the U.K. legal system. Although, it is recognised that this may be difficult to establish for other countries due to differences whereby legal scholars may be familiar with the legal system of their own country but not necessarily so with foreign jurisdictions.[42] The identification of legal issues is often the starting point for the comparisons to be made, irrespective of appearing 'unscientific' or individualistic.[43] It is these considerations which open avenues for further research in contemplation of the legal contribution

38 Fikir ve Sanat Eserleri Kanunu 5846, 1951

39 *Star Athletica LLC v Varsity Brands Inc 799 F. 3d 468 (2015) (6th Cir (US))*

40 Alisiya Blackham, 'When Law and Data Collide: The Methodological Challenge of Conducting Mixed Methods Research in Law' (2022) 49(S1) Journal of Law and Society

41 Mike McConville and Wing Chui, *Research Methods for Law* (Edinburgh 2007) 92

42 Mike McConville and Wing Chui, *Research Methods for Law* (Edinburgh 2007) 93

43 Mike McConville and Wing Chui, *Research Methods for Law* (Edinburgh 2007) 93

to the issue within each jurisdiction.[44] Chapter 3 is the heart of the book, as it specifically forms the foundation for the research relating to the definition of art and the extent to which Couture is art. This may at first instance enhance the philosophical theories perspective of what art is and further demonstrates an individualistic approach to the study; however, it is a crucial step in answering the primary and secondary research questions.[45] Further, for the purposes of understanding the U.K. copyright law and cultural outlook in relation to Couture, it has been necessary to consider the international approaches to Couture and art, and whether there is scope for development within the U.K. system.

Regarding mixed method research, Freshwater is known to have been concerned of mixed method research in relation to a non-critical stance on this methodology.[46] The apprehension derives from the impact regarding how it is 'located, positioned, presented, and perpetuated.'[47] The request put forward by Freshwater is that researchers using a mixed method approach should assume in essence 'incompleteness.'[48] Creswell recognises that this view by Freshwater is essentially encouraging researchers to be inquisitive and to acknowledge the 'messiness' of the mixed method approach in recognition of its 'adolescence.'[49] With these criticisms expressed, the argument raised in this thesis is that the nature of the study would dictate the suitability of the research method. For example, this study would seemingly fail to satisfy the research question if only one type of methodology were applied. The use of multiple methodologies addresses various aspects of the research question and is therefore necessary to generate the relevant findings. Whilst the rhetoric surrounding a mixed method approach may be justified for some scholarly work as being a method which is 'incomplete,' it may serve as a dichotomy whereby the use of varying research methodologies completes the information gap which the other research method cannot answer. For this reason, the perspective from this thesis is that the mixed method research method is suitable to a research subject which is at its very core nuanced, and therefore requires a nuanced research methodology approach.

Comparative law research relating to legislation and the common law is expressed cautiously.[50] This is for the purpose of avoiding undermining the facts with assumptions regarding the translation efficacy pertaining to the doctrines.[51] Further, an advantage of researching the common law is that common law

44 Mike McConville and Wing Chui, *Research Methods for Law* (Edinburgh 2007) 93

45 See chapters 3 and 5, 4

46 John W Creswell, *Research Design: Qualitative, Quantitative, and Mixed Methods Approaches* (Sage 2018) 277

47 John W Creswell, *Research Design: Qualitative, Quantitative, and Mixed Methods Approaches* (Sage 2018) 277

48 John W Creswell, *Research Design: Qualitative, Quantitative, and Mixed Methods Approaches* (Sage 2018) 277

49 John W Creswell, *Research Design: Qualitative, Quantitative, and Mixed Methods Approaches* (Sage 2018) 278; Tashakkori and Teddlie, 2003

50 Mike McConville and Wing Chui, *Research Methods for Law* (Edinburgh 2007) 94

51 Mike McConville and Wing Chui, *Research Methods for Law* (Edinburgh 2007) 94

scholarship tends to place emphasis on the facts.[52] With that said, the incorporation of imagination into legal scholarly research is regarded as a 'virtue' that is rooted in a measured approach which facilitates conceptual perspectives of the law.[53] The rationale of the common law perspective is greatly dependant on 'persuasiveness.' Practical examples are the judge providing a ratio decidendi and a barrister persuading the judge of the validity of their argument.[54] McConville and Chui argue that common law scholarship pertaining to legal practice should actively foster imagination in comparative research, as it is said to unveil the character and mechanisms of international legal systems.[55] Although, criticism of using imaginative comparative law relates to the degree of quantifiable information, since the foundation of imagination can be both 'unpredictable' and 'open-ended.'[56] In consideration of the thesis and information generated through drawing inferences, the nuanced and novel issues which arise in consideration of the legal components dictate that the comparative analysis must be taken proportionately, and the information generated from it is addressed in view of providing a global appreciation. This method is used to circumvent undermining the study, and ultimately digressing from the main issue of examining Couture as an artistic work as listed by s.4 of the CDPA 1988.[57]

The extent of the comparative research approach has not been used in full due to the criticisms that are explored. Although it is understood that comparative law extends beyond comparison of the legal doctrines in different countries,[58] the focus of the study is not solely regarding the different doctrinal legal applications in each jurisdiction. The study considers the cultural approaches to fashion and the impact upon the legal systems in focus. On this basis, in consideration of the cultural influences and approach to art, the analysis of the different legal system approaches within each jurisdiction is considered as potential persuasive legal authority. Further, based on those legal systems, the study considers whether the potential exists for the U.K. to draw influence and reform existing copyright legislation.[59]

Research methods used for the heart of the thesis (chapter 3) rely on research concepts appropriate to art and design.[60] Research methodology combining practical application has only been examined within the last 20 years.[61] The absence of a clear methodological framework has directed art and design researchers to adopt methods used in the social sciences.[62] Gray and Malins express that the position has effectively meant that researchers in art and design either use a 'standard'

52 Mike McConville and Wing Chui, *Research Methods for Law* (Edinburgh 2007) 95
53 Mike McConville and Wing Chui, *Research Methods for Law* (Edinburgh 2007) 97
54 Mike McConville and Wing Chui, *Research Methods for Law* (Edinburgh 2007) 98
55 Mike McConville and Wing Chui, *Research Methods for Law* (Edinburgh 2007) 98
56 Mike McConville and Wing Chui, *Research Methods for Law* (Edinburgh 2007) 98
57 See chapters 3 and 7, 5, 6
58 Mike McConville and Wing Chui, *Research Methods for Law* (Edinburgh 2007) 92
59 Mike McConville and Wing Chui, *Research Methods for Law* (Edinburgh 2007) 92
60 Carole Gray and Julian Malins, 'Research Procedures/Methodology for Artists & Designers' (1993)
61 Carole Gray and Julian Malins, 'Research Procedures/Methodology for Artists & Designers' (1993)
62 Carole Gray and Julian Malins, 'Research Procedures/Methodology for Artists & Designers' (1993) Referring to (Malins, 1993)

methodology, which is not ideal as it could misrepresent the findings, or they will be at risk of using obscure methods that may result in being too precise (relative) to the research project.[63] It is suggested that art design necessitates a 'distinctive approach' that is equal in rigour and accountability and is just as respectable as other research methods used in the social sciences.[64] By and large, analysis drawn on art/design history provides a wealth of 'esoteric' and 'idiosyncratic' material for the way in which the artist/designer works.[65] It is further suggested that the usual science research model, whereby the specific is observed and applied generally, cannot be applied to creative works which are derived through idiosyncratic and random creation methods and will inevitably result in art being 'unique/original.'[66] Whilst this aspect resonates strongly with the research, the disconnect between the law and art has highlighted the necessity for a more nuanced research approach. It is necessary, therefore, to acknowledge that the methodology for the research must reflect the multi-disciplinary nature of the study, but also the fusion of the couturiers' intellectual creative expression (art) with the precise technical requirements necessary to achieve the function of the garment. Moreover, some aspects of Couture can be analysed through the usual social sciences research methods; this is seen within the analysis of the doctrine of functionality, most pertinently a distinction from research on traditional forms of art. For the most part, the study of Couture must consider the integrated functional components as part of the art. For this reason, whilst this opinion is true and does apply to Couture, it cannot apply wholly, due to the implementation of the functionality considerations.[67] The thesis has applied a more varied and nuanced approach to the study and essentially used the social sciences research methods to conduct the study where applicable.

The research method for this study embraces the idiosyncrasy of art with the more precise application of the law. This has resulted in the research methodology application combining the *exclusive* with the *general* scientific methods. The resulting method for this study is identified as refined, and ironically specific to research Couture. This method is supported by the post-modern recommendations by Gray and Malins for research methodology for art and design whereby simultaneously acceptance and critical discussion is articulated.[68] Additionally, traditional and revolutionary views and findings acknowledge the historical position whilst embracing futuristic innovative concepts.[69] The criticism of this method from the perspective of this study is that it does not provide for a precise conclusion and therefore is open to discussion. With that said, the findings presented within this thesis aim to form the basis to narrow down the discussion in identifying Couture as art.

63 Carole Gray and Julian Malins, 'Research Procedures/Methodology for Artists & Designers' (1993)
64 Carole Gray and Julian Malins, 'Research Procedures/Methodology for Artists & Designers' (1993)
65 Carole Gray and Julian Malins, 'Research Procedures/Methodology for Artists & Designers' (1993)
66 Carole Gray and Julian Malins, 'Research Procedures/Methodology for Artists & Designers' (1993)
67 Carole Gray and Julian Malins, 'Research Procedures/Methodology for Artists & Designers' (1993)
68 Carole Gray and Julia Malins, 'Research Procedures/Methodology for Artists & Designers' (1993) (Referring to Rayworth, 1993)
69 Carole Gray and Julian Malins, 'Research Procedures/Methodology for Artists & Designers' (1993)

A post-modern methodology is acknowledged as fostering 'cross-cultural collaboration.'[70] This thesis embraces the cross-cultural concept, not only in art, but also in disciplines, that being 'art and law.' For this reason, a post-modern methodology is the most appropriate in investigation, analysis, and presentation of the findings pertinent to this nuanced study. Whilst Feyerabend's opinion is that anarchism substitutes rationalism, this thesis would argue that the most appropriate methodology for a multi-disciplined/multi-cultural study is to find a synthesis between the two positions as neither would benefit the study wholly, and furthermore one alone would risk polarisation of the findings. Due to this, the position of the thesis in implementation of the post-modernism methodology takes an equal measure of anarchism alongside logical and independent thought for the purposes of responding to the creative pursuit of Couture and the structure of the law simultaneously.

Post-modernism in the social sciences is suggested to be divisive as it fails to provide for an exact resolution or be discharged, continuously cultivating arguments that cannot be determined easily.[71] Moderate post-modernism (a version of post-modernism) is suggested to provide rigour and is absent in rigidity.[72] This point supports the nature of the study which aims to provide arduous arguments for why Couture is art, inviting the reader, the lawyer, the couturier, and the student to deliberate over the conceptual themes put forward throughout this thesis, in consideration of, and through, legal and creative perspectives simultaneously.

The study is not intended to provide rigid arguments, but to present the philosophical views on art and how Couture satisfies these conceptions, if at all. Through the same lens, the study aims to present the legal developments particularly in relation to intellectual creative expression, and the application of judicial decisions for works of such a nature. Post-modernism as a research method relating to philosophy is identified as 'decidedly celebratory' regarding the 'demise of the project of the Enlightenment.'[73] The perspective of this thesis on this post-modern era mindset speaks to a shift in early reasoning and provides a platform for a wide discussion whereby views can be formed through the thorough evaluation of materials sourced. This in turn echoes art, art as a subjective notion which provides the observer with autonomy over reasoning, opinions, and perspectives. Further, the method provides space for deliberation to a greater extent, which allows more time for the reader to form nuanced perspectives prior to conclusions being reached.

70 Carole Gray and Julian Malins, 'Research Procedures/Methodology for Artists & Designers' (1993) (referring to Paul Feyerabend 'Against Method' (1988))

71 Simon Susen, *The 'Postmodern Turn' in the Social Sciences* (Palgrave Macmillan 2015)

72 Christine O'Leary, 'Postmodernism as a Theoretical Framework for Learner Autonomy Research' (2018) 9(3) Studies in Self-Access Learning Journal 342–70

73 Mohammad Khosravishakib, 'The Contributions of Postmodernism Methodology as a Prevailing Practice on Ground of Humanities Sciences' (2012) 2(1) International Journal of Arts

Key Definitions

Throughout the thesis, the following terms are used and thus, a unified definition is intended.

Couture

The word is used to describe Couture works for the U.K. This is due to 'haute Couture' being governed by the Fédération de la Haute Couture et de la Mode in France. France has the designated registration for 'haute Couture' which is legally protected by French law.[74] Due to this fact, only Couture works produced in the U.K. can be referred to as Couture, unless the couturier has membership to the Fédération de la Haute Couture et de la Mode.[75]

Couturier

A fashion designer that creates Couture garments.

Fashion

It is necessary to use the term 'fashion' throughout the thesis at times, to acknowledge Couture as a category of fashion and to provide context when necessary.

Toile

A prototype garment usually made from a light-coloured fabric, most commonly calico.

Tűrkiye

On 26 May 2022, The Republic of Turkey officially changed its name to Tűrkiye in a request submitted to the United Nations Secretary-General.[76] In recognition of this fact, Tűrkiye is used throughout the book.

Tangible Functionality and Intangible Functionality

Two notions/terms, I have developed specifically for this study are:

74 Teg, 'What is Couture? The Guide to High Fashion' (*The Evans Group*, 15 June 2021) <https://tegintl.com/what-is-Couture/> accessed 27 December 2022 and Alexander Fury, 'What Does 'Couture' Actually Mean?' (*New York Times*, 27 January 2017) <https://www.nytimes.com/2017/01/27/t-magazine/fashion/what-does-Couture-actually-mean-fashion-week.html> accessed 29 December 2022

75 Beverly Hills Design Institute, 'Industry/Haute Couture: What is Haute Couture' (*Beverly Hills Design Institute*, 2022) <https://www.bhdi.edu/industry/haute-Couture/what-is-haute-Couture/> accessed 12 June 2022

76 United Nations, 'Türkiye' (*United Nations*, 26 May 2022) <https://www.un.org/en/about-us/member-states/turkiye> accessed 29 March 2024

Tangible functionality:
Relates to the functional element of fashion derived from technical features.
Intangible functionality:
Determined through an incorporeal context, for any purpose other than the basic requirement for the garment. This function exists through the utilisation of the garment, such as self-expression and communication.

Subtraction Method

A method of pattern cutting which is distinct from the traditional process developed by Julian Roberts. The process is achieved by 'removing shapes from a flat material, to create empty spaces for the body to occupy.'[77]

Original Contribution to Knowledge

The original contribution to knowledge of this study has been achieved by specifically concentrating on a category of fashion, Couture. Fashion law as a general concept encompasses numerous areas of legal discipline, such as contract law, commercial law, E.U. law, intellectual property rights, and passing-off. This study specifically considers in detail intellectual property law, most pertinently copyright law, in application to Couture to widen discussions in fashion law.[78] For this reason, the study has engaged in scholarly research to determine what art is as a philosophical concept and the extent to which Couture is art, in its own right. For the purposes of responding to the research question, the analysis has necessitated an original interrelated approach to fashion, art, and law, providing a multi-disciplinary dynamic.[79]

The study adds to the existing body of work in fashion law and specifically widens the existing scholarly discussions in relation to the impact of technical limitations for the grant of copyright. It is important to clarify that this study is *not* asserting that copyright is not possible for Couture absolutely, however it *is* considering the potential legal challenges to copyright protection. For this reason, the original contribution of the study emerges from the nuanced and in-depth analysis between Couture and copyright specifically, which is quite distinct from the existing literature currently available in fashion law. Overall, and most significantly, the thesis puts forward original arguments which support the listing of Couture within s.4 of the CDPA 1988, as an artistic work.

77 Fareeha Masood, 'The World of Pattern Cutting' (*Institute of Making*, 12 July 2021) <https://www.instituteofmaking.org.uk/blog/2021/07/the-world-of-pattern-cutting#:~:text=Subtraction%20pattern%20cutting%20is%20a%20technique%20developed%20by,create%20empty%20spaces%20for%20the%20body%20to%20occupy> accessed 23 October 2023

78 This is due to Couture having a strong influence on the designs generated within the mass manufacturing market, please see chapter 2

79 Please see chapter 4 in consideration of scholarly works by Leo Tolstoy, *What Is Art* (True Sign Publishing 1 March 2021), L Torres and M Kamhi, *What Art is the Esthetic Theory of Ayn Rand* (Open Court 2000) and Nanay Bence, *Aesthetics: A Very Short Introduction* (Oxford University Press 2019)

The study brings forward the link between art, fashion, and the law, and attempts to align the fashion industry requirements with copyright specifically for Couture. In addition, the thesis contributes to knowledge through a visual perspective pertaining to artistry and aesthetics. This is for the purposes of providing an enhanced visual approach to copyright law, particularly relating to my views pertaining to this necessary implementation, in the legal assessment for Couture protection.

Chapter Synopses

Chapter 1

This chapter provides an explanation of what Couture is, a historical overview beginning with Charles Frederick Worth, before considering the French establishment of Fédération de la Haute Couture et de la Mode and the U.K. Association of the Incorporated Society of London Fashion Designers. British couturiers and the fashion industry are presented to provide a backdrop for the questions presented by the book as to the challenges for Couture copyright protection.

Chapter 2

For the purposes of providing a well-rounded analysis, in consideration of extending s.4 of the CDPA to include Couture, existing protections within the intellectual property (IP) framework are examined through patents, design rights, Geographical Indications, passing-off and trade marks. This chapter extends the discussion for the issues and includes a case study to examine the degree copyright protection is afforded to architecture, in a comparative exercise between architecture and Couture. Both follow similar creative processes, although architecture is included within the closed list of protected works under s.4 of the CDPA 1988, and Couture is not.

Chapter 3

This chapter is the heart of the book, this book considers what art is and investigates the extent Couture can be identified as an art form. The chapter explores art theory by Tolstoy and Rand and provides insight into various art types. The concept of artistic craftmanship is explored to provide an understanding of the challenges pertaining to a legally protecting Couture, particularly when questioning whether Couture is a work of *artistic craftmanship*, alone.

Chapter 4

This chapter is solely dedicated to copyright and explores relevant concepts including originality, subject matter, and fixation, amongst others. The thesis question is tested by identifying whether copyright should be allowed to regulate the technical elements of fashion, in dual recognition of the creative innovation within fashion, which may be impacted by copyright limitations.

Chapter 5

Responding to the primary research question, the chapter examines the aspect of technicality and the issue of functionality, which leads to considerations for the monopoly of (technical) function in copyright.

Chapter 6

This chapter examines international legal provisions through a global appreciation approach for international copyright frameworks. The study specifically examines France, Tűrkiye, and the U.S. particularly in light of BREXIT in consideration of good practice and potential future reform.

Chapter 7

Primarily discussing the threshold for copyright from the investigations of the study thus far, the chapter examines the standard expected for copyright protection as it relates to Couture garments. The chapter brings together the findings of the study and considers whether the threshold for copyright protection for Couture is too high. On this basis, considerations extend to whether there is merit in preventing copyright from regulating technical works in consideration of artistic works, specifically Couture. This chapter includes draft legislation.

Figure 1.1 Chanel Dress Spring/Summer 1961 Silk Chiffon and Taffeta V&A S1645-2015 (V&A Chanel 2023 Exhibition)

Acknowledgements

I would like to thank my family and friends for their unwavering love and support. You have given me the strength and fortitude to persevere in this endeavour.

The University of Buckingham: Thanking the supervision team, Dr Patricia Covarrubia and Dr Kerry Purcell. My gratitude also is extended to Sarah Myhill and Professor Luca Turin.

Thanking Couture fashion creators around the globe, continue to inspire!

Abbreviations

BFC	British Fashion Council
BSA	*Bezpečnostni softwarová asociace*
BSI	British Standards Institution
CDPA	Copyright, Designs and Patents Act 1988
CJEU	Court of Justice of the European Union
E.U.	European Union
GI	Geographical Indications
IP	Intellectual Property
LDMA	Literary, Dramatic Musical, and Artistic Works
MBE	Member of the Order of the British Empire
OHIM	Office for Harmonization in the Internal Market (Since March 2016 referred to as the European Union Intellectual Property Office (EUIPO))
PAIS	L'Association de Protection des Industries Artistiques Saisonnieres
SBCII	Southern Building Code Congress Internationals
TFEU	Treaty on the Functioning of the European Union
The code	*Fikir ve Sanat Eserleri Kanunu 5486* (intellectual property legislation of Tűrkiye)
TMA	Trade Marks Act 1994
TRIPS	Agreement on Trade-Related Aspects of Intellectual Property Rights
WTO	World Trade Organisation

1 Understanding Couture and Considerations for Legal Protection

Introduction

This chapter begins with a literature review to introduce the key scholarly articles and judgements which are instrumental in shaping the analysis for the study. The chapter aims to examine what Couture is and the relationship to the wider fashion industry. Initial considerations regarding the connection between Couture and copyright are introduced before the study explores this to a greater extent within the chapters ahead.

To begin, the viewpoint from the perspective of this study looks to broaden views of Couture pertaining to the artistic attributes and moreover, Couture *as* an artwork, in its own right. Broader considerations are rooted in cultural, sociological, and economic generative qualities of Couture within the fashion framework. The historical development of Couture is presented, with a particular focus on the French haute Couture developments. Added to this, enquiries for the study extend to the wider fashion industry relating to the economic contribution fashion makes to the U.K. The study is rooted in considerations from the perspective of the creative process, Couture as art. The chapter aims to examine the objectives of Couture creation as it relates to the creative expression as an *artistic work* and the relationship to commercial viability.

1.1 Couture: What Is It?

Couture is defined by the bespoke qualities intrinsic to the garment, such as the innovative creation, embellishment, and style. These qualities derive from the consumer being at the centre of the creative process. Prototype Couture garment collections are traditionally presented at fashion shows twice a year reflecting the seasons, Spring/Summer and Autumn/Winter.[1] These collections can include a range of garments ranging from tailoring items to day and evening dresses.[2] It is general practice for each garment to be given a name, for example the Dame Vivienne Westwood Bridal Couture collection features gowns named 'Nymph,'

1 Gavin Waddell, *How Fashion Works: Couture, Ready-to-Wear and Mass Production* (Wiley 2004) 1
2 Gavin Waddell, *How Fashion Works: Couture, Ready-to-Wear and Mass Production* (Wiley 2004) 1

DOI: 10.4324/9781003599456-1

'Goddess,' and 'Flora.'[3] The construction and the method of assembly of Couture is associated with 'a work of art . . . where the item transcends dressmaking and becomes true craftmanship.'[4] Haute Couture and Couture are regarded as 'fashion excellence' in consideration of the materials, design, and method of construction, although in recent times, concerns have been raised over skills that have lasted for centuries vanishing.[5] Couture garments often display hand-crafted embellishment such as embroidery or décor through the use of sequins and beads. Pertaining to the creator, the couturier's name is not always tantamount with the fashion house; for example, it is commonplace to see a designer designing for another brand. Karl Lagerfeld for Chanel exemplifies this, a fusion of his own artistic vision, practice, and inspiration with the iconic brand style.[6]

1.2 Defining 'Couture' in This Study

Through the material researched there is much overlap between the use of the terms 'Couture' and 'haute Couture.' Prior to the study expanding into the historical context of the derivation of the art, in summary, the French system has designated registration for 'haute Couture' which is legally protected by French law.[7] On this basis, works not registered with the French establishment of Fédération de la Haute Couture et de la Mode, at this market level, are defined as Couture (this shall be expanded later). The study, therefore, imperatively identifies Couture as an integral part of fashion. For this reason, the term 'Couture' shall be used throughout the study when referring to fashion works in this category, although when referring to the French equivalent, the term 'haute Couture' shall be referenced.

1.3 Historical Foundation

Charles Frederick Worth, an English fashion designer, is understood to be the pioneer for Couture.[8] He started his career working for two textile manufacturers in London, as an apprentice and as a clerk.[9] He later established himself as a designer known to have conquered the Parisian fashion sphere in the later part of

3 Gavin Waddell, *How Fashion Works: Couture, Ready-to-Wear and Mass Production* (Wiley 2004) 1 and Vivienne Westwood, 'Bridal Couture Spring-Summer 2022' (*Vivienne Westwood*, 2022) <https://www.viviennewestwood.com/en/bridal/Couture/2022/> accessed 31 December 2022

4 Gavin Waddell, *How Fashion Works: Couture, Ready-to-Wear and Mass Production* (Wiley 2004) 1

5 Kerry Taylor, *Vintage Fashion & Couture: From Poiret to McQueen* (1st edn, Mitchell Beazley 2017) 205

6 Hamish Bowles, 'Chanel Spring 2019 Couture' (*Vogue*, 22 January 2019) <https://www.vogue.com/fashion-shows/spring-2019-Couture/chanel> accessed 31 January 2023

7 Teg, 'What is Couture? The Guide to High Fashion' (*The Evans Group*, 15 June 2021) <https://tegintl.com/what-is-Couture/> accessed 27 December 2022 and Alexander Fury, 'What Does "Couture" Actually Mean?' (*New York Times*, 27 January 2017) <https://www.nytimes.com/2017/01/27/t-magazine/fashion/what-does-Couture-actually-mean-fashion-week.html> accessed 29 December 2022

8 Elyssa Kostopoulos, 'The Mystique that is Haute Couture: Your Guide to Fashion's Exclusive World' (*RUSSH*, 25 February 2021) <https://www.russh.com/what-is-haute-Couture/> accessed 6 July 2021

9 Jessa Krick, 'Charles Frederick Worth (1825–1895) and the House of Worth' (*The Met*, October 2004) <https://www.metmuseum.org/toah/hd/wrth/hd_wrth.htm> accessed 6 July 2021

Figure 1.2 House of Worth France, 1858–1956, Dress c1880 Pearl-Embroidered White Bengaline – Study From Sargent and Fashion Exhibition 2024, Tate, London

the 19th century[10] and moreover, is said to have been the founding designer of the haute Couture movement.[11] This was in 1858 where the term 'fashion designer' was first generated instead of 'dress maker' to reflect the *artist* within the creator.[12] His designs were known to be recognised for three main elements, and these were the luxurious materials used, the amalgamation of historic fashion influence, and the attention given to form through the fit of the garment.[13]

10 Jessa Krick, 'Charles Frederick Worth (1825–1895) and the House of Worth' (*The Met*, October 2004) <https://www.metmuseum.org/toah/hd/wrth/hd_wrth.htm> accessed 6 July 2021

11 Elyssa Kostopoulos, 'The Mystique That is Haute Couture: Your Guide to Fashion's Exclusive World' (*RUSSH*, 25 February 2021) <https://www.russh.com/what-is-haute-Couture/> accessed 6 July 2021

12 Harpers Bazaar, 'The History of Haute Couture From Humble Beginnings to Present Day' (*Harpers Bazaar*, 19 January 2017) <https://www.harpersbazaar.com/uk/fashion/fashion-news/news/a31123/the-history-of-haute-couture/> accessed 29 October 2024

13 Elyssa Kostopoulos, 'The Mystique That is Haute Couture: Your Guide to Fashion's Exclusive World' (*RUSSH*, 25 February 2021) <https://www.russh.com/what-is-haute-Couture/> accessed 6 July 2021

Figure 1.3 House of Worth Silk Evening Dress C1895 Silk Damask – Study From Sargent and Fashion Exhibition 2024, Tate, London

In France 1868, the 'Chambre Syndicale de la Couture, des Confectionneurs et des Tailleurs pour Dame' was founded.[14] In 1900, the world fair was hosted by the Pavillion of Elegance which showcased many haute Couture designers such as Worth and Doucet.[15] It wasn't until 1908 that the French term 'haute Couture' was used.[16] Haute Couture has been defined as 'unparalleled craftmanship,'[17] histori-

14 Fédération de la haute Couture et de la mode, 'History' (*Fédération de la haute Couture et de la mode*, 2022) <https://fhcm.paris/en/the-federation/history/#:~:text=Founded%20in%201868%20and%20then%20known%20as%20the,de%20la%20Couture%20Parisienne%20on%20December%2014th%201910> accessed 23 December 2022

15 Tim Jackson and David Shaw, *The Fashion Handbook* (Routledge 2006) 30

16 Harpers Bazaar, 'The History of Haute Couture From Humble Beginnings to Present Day' (*Harpers Bazaar*, 19 January 2017) <https://www.harpersbazaar.com/uk/fashion/fashion-news/news/a31123/the-history-of-haute-couture/> accessed 29 October 2024

17 Elyssa Kostopoulos, 'The Mystique That is Haute Couture: Your Guide to Fashion's Exclusive World' (*RUSSH*, 25 February 2021) <https://www.russh.com/what-is-haute-Couture/> accessed 6 July 2021

cally dating back to the 17th century.[18] *Couture* means dressmaking[19] and *haute* is the French word for high,[20] further relating to the nature of the practice, which is for the purposes of creating luxury and exclusive fashion.[21]

Other notable historic haute Couture designers were Doucet known for tailoring,[22] Pingat known as 'nouveatés confectionées,'[23] and Poiret is acknowledged for his artistic innovation specifically within his haute Couture salon known for its extravagant characteristic.[24] In 1910, the establishment of 'Chambre Syndicale de la Couture, des Confectionneurs et des Tailleurs pour Dame' changed the name to Chambre Syndicale de la Couture Parisienne.[25] In 1921, an association was founded by the French press, known as L'Association de Protection des Industries Artistiques Saisonnieres (PAIS), and the primary objective was to protect Couture creations from being reproduced.[26] The Couture works were protected by French copyright law by being photographed on models or mannequins, and the photographs archived in a catalogue.[27] The Chambre Syndicale de la Couture Parisienne name was changed once again to Chambre Syndicate de la Haute Couture in 1945.[28] This amendment reflected the registration of the legal designation of haute Couture (therefore, haute Couture is protected in French law as a *sui-generis* right).[29] Two other Chambre Syndicales emerged in 1973, the Chambre Syndicale

18 Elyssa Kostopoulos, 'The Mystique That is Haute Couture: Your Guide to Fashion's Exclusive World' (*RUSSH*, 25 February 2021) <https://www.russh.com/what-is-haute-Couture/> accessed 6 July 2021

19 Elyssa Kostopoulos, 'The Mystique That is Haute Couture: Your Guide to Fashion's Exclusive World' (*RUSSH*, 25 February 2021) <https://www.russh.com/what-is-haute-Couture/> accessed 6 July 2021

20 Elyssa Kostopoulos, 'The Mystique that is Haute Couture: Your Guide to Fashion's Exclusive World' (*RUSSH*, 25 February 2021) <https://www.russh.com/what-is-haute-Couture/> accessed 6 July 2021

21 Harper's Bazaar, 'The History of Haute Couture From Humble Beginnings to Present Day' (*Harpers Bazaar*, 19 January 2017) <https://www.harpersbazaar.com/uk/fashion/fashion-news/news/a31123/the-history-of-haute-Couture/> accessed 27 December 2022

22 Tim Jackson and David Shaw, *The Fashion Handbook* (Routledge 2006) 31

23 Tim Jackson and David Shaw, *The Fashion Handbook* (Routledge 2006) 31

24 Tim Jackson and David Shaw, *The Fashion Handbook* (Routledge 2006) 31

25 Fédération de la haute Couture et de la mode, 'History' (*Fédération de la haute Couture et de la mode*, 2022) <https://fhcm.paris/en/the-federation/history/#:~:text=Founded%20in%201868%20and%20then%20known%20as%20the,de%20la%20Couture%20Parisienne%20on%20December%2014th%201910> accessed 23 December 2022

26 Fashion ABC, 'Haute Couture Fashion Week' (*Fashion ABC Beta*, 2022) <https://www.fashionabc.org/wiki/haute-Couture-fashion-week/> accessed 27 December 2022

27 Fashion ABC, 'Haute Couture Fashion Week' (*Fashion ABC Beta*, 2022) <https://www.fashionabc.org/wiki/haute-Couture-fashion-week/> accessed 27 December 2022

28 Fédération de la haute Couture et de la mode, 'History' (*Fédération de la haute Couture et de la mode*, 2022) <https://fhcm.paris/en/the-federation/history/#:~:text=Founded%20in%201868%20and%20then%20known%20as%20the,de%20la%20Couture%20Parisienne%20on%20December%2014th%201910> accessed 23 December 2022

29 Fédération de la haute Couture et de la mode, 'History' (*Fédération de la haute Couture et de la mode*, 2022) <https://fhcm.paris/en/the-federation/history/#:~:text=Founded%20in%201868%20and%20then%20known%20as%20the,de%20la%20Couture%20Parisienne%20on%20December%2014th%201910> accessed 23 December 2022

du Prêt-á-Porter des Couturiers et des Créateurs de Mode and the Chambre Syndicale de la Mode Masculine.[30] The three Chambres Syndicales joined forces to be collectively known as Fédération Française de la Couture, du Prêt-a-Porter des Couturiers et des Créateurs de Mode. In 2017, the name was updated to the current form of Fédération de la Haute Couture et de la Mode.[31]

Today, the French Ministry of Industry supports the commission at the Chambres Syndicales de la Haute Couture in approving couturiers each year.[32] The regulations stipulate that a fashion house must have a minimum of 15 employees within the studios and showcase their collections to the media at each fashion season (this is two times per year (Spring/Summer and Autumn/Winter)).[33] Further, the creations must be made entirely by hand.[34] On this basis, designers which are *not* on the list, issued by the Ministry of Industry in Paris, and whom are known as Couture designers are identified as such throughout this study.

It is necessary to distinguish between French and U.K. Couture, since haute Couture is governed by the Fédération de la Haute Couture et de la Mode in France and this study is concerned with the Couture industry in the U.K. and the legislation of the U.K. It is observed that members of the Fédération de la Haute Couture et de la Mode have their works protected in France, whereas the position in the U.K. is the focus for this study as it specifically pertains to the extent copyright protection can be applied, if at all. This is particularly significant in identifying the disconnect between copyright law and the creative process. Most notable are the extensive provisions implemented by the French system to foster and protect Couture works. However, the fundamental question for the U.K. is whether the absence of an equivalent to the French Fédération de la Haute Couture et de la Mode in the U.K. is a contributing factor to Couture not being included within s.4 of the CDPA 1988 as an artistic work.

30 Fédération de la haute Couture et de la mode, 'History' (*Fédération de la haute Couture et de la mode*, 2022) <https://fhcm.paris/en/the-federation/history/#:~:text=Founded%20in%201868%20and%20then%20known%20as%20the,de%20la%20Couture%20Parisienne%20on%20December%2014th%201910> accessed 23 December 2022

31 Fédération de la haute Couture et de la mode, 'History' (*Fédération de la haute Couture et de la mode*, 2022) <https://fhcm.paris/en/the-federation/history/#:~:text=Founded%20in%201868%20and%20then%20known%20as%20the,de%20la%20Couture%20Parisienne%20on%20December%2014th%201910> accessed 23 December 2022

32 Fédération de la haute Couture et de la mode, 'History' (*Fédération de la haute Couture et de la mode*, 2022) <https://fhcm.paris/en/the-federation/history/#:~:text=Founded%20in%201868%20and%20then%20known%20as%20the,de%20la%20Couture%20Parisienne%20on%20December%2014th%201910> accessed 23 December 2022

33 Beverly Hills Design Institute, 'Industry/Haute Couture: What is Haute Couture' (*Beverly Hills Design Institute*, 2022) <https://www.bhdi.edu/industry/haute-Couture/what-is-haute-Couture/> accessed 12 June 2022

34 Sarah Leigh Bannerman, 'Why Are There No Haute Couture Houses in London?' (*Culture Trip*, 22 October 2017) <https://theculturetrip.com/Europe/united-kingdom/england/london/articles/why-are-there-no-haute-Couture-fashion-houses-in-london/> accessed 12 June 2022

Table 1.1 Developments for Couture

Year	Significant development relating to the artistic attributes of Couture
1858	Term: 'Fashion designer' is used in preference to 'dress maker' to correspond to the 'artist' as the creator.[35]
1908	Haute Couture described as high (quality, luxury, and exclusive) dressmaking.

1.4 History: Legally Protecting Couture in the U.K.

Prior to the study progressing, it is necessary to acknowledge the historical development in depth as it relates to the U.K. for couturiers. Mayfair, London, in the 1930s is noted as having an 'expanded retail consumption.'[36] This area of London is understood to have facilitated fashion consumption of luxury fashion products due to the changes in letting agreements in 1928, whereby commercial occupancy increased from a previously mainly residential type.[37] The 'London Couture industry' is said to have been supported at that time through luxury businesses within the area such as 'corsetieres, milliners, goldsmiths, art dealers . . . court dressmakers.'[38] Couturiers originally based in Paris established businesses in central London between 1932 and 1936, notably Edward Molyneux, Elsa Schiaparelli, Dilkusha, Karinska, Robert Piguet, and Jacques Heim.[39]

Historically in the U.K., the Association of the Incorporated Society of London Fashion Designers was established in 1941 by Audrey Withers, who was at the time the Editor-in-chief for *Vogue*.[40] The Chambre Syndicale in Paris was the framework for shaping the Association in the U.K.[41] The archived document Memorandum and Articles of Association of the Incorporated Society of London Fashion Designers was originally drafted on 10 November 1941 and registered 6 January 1942, 3(d) states:

> To assist fashion designers by protecting their original designs, enabling them to exchange information to their mutual advantage, arranging dates for their respective showings, fostering professional and trade interests of

35 Harper's Bazaar, 'The History of Haute Couture From Humble Beginnings to Present Day' (*Harper's Bazaar*, 19 January 2017) <https://www.harpersbazaar.com/uk/fashion/fashion-news/news/a31123/the-history-of-haute-Couture/> accessed 27 December 2022

36 Michelle Jones, *London Couture and the Making of a Fashion Centre* (MIT 2022) 20 referring to Bronwyn Edwards, 'We Are Fatally Influenced by Goods Brought in Bond Street: London, Shopping and the Fashionable Geographies of 1930s Vogue' (2006) 10(1–2) Fashion Theory 73–96

37 Michelle Jones, *London Couture and the Making of a Fashion Centre* (MIT 2022) 20

38 Michelle Jones, *London Couture and the Making of a Fashion Centre* (MIT 2022) 20–1

39 Michelle Jones, *London Couture and the Making of a Fashion Centre* (MIT 2022) 20–1

40 Francesca Steriacci and Joanne Arbuckle, *The A-Z of the Fashion Industry* (Scarecrow Press 2009) 115

41 Francesca Steriacci and Joanne Arbuckle, *The A-Z of the Fashion Industry* (Scarecrow Press 2009) 115

> persons engaged in creating British fashions, developing the standards of skilled workmanship, and representing their views to government and trade bodies to the press.[42]

This provision demonstrates the intention to protect original fashion designs. However, the Association ceased to be in existence after 1974.[43] To put this into context, since 1941 there is potentially an excess of 80 years absence pertaining to the industrial, cultural, and legal development for fashion, more pertinently Couture, in the U.K. In comparison to the French system, the Fédération de la Haute Couture et de la Mode has continued to develop (the French system is explained in depth later).

Today, the British Fashion Council (BFC) is comprised of members (from the fashion industry) for the purposes of 'overseeing, supporting, and advising on key issues facing the British designer industry.'[44] The organisation focuses on key areas such as trade, talent, future considerations for the industry, and intellectual property (mainly relating to design rights), and it also aims to forge and strengthen links to the government to aid fashion designers. The BFC engages in various forums to represent the fashion industry, specifically pertaining to the 'Creative Industries Council,' 'Department for Culture Media & Sport Entertainment & Events Group by Julia Lopez, Minister of State for Creative & Digital,' and 'Government Working Groups on geo-political issues as and when appropriate.'[45] The connections to government organisations and information relating to intellectual property provisions provide designers with a supportive framework, whereby the fashion industry may foster growth and help fashion designers protect their work, similar to the historic Association of the Incorporated Society of London Fashion Designers. However, the BFC does not appear to reach as far as the Fédération de la Haute Couture et de la Mode in France, to reflect the registration for the legal designation of Couture works in the U.K.[46]

1.5 British Couturiers

As the study specifically focuses on the U.K. and the question as to whether Couture is art, the following section shall showcase British couturiers to illustrate Couture as an *art* form; and significantly, the contribution to art made by British couturiers within the U.K.

42 Michelle Jones, *London Couture and the Making of a Fashion Centre* (MIT 2022) 235
43 Michelle Jones, *London Couture and the Making of a Fashion Centre* (MIT 2022) 235
44 British Fashion Council, 'About' (*British Fashion Council*, 2022) <https://www.britishfashioncouncil.co.uk/About/BFC-Network> accessed 27 December 2022
45 British Fashion Council, 'About' (*British Fashion Council*, 2022) <https://www.britishfashioncouncil.co.uk/About/BFC-Network> accessed 27 December 2022
46 Fédération de la haute Couture et de la mode, 'History' (*Fédération de la haute Couture et de la mode*, 2022) <https://fhcm.paris/en/the-federation/history/#:~:text=Founded%20in%201868%20and%20then%20known%20as%20the,de%20la%20Couture%20Parisienne%20on%20December%2014th%201910> accessed 23 December 2022

1.5.1 Bruce Oldfield

Bruce Oldfield is a graduate of St. Martin's School of Art in 1973.[47] He was awarded an OBE in 1990 in honour of his contribution to the British fashion industry and accepted an honorary fellowship from the Royal College of Art.[48] He is defined as 'practicing his art from his London studio,' with influence derived from his love of 'architecture' and 'studio ceramics.'[49]

1.5.2 Oswald Boateng

Oswald Boateng started his career in the 1980s and debuted his first collection in 1994,[50] and following the success of this, his first boutique was opened in London in 1995.[51] In 2003, he was appointed as creative director of menswear at Givenchy, and it was in 2019 that he showcased his first womenswear collection.[52] He returned to London Fashion Week in February 2022 after a 12-year interval.[53] Highlighting the expression deployed for both the designer and the wearer of his garments, he describes his creative ethos as 'Style is an extension of yourself. My approach is to enhance the personality of the wearer by creating an emotional connection between them and the pieces I create.'[54]

1.5.3 Hussein Chalayan

Hussein Chalayan is described as '[o]ne of fashion's most experimental and innovative designers.'[55] His work appears to be influenced by his environment, specifically 'architecture, art, politics, nature and sculpture.' One of his most

47 Michelle Cooper, 'Bruce Oldfield' (*Vogue*, 1 December 2010) <https://www.vogue.co.uk/article/bruce-oldfield-biography> accessed 27 December 2022

48 Michelle Cooper, 'Bruce Oldfield' (*Vogue*, 1 December 2010) <https://www.vogue.co.uk/article/bruce-oldfield-biography> accessed 27 December 2022

49 Bruce Oldfield, 'Bruce Oldfield Couture' (*Bruce Oldfield Couture*, 2022) <https://bruceoldfield-Couture.com/> accessed 29 December 2022

50 Alex Kessler, 'Ozwald Boateng Celebrates Black Excellence With a Grand Homecoming Spectacle in London' (*Vogue*, 23 February 2022) <https://www.vogue.co.uk/fashion/article/ozwald-boateng-celebrates-black-excelleance-with-homecoming-in-london> accessed 27 December 2022

51 Famousfashiondesignersorg, 'Ozwald Boateng' (*FamousFashionDesignersorg*, 2018) <https://www.famousfashiondesigners.org/ozwald-boateng> accessed 27 December 2022

52 Brooke Bobb, 'In Celebration of the 100th Anniversary of the Harlem Renaissance, Ozwald Boateng Brought Fashion to the Apollo Theater' (*Vogue*, 6 May 2019) <https://www.vogue.com/article/ozwald-boateng-show-harlem-the-apollo> accessed 27 December 2022

53 Alex Kessler, 'Ozwald Boateng Celebrates Black Excellence With a Grand Homecoming Spectacle in London' (*Vogue*, 23 February 2022) <https://www.vogue.co.uk/fashion/article/ozwald-boateng-celebrates-black-excelleance-with-homecoming-in-london> accessed 27 December 2022

54 Ozwald Boateng, 'The Core Essence of Ozwald Boateng Tailoring' (*Ozwald Boateng*, 2022) <https://www.ozwaldboateng.co.uk./bespoke-Couture> accessed 27 December 2022

55 Ella Alexander, 'Hussein Chalayan' (*Vogue*, 22 August 2011) <https://www.vogue.co.uk/article/hussein-chalayan-biography> accessed 27 December 2022

notable creations is a coffee table skirt.[56] He was awarded a Member of the Order of the British Empire (MBE) in 2006 for his contribution to the fashion industry, and in 2011, he was appointed as an honorary fellow at the London College of Fashion.[57]

1.5.4 Alexander McQueen

The late Alexander McQueen was regarded as producing garments that were akin to 'costumes' and at times, 'props,'[58] and further, the clothes were noted as having 'theatrical'[59] quality. His first haute Couture collection was debuted in the summer of 1997, which was influenced by Grecian mythology of Jason and the Argonauts.[60] The show was noted to be very theatrical with 'ram's horns . . . pegasus wings and golden rain'; this show was reported as being different to the usual expectations of haute Couture audiences.[61] McQueen was known for his defiant approach to fashion creation and expressed that Paris Couture had been started by Charles Frederick Worth and further went on to make a distinction between the French and U.K. creative approaches: 'Givenchy is 200 million-light years away from what I do . . . One is London, the other is Paris [emphasis added].'[62] This gives insight into the intellectual and creative process employed by McQueen, who respected the longevity of tradition but wanted to dismantle the rules in fashion creativity.[63] McQueen was regarded as an artist, implementing his creative ideas onto clothes instead of a canvas. His 'Couture . . . showmanship' was demonstrated in the Spring/Summer 2005 collection, whereby the giant chessboard formed the stage for showcasing the intricate Couture pieces. The theme comprised of Edwardian influences, bodices, embroidery, tailoring, and floaty dresses.[64] Following his passing, Sarah Burton completed his final collection and is noted as successfully taking the brand forward in his legacy. She is also known for designing the wedding dress for Kate Middleton under the McQueen brand.[65]

56 Ella Alexander, 'Hussein Chalayan' (*Vogue*, 22 August 2011) <https://www.vogue.co.uk/article/hussein-chalayan-biography> accessed 27 December 2022

57 Ella Alexander, 'Hussein Chalayan' (*Vogue*, 22 August 2011) <https://www.vogue.co.uk/article/hussein-chalayan-biography> accessed 27 December 2022

58 Blue 17, 'Incredible Couturiers Alexander Mcqueen' (*Blue 17*, 6 March 2015) <https://www.blue17.co.uk/vintage-blog/incredible-couturiers-alexander-mcqueen/> accessed 6 July 2021

59 Blue 17, 'Incredible Couturiers Alexander Mcqueen' (*Blue 17*, 6 March 2015) <https://www.blue17.co.uk/vintage-blog/incredible-couturiers-alexander-mcqueen/> accessed 6 July 2021

60 Chloe Fox, *Vogue on Alexander McQueen* (Quadrille 2012) 369

61 Chloe Fox, *Vogue on Alexander McQueen* (Quadrille 2012) 379

62 Chloe Fox, *Vogue on Alexander McQueen* (Quadrille 2012) 393

63 Chloe Fox, *Vogue on Alexander McQueen* (Quadrille 2012) 442

64 Sarah Mower, 'Alexander McQueen' (*Vogue*, 7 October 2004) <https://www.vogue.com/fashion-shows/spring-2005-ready-to-wear/alexander-mcqueen> accessed 19 August 2023

65 Emily Sutherland, 'The Ongoing Reign of Alexander McQueen' (*Drapers Online*, 10 February 2020) <https://www.drapersonline.com/news/the-ongoing-reign-of-alexander-mcqueen> accessed 27 December 2022

1.5.5 Dame Vivienne Westwood

The late Dame Vivienne Westwood had her first catwalk show in 1981.[66] The iconic fashion designer was an environmental activist.[67] Known for being influenced by the punk movement since the 1970s, it is at this time that her career into fashion design launched through her boutique on the Kings Road, London, called 'Let it rock.'[68] In the 1990s, she recreated corsetry and re-established it as not only a decorative timeless piece, but also providing a functional purpose in shaping the female form. The corset was featured in many of her collections including in the MacAndreas 1993 tartan collection called Anglomania, whereby the tartan is officially recognised by the 'Scottish register of tartans.'[69] In terms of function, in addition to defining the female form the corset speaks of body positivity, and most recently, the crepe yellow corset worn by the singer Adele was showcased on the November 2021 cover of *Vogue* magazine.[70]

1.6 Couture: The Process

To give context to the effort and dedication given to Couture, the labour in hours is illustrated here,[71] on average it takes 150 hours to create a simple Couture dress,[72] 1000 hours for a Chanel haute Couture jacket,[73] and it takes in excess of 6000 hours to create elaborately embellished Couture dresses.[74]

A closer look at the product development process used within the fashion industry is necessitated to outline the various concepts which are determined by considerations relating to commercial viability. This correlates closely to the idea of the consumer and the perceived concept of fashion providing an 'alluring value.'[75] The

66 Vivienne Westwood, 'Celebrating the History of the Vivienne Westwood Catwalk Complete Collections' (*Vivienne Westwood*, 9 June 2021) <https://blog.viviennewestwood.com/celebrating-the-history-of-the-vivienne-westwood-catwalk-complete-collections/> accessed 6 July 2021

67 Vivienne Westwood, 'Official Website' (*Vivienne Westwood*, 2021) <https://www.viviennewestwood.com/en/> accessed 6 July 2021

68 Megan Boyes, 'Vivienne Westwood' (*Vogue*, 22 April 2008) <https://www.vogue.co.uk./article/vivienne-westwood-biography> accessed 27 December 2022

69 Vivienne Westwood, 'Celebrating the History of the Vivienne Westwood Catwalk Complete Collections' (*Vivienne Westwood*, 9 June 2021) <https://blog.viviennewestwood.com/celebrating-the-history-of-the-vivienne-westwood-catwalk-complete-collections/> accessed 6 July 2021

70 Emily Chan, 'Why Vivienne Westwood's Corsetry Remains Unparalleled' (*Vogue*, 7 October 2021) <https://www.vogue.co.uk/fashion/article/adele-vogue-vivienne-westwood-corset> accessed 27 December 2022

71 The figures relate to haute Couture, although this is not expected to be too different for British Couture, whereby it has not been possible to access data relating to British Couture alone

72 Vogue, 'Couture By Numbers: What Does It Really Take to Make a Collection?' (*Vogue*, 5 July 2020) <https://www.vogue.co.uk./fashion/article/Couture-by-numbers> accessed 27 December 2022

73 Liam Freeman, 'A Rare Look inside the Chanel Haute Couture Ateliers' (*Vogue*, 7 July 2018) <https://www.vogue.co.uk/article/inside-the-chanel-ateliers> accessed 20 January 2025

74 Vogue, 'Couture By Numbers: What Does It Really Take to Make a Collection?' (*Vogue*, 5 July 2020) <https://www.vogue.co.uk./fashion/article/Couture-by-numbers> accessed 27 December 2022

75 Yuniya Kawamura, *Fashion-Ology* (2nd edn, Bloomsbury Academic 2017) 297

initial concept of an idea is developed through the creative method incorporating the design with use of textiles. Further considerations in terms of sourcing of the materials, fabric testing, location, cost, and technology are essential for the purposes of ascertaining suitability to the design. These constructs must be considered in tandem with the garment manufacturing. Marketing models must be evaluated for the purposes of commercial viability along with merchandising, and costing and accounting models shall reflect the desired and expected profit margins. Logistics are crucial when considering the interrelation of trade and manufacturing for the purposes of supply chain management. Each of the concepts shall be explained in the following.

1.6.1 The Design Process

The beginning of the design process stems from not only the designer's creative concept of an idea with the intention of developing this into a tangible form, but it is also influenced by trend forecasts. It is vital that a designer comprehends and interprets trend forecasts for the purposes of attaining business success.[76] Trend forecasting is established as an industry[77] and is said to be in existence since 1915 when colour forecasts were generated by Margaret Hayden Rorke.[78] This was achieved by investigating into the popular textiles in Paris, France, and creating 'colour cards' for distribution to the manufacturing and retail industry.[79] The purpose of trend forecasting was not only for the purposes of establishing the popular trends, but it also served an additional function, which was to reduce the waste being generated and the need to reduce prices of unappealing fashion items.[80] Trend forecasting does not only relate to colour but to 'style'[81] and 'mood.'[82] Trend forecasting influences designers when creating fashion items such as garments and accessories, as the designer will be considering the trends for silhouettes and shapes.[83] In excess of the past 40 years Premiere Vision[84] has established itself as a leading trend forecaster for the 'global fashion industry.'[85] Premiere Vision is an international trade show which provides the opportunity for the fashion industry to network and source products for designer requirements. It stages shows twice a year in Paris, the purpose of which is to showcase the resources necessary for the

76 Tim Jackson and David Shaw, *The Fashion Handbook* (Routledge 2006) 55

77 Gwyneth Holland and Rae Jones, *Fashion Trend Forecasting* (Laurence King Publishing 2017) 22

78 Gwyneth Holland and Rae Jones, *Fashion Trend Forecasting* (Laurence King Publishing 2017) 22

79 Gwyneth Holland and Rae Jones, *Fashion Trend Forecasting* (Laurence King Publishing 2017) 22

80 Gwyneth Holland and Rae Jones, *Fashion Trend Forecasting* (Laurence King Publishing 2017) 22

81 Gwyneth Holland and Rae Jones, *Fashion Trend Forecasting* (Laurence King Publishing 2017) 25

82 Gwyneth Holland and Rae Jones, *Fashion Trend Forecasting* (Laurence King Publishing 2017) 25

83 Gwyneth Holland and Rae Jones, *Fashion Trend Forecasting* (Laurence King Publishing 2017) 29

84 Premiere Vision, 'About' (*Premiere Vision*, 2021) <https://www.premierevision.com/en/about/?> accessed 6 July 2021

85 Premiere Vision, 'About' (*Premiere Vision*, 2021) <https://www.premierevision.com/en/about/?> accessed 6 July 2021

creation of 'cutting-edge ready to wear' fashion.[86] These include 'textile designs,'[87] 'leather,'[88] 'fabrics,'[89] 'furs,'[90] and 'accessories.'[91] The platform[92] also showcases manufacturing firms and is essentially regarded as a business hub for the fashion industries.[93] Trade publications provide insight into the fashion industry.[94] These include reports on market segments, fashion shows, manufacturers, and suppliers.

London Fashion Week is very well known and established by the British Fashion Council.[95] The event usually lasts for six or seven days, is reported to host 50–60 catwalk shows, and draws in the region of 3000 fashion professionals such as buyers, journalists, and photographers from an international background.[96] The exhibition is vital for selling the latest upcoming ranges to overseas buyers.[97]

Designers also gain insight from trade periodicals. Well-established U.K. publications are *Drapers* (including Drapers online[98]) and *The Business of Fashion*.[99] In recent times, social media has also become a significant source of information as it relates to trend forecasting through the publication of vlogs, blogs, and apps such as Tumblr, Pinterest, Instagram, and Snapchat.[100] Trend forecasting must ensure that it is ahead of the cycle when predicting the re-emergence and waning of trends.[101] The re-emergence of trends theoretically is expected every 20 years, and this is believed to be due to the gap between generations, or even nostalgia.[102] The designer will engage in research into trends prior to developing a fashion collection by a variety of means, and these could be through attending a trade show

86 Premiere Vision, 'About' (*Premiere Vision*, 2021) <https://www.premierevision.com/en/about/?> accessed 6 July 2021

87 Premiere Vision, 'About' (*Premiere Vision*, 2021) <https://www.premierevision.com/en/about/?> accessed 6 July 2021

88 Premiere Vision, 'About' (*Premiere Vision*, 2021) <https://www.premierevision.com/en/about/?> accessed 6 July 2021

89 Premiere Vision, 'About' (*Premiere Vision*, 2021) <https://www.premierevision.com/en/about/?> accessed 6 July 2021

90 Premiere Vision, 'About' (*Premiere Vision*, 2021) <https://www.premierevision.com/en/about/?> accessed 6 July 2021

91 Premiere Vision, 'About' (*Premiere Vision*, 2021) <https://www.premierevision.com/en/about/?> accessed 6 July 2021

92 Premiere Vision, 'About' (*Premiere Vision*, 2021) <https://www.premierevision.com/en/about/?> accessed 6 July 2021

93 Premiere Vision, 'About' (*Premiere Vision*, 2021) <https://www.premierevision.com/en/about/?> accessed 6 July 2021

94 Sue Jenkyn Jones, *Fashion Design* (3rd edn, Laurence King 2002) 63

95 Tim Jackson and David Shaw, *The Fashion Handbook* (Routledge 2006) 54

96 Tim Jackson and David Shaw, *The Fashion Handbook* (Routledge 2006) 54

97 Tim Jackson and David Shaw, *The Fashion Handbook* (Routledge 2006) 54

98 Drapers Online, 'News' (*Drapers Online*, 2021) <https://www.drapersonline.com/> accessed 6 July 2021

99 Business of fashion, 'Professional' (*BOF*, 2021) <https://www.businessoffashion.com/> accessed 6 July 2021

100 Gwyneth Holland and Rae Jones, *Fashion Trend Forecasting* (Laurence King Publishing 2017) 34

101 Gwyneth Holland and Rae Jones, *Fashion Trend Forecasting* (Laurence King Publishing 2017) 58

102 Gwyneth Holland and Rae Jones, *Fashion Trend Forecasting* (Laurence King Publishing 2017) 59

such as Premiere Vision, attending catwalk shows, or inspiration acquired through magazines.[103]

A fashion designer's skill set necessitates two main categories, 'creative'[104] and 'technical.'[105] It is suggested that the creative skill requires the designer to conceive innovative designs or to develop novel creations through inspiration acquired from trend forecasts as discussed earlier.[106] The technical requirement relates to an understanding of the materials and how they shall be appropriate to the design, construction of the garment in consideration of the silhouette and fit, and function including the performance.[107] Although it has been stated that two key skills are required for the fashion designer comprising separately of technical and creative, the perspective from this study is that the creative contribution is superior and encompasses the technical aspect. This is because the creative component requires the designer to *ensure* that the Couture design will meet the functional objective of the garment specifically through the pursuit of incorporating artistic craftmanship whilst satiating the aesthetic obligation.

1.6.2 Textiles

The product development process necessitates consideration of the textiles which shall be used and incorporated into the garment. This is a vital consideration as fibres and fabrics influence the product performance and therefore will provide a fundamental role. In recent years, many new and innovative fabrics have been introduced to the fashion industry such as 'Tencel, Tactel, Coolmax, Supplex and Polartec.'[108] To illustrate recent innovation within textiles, a notable development can be seen using nano technology within textiles, which can enhance the function of the product by creating a water- and chemical-resistant structure,[109] a reduction of 'static electricity,'[110] and 'UV absorption, anti-microbial and self-decontamination.'[111] Nanotechnology provides an increased durability, therefore enhancing functionality.[112] The aspect of a textile function is a key consideration of this study in

103 Gwyneth Holland and Rae Jones, *Fashion Trend Forecasting* (Laurence King Publishing 2017) 73
104 Tim Jackson and David Shaw, *The Fashion Handbook* (Routledge 2006) 40
105 Tim Jackson and David Shaw, *The Fashion Handbook* (Routledge 2006) 40
106 Tim Jackson and David Shaw, *The Fashion Handbook* (Routledge 2006) 40
107 Tim Jackson and David Shaw, *The Fashion Handbook* (Routledge 2006) 40
108 Sue Jenkyn Jones, *Fashion Design* (3rd edn, Laurence King 2002) 147
109 Elizabeth Easter, 'Performance Textiles: Institutional Products' (*Association for Linen Management*, September 2006) <https://cdn.ymaws.com/www.almnet.org/resource/resmgr/Certification/Contact_Hour_Articles/047_PerformanceTextiles.pdf> accessed 6 July 2021
110 Elizabeth Easter, 'Performance Textiles: Institutional Products' (*Association for Linen Management*, September 2006) <https://cdn.ymaws.com/www.almnet.org/resource/resmgr/Certification/Contact_Hour_Articles/047_PerformanceTextiles.pdf> accessed 6 July 2021
111 Elizabeth Easter, 'Performance Textiles: Institutional Products' (*Association for Linen Management*, September 2006) <https://cdn.ymaws.com/www.almnet.org/resource/resmgr/Certification/Contact_Hour_Articles/047_PerformanceTextiles.pdf> accessed 6 July 2021
112 Elizabeth Easter, 'Performance Textiles: Institutional Products' (*Association for Linen Management*, September 2006) <https://cdn.ymaws.com/www.almnet.org/resource/resmgr/Certification/Contact_Hour_Articles/047_PerformanceTextiles.pdf> accessed 6 July 2021

consideration for fashion, and it is noted that 'chemical companies'[113] are engaged in creating fabrics with 'performance'[114] characteristics for textile manufacturers.

As the design may intend a particular textile for use, laboratory testing of the fabric may be necessary to ascertain its suitability. This is a more scientific part of the product development process in fashion.[115] Textile testing can be for various purposes such as checking the quality of the chosen material, for the purposes of quality control to assess any faulty batches, and to ensure that the fabric meets the standards required.[116]

The British Standards Institution (BSI) sets standards for many products and services for the U.K.[117] Textile standards are provided for a variety of issues such as durability and safety to name a few. The testing of the fabric is for the purposes of ensuring that the material performs within a range of acceptable standards, as stated by the BSI.

1.6.3 Garment Technology

Once the design is established, the pattern will be drafted, which can be achieved by traditional methods using paper and flat pattern blocks.[118] In addition, the computer program can 'plot the entered measurements.'[119] After the pattern is developed, it can be tested by producing a toile, which is a garment prototype usually made from calico or muslin, in accordance with the design drawings.[120] The toile is usually modelled on a mannequin or model to ensure it meets with the intended Couture creation. The purpose of a toile is to test the pattern when made into a prototype, which provides for the opportunity to identify any issues with fit and to make required alterations accordingly.

1.6.4 Construction

Couture construction methods differ from home-made and mass-produced manufactured products. These may consist of both hand stitching and machine assembly. For example, in Couture tailoring of a jacket, vertical seams may be machine

113 Sue Jenkyn Jones, *Fashion Design* (3rd edn, Laurence King 2002) 148

114 Sue Jenkyn Jones, *Fashion Design* (3rd edn, Laurence King 2002) 148

115 Testex Textile, 'What is the Textile Fabric Testing, Test Method, Test Item Classification' (*Testex Textile*, 21 June 2019) <https://www.testextextile.com/what-is-the-textile-fabric-testing-test-method-test-item-classification/> accessed 6 July 2021

116 Testex Textile, 'What is the Textile Fabric Testing, Test Method, Test Item Classification' (*Testex Textile*, 21 June 2019) <https://www.testextextile.com/what-is-the-textile-fabric-testing-test-method-test-item-classification/> accessed 6 July 2021

117 British Standards Institution, 'How BSI Can Help' (*BSI*, 2021) <https://www.bsigroup.com/en-GB/> accessed 6 July 2021

118 A block is a master template, from which new patterns for designs can be drafted

119 Sue Jenkyn Jones, *Fashion Design* (3rd edn, Laurence King 2002) 180

120 Gaylene Mccaw, 'Do You Toile?' (*CAFA*, 14 October 2020) <https://www.Couturearts.com.au/blog/do-you-toile#:~:text=Toile%20is%20a%20French%20word,translucent%20linen%20or%20cotton%20fabric> accessed 26 March 2020

stitched or sewn by hand.[121] It is suggested that most principal seams are stitched by machine, although 'the hems, inside seams and lining, are completed by hand.'[122] The main difference between mass-manufactured fashion and bespoke Couture construction is that clients of Couture will have the opportunity to be involved from the design process through to the construction and fitting of the garment.[123] Characteristics of Couture garments are more detailed than mass-manufactured products, as the attention to detail is the essential additional contributing factor that defines Couture. For example, Shaeffer illustrates the intricate attention to detail afforded to a Chanel jacket; the collar is noted for being 'trimmed with a black braid . . . the braid was embroidered with the same chenille yarn used to weave the fabric.'[124]

1.7 Fashion as a Concept

Couture is a branch of fashion, and therefore to illustrate the development of Couture within the study, it is necessary to examine the historical development of fashion as a foundation first, particularly as a concept in relation to cultural and societal conventions. According to Kawamura, 1300 was when the first recordings of 'style, fashion, and manner of dress' were documented,[125] although it was not until 1489 that the word *fashion* as it relates to lifestyle and clothing, was recognised in its current form.[126] In terms of lifestyle, clothing can be seen to have been an instrument to communicate the status of an individual within society. This point is pertinent, as in 1509 legislation came into effect for the purposes of restricting the wearing of clothing that was regarded as affluent. The aspect of affluence related to the fabric, colour, and quality, unless the individual belonged to a superior class; therefore, only members of the community who belonged to a high class were permitted to wear such garments.[127] These restrictions pertained to 'any cloth of gold or silver, sables or woollen cloth made outside of England, Wales, Ireland or Calais.'[128] Fashion being subject to an association with class also provided a specific identity to the wearer by visually communicating the wearer's societal background. Whilst the restrictions of 1509 do not have any relevance on society today, Couture designs do have a significant influence on the fashion industry, which is a factor considered next.

It appears that fashion is a cultural, sociological, environmental, and economic concept, time-stamped by the date of creation and treasured in historical chronicles.

121 Claire Shaeffer, *Couture Tailoring* (Laurence King Student & Professional 2021) 6

122 Gavin Waddell, *How Fashion Works: Couture, Ready-to-Wear and Mass Production* (Wiley 2004) 1

123 Ralph & Russo, 'The Couture Process' (*Ralph & Russo*, 2022) <https://ralphandrusso.com/pages/Couture-process> accessed 27 December 2022

124 Claire B Shaeffer 'Couture Sewing: The Couture Cardigan Jacket, Sewing Secrets From a Chanel Collector' (The Taunton Press Inc, 2013) 347

125 Yuniya Kawamura, *Fashion-ology* (2nd edn, Bloomsbury Academic 2017) 263

126 Yuniya Kawamura, *Fashion-ology* (2nd edn, Bloomsbury Academic 2017) 276

127 Richard Thompson Ford, *Dress Codes: How the Laws of Fashion Made History* (Simon & Schuster 2021) 33

128 Richard Thompson Ford, *Dress Codes: How the Laws of Fashion Made History* (Simon & Schuster 2021) 33

Fashion has been stated as being connected to *change*,[129] and not fixed or motionless.[130] Further, it has been considered from the viewpoint of time as being 'now'[131] as it relates to the 'process of rapid style change.'[132] Further, it is considered as sharing an attribute relating to the paradigm of modernism.[133] Fashion is therefore characteristically unstable and pertains to seasons,[134] and for this reason, it appears that the notion of *change* is the catalyst for *fashion* creation.

Conversely, noted is the idea that fashion possesses 'invisible elements'[135] and the 'use'[136] of attire is therefore embraced by 'society'[137] for a temporary time-period, and furthermore, this is attributed to 'cultural values.'[138] However, understanding why this is temporary may lie in the fact of fashion being regarded by the consumer as providing 'alluring value,'[139] and that the consumer by purchasing the fashion item is obtaining the perceived value.[140] It is hereby observed that a *change* in cultural values dictates the appeal and commercial viability of fashion.

Considerations are extended to *fashion* as an *independent* concept, and correspondingly, fashion has been stated as being *the* 'essential value' within attire,[141] whereby if this did not exist, the intrinsic value would not subsist.[142] Hereby, there is the idea of fashion being an independent concept but also being *attached* to garments; and therefore, notions can be developed as to fashion being regarded as an independent intangible commodity, and this shall now be explained further. An attempt to distinguish fashion from 'clothing' has been made;[143] however, both concepts appear to be always addressed concurrently.[144] In other words, fashion as a notion is communicated and exists only through dress. This occurs via the perpetual changing influences of society for a duration, the relevance of which seems dependent on the intrinsic value conferred upon it by cultural expectations and judgements. Therefore, the concept of *fashion* and apparel (dress) appear to be inseparable. Furthermore, the element of the *technical* component of apparel is an inseparable part of fashion. On this basis, questions to consider are whether this makes a garment functional, the extent of functionality, and to what extent is this aspect important. These points shall be considered further on in the study in chapter 5.

129 Tim Jackson and David Shaw, *The Fashion Handbook* (Routledge 2006) 1
130 Yuniya Kawamura, *Fashion-ology* (2nd edn, Bloomsbury Academic 2017) 282
131 Caroline Evans and Allessandra Vaccari, *Time in Fashion* (Bloomsbury 2020) 3
132 Caroline Evans and Allessandra Vaccari, *Time in Fashion* (Bloomsbury 2020) 3
133 Lars Svendsen, *Fashion: A Philosophy* (Reaktion Books 2006) 70
134 Rebecca Arnold, *Fashion: A Very Short Introduction* (Oxford University Press 2009) 50
135 Yuniya Kawamura, *Fashion-ology* (2nd edn, Bloomsbury Academic 2017) 296
136 Yuniya Kawamura, *Fashion-ology* (2nd edn, Bloomsbury Academic 2017) 296
137 Yuniya Kawamura, *Fashion-ology* (2nd edn, Bloomsbury Academic 2017) 297
138 Yuniya Kawamura, *Fashion-ology* (2nd edn, Bloomsbury Academic 2017) 297
139 Yuniya Kawamura, *Fashion-ology* (2nd edn, Bloomsbury Academic 2017) 297
140 Yuniya Kawamura, *Fashion-ology* (2nd edn, Bloomsbury Academic 2017) 297
141 Yuniya Kawamura, *Fashion-ology* (2nd edn, Bloomsbury Academic 2017) 303
142 Yuniya Kawamura, *Fashion-ology* (2nd edn, Bloomsbury Academic 2017) 303
143 Yuniya Kawamura, *Fashion-ology* (2nd edn, Bloomsbury Academic 2017) 282
144 Yuniya Kawamura, *Fashion-ology* (2nd edn, Bloomsbury Academic 2017) 282

Figure 1.4 Day Dress V&A Museum no. T.155-1937

When considering apparel, the idea that fashion is about 'self-adornment' and the 'presentation' of oneself is a key factor, because the concept of *fashion* as dress provides for the opportunity for communication by consumers to the external environment.[145] Once the consumer perception of value diminishes, a transition into the next *fashion* is inevitable, and so is the enduring cycle. This can be supported by a historic theoretic approach to fashion which has established the idea that fashion inhabits its own death, which is observed through the transitions and cycles of fashion.[146] To understand such concepts, the fashion industry is examined next for the purposes of illustrating the current position of the U.K. market and how it operates.

145 Frances Corner, *Why Fashion Matters* (Thames & Hudson 2014) 22
146 Lars Svendsen, *Fashion: A Philosophy* (Reaktion Books 2006) 567

1.8 The U.K. Fashion Industry

As mentioned earlier, fashion is supported by the BFC, a registered charity,[147] and it is instrumental in building a network within the U.K. fashion industry which actively supports 'diversity'[148] as a 'responsible'[149] and 'creative business.'[150] The U.K. fashion industry is established for influencing trends globally,[151] and the U.K. is recognised for its expertise and innovative designs.[152]

The United Kingdom supports fashion education through the many degree courses available at leading art and design institutions such as the London College of Fashion and Central Saint Martins. Both schools are part of the University of the Arts, London, and are among the top fashion schools in London.[153] Further, the University of the Arts, London, is the largest institute solely dedicated to art, fashion, the performing arts, and design courses for higher education. It has produced world leading designers such as Stella McCartney and the late Alexander McQueen.[154] Notably, Central Saint Martins has been awarded museum status, and this is indicative of the contribution to the arts, and testament to the value given to the work produced.[155] Courses in fashion are seen to integrate business concepts and design to meet the needs of the industry.[156] Although the U.K. is a global market leader in fashion and textiles, it was reported in 2015 that to maintain this position, investment must be put into skilled personnel.[157] With this considered, fashion

147 BFC, 'The BFC Has Incorporated All Its Charities to Form the BFC Foundation' (*British Fashion Council*, 2020) <https://www.britishfashioncouncil.co.uk./About> accessed 6 July 2021

148 British Fashion Council, 'The British Fashion Council Strengthens British Fashion in the Global Economy as a Leader in Creative, Responsible Businesses' (*British Fashion Council*, 2020) <https://www.britishfashioncouncil.co.uk./home> accessed 6 July 2021

149 British Fashion Council, 'The British Fashion Council Strengthens British Fashion in the Global Economy as a Leader in Creative, Responsible Businesses' (*British Fashion Council*, 2020) <https://www.britishfashioncouncil.co.uk./home> accessed 6 July 2021

150 British Fashion Council, 'The British Fashion Council Strengthens British Fashion in the Global Economy as a Leader in Creative, Responsible Businesses' (*British Fashion Council*, 2020) <https://www.britishfashioncouncil.co.uk./home> accessed 6 July 2021

151 Creative Industries Council, 'Fashion: Why the U.K.?' (*CIC*, 14 January 2021, updated on 13 April 2021) <https://www.thecreativeindustries.co.uk/site-content/industries-fashion-fashion-why-the-U.K?> accessed 6 July

152 Creative Industries Council, 'Fashion: Why the U.K.?' (*CIC*, 14 January 2021, updated on 13 April 2021) <https://www.thecreativeindustries.co.uk/site-content/industries-fashion-fashion-why-the-U.K?> accessed 6 July

153 T Laura, 'Top Fashion Schools Around the World' (*QS*, April 2021) <https://www.topuniversities.com/courses/art-design/top-fashion-schools-around-world> accessed 25 October 2021

154 Times Higher Education, 'University Rankings, University of the Arts' (*Times Higher Education*, 2021) <https://www.timeshighereducation.com/world-university-rankings/university-arts-london> accessed 25 October 2021

155 Times Higher Education, 'University Rankings, University of the Arts' (*Times Higher Education*, 2021) <https://www.timeshighereducation.com/world-university-rankings/university-arts-london> accessed 25 October 2021

156 Creative Industries Council, 'Fashion: Why the U.K.?' (*CIC*, 14 January 2021 updated on 13 April 2021) <https://www.thecreativeindustries.co.uk./site-content/industries-fashion-fashion-why-the-U.K> accessed 6 July

157 Wendy Malem and others, 'High-End & Designer Manufacturing Report' [2015] Protecting Existing Resource and Encouraging Growth and Innovation – Commissioned by the British Fashion

is a *multi-billion-dollar business.*[158] The fashion industry is observed to consist of industries that interlink, stemming from manufacturing to promotional activities.[159]

1.9 Market Levels

Market levels of the fashion market can be divided into sub-groups, although for the purposes of this study, three market levels shall be examined. The consumer has been referenced earlier when considering 'value,' and therefore the vast influence consumers have on the direction of fashion is significant. Consumers purchase fashion for a variety of reasons, including replacing an older version of a product, a passtime or even for the purposes of expressing the self through fashion.[160] It is suggested that the modern-day consumer is complicated, particularly as it relates to expression of the self at different stages of life.[161]

The consumer is described as 'the stylist,'[162] and they are regarded as not wanting to wear a set of clothes from the same brand and are mixing brands from all market levels. Yet, the market levels this study examines are Couture, luxury ready to wear, and high street. Each level is examined as follows, although the main focus and emphasis is placed on the Couture markets as it is the fundamental influencer for the levels below.

1.9.1 Couture

The Couture category of fashion is identified as the most significant market level for fashion due to the influence it has on the market levels below it. For example, high street brands can interpret the Couture trends to produce more cost-efficient derivatives as it relates to fabric and 'simpler patterns.'[163]

1.9.2 Ready to Wear Luxury

It is said that Paul Smith and Burberry are brands which occupy the luxury ready to wear fashion level.[164] The pricing of the luxury ready to wear market reflects the exclusivity of the brands, and therefore identifying luxury fashion brands

---

Council, U.K. Fashion & Textile Association, Creative Skillset and Marks & Spencer Research by Oxford Economics and Glasgow Caledonian University

158 *Tim Jackson and David Shaw, The Fashion Handbook (Routledge 2006) 1*

159 Rebecca Arnold, *Fashion: A Very Short Introduction* (Oxford University Press 2009) 48

160 Tim Jackson and David Shaw, *The Fashion Handbook* (Routledge 2006) 127

161 Tim Jackson and David Shaw, *The Fashion Handbook* (Routledge 2006) 207

162 Mark Tungate, *Fashion Brands* (2nd edn, Kogan Page 2008) 248

163 Fashion Addicted, 'Does Haute Couture Affect High Street Style?' (*Fashion Addicted*, 13 January 2014) https://duncanozann.wordpress.com/2014/01/13/does-haute-couture-affect-high-street-style/ accessed 26 March 2022

164 Shatakshi Tiwari, 'Top British Luxury Brands' (*Luxury Abode*, 3 June 2020) <https://www.luxuryabode.com/blog/top-british-luxury-fashion-brands/artid123> accessed 31 March 2022

is said to be dependent on 'the size of the markup it commands.'[165] A luxury fashion brand can also be identified through the route of its sales, for example the merchandise being sold in company owned boutiques or 'high end' department stores.[166] In terms of marketing luxury ready to wear fashion, advertisements often tell a story, a conceptual myth to create mystical curiosity amongst its consumers.[167] Relevant to the objectives of this thesis is the fact that when marketing, advertisements may show a fashion product featured in the Couture show, although it is not sold as part of the ready to wear range.[168] This is significant for the purposes of the thesis because it demonstrates the impact of Couture on the wider industry as it relates to sales for lower market levels and influence over design concepts.

It is hereby observed that the luxury ready to wear market reflects the historical sociological connotations discussed earlier. Although, the luxury fashion market is experiencing a pivotal shift in traditional fashion concepts. Luxury fashion is said to be an indicator of an individual's political, social, and economic status.[169] However, the marker of the sociological status appears to have shifted from the type of garment worn to an emphasis on the brand. Today, luxury brands can produce fashion garments such as 'hoodies' which were not traditionally identified as a luxury garment.[170] A further change noted is that consumers of luxury fashion are choosing unique garments over craftmanship, a concept traditionally associated with luxury fashion.[171] Moreover, craftmanship is a key consideration of this thesis in relation to copyright and shall be explored in depth, in chapters 4–7. With these notions in mind, the next section shall look at high street fashion.

1.9.3 High Street

The high street level exists as tiers, and this is perceived through the quality, style, and pricing ranges of fashion apparel sold at this level. U.K. brands such as LK Bennett[172] and Reiss[173] sit at the higher market level, whilst Marks and Spencer[174] is established at the middle market for the high street, and fast fashion brands such

165 Don Thompson, *The Curious Economics of Luxury Fashion* (3rd edn, e-book 2022) 15
166 Don Thompson, *The Curious Economics of Luxury Fashion* (3rd edn, e-book 2022) 16
167 Don Thompson, *The Curious Economics of Luxury Fashion* (3rd edn, e-book 2022) 16
168 Don Thompson, *The Curious Economics of Luxury Fashion* (3rd edn, e-book 2022) 18
169 Harry Hurt, 'Luxury, and How It Became Common' (*The New York Times*, 19 August 2007) <https://www.nytimes.com/2007/08/19/business/yourmoney/19shelf.html> accessed 26 March 2022
170 Kati Chitrakorn, 'What Makes a Popular Luxury Fashion Brand?' (*Vogue Business*, 5 June 2020) <https://www.voguebusiness.com/companies/what-makes-a-popular-luxury-fashion-brand> accessed 26 March 2022
171 Kati Chitrakorn, 'What Makes a Popular Luxury Fashion Brand?' (*Vogue Business*, 5 June 2020) <https://www.voguebusiness.com/companies/what-makes-a-popular-luxury-fashion-brand> accessed 26 March 2022
172 LK Bennett, 'Fashion' (*LK BENNETT*, 2021) <https://www.lkbennett.com/> accessed 6 July 2021
173 Reiss, 'Fashion' (*Reiss*, 2021) <https://www.reiss.com/> accessed 6 July
174 M&S, 'M&S' (*Marks and Spencers*, 2022) <https://www.marksandspencer.com/?msclkid=c0eb86e7ad8a11ec9c056fb791e72995> accessed 26 March 2022

as Peacocks[175] and Matalan[176] sit at a lower level. Fast fashion has been developed to meet consumer demand for 'on-trend clothing.'[177]

Based on the preceding information regarding the high street garments as it pertains to fulfilling a consumer demand for trends, and producing wardrobe staples, the thesis question cannot be tested against these factors for the purposes of copyright protection. The reason for this is that as seen in the luxury ready to wear market, design concepts become diluted as they are realised further down the market levels. This further supports the thesis question in applying to Couture only.

1.10 Couture as an Artistic Fashion Concept: Cultural and Societal Associations

Fashion is described as 'performative,'[178] and not just being an 'image'[179] or 'object.'[180] The word *perform*[181] suggests that there is activity, that fashion is not a static concept, and that it changes to reflect sociological, cultural, and economic developments as it relates to the artistic attributes. On this basis, the value of art is explored for the purposes of ascertaining an understanding as to the artistic value of Couture.

1.10.1 The Value of Art

The value of art is understood to be appreciated in different forms, such as historical, patriotic, symbolic, and financial societal value.[182] Historically, art is said to connect culture and time; patriotically, it can showcase national pride in artistic accomplishments.[183] For example, the Diana memorial fountain is a tribute landmark to the late Princess Diana of Wales. The societal value of art is reflected through the artworks as responding to social issues, such as race, religion, and culture for the purpose of communicating to the collective.[184]

So far, the value of art has been observed as intrinsic value found within the concepts discussed. In terms of monetary value, it is suggested that a more conservative approach is emerging amongst buyers in favour of historical pieces rather than those associated with a celebrity.[185] It is suggested that when art is commercialised,

175 Peacocks, 'Peacocks' (*Peacocks*, 2022) <https://www.peacocks.co.uk/?msclkid=2eb85589ad8a11ec85599828b97029cc> accessed 26 March 2022

176 Matalan, 'Matalan' (*Matalan*, 2022) <https://www.matalan.co.uk./?msclkid=4133f4f3ad8b11ec8111c3aa3ccb7da1> accessed 26 March 2022

177 Leena Oijala, 'What is Fast Fashion' (*Leaf*, 2022) <https://www.leaf.tv/articles/what-is-fast-fashion/> accessed 26 March 2022

178 Caroline Evans and Allessandra Vaccari, *Time in Fashion* (Bloomsbury 2020) 3

179 Caroline Evans and Allessandra Vaccari, *Time in Fashion* (Bloomsbury 2020) 3

180 Caroline Evans and Allessandra Vaccari, *Time in Fashion* (Bloomsbury 2020) 3

181 *Cambridge, Dictionary (Cambridge University Press 2011)*

182 Obelisk Art History LLC, 'The Value of Art Why Should We Care About Art?' (*Obelisk Art History*, 2022) <https://arthistoryproject.com/essays/the-value-of-art/> accessed 15 July 2022

183 Obelisk Art History LLC, 'The Value of Art Why Should We Care About Art?' (*Obelisk Art History*, 2022) <https://arthistoryproject.com/essays/the-value-of-art/> accessed 15 July 2022

184 Obelisk Art History LLC, 'The Value of Art Why Should We Care About Art?' (*Obelisk Art History*, 2022) <https://arthistoryproject.com/essays/the-value-of-art/> accessed 15 July 2022

185 Michael Findlay, *The Value of Art* (Kindle edn, Prestel 2014) 8

the value is understood to be determined and sustained by '[h]uman stipulation and declaration.'[186] The price of artwork is set following negotiations between artist and publisher/dealer.[187] A new body of art introduced to the market by an artist establishes the price through the size of the work, because public opinion has not formed regarding the types of art available by the artist.[188] The medium of the artwork (e.g. oil, pastel, gouache, water colour) in addition to the colour can impact the price; for example, monochrome works are said to be cheaper.[189]

The creative choices utilised for concepts, methods, and materials that a couturier uses reflect those equivalents in fine art creation. In fine art, an artist working with oil and creating a very large piece shall determine the price based on scale and medium used. A couturier would work out the cost based on the processes, materials, knowledge, and craftmanship used. On this basis, both artistic practices carry common traits which contribute to the value of the arts, in summary these are: knowledge, skill, craftmanship, specific materials, innovative concepts, historical/traditional influence, and possibly practices and an appreciative market.

To ascertain the justifications of the price of Couture, a comparison between fine art and Couture (assuming Couture is a conceptual work of art) follows. As a starting point, there are parallels with fine art and Couture, particularly in how the markets approach and react to art forms. In consideration of the pricing for Couture, the more embellished works are the more expensive.[190] To illustrate the value of fine art, it is noted that the painting *Abstraktes Bild* by Gerhard Richter was sold for £21.3 million in 2012.[191] Moreover, in consideration of Couture, if cultural heritage and traditional knowledge are integrated into Couture designs, the value of the garment increases. This is seen in Kristina Viirpalu's designs, whereby fine textiles artisans skilled in traditional Estonian embroidery and knitting methods are employed for the creation of Couture, combined with modern design concepts.[192] Similarly, Jiri Kalfar recognises Couture as requiring '[p]recision, knowledge, and experience' together with the use of multiple artisans, which increases the price of Couture.[193] To implement the technical components to art forms would lead to enquiries as to whether art can be technical.

186 Michael Findlay, *The Value of Art* (Kindle edn, Prestel Verlag 2014) 16

187 Michael Findlay, *The Value of Art* (Kindle edn, Prestel Verlag 2014) 19

188 Michael Findlay, *The Value of Art* (Kindle edn, Prestel Verlag 2014) 19

189 Michael Findlay, *The Value of Art* (Kindle edn, Prestel Verlag 2014) 21, 26

190 Couture Notebook, 'All You Need to Know About Haute Couture' (*Couture Notebook*, 2022) <https://Couturenotebook.com/haute-Couture-definition-clients-and-prices> accessed 18 July 2022

191 Georgina Adam, 'Why is Art So Expensive?' (*BBC*, 2 May 2013) <https://www.bbc.com/culture/article/20130417-why-is-art-so-expensive> accessed 26 March 2023

192 DiBoscio Chere, 'Why Is Couture So Expensive?' (*Eluxe Magazine*, 15 October 2020) <https://eluxemagazine.com/fashion/why-Couture-is-so-expensive-3-perspectives/> accessed 18 July 2022

193 DiBoscio Chere, 'Why Is Couture So Expensive?' (*Eluxe Magazine*, 15 October 2020) <https://eluxemagazine.com/fashion/why-Couture-is-so-expensive-3-perspectives/> accessed 18 July 2022

1.10.2 Technicality and Functionality

Art containing technical attributes may span across varying industries. The term 'technical artist' is linked to artists who develop video games.[194] Conversely, the University of East London currently provides for a fine art technology degree, whereby the focus of technicality is a feature of fine art.[195] The technical elements pertaining to art are taught through workshops as they relate to contemporary 'practice' inclusive of digital 'tools.'[196]

How does technicality relate to fashion and to what extent? In 2016, the Museum of Fine Art, Boston hosted an exhibition on 'fashion and technology' with pieces exhibited by high profile designers such as 'Iris Van Herpen, Viktor & Rolf, Alexander McQueen and Mary Katrantzou.'[197] The exhibition focused on technical features that pertain to digital technology such as 3D printed works, although as spectacular as technology can make a garment, technical aspects of fashion works are inherent as natural features.[198] Whilst these works appear to have artistic value, how would these works be defined and protected by the law, if at all? Pursuant to s.4 of the CDPA 1988, Couture is not listed within the apparent closed list of protectable subject matter. The traditional technicality of garments is integral to the performance, such as an elastic waist, a sleeve hole, a dart in the breast or waist to add shape and to avoid gaping loose fabric that may be unflattering to the wearer. In other words, in as much as the fashion is designed for aesthetic appeal, the objective moves beyond the garment to the wearer for the purposes of adornment, aesthetics, and performance. On this basis, the study shall begin to break down the various elements of Couture to assess the extent to which it may be categorised as an artistic work under s.4 of the CDPA 1988.

The aspect of technicality relates to functionality, and in addition, fashion is regarded as something which is malleable, time-relevant, and necessary to the individual from the perspective of societal considerations, whether the necessity is bourn through cultural, environmental, or economic implications. It is clear to see how the concept of fashion sits somewhere in between the practical considerations and creative pursuits. Fashion is a wide concept that extends to design, art, and culture. However, Couture is influenced and developed by the implementation of other considerations such as commerce, function, and digital innovation. Examined next is the idea of Couture fusing the aspects of creativity and function in terms of the

194 Sokanu Interactive Inc, 'What Does a Technical Artist Do?' (*Career explorercom*, 2023) <https://www.careerexplorer.com/careers/technical-artist/> accessed 11 February 2023

195 University of East London, 'BA (Hons) Fine Art Technology' (*University of London*, 2023) <https://www.uel.ac.uk./undergraduate/courses/ba-hons-fine-art-technology> accessed 11 February 2023

196 University of East London, 'BA (Hons) Fine Art Technology' (*University of London*, 2023) <https://www.uel.ac.uk./undergraduate/courses/ba-hons-fine-art-technology> accessed 11 February 2023

197 Cassidy Olsen, 'High Fashion Meets High-Tech Innovation at MFA's #techstyle' (*The Tufts Daily*, 9 March 2016) <High fashion meets high-tech innovation at MFA's #techstyle – The Tufts Daily> accessed 29 October 2024

198 Cassidy Olsen, 'High Fashion Meets High-Tech Innovation at MFA's #techstyle' (*The Tufts Daily*, 9 March 2016) <High fashion meets high-tech innovation at MFA's #techstyle – The Tufts Daily> accessed 29 October 2024

performance of the product, or more accurately, the aspect pertaining to technicality which serves the usefulness.

1.11 The Relationship Between Couture and Copyright

Copyright is a right which exists to protect works against copying without the permission of the creator.[199] The considerations for this study are how within this legal provision Couture could be best protected, if at all. Copyright can be a complex issue when considering an international brand as the copyright laws are only applicable within the jurisdiction it applies.[200] The Copyright Designs and Patents Act 1988 is the main legislative provision for copyright within the U.K. Copyright protects a range of creative works such as literary, dramatic, and musical works,[201] databases,[202] artistic works,[203] sound recordings,[204] films,[205] and broadcasts,[206] amongst others.

Couture has been discussed earlier in consideration of an art form; therefore the study shall consider the extent to which Couture is an artistic work. This would lead to an examination as to the extent Couture should be protected in law. S.4 of the CDPA 1988 appears to protect *artistic works* through a closed list system for specific subject matter, such as a graphic work, photograph, sculpture, collage, a work of architecture being a building or a model for a building, or a work of artistic craftsmanship. Here, two issues arise for the study, and they are:

1. The apparent closed list categories of works, whereby Couture is not included; and
2. How Couture could be defined under s.4 of the CDPA 1988.

These two points raise significant enquiries for the study in that firstly, why is Couture not listed within the apparent closed list of works? Additionally, it is necessary within this chapter to understand the relationship between Couture and copyright, in providing a foundation for the deeper examination to follow throughout the research presented. These issues shall continue to be considered throughout the study, mainly in chapters 4 to 7.

It has been argued that fashion should be regarded as an 'original artistic work.'[207] However, contrarily, it has further been established that case law is not

199 Gov.uk, 'How Copyright Protects Your Work' (*Gov.uk*, 2020) <https://www.gov.uk./copyright > accessed 6 July 2021

200 Sue Jenkyn Jones, *Fashion Design* (3rd edn, Laurence King 2002) 94

201 Copyright, Designs and Patents Act 1988, s.3

202 Copyright, Designs and Patents Act 1988, S.3A

203 Copyright Designs and Patents Act 1988, S.4

204 Copyright Designs and Patents Act 1988, S.5A

205 Copyright, Designs and Patents Act 1988, S.5B

206 Copyright Designs and Patents Act 1988, S.6

207 Iona Silverman, 'Copyright and Fashion: A U.K. Perspective' (*WIPO*, June 2014) <https://www.WIPO.int/WIPO_magazine/en/2014/03/article_0007.html> accessed 31 May 2021

necessarily supportive of this.[208] It is suggested that the ideal position for fashion would be for it to be recognised under s.4(c) as a work of artistic craftmanship.[209] This study is narrower in scope of fashion works and examines the category of Couture only, specifically as the substantive element (this is established in relation to the art of Couture creation, practice, and components contained within a Couture garment). The study argues that *Couture is* art and should be included within the apparent closed list under s.4 of the CDPA 1988; the study is *not* advocating for the inclusion of all fashion works within the provision.

To facilitate the research, it is necessary to identify where the art in Couture is. Does art exist within elements of Couture, or are we to perceive Couture as a conceptual work of art? Further, the issue of aesthetics is a paramount consideration for Couture and success amongst clientele, as it is this which may speak to commercial viability. The derivative question would therefore be, does art therefore facilitate aesthetics? This aspect acknowledges a pragmatic concern as it relates to commercial viability of a product and therefore encourages considerations as to how they relate to the value of art and copyright protection. These questions shall be considered throughout the study, although mainly throughout chapters 4–7.

Interim Conclusion

In summary from the preceding discussion, historically fashion has been used as a tool to communicate status, therefore it addresses the societal hierarchy, and the culture adopted in terms of lifestyle. Couture is a category of fashion which reflects these notions.

Traditionally, Couture had developed as a specific category of fashion. The artistic form of fashion was recognised in 1858 through the term 'fashion designer' being used in preference for 'dress maker.'[210] This is a significant development to outline and illustrate the artistic nature of Couture. Although the English fashion designer Charles Frederick Worth is understood to be the pioneer for Couture, the developments in France since 1868 have highlighted the different approaches to the value placed on the art form by the fashion industry and relevant institutions, which have resulted in varying approaches to Couture today.[211] This does raise the question as to whether the absence within the U.K. of a comparable regulatory body (specifically for Couture) to the French Fédération de la Haute Couture et

208 Iona Silverman, 'Copyright and Fashion: A U.K. Perspective' (*WIPO*, June 2014) <https://www.WIPO.int/WIPO_magazine/en/2014/03/article_0007.html> accessed 31 May 2021

209 Iona Silverman, 'Copyright and Fashion: A U.K. Perspective' (*WIPO*, June 2014) <https://www.WIPO.int/WIPO_magazine/en/2014/03/article_0007.html> accessed 31 May 2021

210 Harper's Bazaar, 'The History of Haute Couture From Humble Beginnings to Present Day' (*Harper's Bazaar*, 19 January 2017) <https://www.harpersbazaar.com/U.K./fashion/fashion-news/news/a31123/the-history-of-haute-Couture/> accessed 27 December 2022

211 Elyssa Kostopoulos, 'The Mystique That is Haute Couture: Your Guide to Fashion's Exclusive World' (*RUSSH*, 25 February 2021) <https://www.russh.com/what-is-haute-Couture/> accessed 6 July 2021

Figure 1.5 Chanel Spring/Summer 1965 Agra Lame by Bucol Patrimoine de CHANEL Paris HC. PE.1965.5 (V&A Chanel 2023 Exhibition)

de la Mode is a contributing factor as to the reason Couture does not seem to be specifically protected as an art form, by s.4 of the CDPA 1988 as an artistic work.

Further, it is questioned as to the extent that the dissolution of the Association of the Incorporated Society of London Fashion Designers (that was initially established in 1941) has impacted the development of the U.K. legislation. The potential for the Association to have been developed as the equivalent institution to the French Fédération de la Haute Couture et de la Mode in the U.K. has ceased to be proven through its demise. For this reason, in relation to the development and investment in Couture, it appears that the U.K. is in deficit of approximately 80 years in comparison to France. Although the British Fashion Council (BFC) oversees and supports the fashion industry in the U.K., a body to support Couture exclusively is absent.

The process of Couture appears to be reliant on the fashion notion of 'change,'[212] identified within the discussion as a catalyst for fashion creation and moreover that the consumer is the significant instigator of the 'change,' which is based on the consumer's perception of value as it relates to the product.[213] On this basis, Couture provides the consumer with the opportunity and space to be instrumental in the Couture creation process. Whilst Couture is derived through artistic practice as part of fashion, fashion is identified as being an independent intangible commodity, something that is attached to a fashion product, whereby scholars address both simultaneously.[214] Within the discussion also exists the *concept of fashion* being inseparable from the product. In addition to this, the identification of the technical component of Couture cannot be disconnected from the product either as a concept or physically. The concept of fashion as an independent commodity being inseparable from the product itself, and the technicality of the product is an integral and natural part of Couture. This indicates that those elements exist naturally, and with exception to the designer, remain outside of the control of any other authority. To develop this concept, the couturier is the only individual who can incorporate artistic craftmanship, innovate, and implement all the intrinsic features that are expected as components of Couture. This discussion thus far has signalled the incorporation of the technical elements of Couture, which cannot be separated from the creative process, and further that the creative skill is required to accommodate the technical component specifically. The couturier's skill therefore must be engaged for the purposes of creating the art form, whereby the technical aspects are *part of the art*.

At this point, it is necessary to acknowledge that the study has only introduced the concept of copyright and the relationship to Couture. For a balanced view, it is necessary to analyse the wider IP framework of legislation and case law, in consideration of the application to Couture within the next chapter.

212 Tim Jackson and David Shaw, *The Fashion Handbook* (Routledge 2006) 1
213 Yuniya Kawamura, *Fashion-ology* (2nd edn, Bloomsbury Academic 2017) 297
214 Yuniya Kawamura, *Fashion-ology* (2nd edn, Bloomsbury Academic 2017) 282

2 Broader Considerations

The Wider Intellectual Property Law Framework, in Response to Couture as Art

Introduction

This chapter examines the wider IP framework, regarding the different legal approaches of each IP right. The chapter is significant as the IP framework has been established to protect categories of works, and therefore, depending on the nature of the work, an appropriate IP right should apply and protect the work in question. The scope of the chapter is mainly from the perspective of the U.K. and E.U. legislation, aiming to identify the symmetry between the two and establishing the position for works in both regimes. The chapter concludes with a case study on architecture whereby a comparison is made to Couture as an artistic work for the purposes of contributing to the assessment regarding the threshold for copyright protection within s.4 of the CDPA 1988. Pertinently, the chapter invites considerations as to whether copyright is the most appropriate IP right for Couture.

2.1 The Connection Between Patents and Couture

The main considerations regarding patents relate to the invention of Couture and whether this concept aligns with the criteria for the purposes of patent protection. Patents protect an invention 'that can be made or used . . . new and inventive.'[1] A patent will protect an invention, and legal action can be taken against an individual who infringes the patent.[2] Patents are described as incorporating 'technical, commercial and legal documents.'[3] The legal document for a patent sets out the reason for why the patent is 'necessary' and the solution the patent is intended to provide.[4] In other words, patents protect the *function* of the invention, the technical aspect of a product, a *process*. To elaborate, a patent is an exclusive right given to an individual, based on the disclosure of the technical information concerning the invention.[5]

1 Gov.uk, 'Patenting Your Invention' (*Gov.uk.*, 2021) <https://www.gov.uk./patent-your-invention> accessed 30 August 2021

2 Gov.uk, 'Patenting Your Invention' (*Gov.uk.*, 2021) <https://www.gov.uk./patent-your-invention> accessed 30 August 2021

3 L Bentley and others, *Intellectual Property Law* (6th edn, Oxford University Press 2022) 409

4 Rosie Burbridge, *European Fashion Law* (Edward Elgar 2019) 97

5 L Bentley and others, *Intellectual Property Law* (6th edn, Oxford University Press 2022) 409

DOI: 10.4324/9781003599456-2

2.1.1 *Novelty*

'New' or 'novelty'[6] is related to the concept of the 'state of the art,' and therefore for a patent to be recognised as new for the purposes of a patent registration, must not be part of the 'state of the art.'[7] The concept of 'state of the art' comprises of globally available subject matter in existence before the invention's priority date.[8] The aspect of *new* can be compromised if the patentable invention is disclosed prior to a registration application. This may, for example, arise through the publication on social media.[9] Identified is the aspect of novelty being 'quantitively' distinguishable from prior disclosures as it relates to the confidential nature of the technical information being withheld from the public domain.[10] Differentiation between novelty and an inventive step is identified as a 'qualitative' feature to establish whether a monopoly over the patent is justifiable.[11] In consideration of the justifications for the grant of a monopoly, it is expressed that the public are only happy to pay the patent monopoly costs provided that the information which is not ordinarily available to them is granted.[12]

In consideration of Couture, the requirement of novelty regarding the integral technical elements is significant, since most functional parts on products are not regarded as new. Consider items which are used to support apparel such as zips, hook and eye fastenings, and shoulder pads.[13] Therefore, would a *novel type* of supportive component for apparel such as a fastening be regarded as new? This would depend on the creative *and* design process for the functional part of the product, for instance, an innovative way the garment is assembled and held together, such as a shoulder strap for a summer top. The tie could be regarded as the product, although the assembly of the tie to provide the *function* of aligning, and fastening the garment together, is the *process*.

2.1.2 *Capable of Industrial Application*

The requirement that a patent must be capable of industrial application necessitates that it should not solely be an intellectual invention or that of an abstract concept, but it should subsist of 'concrete and technical character.'[14] The concept of *industry* is wide, and this may include not for profit and agricultural enterprises, therefore industrial application is defined as an invention which can be utilised and

6 The Patents Act 1977, s.1(1); European Patents Convention 2000, Art 52(1) (ex European Patents Convention 1973, Art 52(1))
7 The Patents Act 1977, s.2(1); European Patents Convention 2000, Art 54(1)
8 L Bentley and others, *Intellectual Property Law* (6th edn, Oxford University Press 2022) 557
9 Rosie Burbridge, *European Fashion Law* (Edward Elgar 2019) 97
10 L Bentley and others, *Intellectual Property Law* (6th edn, Oxford University Press 2022) 557
11 L Bentley and others, *Intellectual Property Law* (6th edn, Oxford University Press 2022) 557
12 L Bentley and others, *Intellectual Property Law* (6th edn, Oxford University Press 2022) 557
13 Please see 1.5.1 referring to Annette Fischer, and Kiran Gobin, *Construction for Fashion Design* (2nd edn, Bloomsbury 2017) 145
14 L Bentley and others, *Intellectual Property Law* (6th edn, Oxford University Press 2022) 589

created within *any* type of industry.[15] The invention must demonstrate a 'useful purpose'[16] which is defined by its 'practical application' or 'concrete benefit.'[17]

In consideration of Couture as it relates to industrial application,[18] a conflict between s.1(2)[19] and s.4 of the Act[20] as s.1.(2) is viewed[21] as overriding s.4 as it pertains to 'industrial application.' Although it may be argued that s.4 may be asserted as protecting functional features for the purposes of industrial application, this could be challenged if the functional features are dictated by aesthetic qualities. Noted is that the duration of a patent is shorter than it is for copyright and, trade mark protection further deliberated is the 'commercial uses' for the patent.[22] On this basis, significant is the 'limited monopoly' conferred to the inventor, only granted following an 'onerous registration process.'[23]

2.1.3 Patent for Products

A product patent protects the product and entitles the owner of the patent to a high degree of control over the patent as S.60(1)(a) states: '(a)where the invention is a product, he makes, disposes of, offers to dispose of, uses or imports the product or keeps it whether for disposal or otherwise.'[24] Suggested is that the purpose of the high level of protection is to limit the competition for identical products.[25] On this basis, liability is absolute and essentially makes 'knowledge of the defendant's activities irrelevant in consideration of those activities controlled by the patent owner.'[26]

2.1.4 Patents Derived Through a Process

Patents for a process permit the owner to use or offer the use of the patent within the U.K.[27] As it relates to infringement, unlike the product patent, the liability for a

15 L Bentley and others, *Intellectual Property Law* (6th edn, Oxford University Press 2022) 590

16 L Bentley and others, *Intellectual Property Law* (6th edn, Oxford University Press 2022) 551

17 L Bentley and others, *Intellectual Property Law* (6th edn, Oxford University Press 2022) 551 referring to *Max-Planck/BDPI phosphatase*, T870/04 [2006] EPOR 14[6],[7], [21], *Zymogenetics/Hematopoietic cytokine receptor*, T 898/05 [2007] EPOR 2, [4], cited with approval by the Supreme Court in *Human Genome Sciences v Eli Lilly* [2011] U.K.SC 51, [107]

18 Tomruk Űstűnkaya, 'Fashion Law: The Limitation Conundrum of the Patents Act 1977' (2020) 42(10) EIPR 621

19 The Patents Act 1977, s.1(2)

20 The Patents Act 1977, s.4

21 Tomruk Űstűnkaya, 'Fashion Law: The Limitation Conundrum of the Patents Act 1977' (2020) 42(10) EIPR 621

22 L Bentley and others, *Intellectual Property Law* (6th edn, Oxford University Press 2022) 409

23 L Bentley and others, *Intellectual Property Law* (6th edn, Oxford University Press 2022) 409

24 L Bentley and others, *Intellectual Property Law* (6th edn, Oxford University Press 2022) and PA 1977 s.60(1)(a)

25 Your Patent Team, 'What is the Difference Between Product and Process Patent in India?' (*Your Patent Team*, 2019) <https://yourpatentteam.com/hrf_faq/difference-between-product-and-process-patent/> accessed 18 October 2021

26 L Bentley and others, *Intellectual Property Law* (6th edn, Oxford University Press 2022) 649 referring to *Schenck v Universal Balancing* [2012] E.W.H.C. 1920, [86]

27 L Bentley and others, *Intellectual Property Law* (6th edn, Oxford University Press 2022) 658

process patent is not absolute. The defendant's knowledge is relevant as it relates to the unauthorised use of the patent resulting in an infringement.[28] When considering obtaining a patent derived through a process, the wording of the convention is said to be problematic for protection in relation to the end-product.[29] This is because claims are often deferred to an intermediary product due to the limitation of the requested 'directly obtained' condition.[30] Limitations pertain to the requirement of the product being a 'sequential step of the process,' and further that protection is afforded to only products that are 'directly obtained' by this process.[31]

To consider this within the context of textiles for use in Couture, lyocell (Tencel brand),[32] viscose, and modal are noted to be almost identical but derived through different processes.[33] In relation to the distinguished characteristics, the manufacturing process that produces lyocell is described as 'a by-product of the different production method, in that the internal structure of the fibre is more uniform which further improves its ability to absorb water.'[34] Tencel is noted to have advanced characteristics relating to 'moisture absorbency and breathability.'[35] Significantly, these differences exist due to the manufacturing processes for each.[36] Inventions for Couture other than the textile used for the product such as a fastening, a hood, a belt, corsetry, support, and shape enhancing inventions engage the design process.[37] Therefore, the design for the creation and construction of the technical product is specifically an intentional objective, and it is argued, therefore, that it is not a derivative or by-product of the Couture garment.

However, the creation of Couture could be regarded as a process, for the purpose of understanding the rationale for a patent as it relates to products derived through a

28 L Bentley and others, *Intellectual Property Law* (6th edn, Oxford University Press 2022) 658

29 L Bentley and others, *Intellectual Property Law* (6th edn, Oxford University Press 2022) 658

30 Jobst Wibbelmann, 'Protection of "Products Directly Obtained By Processes" According to Article 64(2) EPC' (1996) 18(3) EIPR 174–76

31 Jobst Wibbelmann, 'Protection of "Products Directly Obtained By Processes" According to Article 64(2) EPC' (1996) 18(3) EIPR 174–76

32 Tencel is the brand name for lyocell – http://www.madehow.com/Volume-5/Lyocell.html (Courtaulds are the owners of a patent for the process for the manufacture of lyocell fibre.) Patent No: 5725821, Process for the manufacture of Lyocell fibre, March 10, 1998, Inventors: James Martin Gannon, Ian Graveson, Simon Ashley Mortimer. Assignee: Courtaulds Fibres (Holdings) Limited

33 Robert Kay, 'Viscose Vs Modal Vs Lyocell- Difference?' (*Robert Owen Undershirts*, 30 April 2017) <https://www.undershirts.co.uk./blogs/research/viscose-vs-modal-vs-lyocell> accessed 3 October 2021

34 Robert Kay, 'Viscose Vs Modal Vs Lyocell- Difference?' (*Robert Owen Undershirts*, 30 April 2017) <https://www.undershirts.co.uk./blogs/research/viscose-vs-modal-vs-lyocell> accessed 3 October 2021

35 Robert Kay, 'Viscose Vs Modal Vs Lyocell- Difference?' (*Robert Owen Undershirts*, 30 April 2017) <https://www.undershirts.co.uk./blogs/research/viscose-vs-modal-vs-lyocell> accessed 3 October 2021

36 Robert Kay, 'Viscose Vs Modal Vs Lyocell- Difference?' (*Robert Owen Undershirts*, 30 April 2017) <https://www.undershirts.co.uk./blogs/research/viscose-vs-modal-vs-lyocell> accessed 3 October 2021

37 Please see chapter 1

process. To consider this point, the case of *Pioneer Electronics Capital, Inc*[38] is significant. This case illustrates the concept of the product being *directly obtained*. The claimant had brought two actions against *Warner Music Manufacturing* for the patents relating to the manufacturing process of optical discs (CDs).[39] The claim against the defendants was rooted in an infringement action under s.60(1)(c) of the Patents Act 1977. The defendants attempted to strike out the claims and argued that the CDs they manufactured were different when contrasted with the claimants patented process and therefore the defendants' CD manufacturing process was not 'directly obtained.'[40] Further, the defendants submitted that to construe the findings differently by disregarding the word 'directly' would infer that a 'casual' correlation would establish infringement.[41] The claimant's relied on a factual analysis of whether the product was obtained directly, and further they argued on the definition of 'directly' asserting that it did not pertain to the product being an immediate result of the process.[42]

The decision ultimately rested with 'directly obtained' being understood as the first product derived from the process. The decision by Aldous J sought clarity of the issue for the public, but moreover, fairness for the patentee. The decision was noted to illustrate the court's enthusiasm to consider reviews from other E.U. states and the need for consistency.[43] On appeal, it was held that the CDs were regarded as distinguishable from the master CDs. The derivation of the Warner's discs was from the master disc, although the manufacturing process to achieve the end-product necessitated a further three steps. Due to the differences in obtaining the product through a different process, the master discs were not capable of achieving the same operation.[44]

2.1.5 Pragmatic Considerations: Couture and Patents

When considering Couture as subject matter, it is necessary to ask whether the functional component is *the* product, such as the shoulder tie described earlier. Based on this example, in evaluating the U.K. approach it is necessary to question whether the 'direct product of the process'[45] is either lost within the subject matter

38 *Pioneer Electronics Capital, Inc. and Another v Warner Music Manufacturing Europe GmbH and Another, [1995] R.P.C. 487; [1995] 1 WLU.K. 464 (Ch D (Patents Ct)), 24 January 1995, Aldous J*

39 *Pioneer Electronics Capital Inc v Warner Music Manufacturing Europe GmbH* [1995] R.P.C. 487; [1995] 1 WLU.K. 464 (Ch D (Patents Ct))

40 Fiona Russell and Heidi Hurdle, 'What is the Direct Product of a Patented Process?' (1995) 17(5) EIPR 249

41 Fiona Russell and Heidi Hurdle, 'What is the Direct Product of a Patented Process?' (1995) 17(5) EIPR 249

42 Fiona Russell and Heidi Hurdle, 'What is the Direct Product of a Patented Process?' (1995) 17(5) EIPR 249

43 Fiona Russell and Heidi Hurdle, 'What is the Direct Product of a Patented Process?' (1995) 17(5) EIPR 249

44 *Pioneer Electronics Capital, Inc. and Another v Warner Music Manufacturing Europe GmbH and Another* [1997] R.P.C. 757

45 *Pioneer Electronics Capital, Inc. and Another v Warner Music Manufacturing Europe GmbH and Another* [1997] R.P.C. 757

or, in fact, defines the subject matter.[46] With the U.K. now having exited from the E.U., it is necessary to look at the situation from the perspective of the U.K. specifically. For this, s.60 of the Patents Act 1977 is a necessary consideration. S.60(1)(c) states:

> 1) Subject to the provisions of this section, a person infringes a patent for an invention if, but only if, while the patent is in force, he does any of the following things in the United Kingdom in relation to the invention without the consent of the proprietor of the patent, that is to say – (c)where the invention is a process, he disposes of, offers to dispose of, uses or imports any product obtained directly by means of that process or keeps any such product whether for disposal or otherwise.

Noted in the preceding is that different processes produce different filament yarns for almost identical textiles, namely lyocell (Tencel brand),[47] viscose, and modal.[48] This point is significant because it highlights the fact that when there is an intentional alteration of the process at any given stage, it will alter the end-product. For this reason, argued is the concept of creativity being a fundamental element to patents, in that the creative method dictates the purpose, and therefore the process, of the invention from which the product shall be derived. Couture is a creative process, but also the concept of aesthetics is a significant consideration as a natural part of the product; therefore, by altering the design process, potentially a different end-product relating to the *aesthetic* shall be achieved. If Couture is to be regarded as a creative pursuit, the relationship between aesthetics, creativity, and patents must be explored to understand the rationale for exclusions for aesthetic and artistic subject matter.

2.2 Couture: Design in Law Defined

The connection between Couture and design rights appears to be a natural consideration when protecting fashion designs; this section attempts to address the extent to which design rights afford protection to fashion. Further, design rights are analysed to identify whether the concept of design from a designer's perspective and the view of the courts are in alignment, and finally, whether any disparity may be problematic.

The concept of 'design' being noted as necessitating 'investment, time and money'[49] introduces the argument that there exists the necessity to protect 'successful' designs from being copied.[50] Design rights legislation is specifically concerned with

46 Jobst Wibbelmann, 'Protection of "Products Directly Obtained by Processes" According to Article 64(2) EPC' (1996) 18(3) EIPR 174–76

47 Tencel is the brand name for Lyocel – http://www.madehow.com/Volume-5/Lyocell.html

48 Robert Kay, 'Viscose Vs Modal Vs Lyocell-Difference?' (*Robert Owen Undershirts*, 30 April 2017) <https://www.undershirts.co.uk/blogs/research/viscose-vs-modal-vs-lyocell> accessed 3 October 2021

49 Bentley and others, *Intellectual Property Law* (6th edn, Oxford University Press 2022) 732 referring to M Levin, 'Recent Developments in Nordic Design Protection' (1988)

50 L Bentley and others, *Intellectual Property Law* (6th edn, Oxford University Press 2022) 733

the appearance and shape of products which are manufactured.[51] In relation to the design process and the designer exercising creative expression, design freedom is recognised as attracting protection, whereas a design limited in scope for development will not attract protection; an example is 'cable connection.'[52] The designer's creativity is seldomly suggested as being recognised as a justification for legal protection of designs; on the contrary, utilitarian concepts provide arguments justifying protection based on investment considerations.[53] To reflect on the justifications for protection of designs, the design process links both utilitarian and creative elements through notions of creativity, artistry, and technicality. Suggested is that it is 'not acceptable' for a monopoly right to be granted to an individual based on the appearance of a product.[54] The most common theme observed for product design is the aesthetic attributes it lends to enhance the product's appearance and commercial qualities, particularly in consideration for the product's viability for the market. This concept can be applied to many types of designs such as Couture, furniture, and technical products such as laptops or mobile phones. Therefore, aesthetics, creativity, and technicality are generally established in unison throughout the design process and are intrinsically connected.

The discussion that follows will focus on the design rights in the U.K. and the E.U. This is for the purposes of ascertaining an understanding of how the legal provisions reflect on design concepts in law. In the U.K., two types of design rights exist, the registered design right and the unregistered design right, and the E.U. provisions are referred to as the community design right.

2.2.1 Registered Design Right

Legal protection for designs are provided for by the Registered Designs Act 1949, although this was amended in 2001.[55] An application to register a design must be made through the Intellectual Property Office and further, industrial designs can be registered internationally by virtue of the Hague Agreement.[56] The registration process necessitates a product to be identified pertaining to the application of a specific design to a product, which is merely a procedural aspect and is for the purposes of classifying the design and enabling searches, although the design is not restricted to

51 Judith Embley, Keir Bamford and Nick Hancock, *Commercial and Intellectual Property Law and Practice* (CLP 2021) 702

52 Judith Embley, Keir Bamford and Nick Hancock, *Commercial and Intellectual Property Law and Practice* (CLP 2021) 704

53 L Bentley and others, *Intellectual Property Law* (6th edn, Oxford University Press 2022) 733

54 Judith Embley, Keir Bamford and Nick Hancock, *Commercial and Intellectual Property Law and Practice* (CLP 2021) 702

55 L Bentley and others, *Intellectual Property Law* (6th edn, Oxford University Press 2022) 742

56 Prior to 13 June 2018, industrial designs could be registered by virtue of the Intellectual Property Act 2014 which enabled the U.K. to apply the Hague Agreement. Since becoming a member, it is possible for the U.K. to register up to 100 designs across 68 signatories to the Agreement. Please see: Gov.uk., 'Hague Agreement for the International Registration of Industrial Designs' (*Gov.uk.*, 2018) <https://www.gov.uk./government/publications/hague-system-design-protection-for-applicants/hague-agreement-for-the-international-registration-of-industrial-designs> accessed 18 October 2021

the product listed in the registration form.[57] Further, a limit of seven design images can be included on the registration form.[58] The Designs Act 1949, s.1(2) defines a design as 'the appearance of the whole or a part of a product resulting from the features of, in particular, the lines, contours, colours, shape, texture or materials of the product or its ornamentation.'[59]

2.2.2 Unregistered Design Right

The unregistered design is defined under s.213(2) of the CDPA as the 'design right.'[60] A requirement for the design to be 'original' is expressed as 'not common place in a qualifying country in the design field in question.'[61] This is noted as an overlap between design rights and copyright, as the originality requirement for a design right pursuant to the CDPA is the same as for the originality requirement in copyright. Further, for the design to be protected by the right, the design must be logged in a document or produced to a design specification.[62]

2.2.3 Community Design Right

The E.U. protection for design rights is pursuant to the Community Design Right 6/2002 which is defined under Article 3(a) as 'the appearance of the whole or part of a product resulting from the features of, in particular, the lines, contour, colours, shape, texture and/or materials of the product itself and/or its ornamentation.'[63]

2.2.4 Novelty

A valid design must be regarded as being new in law. This aspect is reflected in the U.K. registered design legislation, E.U. Community registered and unregistered designs.[64] The aspect of new relates to products which must be absent of identical designs that comprise of similar features already available to the public prior to the date of application; these are referred to as the *prior art.*[65] This aspect is concerned with whether the design is recognised by persons relevant to the sector.[66] The sector is referring to the location of the prior art and *not* the sector as it relates to the

57 L Bentley and others, *Intellectual Property Law* (6th edn, Oxford University Press 2022) 744
58 Rosie Burbridge, *European Fashion Law* (Edward Elgar 2019) 92
59 Registered Designs Act 1949, s1(2)
60 Judith Embley, Keir Bamford and Nick Hancock, *Commercial and Intellectual Property Law and Practice* (CLP 2021) 719
61 CDPA 1988 S.213(1) and Judith Embley, Keir Bamford and Nick Hancock, *Commercial and Intellectual Property Law and Practice* (CLP 2021) 719
62 CDPA 1988, s.213(6) and Judith Embley, Keir Bamford and Nick Hancock, *Commercial and Intellectual Property Law and Practice* (CLP 2021) 719
63 Community Design Directive, Art 3(a) and L Bentley and others, *Intellectual Property Law* (6th edn, Oxford University Press 2022) 750
64 L Bentley and others, *Intellectual Property Law* (6th edn, Oxford University Press 2022) 766
65 *L Bentley and others, Intellectual Property Law (6th edn, Oxford University Press 2022) 766*
66 Judith Embley, Keir Bamford and Nick Hancock, *Commercial and Intellectual Property Law and Practice* (CLP 2021) 710 referring to Registered Design Right 1948, s. 1B(6)(a)

product.[67] The implication of this places limitations on a registered design for use on another product, say a registered design for a ballet shoe would be restricted for use as a decorative porcelain ornament.[68] The burden of opposing a 'prior art' is for a third party and not a search by the design registry. This method of comparison of new designs contrasted with existing products is noted as an objective test, similar to the originality test in copyright.[69] The similarities between the two IP rights as they relate to novelty have historically been suggested as bringing into existence 'confusion' between the two systems.[70] This is due to design rights being concerned with novelty and individual character whereas in copyright the protection criterion is originality and as a result, the reasons for bringing an action within each IP right are distinct.[71]

2.2.5 *Individual Character*

The individual character is dependent on a concept based on the 'overall impression' upon an 'informed user,' which is an individual acquainted with designs for a particular sector.[72] In *JChoo (Jersey) Ltd v Towerstone Ltd*,[73] the 'informed user' was defined as an individual who understood handbag design.[74] Contention had arisen due to the overall impression and quality of the bags appearing to be the same.[75] Design freedom is significant because for a design to be recognised as having individual character, the designer should be seen to have exercised and implemented innovative design concepts. This is the distinguishing factor between the new design and those currently available on market.[76]

2.2.6 *Application of Design Law*

In ascertaining the method of analysis of design in the courts, it is necessary to consider the *Magmatic* case.[77] Here the court considered the design of two children's cases with a 'ride on' feature. The *Magmatic* case was called a 'Tunki' whilst PMS had imported and sold similar designs called 'Kiddee'; both companies produced

67 Judith Embley, Keir Bamford and Nick Hancock, *Commercial and Intellectual Property Law and Practice* (CLP 2021) 710. Please see: *Green Lane Products Ltd v PMS International Group Ltd* [2007] E.W.H.C. 1712
68 Judith Embley, Keir Bamford and Nick Hancock, *Commercial and Intellectual Property Law and Practice* (CLP 2021) 710
69 L Bentley and others, *Intellectual Property Law* (6th edn, Oxford University Press 2022) 750 Originality is discussed in chapter 4
70 Estelle Declayre, *The Copyright/Design Interface* (Cambridge 2017) 8
71 Estelle Declayre, *The Copyright/Design Interface* (Cambridge 2017) 8
72 The informed user was identified in *J Choo (Jersey) Ltd v Towerstone Ltd* [2008] E.W.H.C. 346 as an individual possessing knowledge of handbag design. Judith Embley, Keir Bamford and Nick Hancock, *Commercial and Intellectual Property Law and Practice* (CLP 2021) 711
73 *J Choo (Jersey) Ltd v Towerstone Ltd* [2008] E.W.H.C. 346
74 *J Choo (Jersey) Ltd v Towerstone Ltd* [2008] E.W.H.C. 346
75 *JChoo (Jersey) Ltd v Towerstone Ltd* [2008] E.W.H.C. 346 (Ch); [2008] F.S.R. 19
76 Judith Embley, Keir Bamford and Nick Hancock, *Commercial and Intellectual Property Law and Practice* (CLP 2021) 711
77 *Magmatic Ltd v PMS International Ltd* [2016] U.K.SC 12; [2016] 4 All E.R. 1027; [2016] 3 WLU.K. 280 (SC)

designs which were animal and insect themed. The judge had highlighted that the community registered design (CRD) pertained to the shape of the case, and other aspects of the 'Kiddee' design should therefore be ignored. In terms of the *overall user impression* of the 'Kiddee' case, it was concluded in the initial case that it was the same as that produced by the CRD.[78] PMS asserted that the judge had erred in not only interpreting the CRD but also in considering the surface decoration on the Kiddee case. Pertinent to the discussion and analysis on design is the method by which the judge had reached his decision, as it was noted he had failed to 'appreciate' in considering the CRD as a whole.[79] The deliberation of the designs included a global assessment pertaining to how the designs were to be utilised. On appeal, it was held that the *method* by which the judge applied the principles for his decision were problematic. It was held that the Kiddee case's shape was influenced by the colours being two-tone. It was further held that a disparity of the overall shape conveyed a different impression from that of the CRD. The same principles should have been applied to both the animal and insect versions of the cases, and noted were the details such as whiskers and stripes on the flanks producing an overall impression of a tiger. Further, the judge had erred in the lack of consideration afforded to the surface decoration of the Kiddee case and the contrast in colour between the body and the wheels of the case in the CRD.[80]

The decision rested with the overall impression of the two cases being regarded very differently. It was held that the judge should have decided that the Kiddee case had not infringed the CRD.[81] In 2016, the case reached the Supreme Court,[82] where the decision of the Court of Appeal was upheld as the Kiddee cases not being regarded as infringing the CAD greyscale drawings of the Trunki CRD. The case has been noted for the importance of accurate representations[83] and further that several applications may be necessary for the protection of different aspects of the design.[84] Further, it has illuminated positive aspects of the U.K. design right in that the inclusion of a narrative setting out restrictions relating to the extent of protection claimed is permitted.[85] One of the main criticisms of the case pertains to capricious representations exacerbating the absence of a decision on the part of the Supreme Court.

The implications of this case as it relates to Couture from the perspective of this book are that the *attention to detail* during a court hearing must be to the equivalent extent as at the time of creation/designing. However, the basis for this legal

78 *Magmatic Ltd v PMS International Ltd* [2014] E.W.C.A. Civ 181

79 *Magmatic Ltd v PMS International Ltd* [2014] E.W.C.A. Civ 181

80 *Magmatic Ltd v PMS International Ltd* [2014] E.W.C.A. Civ 181 paras 41–48

81 *Magmatic Ltd v PMS International Ltd* [2014] E.W.C.A. Civ 181 paras 49–55

82 *Magmatic Ltd v PMS International Ltd* [2016] U.K.SC 12; [2016] 4 All E.R. 1027; [2016] 3 WLU.K. 280 (SC)

83 Sara Ashby, 'The U.K. Supreme Court and the Trunki Case: Missed Opportunities, Mysteries and Misunderstood' (2016) 38(9) EIPR 527 referring to Lindner [2010] E.C.D.R. 1 at [33]

84 Sara Ashby, 'The U.K. Supreme Court and the Trunki Case: Missed Opportunities, Mysteries and Misunderstood' (2016) 38(9) EIPR 527

85 Sara Ashby, 'The U.K. Supreme Court and the Trunki Case: Missed Opportunities, Mysteries and Misunderstood' (2016) 38(9) EIPR 527

reasoning is that whilst considerations are given to surface decoration, colours, and shapes by a designer (or design team), ultimately producing designs that are viable for the commercial market, a disproportionate interpretation by the court of those elements may dominate the legal decision.

To explain this further, in the initial case, the key problem identified was the *method* for the judge's decision. The pertinent point identified from the perspective of this study is the notion of 'appreciation' for the design, as a whole concept. In other words, not dividing the design into various components, such as shape, colour, etc, risks overlooking *appreciation* for the product in its entirety. However, if the design is to be meticulously examined for each component it is comprised of, it is argued that this must be exercised with caution. To elaborate, it is necessary to consider the decision in *Austretherm v Termo Organika*[86] and *Lindner*[87] in consideration of Article 8(1) of Community Design Right 6/2002. It argued that the *details* of the design should be considered as an *integral* part of the product and not be considered for the *impact* of those details upon an *entire product*. The reason for this is because to consider the *impact* on the design as it relates to each individual component, shall give effect to an absence of *appreciation* for the product as a whole concept. To summarise this argument, we can see a paradoxical emergence of how the design right may in fact be in operation. This is that for infringement cases, it appears that it is necessary to consider all details of the design to appreciate the product as a whole, but in cases relating to validity of a design, an over-zealous approach to the design details may bring about a narrow interpretation of the legislation. Although this problem is identified relating to an inconsistent approach to design law in relation to validity and infringement, the solution is not clear either. The legislation appears to necessitate a review for the purposes of seeking to align the *effect* of the provisions to designs.

2.2.7 The Copyright and Design Intersection

Copyright protection attempts to exclude industrially manufactured products from copyright protection and in addition, a design recorded within a document whereby a product has been created from the specification is also excluded under s.51 of the CDPA 1988.[88] With this said, whilst copyright can protect the design drawings, it does not protect against a product being reproduced from those drawings in 3D form by virtue of s.51.

Further complications for the implications for Couture are that the likelihood of a fashion product being protected by a design right is unlikely. This is based on the criteria for exclusions regarding the appearance and shape. However, under this

86 *Austretherm v Termo Organika, Case R 998/2013-3*

87 *Lindner (R-690/2007-3), 22 October 2009 at [42]*

88 Judith Embley, Keir Bamford and Nick Hancock, *Commercial and Intellectual Property Law and Practice* (CLP 2021) 731

provision, the design drawings for Couture can be protected.[89] With this said, there are further significant complications for Couture being protected in design law.

The complexity is rooted in Couture being considered from the perspective of this study as an artistic work; design is technical, and therefore the design drawings will not protect the *artistry* within the product, only the drawings for the design. The design from the perspective of this thesis is considered as the *skeleton* for the Couture garment. Although, the *artistry* is considered as the body. The artistry can be described as an embellishment, and additional work consisting of intellectual creation, which is applied in addition to and beyond the initial skeleton. On this basis, design rights appear to fall short of protecting Couture adequately as an *artistic work* and can only protect the *skeleton*, the design, consisting of the design drawings. Further, pursuant to s.236 of the CDPA 1988, when considering the hypothetical scenario whereby in the instance that copyright shall subsist in a Couture garment, which includes a design right, 'it is not an infringement of design right in the design to do anything which is an infringement of the copyright' of the Couture garment.[90] However, copyright can be applied to a three-dimensional article (a made product) for a registered design.[91]

For an unregistered design to be capable of protection it necessitates *novelty* of the design which is akin to the 'originality' requirement for copyright. This is a significant point as it is apparent that originality and novelty are not regarded as the same in law. For this reason, the study observes and indications point towards Couture potentially not being capable of being *new*. This is because fashion is re-generated every 20 years or so, as a re-generation of trends as discussed in chapter 1.[92] Creators implement influences from existing 'things' and may incorporate influences which are not necessarily *new* but when incorporated into a design, are regarded as original when assessing the whole product. Furthermore, it is observed that design rights are centred on the technicality rather than the art and aesthetics of the design, and it is this point which supports the basis for this study being focused specifically on copyright protection for Couture.

2.2.8 Developments in E.U. Design Law

In addressing the design rights and copyright interface, Declayre states: 'The Design Directive legislated very minimally on the interface as the EU legislature only required Member States to cumulate copyright and design laws without

89 S.51 CDPA 1988

90 Please see Judith Embley, Keir Bamford and Nick Hancock, *Commercial and Intellectual Property Law and Practice* (CLP 2021) 732

91 Please see *Flashing Badge Co Ltd v Groves* [2007] E.W.H.C. 1372 (Ch), where the defendant had imported badges with a flashing feature identical to the claimant's badges, whereby copyright was owned in the surface decoration. Although the defendant raised the defence under s.51, Rimer J expressed the design was surface decoration and therefore was not within the parameters of a 'design document' and was held to be an infringement of copyright. Also see: Judith Embley, Keir Bamford and Nick Hancock, *Commercial and Intellectual Property Law and Practice* (CLP 2021) 732

92 Gwyneth Holland and Rae Jones, *Fashion Trend Forecasting* (Laurence King Publishing 2017) 59

specifying rules to regulate the overlap (Article 17 Design Directive, Article 96. Design Regulation and Article 9. Infosoc Directive).'[93]

A major development was seen in E.U. law in the case of *Flos*.[94] The case concerned a dispute over the reproduction of the 'Arco lamp' design, which *Flos SpA* ('Flos'), asserted that it was the owner of the property rights, against Semeraro Casa e Famiglia SpA ('Semeraro').[95] The question for the court was whether a design which was in the public domain prior to the enforcement of Directive 98/71 could be protected under copyright. Secondly, the court was to determine whether the manufactured and marketed product which imitates the shape of the design, which was in the public domain, could impact the eligibility of copyright protection of the design, and whether a transitional period during which protection is excluded could be established.

Flos established that Article 17 of Directive 98/71 EC of the European Parliament and of the Council of 13 October 1998 on the legal protections of designs must be interpreted as Member States must not deny copyright protection to designs where the originality criteria are established. Due to this ruling, the U.K. repealed s.52 of the CDPA 1988, whereby the copyright term was 25 years.[96] S.51 of the CDPA was not repealed. Some E.U. countries, namely Portugal, U.K., Italy, and the Czech Republic, argued that both Article 17 of the Directive on the legal protection of designs (98/71/EC) and Article 96(2) of the Community Design Rights legislation (6/2002) should be read together with the *Flos* and *Infopaq* (considered in chapter 4) rulings, whereby the Member State should provide for the scope, conditions, and level of protection.[97] Declayre addresses the *Flos* judgement: 'which seemingly imposes the author's own intellectual creation level of originality for unregistered designs but leaves the originality for registered designs to Member States, has created even more uncertainty.'[98]

In consideration of *Flos*, whilst some Member States have argued that the E.U. legislation should have been read together with the decision, and from the perspective of this thesis, this is a point that is agreed with. The more significant aspect of the decision is that it highlights the disconnect between the E.U. legislative provisions

93 Estelle Declayre, *The Copyright/Design Interface* (Cambridge 2017) 1

94 *Flos SpA v Semeraro Casa e Famiglia SpA* Case C-168/09

95 *Flos SpA v Semeraro Casa e Famiglia SpA* Case C-168/09

96 Adam Rendle and Louise Popple, 'Important CJEU Ruling Could Mean Copyright Protection is Available for All Original Designs' (*Taylor Wessing*, 9 January 2020) <https://www.taylorwessing.com/en/insights-and-events/insights/2020/01/important-CJEU-ruling-could-mean-copyright-protection-is-available-for-all-original-designs#:~:text=A%20work%20will%20be%20its%20author%27s%20own%20intellectual,constraints%20which%20leave%20no%20room%20for%20creative%20freedom> accessed 29 August 2023

97 Adam Rendle and Louise Popple, 'Important CJEU Ruling Could Mean Copyright Protection is Available for All Original Designs' (*Taylor Wessing*, 9 January 2020) <https://www.taylorwessing.com/en/insights-and-events/insights/2020/01/important-CJEU-ruling-could-mean-copyright-protection-is-available-for-all-original-designs#:~:text=A%20work%20will%20be%20its%20author%27s%20own%20intellectual,constraints%20which%20leave%20no%20room%20for%20creative%20freedom> accessed 29 August 2023

98 Estelle Declayre, *The Copyright/Design Interface* (Cambridge 2017) 2

and individual Member State autonomy on application. The *Flos* decision appears to infer an attempt at harmonising the approach and application to design protection, although in doing so, could this in fact be overlooking the significance of subject matter? To elaborate, different Member States may approach design protection differently; for example, as mentioned earlier, the approach France has to fashion may mean that its application of the Directive on the legal protection of designs (98/71/EC) and Article 96(2) of the Community Design Rights legislation (6/2002), could in fact have resulted in a slightly different approach in relation to the scope, conditions, and level of protection applied in France in comparison to the U.K. The *Flos* decision may therefore have provided more scope for protection in consideration of interpretation of the originality criteria by Member States.

On 28 November 2022, a new Regulation of the European Parliament and of the Council amending Council Regulation (EC) No 6/2002 on Community designs and repealing Commission Regulation (EC) No 2246/2002 was proposed. The purpose of the new proposal is explained at paragraph 3, as being developed based on the conclusions of the 11 November 2020 IP Policy and reconsideration of the industrial design system within the E.U. The main aim is to modernise the industrial design protection system and make it more attractive to designers, small and medium sized businesses.[99] The most significant consideration for this study is the implications for effectively a culminative design and copyright protection. This is seen in paragraph 33 whereby it is stated 'allowing designs protected by E.U. design rights to be protected as copyright works.'[100] The implication of this is for a design to have a much longer protection period once it transitions to copyright, and therefore to be protected for 70 years after the death of the author under copyright law, provided for by Directive 2006/116/EC of the European Parliament and of the Council of 12 December 2006 on the term of protection of copyright and certain related rights.[101]

In analysis of the implications of this, from the perspective of this study, it is necessary to examine the position as it relates specifically to the categorisation for fashion, in relation to both the categorisation in law and categorisation for the industry. This study would assert that Couture be protected as an artistic work in law, and therefore requires copyright protection; all other fashion works outside of Couture (industrial designs) should be protected under the design right. The implication of the new proposal is that all other fashion works, which are mainly produced and manufactured at high street level, may have the potential to be protected under the copyright duration instead of the maximum 25-year duration conferred by Article 12 of Council Regulation (EC) No 6/2002 for the industrial design right. Whilst the U.K. is no longer a member of the E.U. and therefore these provisions are not binding upon it, the influential effect is a consideration for the U.K. design

99 Regulation of the European Parliament and of the Council amending Council Regulation (EC) No 6/2002

100 Regulation of the European Parliament and of the Council amending Council Regulation (EC) No 6/2002

101 Directive 2006/116/EC of the European Parliament and of the Council of 12 December 2006 on the Term of Protection of Copyright and Certain Related Rights

and copyright provisions in terms of the potential to develop the U.K. approach in the future.

2.3 Geographical Indications

Absent from earlier studies relating to analysis on the law and Couture is an evaluation of Geographical Indications (GIs).[102] The most significant characteristic of a GI is that 'the product must . . . originate from a specific location.'[103] Stilton cheese and champagne, for example, are well-known products which are protected by a GI.[104]

In consideration of Brexit and the position of the U.K., from January 2021, the U.K. introduced new 'GI schemes'[105] for the purposes of protecting products from England, Scotland, and Wales. GIs for the E.U. protect products in the E.U. and Northern Ireland.[106] GIs have an interaction with trade marks in so much as during the trade mark process carried out by the Intellectual Property Office, if it is found that a GI is registered, a trade mark will not be granted if a conflict exists.[107] Further, the historical roots of GIs are valued, and it is asserted that this history should not be overlooked for the purposes of one international standard.[108] On this basis, it is also argued that the development of GI protection must be set within the confines of TRIPS.[109]

To consider the position for the E.U., the European commission is noted as developing a strong system for agricultural products, although for non-agricultural products, 'there is currently no such system.'[110] The implications of this are 'an unlevel playing field in the single market.'[111] To be protected by a GI the product must correspond with a place.[112] Although currently, an E.U.-wide GI protec-

102 Tomruk Űstűnkaya, 'Artificial Intelligence: Friend or Foe to Fashion in Consideration of the Functionality Doctrine?' (2020) 42(1) EIPR 13 and Tomruk Űstűnkaya, 'The Functionality Doctrine: The Challenges to Fashion Copyright' (2020) 42(3) EIPR 156 and Tomruk Űstűnkaya, 'Fashion Law: The limitation Conundrum of the Patents Act 1977' (2020) 42(10) EIPR 621 and Tomruk Űstűnkaya, 'The Functionality Doctrine: Is 3D Printing Challenging Rigidity in Fashion Law?' (2020) 42(5) EIPR 286

103 Rosie Burbridge, *European Fashion Law* (Edward Elgar 2019) 14

104 Rosie Burbridge, *European Fashion Law* (Edward Elgar 2019) 14

105 Gov.UK, 'Guidance, Trade Marks and Geographical Indications' (*Gov.uk*, 2021) <https://www.gov.uk./guidance/trade-marks-and-geographical-indications> accessed 30 August 2021

106 Gov.UK, 'Guidance, Trade Marks and Geographical Indications' (*Gov.uk*, 2021) <https://www.gov.uk./guidance/trade-marks-and-geographical-indications> accessed 30 August 2021

107 Gov.UK, 'Guidance, Trade Marks and Geographical Indications' (*Gov.uk*, 2021) <https://www.gov.uk./guidance/trade-marks-and-geographical-indications> accessed 30 August 2021

108 Rhonda Chesmond, 'Protection or Privatisation of Culture? The Cultural Dimension of the International Intellectual Property Debate on Geographical Indications of Origin' (2007) 29(9) EIPR 379

109 Rhonda Chesmond, 'Protection or Privatisation of Culture? The Cultural Dimension of the International Intellectual Property Debate on Geographical Indications of Origin' (2007) 29(9) EIPR 379

110 Catherine Seville, 'Intellectual Property' (2011) 60(4) ICLQ 1039

111 Catherine Seville, 'Intellectual Property' (2011) 60(4) ICLQ 1039

112 Rosie Burbridge, *European Fashion Law* (Edward Elgar 2019) 14

tion system does not exist for non-agricultural goods. The protection mechanisms are in place in some E.U. countries at national and regional levels for the protection on some products, for example 'Solingen knives.'[113] France does protect all non-agricultural GI products.[114]

The outcome of a varying level of legal protection across the E.U. is that a producer of a non-agricultural product must file for the IP protection in each country of obtainability.[115] Similarly with the U.K.,[116] producers could alternatively rely on a trade-mark for the protection of their goods.[117] In terms of developing the GI system across the E.U., the focus for development is noted to be for the objective of harmonising 'the fragmented system.'[118] Further regarding the IP plan, announced is the consideration for a protective process across the E.U. for industrially produced goods and handicrafts of geographical origin.[119]

2.3.1 TRIPS

Article 22.1 of TRIPS provides for the protection of Geographical Indications (for signatories to the TRIPS agreement) as:

> 1. Geographical indications are, for the purposes of this Agreement, indications which identify a good as originating in the territory of a member, or a region or locality in that territory, where a given quality, reputation, or other characteristic of the good is essentially attributable to its geographical origin.[120]

The type of protection provided by GIs is for right holders to be able to prevent third parties from using it, specifically as it relates to not meeting the standards of

113 European Commission, 'Geographical Indications for Non-Agricultural Products' (*European Commission*, 2021) <https://ec.europa.eu/growth/industry/policy/intellectual-property/geographical-indications/non-agricultural-products_en> accessed 30 August 2021

114 European Commission, 'Geographical Indications for Non-Agricultural Products' (*European Commission*, 2021) <https://ec.europa.eu/growth/industry/policy/intellectual-property/geographical-indications/non-agricultural-products_en> accessed 30 August 2021

115 European Commission, 'Geographical Indications for Non-Agricultural Products' (*European Commission*, 2021) <https://ec.europa.eu/growth/industry/policy/intellectual-property/geographical-indications/non-agricultural-products_en> accessed 30 August 2021

116 Gov.UK., 'Guidance, Trade Marks and Geographical Indications' (*Gov.uk*, 2021) <https://www.gov.uk./guidance/trade-marks-and-geographical-indications> accessed 30 August 2021

117 European Commission, 'Geographical Indications for Non-Agricultural Products' (*European Commission*, 2021) <https://ec.europa.eu/growth/industry/policy/intellectual-property/geographical-indications/non-agricultural-products_en> accessed 30 August 2021

118 European Commission, 'Geographical Indications for Non-Agricultural Products' (*European Commission*, 2021) <https://ec.europa.eu/growth/industry/policy/intellectual-property/geographical-indications/non-agricultural-products_en> accessed 30 August 2021

119 European Commission, 'Geographical Indications for Non-Agricultural Products' (*European Commission*, 2021) <https://ec.europa.eu/growth/industry/policy/intellectual-property/geographical-indications/non-agricultural-products_en> accessed 30 August 2021

120 TRIPS Article 22 (1)

the GI,[121] this is pursuant to Article 22 (a). However, a right holder of a GI does not prevent a third party from creating a product utilising the same standards as those used for the GI.[122]

Article 24 of TRIPS provides for;

> International Negotiations; Exceptions: 1. Members agree to enter into negotiations aimed at increasing the protection of individual geographical indications under Article 23. . . . In the context of such negotiations, Members shall be willing to consider the continued applicability of these provisions to individual geographical indications whose use was the subject of such negotiations.

The preceding provision (Article 24 TRIPS) brings forward the notion of protection of Geographical Indications through negotiating processes on an international basis. This is a key feature of the legal framework for GIs specifically as it relates to fashion being a global enterprise. Further, the provision is regarded as enabling the introduction of products from different geographical locations and therefore being instrumental for the awareness and trade of those international communities.

Three specific ways of protecting a GI are:

- A suis generis right (a special system of protection).
- The use of certification or marks such as trade marks.
- Business practice systems which may include administrative procedures for the approval of products.[123]

2.3.2 Geographical Indications and Couture

WIPO states that Geographical Indications (GI) can be used for 'agricultural products, food stuffs, wine and spirit drinks, handicrafts and industrial products.'[124] This does provide scope for fashion in two areas, which appear to be in handicrafts and industrial products, provided there is a clear correlation between the geographical

121 WIPO, 'Geographical Indications What is a Geographical Indication?' (*WIPO*, 2021) <https://www.WIPO.int/geo_indications/en/#:~:text=A%20geographical%20indication%20right%20enables%20those%20who%20have,product%20does%20not%20conform%20to%20the%20applicable%20standards> accessed 30 August 2021

122 WIPO, 'Geographical Indications What is a Geographical Indication?' (*WIPO*, 2021) <https://www.WIPO.int/geo_indications/en/#:~:text=A%20geographical%20indication%20right%20enables%20those%20who%20have,product%20does%20not%20conform%20to%20the%20applicable%20standards> accessed 30 August 2021

123 WIPO, 'Geographical Indications What is a Geographical Indication?' (*WIPO*, 2021) <https://www.WIPO.int/geo_indications/en/#:~:text=A%20geographical%20indication%20right%20enables%20those%20who%20have,product%20does%20not%20conform%20to%20the%20applicable%20standards> accessed 30 August 2021

124 WIPO, 'Geographical Indications What is a Geographical Indication?' (*WIPO*, 2021) <https://www.WIPO.int/geo_indications/en/#:~:text=A%20geographical%20indication%20right%20enables%20those%20who%20have,product%20does%20not%20conform%20to%20the%20applicable%20standards> accessed 30 August 2021

place of construction and the product.[125] The Geneva Act 2015, of the Lisbon treaty, facilitated multilateral protection for GIs outside of the wines and spirits category.[126] The treaty facilitates 'maximum flexibility' for the purposes of taking into account regional and national designations.[127]

Handicrafts that may be worn have the potential to be protected by Geographical Indications, for example ponchos from Peru or wooden clogs from the Netherlands. Although most pertinent to Couture in connection to GIs is textiles and therefore apparel maybe constructed from fabric which has GI protection.

The Ponchampally Ikat from Ponchampally, in Andra Pradesh, India is noted as the first textile to be registered in 2005 as a GI.[128] In Thailand, it is noted that whilst 60 villages produce the textile called Sakon Nakhon, which is a 'hand-spun, handwoven Indigo-dyed cotton'[129] from the Sakon Nakhon province, only seven villages are protected by the GI.[130] In India, it is noted that GIs have been registered for at least 15 types of textiles[131] and that embroidery types have also been registered, such as: the Kasuti,[132] Kutch,[133] and Sujini.[134]

125 WIPO, 'Geographical Indications What is a Geographical Indication?' (*WIPO*, 2021) <https://www.WIPO.int/geo_indications/en/#:~:text=A%20geographical%20indication%20right%20enables%20those%20who%20have,product%20does%20not%20conform%20to%20the%20applicable%20standards> accessed 30 August 2021

126 Chomwan Weeraworawit, 'Geographical Indications and the Textiles Industry in Developing Countries: The Case for Multilateral Protection' (*Fordham Institute*, April 2019) <https://fordhamipinstitute.com/wp-content/uploads/2019/04/Chomwan_Fordham-2019_GIs-and-multilateral-protection_reduced-size.pdf> accessed 30 August 2021

127 WIPO, 'Summary of the Geneva Act of the Lisbon Agreement' (*WIPO*, 2020) <https://www.WIPO.int/treaties/en/registration/lisbon/summary_lisbon-geneva.html> accessed 30 August 2021

128 Chomwan Weeraworawit, 'Geographical Indications and the Textiles Industry in Developing Countries: The Case for Multilateral Protection' (*Fordham Institute*, April 2019) <https://fordhamipinstitute.com/wp-content/uploads/2019/04/Chomwan_Fordham-2019_GIs-and-multilateral-protection_reduced-size.pdf> accessed 30 August 2021

129 Chomwan Weeraworawit, 'Geographical Indications and the Textiles Industry in Developing Countries: The Case for Multilateral Protection' (*Fordham Institute*, April 2019) <https://fordhamipinstitute.com/wp-content/uploads/2019/04/Chomwan_Fordham-2019_GIs-and-multilateral-protection_reduced-size.pdf> accessed 30 August 2021

130 Chomwan Weeraworawit, 'Geographical Indications and the Textiles Industry in Developing Countries: The Case for Multilateral Protection' (*Fordham Institute*, April 2019) <https://fordhamipinstitute.com/wp-content/uploads/2019/04/Chomwan_Fordham-2019_GIs-and-multilateral-protection_reduced-size.pdf> accessed 30 August 2021

131 Pranjal Shirwaikar, 'Fashion Copying and Design of the Law' (2009) 14 Journal of Intellectual Property Rights 113–21

132 Embroidery of Karnataka – Pranjal Shirwaikar, 'Fashion Copying and Design of the Law' (2009) 14 Journal of Intellectual Property Rights 113–21

133 Embroidery from Gujarat – Pranjal Shirwaikar, 'Fashion Copying and Design of the Law' (2009) 14 Journal of Intellectual Property Rights 113–21

134 Pranjal Shirwaikar, 'Fashion Copying and Design of the Law' (2009) 14 Journal of Intellectual Property Rights 113–21

Tartan is considered a textile and is noted to be in alignment with a GI, although specific legislation protects tartan under the Scottish Tartan Bill 2008.[135] Further, the islands of Harris produce Harris Tweed pursuant to the Harris Tweed Act 1993.[136] This legislation was brought into existence for the purposes of maintaining 'authenticity, standard and reputation.'[137] In addition, the legislation goes further to state that the purpose of the legislation is for the prevention of the sale of 'Harris Tweed,' should the textile not fall within the parameters of the definition.[138] This Act is very much like the Geographical Indication provision as stipulated by TRIPS Article 22.1 and 23.1. The imperative question therefore is whether the GI system of protection requires expanding for textiles and wider considerations extended to fashion goods.

It is noted that Scotland has recognised the intrinsic and economic value being afforded to the intangible cultural heritage production of tartan. The GI system appears to be a novel method of protection and applicable to products of designated origin, although disparity regarding GI protection and textile/fashion production does not appear to be widely administered or perhaps recognised. The GI system of protection is observed for the purposes of this chapter as an alternative IP mechanism for Couture, although the system appears to still be developing. On this basis, there is an absence of information for fashion products pertaining to geographical locations, potentially capable of registration. Finally, it is observed that products with GI protection can be used within a fashion product, such as a textile or embroidery, to create a Couture garment.

2.3.3 Geographical Indications: The Relationship Between GIs and French Designation of Haute Couture

In relation to haute Couture, the French system may be considered as the intersection between art and the law in the protection of Couture works. The French legal system protects 'haute Couture' by the designated registration but no specific geography.[139] Therefore, as haute Couture is of specific legal designation, the protection of haute Couture as a Geographical Indication (France) is a consideration.[140] The qualification of haute Couture must be the work of a couturier that is a member

135 Scottish Register of Tartans Bill (SP Bill 8) as introduced in the Scottish Parliament on 25 March 2008

136 Harris Tweed Act 1993, Scotland

137 Megan Rae Blakley, 'Pattern Recognition: Governmental Regulation of Tartan and Commodification of Culture' (2015) 22(4) International Journal of Cultural Property 487

138 Megan Rae Blakley, 'Pattern Recognition: Governmental Regulation of Tartan and Commodification of Culture' (2015) 22(4) International Journal of Cultural Property 487

139 Teg, 'What is Couture? The Guide to High Fashion' (*The Evans Group*, 15 June 2021) <https://tegintl.com/what-is-Couture/> accessed 27 December 2022 and Alexander Fury, 'What Does "Couture" Actually Mean?' (*New York Times*, 27 January 2017) <https://www.nytimes.com/2017/01/27/t-magazine/fashion/what-does-Couture-actually-mean-fashion-week.html> accessed 29 December 2022

140 WIPO, 'Frequently Asked Questions: Geographical Indications' (*WIPO*, 2023) <https://www.WIPO.int/geo_indications/en/faq_geographicalindications.html> accessed 17 January 2023

of the Fédération de la Haute Couture et de la Mode, and the garments must meet the standards as set by the Fédération. In terms of meeting the requirements as a Geographical Indication, the only issue remaining is the quality, reputation, and characteristics must also originate from France.[141] With this established, it seems unlikely that any haute Couture works by members of the Fédération that are produced outside of France would obtain Geographical Indication protection, as there must exist a connection between the qualities and the original geographical place of production.[142]

2.4 Trade Marks and Considerations for Couture

The connection between trade marks and Couture relates to a distinguishable mark which identifies the fashion brand. Registered trade marks in the U.K. are protected by the Trade Marks Act 1994 (TMA).[143] A trade mark is considered as an identity of the origin, described under s.1(1) of the TMA as 'any sign capable of being represented graphically which is capable of distinguishing goods or services of one undertaking from those of other undertakings.'[144] 'A trade mark may in particular, consist of words (including personal names), designs, letters, numerals colours, sounds, or the shape of goods or their packaging.'[145] Therefore, the purpose of a trade mark is to indicate the origin of the goods or services as it relates to aspects of trade.[146] Harmonisation for the trade mark framework has developed across the E.U. and through international conventions such as the Agreement on Trade-Related Aspects of International Property Rights (TRIPs) and the Singapore Trade Mark Law Treaty.[147] The process of registration of trade marks shall lead the discussion on this topic, as follows.

2.4.1 Registration

It is observed that registration of trade marks provides an unlimited protection for the purposes of use within the context of trade, and further, the duration of protection can last for ten years whereby after this time, an option to renew for ten-year periods after the initial registration is possible.[148] Exclusive rights are conferred to

141 WIPO, 'Frequently Asked Questions: Geographical Indications' (*WIPO*, 2023) <https://www.WIPO.int/geo_indications/en/faq_geographicalindications.html> accessed 17 January 2023

142 WIPO, 'Frequently Asked Questions: Geographical Indications' (*WIPO*, 2023) <https://www.WIPO.int/geo_indications/en/faq_geographicalindications.html> accessed 17 January 2023

143 Judith Embley, Keir Bamford and Nick Hancock, *Commercial and Intellectual Property Law and Practice* (CLP 2021) 554

144 The Trade mark Act 1994, s.1(1)

145 The Trade mark Act 1994, s.1(1)

146 Judith Embley, Keir Bamford and Nick Hancock, *Commercial and Intellectual Property Law and Practice* (CLP 2021) 554

147 Judith Embley, Keir Bamford and Nick Hancock, *Commercial and Intellectual Property Law and Practice* (CLP 2021) 554

148 Judith Embley, Keir Bamford and Nick Hancock, *Commercial and Intellectual Property Law and Practice* (CLP 2021) 555

the owner of the trade mark by virtue of s.9(1) of the TMA, and further, the owner of the registered trade mark may sue for damages. If the mark is not used it can be become invalid on this basis.[149] Trade marks in fashion provide for a distinct and recognisable identity for the brand, and these may consist of such components as colour or shape.

2.4.2 Absolute Grounds for Refusal

The position in the U.K. for absolute refusal of a trade mark is provided for by s.3 of the TMA 1994. A sign will be refused registration when the sign does not fulfil s.(1) of the TMA 1994, or for being devoid of distinctive character, a sign which exclusively designates quality, geographical origin, quantity, or where it is indicative of other products and services.[150] Further, any sign which has 'become customary in the current language or in the bona fide and established practices of trade.'[151] The community trade mark reflects the U.K. provision as it relates to a distinguishing mark. Article 3(1)(b) does not permit registration for signs whereby consumers cannot identify the sign as 'reliably' representing 'the commercial origin of the product.'[152]

2.4.3 Relative Grounds for Refusal

Relative grounds for refusal of a trade mark are provided by s.5 of the TMA. The relative grounds exclusion refers to the new mark conflicting with a mark which has already been registered. Further, the implementation of the trade marks Directive has implications as it relates to an existing IP right over a geographic indication, in that a trade mark registration may not be possible.[153]

2.4.4 Characteristics: Colour and Shape

A colour mark is observed as being devoid of distinctive character.[154] Registration for a trade mark for colour is considered through popular products particularly the correlation of a colour to a brand, which appears to be a strategy

149 Judith Embley, Keir Bamford and Nick Hancock, *Commercial and Intellectual Property Law and Practice* (CLP 2021) 557

150 Please see *Peek & Cloppenburg v OHIM* [2006] ETMR 35 as it relates to geographic origin, this case demonstrates a more relaxed attitude within the context of community trade mark applications. Judith Embley, Keir Bamford and Nick Hancock, *Commercial and Intellectual Property Law and Practice* (CLP 2021) 564

151 Judith Embley, Keir Bamford and Nick Hancock, *Commercial and Intellectual Property Law and Practice* (CLP 2021) 564

152 L Bentley and others, *Intellectual Property Law* (6th edn, Oxford University Press 2022) 994 referring to *Nichols v Registrar*, Case C-404/02 [2004] ECRI-8499, [43]

153 Directive (EU) 2015/2436 of the European Parliament and of the Council of 16 December 2015 to approximate the laws of the Member States relating to trade marks (recast) (Text with EEA relevance)

154 L Bentley and others, *Intellectual Property Law* (6th edn, Oxford University Press 2022) 994

which provides commercial recognition. However, observed is that public policy considerations essentially limit obtaining a colour mark for the creation of a monopoly right.[155] This is illustrated in the case of *Libertel Groep v Benelux-Merkenbureau*[156] where it was held that a colour may be regarded as having distinct character, and whilst colours can be registered, the criteria for registration is limited, as a requirement exists to provide information as it relates to the extent and where the colour shall be utilised.[157] When considering shape marks, the concept of a sign being devoid of distinct character is noted by the courts as applying the same test as for 'word or device marks,' the consumer approach to shape marks is distinct.[158] The reason put forward for this is because consumers are not likely to view a shape as communicating or in fact pertaining to a particular brand.[159]

The registration of a mark which produces a technical result will not be permitted. This reflects the public policy considerations discussed earlier in colour as they relate to considerations surrounding the prevention of creating a business monopoly.[160] Invisible functioning parts of a mark are subject to an exclusion for registration, although on the other hand when the aesthetics of a mark are enhanced, the challenge of 'substantial value' will be prevalent as a ground for refusal of the mark, pursuant to Article 3(1)(e)(ii) of Directive 2008/95.[161] (Technical function is examined in more detail in chapter 5.) Next a discussion on the relevance of an action in passing-off is presented, in consideration of a supportive legal mechanism to creators, outside of IP rights.

2.5 Passing-Off and the Relationship to Couture

The relationship between Couture and passing-off is one that is upheld by pragmatic commercial considerations for protecting the brand. The goodwill in fashion generally, is considered as the foundation for recognition and value of the brand. Passing-off is an action that is considered as a tort, and it is the idea of a someone taking advantage of another's goodwill and must be in connection to commercial pursuits.[162] A defendant assumes either a distinguishing sign or mark associated

155 Rosie Burbridge, *European Fashion Law* (Edward Elgar 2019) 41
156 *Libertel Groep BV v Benelux-Merkenbureau (C-104/01) E.U:C:2003:244; [2005] 2 CMLR. 45*
157 *Libertel Groep BV v Benelux-Merkenbureau* (C-104/01) E.U:C:2003:244; [2005] 2 CMLR. 45
158 L Bentley and others, *Intellectual Property Law* (6th edn, Oxford University Press 2022) 996 referring to Linde AG, *Winward Industries, Radio Watch Co Ltd*, Joined cases C-53/01, C-54/01, and C-55/01 [2003] ECRI-3161, [42], [46], [49]; *KWS Saat AG v OHIM*, Case 447/02P [2004] ECR I-10107, [8]
159 L Bentley and others, *Intellectual Property Law* (6th edn, Oxford University Press 2022) 996
160 Rosie Burbridge, *European Fashion Law* (Edward Elgar 2019) 41
161 Rosie Burbridge, *European Fashion Law* (Edward Elgar 2019) 41
162 Judith Embley, Keir Bamford and Nick Hancock, *Commercial and Intellectual Property Law and Practice* (CLP 2021) 538 referring to *Kean v McGivan* [1982] F.S.R. 119

with another's brand as their own which will be confusing to consumers.[163] The distinguishing factors may be either logos or names.[164] *Reckitt & Colman* is the leading authority on passing-off in the U.K. as it established the criteria for a claim.[165] Three-elements must be proven, and they are goodwill, misrepresentation (which leads to confusion), damage (leading to loss). These elements are examined next.

2.5.1 Goodwill

This has been described as 'the attractive force which brings in custom.'[166] Goodwill is identified as being *the* 'benefit and advantage of the good name . . . reputation' as it relates to a business.[167] This is the concept which generates the custom from consumers, which the business has developed over time through the reputation.[168] In the case of *Alan Kenneth McKenzie v Associated Newspapers*, the claimant protected his reputation as a diary writer.[169] Joseph Raz expresses value in goodwill two ways, which are having 1. Instrumental value and 2. Intrinsic value. '[S]omething is instrumentally good if its value derives from the fact that it makes certain consequences more likely, or that it can contribute to producing more consequences.'[170]

2.5.2 Misrepresentation

The element of misrepresentation can come into existence by the defendant either expressly or impliedly representing the origin of the products or services being that of the claimant's business.[171] Passing-off was established in *United Biscuits*[172] where the packaging of the two commercial enterprises confused consumers as the defendant's packaging was very reminiscent of the claimant's.[173]

163 Judith Embley, Keir Bamford and Nick Hancock, *Commercial and Intellectual Property Law and Practice* (CLP 2021) 538

164 Judith Embley, Keir Bamford and Nick Hancock, *Commercial and Intellectual Property Law and Practice* (CLP 2021) 538 referring to names*: Neutrogena Corporation and Another* [1996] R.P.C. 473) and *Harrods Ltd v Harrodian School Ltd* [1996] R.P.C. 697)

165 *Reckitt & Colman Products Ltd v Borden Inc* (No.3) [1990] 1 W.L.R. 491; [1990] R.P.C. 341 HL

166 Rosie Burbridge, *European Fashion Law* (Edward Elgar 2019) 341 referring to Lord Macnaughton in *IRC v Muller and Co's Margarine* [1901] A.C. 217 at 223

167 L Bentley and others, *Intellectual Property Law* (6th edn, Oxford University Press 2022) extract from *IRC v Muller and Co's Margarine* [1901] A.C. 217

168 L Bentley and others, *Intellectual Property Law* (6th edn, Oxford University Press 2022) 790

169 Judith Embley, Keir Bamford and Nick Hancock, *Commercial and Intellectual Property Law and Practice* (CLP 2021) 542 and *Alan Kenneth McKenzie v Associated Newspapers* [1998] R.P.C. 261

170 Joseph Raz, *Morality and Freedom* (Oxford University Press 1986)

171 L Bentley and others, *Intellectual Property Law* (6th edn, Oxford University Press 2022) 854

172 *United Biscuits (U.K.) Ltd v Asda Stores Ltd [1997] R.P.C. 513*

173 Judith Embley, Keir Bamford and Nick Hancock, *Commercial and Intellectual Property Law and Practice* (CLP 2021) 542 referring to *United Biscuits (U.K.) Ltd v Asda Stores Ltd* [1997] R.P.C. 513

2.5.3 Damage

Damage must be proven by the claimant as lost revenue due to the confusion of consumers with the products or services of the businesses.[174] The confusion would occur because of the defendant using the goodwill of the claimant.[175] Goodwill and fashion are explored in the following.

2.5.4 Implications of Passing-Off Within the Fashion Industry

In *Westwood v Knight* the action for passing-off had arisen following Mr Knight using a logo which was very reminiscent of Dame Westwood's trade mark.[176] Here the damage had occurred to Dame Westwood's brand, as she had lost revenue from her 'Destroy' logo and further this was due to consumers being confused when purchasing Mr Knight's merchandise, thinking they were buying Westwood's products. Mr Knight was held to have infringed Dame Westwood's mark. Mr Knight was held to be taking advantage of Dame Westwood's goodwill, and although the logos were created in the 1970s and were not being used by Dame Westwood at the time of the trial, the action in passing-off was successful. The crucial point observed by the cases of *Reckitt & Colman*[177] and *Westwood v Knight*[178] is the *value* of the goodwill of a brand. In other words, passing-off is a valuable legal protective mechanism for the reputation of the brand which is pertinent to sustaining its success. The intrinsic value of goodwill is expressed by Raz not being a derivative of instrumental value but an independent factor.[179] Raz uses art as an example and expresses that art works are to be valued for themselves. On this basis, it is noted that when applied to Couture, this notion conveys that the goodwill of the brand is rooted within the 'intangible assets of the brand attributing to the intrinsic value.'[180] To expand on this point the analysis in chapter 1 brings forward the non-physical purpose of fashion such as communication as evaluated by Barnard,[181] and the role of semiotics as examined by Sapir.[182] Ng asserts that the intrinsic value extends to 'more' than the reputation of the brand but that it also employs principles that connect to societal communities which ultimately influence business decisions.[183]

The rationale for this study consists of the fact that the technical aspects of fashion which contribute to its function run parallel with aesthetic considerations and therefore these are an intrinsic part, and it further is regarded herein as contributing

174 Rosie Burbridge, *European Fashion Law* (Edward Elgar 2019) 343
175 Rosie Burbridge, *European Fashion Law* (Edward Elgar 2019) 341
176 *Westwood v Knight* [2010] E.W.P.C.C. 16
177 *Reckitt & Colman Products Ltd v Borden Inc (No.3) [1990] 1 W.L.R. 491; [1990] R.P.C. 341 HL*
178 *Westwood v Knight [2010] E.W.P.C.C. 16*
179 Joseph Raz, *Morality and Freedom* (Oxford University Press 1986)
180 Tomruk Űstűnkaya, 'Fashion Law: Exploration Through Trademarks and Passing-Off' (2021) 43(3) EIPR 181
181 Malcom Barnard and A Reader, *Fashion Theory* (2nd edn, Routledge 2020) 115
182 Malcom Barnard and A Reader, *Fashion Theory* (2nd edn, Routledge 2020) 115
183 Catherine W Ng, 'The Law of Passing Off: Goodwill Beyond Goods' (2016) 47(7) IIC 817

to the goodwill of the brand.[184] Passing-off is considered a useful remedy in terms of the considerations given to goodwill as a property right and thus a valuable protective mechanism for businesses.[185] On this basis, the thesis question must be tested to ascertain whether copyright protection should be widened to protect fashion works, due to the intrinsic value based within the functional components.

2.6 Case Study: Architecture-Couture Parallel

This case study shall attempt to explore the parameters of copyright law in relation to architecture, for the purpose of understanding and defining art in copyright law, namely s.4 of the CDPA 1988, and the extent the law is applied equally. The overriding objective is to understand whether the law and the artistic notions of art are aligned, specifically in consideration of functional art forms, such as architecture, to gain a clearer perspective for the legal position for Couture. S.4 of the CDPA 1988, does not include fashion or Couture as an artistic work.

Fashion has been said to be seen as the 'stepchild' of the art world, 'the less worthy creative form,' and for this reason it is significant that Couture is accepted by law as art in as much as architecture is.[186] The position of the thesis is that art is not confined to static and traditional notions of *what* art is, such as traditional fine art painting, but extends to collage, sculpture, performance, dance, digital, and 3D forms of art. Art is therefore regarded as an evolving practice, whereby the response to the creative process is dictated by innovative developments, and further, societal and cultural changes. Further, limitations are those dictated by the technical function for example. The culmination of these factors therefore results in work which is not necessarily wholly the intellectual creation of the author, but to an extent, dictated by the obligatory requirements, prior to the author beginning to create.

Well-known historical architectural works include the Casa Batlló, Barcelona, Spain by Gaudi, which is identified as 'a true work of art'; the Acropolis in Athens, Greece and part of the Pisa Cathedral, Italy, known as the Leaning Tower of Pisa.[187] Today, the evolving commercial sphere influences creativity, and therefore it is necessary for creators to respond to market constraints, and in turn, it places limitations on the creative process and end-product.

Since ancient civilisation, architecture has been established as an art form.[188] Architecture has been compared to performance art, whereby the architect is

184 Please see: Tomruk Űstűnkaya, 'Fashion Law: Exploration Through Trademarks and Passing-Off' (2021) 43(3) EIPR 181

185 Tomruk Űstűnkaya, 'Fashion Law: Exploration Through Trademarks and Passing-Off' (2021) 43(3) EIPR 181 referring to *Irvine v Talksport Ltd* [2003] E.W.C.A. Civ 423; [2003] E.M.L.R. 26 referring to *British American Glass Co v Winton Products (Blackpool)* [1962] R.P.C. 230 in *Irvine v Talksport* [2003] E.M.L.R. 26 at [31]. 165

186 Paola antonelli michelle millar fisher, 'Announcing Items: Is Fashion Modern?' (*Inside Out*, 5 April2016)<https://www.moma.org/explore/inside_out/2016/04/05/announcing-items-is-fashion-modern/> accessed 20 September 2023

187 Casa Batlló, 'History of Casa Batlló' (*Casa Batlló Gaudi Barcelona*, 2021) <https://www.casabatllo.es/en/antoni-gaudi/casa-batllo/history/> accessed 30 August 2021

188 Matthew Rimmer, 'Crystal Palaces: Copyright Law and Public Architecture' (2002) 14(2) Bond Law Review 320–46 <https://ssrn.com/abstract=600865>

perceived as a director, and the people who use the buildings are viewed as meaningfully engaging with the building, within a given location.[189] Likewise, the wearer of Couture will use the garment for the purposes of adornment and possibly within the context of a specific occasion. In other words, both the building and the Couture garment have a distinct conceptual use, and therefore could be regarded as functional. Furthermore, both the Couture garment and the building necessitate technical components, such as doors, windows, balconies, and lifts for a building, whereas the Couture garment requires fastenings and construction techniques which allow for movement.

When the director Peter Brook abandoned the stage during a public speaking engagement in favour of the classroom, the director could engage in a two-way dialogue with his audience as individuals, rather than a one-way talk to a collective.[190] Furthermore, what is said to have taken place is an exchange of attention between the two parties. The concept of *attention* is discussed in chapter 3 in relation to aesthetics; art need only to hold attention of the audience to be regarded as aesthetic. Here, it is apparent that an architectural building (work) which provides for the utilisation of the space holds the potential to be art. In parallel, these concepts exist within Couture. Firstly, the stage in the building was described as a 'one-way glass'; when Couture is being modelled on the catwalk, the artistry is one way.[191] However, when the director in the earlier example moved to a classroom, the interaction with the audience became a two-way dialogue. When Couture is worn and exhibited in a natural environment, i.e. an occasion such as an evening dinner, the wearer becomes part of the art. *Attention* is directed towards the wearer, and the Couture garment will have satisfied the definition of aesthetic deriving from the attention paid to the wearer. The function of Couture therefore is more than its technical attributes, but it also extends to the art, and the function of art goes beyond the traditional concept of creativity.

2.6.1 Architectural Process

The architectural process consists of the following steps:

1. Conceiving the idea and understanding the client's requirements for a building project. This includes ascertaining the parameters in which the building must be created such as the location, existing structures, and planning regulations.[192]

189 Gray Read, *Introduction: The Play's the Thing Architecture as Performance Art* (Routledge 2013) 1

190 Gray Read, *Introduction: The Play's the Thing Architecture as Performance Art* (Routledge 2013) 1

191 Gray Read, *Introduction: The Play's the Thing Architecture as Performance Art* (Routledge 2013) 3

192 Mima Studios, 'Stages of Architectural Design' (*Mima Studios*, 2022) <https://mim.archi/blog/architecture/stages-of-architectural-design/> accessed 20 September 2023

2. Development of the architectural project through planning, sketches, consideration of materials, and space.[193]
3. Development of the building design showcasing exterior and interior drawings. Today this usually includes the use of 3D software.[194]
4. Construction plans are developed through the preliminary work (outlined in points 1–3) to showcase the building design.[195]
5. Construction stage.[196]

A definition of architecture:

> [a]rchitecture, the art and technique of designing and building, as distinguished from the skills associated with construction. The practice of architecture is employed to fulfil both practical and expressive requirements, and thus it serves both utilitarian and aesthetic ends. Although these two ends may be distinguished, they cannot be separated, and the relative weight given to each can vary widely.[197]

The most striking pertinent words regarding the preceding definition shall be discussed to ascertain not only the similarities with the thesis findings on Couture but also in understanding 'art' as a functional form. The first phrase from the preceding quote is 'the art and technique of designing' which invariably implies that design is an intrinsic part of the art of architecture, which as the study has unearthed, is the same for Couture.[198] Architecture is said to 'fulfil both practical and expressive requirements'; this is exactly the same for Couture, as when creating a Couture garment the couturier must create around the existing practical limitations.[199] The quote for architecture acknowledges both the aesthetic and utilitarian nature of architecture and essentially recognises that they cannot be separated. This point is significant as the quote acknowledges the industry definition and standard for architecture recognises that the utilitarian and aesthetic components exist in unison for the purposes of realising a *complete whole concept* of architecture, and the same would apply to Couture. For this reason, it is significant that whilst industry practice does

193 Mima Studios, 'Stages of Architectural Design' (*Mima Studios*, 2022) <https://mim.archi/blog/architecture/stages-of-architectural-design/> accessed 20 September 2023
194 Mima Studios, 'Stages of Architectural Design' (*Mima Studios*, 2022) <https://mim.archi/blog/architecture/stages-of-architectural-design/> accessed 20 September 2023
195 Mima Studios, 'Stages of Architectural Design' (*Mima Studios*, 2022) <https://mim.archi/blog/architecture/stages-of-architectural-design/> accessed 20 September 2023
196 Mima Studios, 'Stages of Architectural Design' (*Mima Studios*, 2022) <https://mim.archi/blog/architecture/stages-of-architectural-design/> accessed 20 September 2023
197 Britannica, 'Architecture' (*Britannica*, 17 August 2023) <https://www.britannica.com/topic/architecture> accessed 20 September 2023
198 Mima Studios, 'Stages of Architectural Design' (*Mima Studios*, 2022) <https://mim.archi/blog/architecture/stages-of-architectural-design/> accessed 20 September 2023
199 Mima Studios, 'Stages of Architectural Design' (*Mima Studios*, 2022) <https://mim.archi/blog/architecture/stages-of-architectural-design/> accessed 20 September 2023

not separate the elements, or moreover discriminate between aesthetic and utilitarian features, the significant question remaining is, why does copyright law?

2.6.2 The U.K.

The Copyright Act 1911 protected architectural works of *art* relating to the design and not the means by which it was constructed.[200] This is noteworthy as this piece of legislation also infers that design is a part of the *art*. The Copyright, Designs and Patents Act 1988 protects architecture under s.4(1)(b) 'a work of architecture being a building or a model for a building.'[201] This is significant as s.4 is specifically for artistic works. In the case of *Signature Realty Ltd v Fortis Developments Ltd and another*[202] the High Court held that the architect's copyright was infringed when the drawings were used by the property developer to build according to those specifications.[203]

Barron identifies through the work of Jaszi and Woodmansee that the law on copyright fails to recognise 'many forms and genres of contemporary Western art.'[204] This is significant when considering Couture as an artistic work (from the perspective of this book) is absent from the closed list in the CDPA 1988 (whereas architecture is included). Barron additionally is of the opinion that the words 'artistic works' are only limited to identify the categories listed within the provision. Barron further argues that the closed list employs a 'taxonomic' approach in the portrayal of the protected works within the list, and observes the apparent commitment to those categories.[205] With that said, any works going beyond the parameters of those categories cannot be described as artistic works in law, and this opinion very much supports the fundamental findings of the study.[206] Further put forward is the notion that architecture is not required to possess fine art characteristics to satisfy the classification of an artistic work.[207] In relation to the artistic quality, which Barron identifies as an evaluative aesthetic subjective notion, the legislative concern is to deter the courts from being embroiled in subjective assessments. This is a significant point, because as art practice evolves beyond the traditional fine arts and yet the legislation lists architecture as an artistic work within s.4 of the CDPA 1988, and the evaluative subjectivity left to the legislative process is a consequence of what has been determined by the law already. The law, by listing architecture as

200 Matthew Rimmer, 'Crystal Palaces: Copyright Law and Public Architecture' (2002) 14(2) Bond Law Review 320–46 <https://ssrn.com/abstract=600865>

201 Copyright Design and Patents Act 1988, s.4 (1)(b)

202 *Signature Realty Ltd v Fortis Developments Ltd and another [2016] E.W.H.C. 3583 (Ch)*

203 *Signature Realty Ltd v Fortis Developments Ltd and another [2016] E.W.H.C. 3583 (Ch)*

204 Anne Barron, 'Copyright Law and the Claims of Art' <https://ssrn.com/abstract=346361 or http://dx.doi.org/10.2139/ssrn.346361>

205 Anne Barron, 'Copyright Law and the Claims of Art' <https://ssrn.com/abstract=346361 or http://dx.doi.org/10.2139/ssrn.346361>

206 Anne Barron, 'Copyright Law and the Claims of Art' <https://ssrn.com/abstract=346361 or http://dx.doi.org/10.2139/ssrn.346361>

207 Anne Barron, 'Copyright Law and the Claims of Art' <https://ssrn.com/abstract=346361 or http://dx.doi.org/10.2139/ssrn.346361> Please see: Hugh Laddie and others, *The Modern Law of Copyright and Designs* (3rd edn, Butterworths 2000) 194

an artistic work within s.4 of the CDPA 1988, inadvertently invites the definition of an artistic work to be further examined.

2.6.3 The U.S.

The U.S. legislates for architecture through the Architectural Copyright Act.[208] The legislative provision was developed through the essential requirement for endorsing the Berne Treaty. Tang argues that the architect Grave's congressional guidelines for the Act are restrictive in the definition of an architectural work and therefore impact upon the legal analysis.[209] Tang argues that arguments raised for concerns against copyright due to economic concerns are simplistic.[210]

Tang argues that the 'total concept and feel' test put forward in the case of *Shine v Childs* should be exercised in consideration of the guidelines of the Act.[211] The test determines the similarity between the two works in infringement cases by observations derived from the jury or ordinary observer.[212] The test effectively establishes infringement if the ordinary observer fails to distinguish between the differences in the aesthetic appeal of the two works and regards them as the same.[213] The case concerned an alleged infringement of Shine's design (claimant) of the Freedom Tower at the World Trade Centre by Childs (defendant) design. The drawings were copied by Childs when Shine was a post-graduate student in architecture. Tang asserts that the standard used for the case promoted progress 'in the architectural field.' Further, Tang expresses that architecture should be avant-garde rather than only satisfying a market demand. Tang identifies 'undue monopolies on useful forms' within the copyright framework, particularly when applied to architecture. The useful articles concept pursuant to the Copyright Act 1976 results in such works being denied copyright protection as intellectual property within the work could be protected by other means such as a design patent (equivalent of design law in the U.K. or the community design regulations in the E.U.). Tang acknowledges that the attempt in attainting copyright of architecture is as onerous as the attempt in attaining copyright for fashion and significantly that due to

208 Architectural Works Copyright Protection Act, Pub. L. No. 101–650, § 701–06, 104 Stat. 5133 (codified in scattered sections of 17 U.S.C.)

209 Xiyin Tang, 'Narrativizing the Architectural Copyright Act: Another View of the Cathedral (June 22, 2013)' (2013) 21(1) Texas Intellectual Property Law Journal <https://ssrn.com/abstract=2169090>

210 Xiyin Tang, 'Narrativizing the Architectural Copyright Act: Another View of the Cathedral (June 22, 2013)' (2013) 21(1) Texas Intellectual Property Law Journal <https://ssrn.com/abstract=2169090>

211 Xiyin Tang, 'Narrativizing the Architectural Copyright Act: Another View of the Cathedral (June 22, 2013)' (2013) 21(1) Texas Intellectual Property Law Journal <https://ssrn.com/abstract=2169090>

212 Jeffrey Brown, 'Too Close for Comfort' (*Architect Magazine*, 2 November 2007) <https://www.architectmagazine.com/practice/too-close-for-comfort_o> accessed 19 September 2023 and Shine, 382 F. Supp. 2d

213 Jeffrey Brown, 'Too Close for Comfort' (*Architect Magazine*, 2 November 2007) <https://www.architectmagazine.com/practice/too-close-for-comfort_o> accessed 19 September 2023 and Shine, 382 F. Supp. 2d

Table 2.1 Parallels Between Architecture and Couture

Architecture	*Couture*
Idea conception - understanding the clients' requirements for a building project	Conception of the idea through research of trend forecasts and cultural trends
Development of the architectural project through planning, sketches, consideration of materials, and space	Illustrations of Couture garments including more detailed designs
Development of the building design – modelling	Textile sourcing
Construction plans	Toile/prototype creation of the designs
Construction	Construction

the considerations relating to the effect of protection on the fashion industry, in whether it would increase or decrease innovation. Another key observation by Tang is that limitations on originality have subsequently been noted in the latter case of *Harvester, Inc. v Rule Joy Trammell + Rubio, LLC* by the district courts due to '(1) market demands, (2) building codes and manufacturers' clearance directives, [and] (3) functional demands.'[214] Put forward is that the Act essentially pigeonholes the architect as servicing society with building creations, and this is viewed in contrast to the 'speculative' architect that wants to instigate change in building creations in order to reshape the societal future.[215] Tang acknowledges the approach of modernists Corbusier and Colquhoun and the notions of aestheticism and beauty. On this basis, the process of creation is understood to be a developmental route which may in fact result in the work not necessarily arriving at the intended destination.

Conclusion

The case study primarily demonstrates the legal position for architecture as an artistic work in copyright, and significantly highlights the legal position for Couture. This is due to the fact that whilst both architecture and Couture are very different disciplines, in practice they both primarily consist of creative processes which are very similar. Further, both disciplines comprise of design to attain the final product (a Couture garment or a building). This is supported by the Copyright Act 1911, which listed architectural works as art, specifically relating to the design which affirms design as an inherent part of the art. Further, architecture is protected by s.4 of the CDPA.[216] On this basis, the question from the perspective of the thesis is, why is architecture listed as an artistic work under s.4 of the CDPA 1988 and Couture is not? In the interests of a level playing field, any arguments relating to function deriving from technical considerations as exemptions to copyright if applied to Couture would therefore be

214 716 F. Supp. 2d 428, 440 (E.D. Va. 2010)

215 Xiyin Tang, 'Narrativizing the Architectural Copyright Act: Another View of the Cathedral (June 22, 2013)' (2013) 21(1) Texas Intellectual Property Law Journal <https://ssrn.com/abstract=2169090>

216 Matthew Rimmer, 'Crystal Palaces: Copyright Law and Public Architecture' (2002) 14(2) Bond Law Review 320–46 <https://ssrn.com/abstract=600865>

Figure 2.1 Hubert De Givenchy 1960 Dress Created for Audrey Hepburn in *Breakfast at Tiffany's* Saatchi Gallery Tiffany Exhibition 2021

required to apply to architecture. The case-study illustrates the disparity through the application of the law for different subject matter. Noted is the current legislative view, as to what art is in copyright – ***End of Case Study***.

Interim Conclusion

The interim conclusion presented illustrates the relationship between art and copyright law, specifically in relation to the necessity to define artistic works within s.4 of the CDPA 1988 to a wider extent. Whether Couture is considered as an artistic work in law is yet to be determined, although as art and creativity are a natural part of the fashion creation process, it is difficult to see a more appropriate IP right other than copyright to protect Couture under s.4 of the CDPA 1988. In addition, the case study demonstrates the inequality amongst subject matter, namely Couture and architecture, as whilst architecture is a protected artistic work under s.4 of the CDPA 1988, Couture is not. Therefore, the inclusion of Couture would serve to balance the provision, in consideration of the inclusion of architecture.

The findings so far have highlighted the limitations relating to the wider IP framework for the protection of Couture. Design rights are more concerned with the technicality of a design for commercial purposes. The *Magmatic* case demonstrates that the scope of rights has widened in the consideration of the essential design components, for the purposes of appreciating the product as a whole, and therefore the scope of limitations appears narrowed.[217] Trade marks are concerned with strategical marks in identification of a business, and copyright protects artistic works.[218] It is apparent that patents protect a process, and as seen in *Pioneer Electronics Capital, Inc*[219] the different processes produce different products which may be significant for Couture.

The legal response to art is rooted in the differences between the common law and civil law, and the function of the judges within each is integral to the decision process. How Couture is regarded by the common law will depend on legal precedent, irrespective of the differing subject matter within the case being applied. Considerations extend to Couture being derived through a creative process which is essentially an artistic practice; and copyright is for the purposes of protecting artistic works.[220] The next chapter explores Couture as an artistic work.

217 *Magmatic Ltd v PMS International Ltd* [2016] U.K.SC 12; [2016] 4 All E.R. 1027; [2016] 3 WLU.K. 280 (SC)

218 CDPA, s1(a)

219 *Pioneer Electronics Capital, Inc. and Another v Warner Music Manufacturing Europe GmbH and Another, [1995] R.P.C. 487; [1995] 1 WLU.K. 464 (Ch D (Patents Ct)), 24 January 1995, Aldous J*

220 CDPA, S.1(a)

3 'Couture,' an Artistic Work?

Introduction

The objective of this chapter is to establish how art can be identified within Couture and whether Couture can be regarded as a conceptual work of art in its own right. The chapter examines the French notion of Droit D'Ateur in consideration of the relationship between the work and author, and the relevance to copyright protection. Further, the chapter evaluates the significance of aesthetics and commercial viability in consideration of Couture. The primary thesis question specifically tests whether copyright legislation must widen the criterion of 'artistic works' to include Couture garments. For this reason, the heart of this chapter rests on the notion of art, and therefore the argument raised is that copyright law shall reflect the artistic value by incorporating Couture into s.4 of the CDPA 1988 as an artistic work. The secondary research question addressed is: To what extent is Couture defined as art, in law?

The first task of this chapter is to determine the extent to which Couture can be defined as an artistic work, which may lead to considering whether Couture can be incorporated into the CDPA 1988. The CDPA 1988 appears to provide for a closed list of artistic works, of which Couture is absent:

S.4 'Artistic works.

(1) In this Part "artistic work" means –
(a) a graphic work, photograph, sculpture or collage, irrespective of artistic quality,
(b) a work of architecture being a building or a model for a building, or
(c) a work of artistic craftsmanship.'[1]

3.1 Defining Art: Philosophical Theories

Philosophical insight into the definition of art and associated characteristics is crucial to determine whether Couture can be defined as an artistic work. The Oxford English Dictionary defines art as: '1 The expression of creative skill in visual form.

1 CDPA 1988, s.4(1)

DOI: 10.4324/9781003599456-3

2 Paintings, drawings, and sculpture. 3 (the arts) creative activities such as painting, music, and drama. 4 a skill. Artwork illustrations to be included in a publication.'[2]

An artist is defined as: '1. a person who paints or draws 2. a person who performs any of the creative arts.'[3]

The preceding definition of art appears to identify specific characteristics such as 'expression of creative skill,' 'creative activities,' 'a skill.'[4] Consequently, an artist is defined as a person 'who performs any of the creative arts.'[5]

Primarily, the work of Tolstoy and Rand are examined to assert the definition of art and to determine the extent to which these definitions may be applied to Couture. The thesis aim is to be critical in the analysis. The critical objective of the assessment is merely to draw inferences on the philosophical views, deducing the necessary information, so as when applied to Couture, this may contribute to forming an understanding as to whether Couture is art and the couturier is an artist.

Tolstoy theorises art as a 'false view of life' and puts forward the theory that the value of art would be absent without such a false perception.[6] He observes that art is not in existence for its own good but proportionately can be '[v]aluable . . . objectionable . . . serviceable . . . or harmful.'[7] Tolstoy identifies that a common definition of art is absent due to most ideas of art being derived from the notion of beauty.[8] Tolstoy appears to define art as a multi-faceted concept that is not compelled to radiate beauty. (Although, as Tolstoy's work has been subject to interpretation, the viewpoint from this thesis is that the notion of beauty potentially relates to aesthetic considerations.) Tolstoy's view on art is that it does not have to be beautiful. In his work, Tolstoy identifies the definitions of art put forward by Schiller, Darwin, and Spencer and examines the work of Grant Allen.[9] The first definition of art is:

> 1a [A]rt is an activity arising even in the animal Kingdom and springing from sexual desire and the propensity to play,[10] and accompanied by a pleasurable excitement of the nervous system.[11]

The second definition of art referred to by Tolstoy is:

> 1b [A]rt is the external manifestation, by means of lines, colours, movements, sounds, or words, of emotions felt by man.[12]

2 Charlotte Buxton, *Oxford English Dictionary* (8th edn, Oxford University Press 2013) 27
3 Charlotte Buxton, *Oxford English Dictionary* (8th edn, Oxford University Press 2013) 27
4 Charlotte Buxton, *Oxford English Dictionary* (8th edn, Oxford University Press 2013) 27
5 Charlotte Buxton, *Oxford English Dictionary* (8th edn, Oxford University Press 2013) 27
6 Leo Tolstoy, *What Is Art* (True Sign Publishing 1 March 2021) 37
7 Leo Tolstoy, *What Is Art* (True Sign Publishing 1 March 2021) 172
8 Leo Tolstoy, *What Is Art* (True Sign Publishing 1 March 2021) 171
9 Leo Tolstoy, *What Is Art* (True Sign Publishing 1 March 2021) 1167
10 Leo Tolstoy referring to Schiller, Darwin and Spencer, *What Is Art* (True Sign Publishing 1 March 2021) 1167
11 Leo Tolstoy referring to Grant Allen, *What Is Art* (True Sign Publishing 1 March 2021) 1167
12 Leo Tolstoy referring to Vérnon, *What Is Art* (True Sign Publishing 1 March 2021) 1167

The third definition:

> [A]rt is the production of some object, or passing action, which is fitted not only to supply an active enjoyment to the producer, but to convey a pleasurable impression to several spectators or listeners, quite apart from any personal advantage to be derived from it.[13]

Tolstoy describes 1a as a definition which is not 'exact' as the definition digresses to the derivation point of the art, instead of art being deliberated as the substantive matter itself.[14] In relation to 1b, Tolstoy identifies that this definition is also 'inexact' as it is akin to other 'human activities,' which identify art as pertaining to actions of humans, such as the 'preparation of handsome clothes, pleasant scents and even of victuals.'[15] The second definition, understanding art through expression by the use of colours, lines emotions, and sounds, as put forward by Vérnon, is regarded by Tolstoy as 'inexact' due to the creator only expressing some emotions and not others, although moreover that the 'manifestation of emotion is not art.'[16] In consideration of the third definition by Sully, Tolstoy again expresses this as 'inexact,' as not all art affords pleasure to the viewer and identifies that some forms of 'heart-rendering scenes' from a 'gloomy' poem are artistic works.[17]

It appears that Tolstoy's observation of art is much wider and less limited in scope in comparison to his contemporaries. Tolstoy's view on art is understood here as a live concept, inclusive of the moment in which it is being created until the time it is experienced by the person viewing/hearing the work. It is a conceptual experience, therefore viewed as placing the creator of the art and the individual experiencing the work within close proximity to each other, as both shall experience the same emotive effect.[18] Tolstoy's theory of 'infection' ultimately rests on the principle that the art can evoke emotive disturbance within the observer. The theory of 'infection' is presented as a neutral concept that is not concerned with either good or bad notions of morality, and the emphasis is on transferable feelings, whereby the feelings of the creator are transmitted through the art, to the observer, whilst experiencing the art.[19] In summary, the art evokes within the observer (of the art) emotions of the artist when creating the piece; if these feelings are happy, the observer shall be infected with happiness, and if sorrowful, then feelings of sadness shall be experienced.[20]

13 Leo Tolstoy referring to Vérnon, *What Is Art* (True Sign Publishing 1 March 2021) 1167
14 Leo Tolstoy, *What Is Art* (True Sign Publishing 1 March 2021) 1172
15 Leo Tolstoy, *What Is Art* (True Sign Publishing 1 March 2021) 171
16 Leo Tolstoy, *What Is Art* (True Sign Publishing 1 March 2021) 1169
17 Leo Tolstoy, *What Is Art* (True Sign Publishing 1 March 2021) 1180
18 Leo Tolstoy, *What Is Art* (True Sign Publishing 1 March 2021) 1186
19 Leo Tolstoy, *What Is Art* (True Sign Publishing 1 March 2021) 187
20 Leo Tolstoy, *What Is Art* (True Sign Publishing 1 March 2021) 187

Similarly to Tolstoy, Rand's perception and approach to art essentially draws parallels with human nature[21] and thus, relating to 'cognitive' requirements such as 'emotional complexity.'[22] Art is identified by Rand as being a 'need' and a requirement of 'human consciousness.'[23] However, the work of Witold Rybczynski differs from Rand's theories in that he recognises the contemporary considerations of the implementation of art within industrial settings in contrast to the traditional fine art perspective of Rand.[24] Rybczynski acknowledges fashion in comparison to architecture as a 'task of mating utility with beauty.'[25] This notion can be applied to Couture, in consideration of the materials, design, form, and the impression the garment shall leave on the observer.

In the U.S., the National Foundation on Arts and Humanities Act 1965 is referenced by Rand in relation to the key term definition of 'the arts.'[26] The main point of interest from the perspective of this study is the category for utilitarian works, whereby fashion design is included.[27] The list including fashion design is referenced as 'major art forms' in s.952 (b) under the section 'Definitions.'[28] One of the criticisms Rand makes when referencing the work of writer Dobbs is that fine arts are not distinguished from popular or applied arts.[29] Rand's criticism extends to the viewpoint that the four disciplines referenced in Dobb's work, 'art-making, art criticism, art history, and esthetics' are absent in any conceptual understanding and therefore 'lack substance.'[30] In defining art, Rand's conclusions appear to be arguably very narrow in scope, particularly seen from the perception of contemporary art forms such as 'conceptual, incendiary or pop' as not being within the definition of art.[31] Moreover, in consideration of Rand's definition of art, fashion appears to fall outside of this meaning.[32]

21 Louis Torres and Michelle Kamhi, *What Art is the Esthetic Theory of Ayn Rand* (Open Court 2000) 109
22 Louis Torres and Michelle Kamhi, *What Art is the Esthetic Theory of Ayn Rand* (Open Court 2000) 109
23 Louis Torres and Michelle Kamhi, *What Art is the Esthetic Theory of Ayn Rand* (Open Court 2000) 24
24 Louis Torres and Michelle Kamhi, *What Art is the Esthetic Theory of Ayn Rand* (Open Court 2000) 42
25 Louis Torres and Michelle Kamhi, *What Art is the Esthetic Theory of Ayn Rand* (Open Court 2000) 294 Referring to Witold Rybczynski, "Gentlemen, Here Is the Winner," review of Architectural Competitions, by Cees de Jong and Erik Mattie, Times Literary Supplement, 11 August 1995, 19
26 Louis Torres and Michelle Kamhi, *What Art Is the Esthetic Theory of Ayn Rand* (Open Court 2000) 294 Jeffrey Lependorf, 'Law Creating NEA is a Work of Art in Itself' (*Blue Mountain Center*, 2022) <https://commons.bluemountaincenter.org/law-creating-nea-is-a-work-of-art-in-itself/#:~:text=On%20a%20sunny%20September%2029%20th%20in%20the,Ansel%20Adams%20the%20pens%20used%20to%20sign%20it> accessed 9 July 2022
27 Please see: The National Foundation on Arts and Humanities Act 1965, s.952 (b)
28 Please see: The National Foundation on Arts and Humanities Act 1965, s.952 (b)
29 Louis Torres and Michelle Kamhi, *What Art Is the Esthetic Theory of Ayn Rand* (Open Court 2000) 212. Please see: and Stephen Dobbs, *Learning In and Through Art: A Guide to Discipline-Based Art Education* (Getty Publications 1998) 66
30 Louis Torres and Michelle Kamhi, *What Art Is the Esthetic Theory of Ayn Rand* (Open Court 2000) 299
31 Louis Torres and Michelle Kamhi, *What Art Is the Esthetic Theory of Ayn Rand* (Open Court 2000) 317
32 Louis Torres and Michelle Kamhi, *What Art Is the Esthetic Theory of Ayn Rand* (Open Court 2000) 317

Predominantly, the aforementioned views of Tolstoy and Rand shall be applied to Couture to begin the process of understanding whether Couture fits within each of those perceptions of art, or whether Couture can be established as a work of art. Tolstoy defines art as a false view of life,[33] and further, that art may carry both positive and negative effects through transference of feelings from the creator to the individual experiencing the art.'[34] These notions would fit with the concept of Couture as explained later. To consider Couture as a false notion of life, Couture is far removed from the fundamental idea of life and extends to notions of status, wealth, and exclusivity. These concepts are regarded from the perspective of this thesis as a 'false notion of life.' If we are to contemplate the true notion of life, this would possibly be understood as the fundamental generic attributes and common characteristics of human nature, shared by all humans. The adorning of the body with clothes and decoration comes secondary to the notion of life derived from cultural practices and values. The creation of Couture is therefore considered to be a cultural practice that would align with Tolstoy's theory akin to a false notion of life.[35] In consideration of Tolstoy's' 'false notions of life' theory and Rybczynski's contemporary implementation of art within industrial settings, Couture shall now be analysed in relation to the fashion designer's consideration of economic, environmental, and ethical concerns through the creative expression.

Rand's theories would not apply to Couture, and it would appear that Rand would not recognise Couture as a conceptual work of art. Rand appears to express a preference for classic or traditional art forms, and whilst Rand's observations rest on a bio-centric approach, similar to Tolstoy, the scope for defining art seems narrow. This is evidenced in the argument against the National Foundation on Arts and Humanities Act 1965, s.952, whereby fashion design is included as a major art form.[36] Further, Rand argues on the work of Dobbs, which recognises that the four categories (listed by Dobbs) may expand or change.[37] When applied to Couture, we can see that fashion is perpetually derivative, and changes regarding advancing technological and industrial practices impact the creative process for Couture.

In relation to testing the thesis question, therefore, through the above analysis, Rand's definition of art would not support that copyright legislation must widen the criterion of 'artistic works' to include Couture garments. Whilst Rand's view on art aligns with the traditional methods used to create fine art, and although Couture is not fine art, Couture employs the artistic methods and processes for the creation of an artwork. For this reason, Couture aligns very closely with the ideas expressed by Dobbs whereby art is perceived as having the capacity to expand and change, particularly relative to time and the sociological impact as reflected in the creative expression. In summary, the theory of Rand appears to support and perceive art as classic traditional art forms, such as fine art, whereas Dobbs sees art with the potential to develop and change, which corelates to variable factors in society and/or epoch.

33 Leo Tolstoy, *What Is Art* (True Sign Publishing 1 March 2021) 171

34 Leo Tolstoy, *What Is Art* (True Sign Publishing 1 March 2021) 172

35 Leo Tolstoy, *What Is Art* (True Sign Publishing 1 March 2021) 33

36 Please see: The National Foundation on Arts and Humanities Act 1965, s.952 (b)

37 Louis Torres and Michelle Kamhi, *What Art Is the Esthetic Theory of Ayn Rand* (Open Court 2000) 301

3.2 Art Theory Applied to Couture

Conversely, Couture may be regarded as objectionable. For instance, consider the 2000 Spring/Summer collection by John Galliano titled 'Couture Homeless' for Dior, where activists had protested outside the Dior boutique, Avenue Montaigne in Paris, in response to the collection.[38] The harmful notion of Couture could be attributed to environmental concerns, although this is addressed most frequently by adopting sustainability policies and pledges, as in the case of Vivienne Westwood,[39] Stella McCartney,[40] and Victoria Beckham to name a few British designers.[41] Tolstoy's concept of 'infection' can be considered together with Couture, particularly when assessing audience reactions to the bi-annual fashion show presentations.[42] Often press releases are delivered through the media, encapsulating the emotive response to the garments. For example, an extract from *Elle* magazine reporting on the Dior Autumn/Winter 2022 collection states: 'Tradition, as it relates to why and how we dress, was a prominent theme throughout, with garments paying sartorial tribute to different countries and cultures, the underlying message being that we all belong together.'[43]

In applying Tolstoy's theory of 'infection' to this collection, it is seen that the observer of the show is unified with the emotions evoked by the Autumn/Winter 2022 collection created by Dior.[44] This Dior collection speaks to sociological challenges and is significant because it is understood to be placed against the backdrop of challenging times, which forms the basis of the collection and therefore, is part of the art. The clothes are arguably beautiful (as a matter of taste, and a subjective notion), although the endeavour for the collection was to communicate the sociological and cultural challenges of our time, in other words, the creator is 'infecting' the observer and beauty is not necessarily the *only* point of focus. Therefore, based on the preceding analysis, Couture appears to fulfil Tolstoy's notion of 'infection,' which establishes the emotive response by the observer to the art.

On this basis, Couture should be considered within the context of conceptual works of art which are developed through evolution (changing/developing) of ideas, and in this instance, Couture as a conceptual work of art.[45] As the study

38 Admin, 'John Galliano and the Representation of the Homeless: When Fashion Changes Society' (*Slogan Observer*, 17 January 2022) <https://slogan.observer/blog/2022/01/17/john-galliano-and-the-representation-of-the-homeless-when-fashion-changes-society/> accessed 9 July 2022 and please see Leo Tolstoy, *What Is Art* (True Sign Publishing 1 March 2021) 171 regarding 'objectionable'

39 Vivienne Westwood, 'Our Approach' (*Vivienne Westwood*, 2022) <https://www.viviennewestwood.com/en/our-approach/> accessed 9 July 2022

40 Stella McCartney, 'Our Commitments' (*Stella McCartney*, 2022) <https://www.stellamccartney.com/gb/en/sustainability/our-commitments.html> accessed 9 July 2022

41 Luxiders, 'Victoria Beckham' (*Luxiders*, 2022) <https://luxiders.com/sustainable-brands-victoria-beckham/> accessed 9 July 2022

42 Leo Tolstoy, *What Is Art* (True Sign Publishing 1 March 2021) 187

43 Ellecom, 'Dior's Couture Collection Wants to Bring Beauty to An Ugly World' (*Elle*, 4 July 2022) <https://www.elle.com/fashion/a40500543/dior-Couture-collection-fall-2022/> access ed 9 July 2022

44 Leo Tolstoy, *What Is Art* (True Sign Publishing 1 March 2021) 175

45 Louis Torres and Michelle Kamhi, *What Art Is The Esthetic Theory of Ayn Rand* (Open Court 2000) 301

is testing the thesis question regarding Couture as a conceptual work of art, in pragmatic terms, it is necessary to understand what 'conceptual art' means, to understand the extent to which the analysis supports the thesis question, as discussed next.

3.2.1 Conceptual Works of Art

Conceptual art is understood to have the most significant emphasis on the idea attributed to the artwork.[46] Goldie and Shellekens identify two approaches to conceptual art, that is, historical and philosophical.[47] Historically, works produced between 1966 and 1972, during the conceptual art movement, are regarded as such.[48] Philosophically, artworks produced outside of this time frame qualify as conceptual pieces due to the common traits, such as the elimination of the element of 'sensory pleasure.'[49] To illustrate this, critical art making is central to the movement, as it relates to activism in promoting views.[50] An example is the work of Marcel Duchamp, noted to be the first conceptual art artist, known for his work titled Fountain (1917), a urinal with a signature of R.Mutt.[51]

The materials used by a conceptual artist are those which will most suitably complement the communication of the idea.[52] The artist considers the preparation, organisation, and decision-making for the artwork *prior* to the obligatory accomplishment of the art. Conceptual art is recognised as a type of contemporary and modern art.[53] The Dada, Cubist, Abstract Expressionist, and Pop-art movements formed the basis for conceptual art, whereby art could extend beyond the parameters of traditional norms through experimentation.[54] In consideration of Couture, and in applying these concepts, Amanda Thompson's creations appear to reflect this artistic practice through 'exploration of textures, shapes, skills and thread, combined with a heady mix of adventure and imagination, all coalesce into pieces that offer up a timeless style.'[55] Next, the discussion shall extend to the notion of Couture as conceptual art, where themes in this next section shall be revisited in application to Couture further on.

46 Tate, 'Conceptual Art' (*Tate*, 2022) <https://www.tate.org.uk/art/art-terms/c/conceptual-art> accessed 9 July 2022

47 P Goldie and E Shellekens, *Philosophy and Conceptual Art* (Oxford University Press 2007) xi

48 P Goldie and E Shellekens, *Philosophy and Conceptual Art* (Oxford University Press 2007) xi

49 P Goldie and E Shellekens, *Philosophy and Conceptual Art* (Oxford University Press 2007) xii

50 P Goldie and E Shellekens, *Philosophy and Conceptual Art* (Oxford University Press 2007) xii

51 Tate, 'Conceptual Art' (*Tate*, 2022) <https://www.tate.org.uk./art/art-terms/c/conceptual-art> accessed 9 July 2022

52 Tate, 'Conceptual Art' (*Tate*, 2022) <https://www.tate.org.uk./art/art-terms/c/conceptual-art> accessed 9 July 2022

53 Art in Context, 'Conceptual Art: An Exploration of the Conceptualist Art Movement' (*Art in Context*, 8 December 2021) <https://artincontext.org/conceptual-art/> accessed 9 July 2022

54 Art in Context, 'Conceptual Art: An Exploration of the Conceptualist Art Movement' (*Art in Context*, 8 December 2021) <https://artincontext.org/conceptual-art/> accessed 9 July 2022

55 Amanda Thompson, 'Atelier' (*Amanda Thompson Couture*, 2024) <https://www.amandathompson Couture.co.uk/atelier> accessed 15 October 2024

3.2.2 The Role of Aesthetics

The preceding discussion has touched on aesthetics in consideration of art and its philosophy. This concept is understood to be connected primarily to the idea of most aesthetic notions being connected strongly to beauty, while as referenced earlier, Tolstoy does not agree with art always being beautiful.[56] The relationship between art and aesthetics is now explored through an analysis of what aesthetics is. The origin of the word 'aesthesis' is Greek, which is understood to mean 'perception.'[57] Historically, in 1750 the concept of aesthetics was presented by the philosopher Alexander Baumgarten, as meaning 'sensory experiences.'[58] To understand this, we can consider the sensory experiences through our everyday lives whilst choosing products or food, perhaps most associated with things we like, and to our taste. Aesthetics is said to be an important part of our lives, and therefore it is not only applicable to art. Bence believes that '[i]f an experience is worth having for you, it thereby becomes a potential subject of aesthetics.'[59]

Bence regards aesthetics in two ways, first, as an engagement, therefore doing something, and second, as the aspect of experience, describing what is felt.[60] If we consider engagement with aesthetics, then when observing, analysing, or evaluating art or other types of creative works, it is inevitable that the aesthetic experience in how an individual feels will follow. The notion of beauty was recognised by Tolstoy as being the element that formed the basis for most definitions of art. This notion that Tolstoy recognised as 'beauty' is established from the perspective of this study, as Tolstoy referring to aesthetics.

Moving from the perception of engagement, the second is the experience. Bence characterises beauty as a descriptor for an experience, and questions what beauty is.[61] Based on this reasoning, the question arises of whether something that is aesthetic can be distinguished from that which is beautiful, but how? Bence analyses the concept of pleasure and identifies aesthetic pleasure as sustained and, therefore, a motivating concept.[62] This is characterised by looking at a painting and engaging with it; the pleasure derived from looking at the painting sustains the ongoing engagement.[63] Bence further identifies 'emotion' as an integral part of the aesthetic experience, which is observed in many cultures such as Islamic, Sanskrit, Japanese, and Chinese.[64] Similarly to Bence, Kant is recognised for his observations of 'judgments of beauty were grounded in features of the object itself.'[65] Kant

56 Nanay Bence, *Aesthetics: A Very Short Introduction* (Oxford University Press 2019) 8 and Britanica, 'Aesthetics Philosophy' (*Britanica*, 2022) <https://www.britannica.com/topic/aesthetics> accessed 12 July 2022

57 Nanay Bence, *Aesthetics: A Very Short Introduction* (Oxford University Press 2019) 2

58 Nanay Bence, *Aesthetics: A Very Short Introduction* (Oxford University Press 2019) 2

59 Nanay Bence, *Aesthetics: A Very Short Introduction* (Oxford University Press 2019) 3

60 Nanay Bence, *Aesthetics: A Very Short Introduction* (Oxford University Press 2019) 3

61 Nanay Bence, *Aesthetics: A Very Short Introduction* (Oxford University Press 2019) 8

62 Nanay Bence, *Aesthetics: A Very Short Introduction* (Oxford University Press 2019) 8

63 Nanay Bence, *Aesthetics: A Very Short Introduction* (Oxford University Press 2019) 8

64 Nanay Bence, *Aesthetics: A Very Short Introduction* (Oxford University Press 2019) 16

65 Anjan Chatterjee, *The Aesthetic Brain* (Oxford University Press 2014) 118

considered the interaction between individual 'perception, intellect and imagination' with those of 'beautiful objects' and the notion of having a fondness for something without necessarily wanting it.[66] Therefore, beauty is understood as being the concept that draws interest to the creation. Conversely, Bence identifies the element of 'attention' being the missing link in ascertaining the aesthetic as beautiful, and an emotional experience.[67] Attention is identified as the component that can characterise the aesthetic experience as either a success or a failure.[68] To widen the discussion, Bence observes that to understand artefacts on a global level, a 'conceptual framework' must be developed that is capable of communicating on artefacts irrespective of the cultural/traditional background it derives from.[69]

Following on from the earlier discussion regarding the concepts of art, international law that regulates protection for artistic works is the Berne Convention. The Berne Convention is understood as providing a framework for copyright protection for artistic works, and while this international convention is soft law, the World Trade Organization has integrated it via the TRIPS Agreement (minus the moral rights), which is hard law. Therefore, E.U. countries as well as the U.K. (who are WTO members) shall adapt their national legislation or must interpret and develop the guidance of the word 'artistic works' through common law and domestic legislative provisions. The most pertinent observation relevant to the thesis question is whether Couture could be defined as an artistic work under Article 2 of the Convention.[70] The Convention states:

> **Article 2**
>
> (1) The expression "literary and artistic works" shall include every production in the literary, scientific and artistic domain, whatever may be the mode or form of its expression, such as . . . dramatic or dramatico-musical works; choreographic works and entertainments in dumb show; musical compositions with or without words; cinematographic works to which are assimilated works expressed by a process analogous to cinematography; works of drawing, painting, architecture, sculpture, engraving and lithography.

The Article does not prescribe the exact type of artistic work, although it does provide some examples. Yet, what is significant is at the start of Article 2(1), that is 'every production in the literary, scientific and *artistic domain*, whatever the mode or form of its expression' [emphasis added]. Based on this construction, an artistic work appears to be any produced work which is created by its 'form and materials' reflecting the expression of the artist. This inevitably denotes an open list that shall

66 Anjan Chatterjee, *The Aesthetic Brain* (Oxford University Press 2014) 118
67 Nanay Bence, *Aesthetics: A Very Short Introduction* (Oxford University Press 2019) 21
68 Nanay Bence, *Aesthetics: A Very Short Introduction* (Oxford University Press 2019) 28
69 Nanay Bence, *Aesthetics: A Very Short Introduction* (Oxford University Press 2019) 93
70 The Berne Convention for the Protection of Literary and Artistic Works, 1886, Article 2 (1)

include all works of art including Couture, if Couture can potentially be established as an artwork, due to the nature of the creation.

3.3 Establishing Art in Couture

Fashion designer Zandra Rhodes expresses that fashion is an art form. Whether it is referred to as decorative or applied art, artistic expression is comprised in fashion to the same degree as in other art forms, such as paintings or pottery.[71] However, Alice Rawsthorn, a design critic and author, does not think fashion is art, as fashion has a practical purpose and art does not.[72] These two opposing views demonstrate the difference between design and art. When concerned with design, it is often how the practical aspects of the 'thing' are created and presented, whereas art, as referenced earlier in the chapter rests on notions of expression of creativity and the feelings invoked within the observer of the art as an experience. These two opposing views also highlight another critical difference between fashion and Couture. Whilst Couture is understood to be a category of fashion, the artistic element is key to its very platform. The platform to showcase the work as art, the place at which Couture sits within the fashion framework, is at the top. From here, the trends and ideas for the high street are generated. For this reason, when looking at fashion specifically, the design element and the practical nature of fashion may be *the* more prominent feature. In relation to the law, copyright appears to be the preferential legal protective mechanism for Couture, and design rights for fashion. Couture is noted as being art due to encompassing elements such as 'creative thinking and a way to inspire.'[73] Both elements reaffirm the innovative and influential nature of art, in that it presents a creative new concept that has the potential to influence future creations. Well-known English Couture designers are Norman Hartnell and Hardy Amies, and both had established appointment to the Queen.[74]

In fashion, Couture works display innovative concepts that may relate to the form, colour, construction, design feature, or materials, and as discussed earlier, Couture works influence the market levels below, such as high street brands. Therefore, the artistic nature of Couture is reasserted as an evolving conceptual work of art.[75] A fashion show itself can become part of the art presented for the collection. For example, the *artist* Kim Keever collaborated with Iris Van Herpen, a Couture designer, to enhance the fashion show experience.[76] This included '[l]aser lighting . . . , floating clouds' and the movements of the models were described as

71 The Guardian, 'Is Fashion a True Art Form?' (*The Guardian*, 13 July 2003) <https://www.theguardian.com/artanddesign/2003/jul/13/art.artsfeatures1> accessed 23 June 2023

72 The Guardian, 'Is Fashion a True Art Form?' (*The Guardian*, 13 July 2003) <https://www.theguardian.com/artanddesign/2003/jul/13/art.artsfeatures1> accessed 23 June 2023

73 Issiah Lawrence, 'Does the World of Haute Couture and Design Still Belong in Art?' (*Art Dealer Street*, 14 May 2021) <https://www.artdealerstreet.com/single-post/does-the-world-of-haute-Couture-and-design-still-belong-in-art#:~:text=Haute%20Couture%20is%20considered%20a,and%20a%20way%20to%20inspire> accessed 25 June 2022

74 Tim Jackson and David Shaw, *The Fashion Handbook* (Routledge 2006) 32

75 See *4.4.4 Derivative Works*

76 Issiah Lawrence, 'Does the World of Haute Couture and Design Still Belong in Art?' (*Art Dealer Street*, 14 May 2021) <https://www.artdealerstreet.com/single-post/does-the-world-of-haute-

Figure 3.1 Ball Dress – Norman Hartnell c1953 V&A Museum no. T.88-2016

'[g]littering fireflies.'[77] Significantly, Iris Van Herpen has described her clients as 'art clients,' clearly placing emphasis on Couture as art.[78]

Couture-and-design-still-belong-in-art#:~:text=Haute%20Couture%20is%20considered%20a,and%20a%20way%20to%20inspire> accessed 25 June 2022
Please see *4.4.4 Derivative Works*

77 Issiah Lawrence, 'Does the World of Haute Couture and Design Still Belong in Art?' (*ArtDealerStreet*, 14 May 2021) <https://www.artdealerstreet.com/single-post/does-the-world-of-haute-Couture-and-design-still-belong-in-art#:~:text=Haute%20Couture%20is%20considered%20a,and%20a%20way%20to%20inspire> accessed 25 June 2022
Please see *4.4.4 Derivative Works*

78 Ellie Pithers, 'Iris van Herpen Fall 2022 Couture' (*Vogue*, 2022) <https://www.vogue.com/fashion-shows/fall-2022-Couture/iris-van-herpen> accessed 12 February 2023

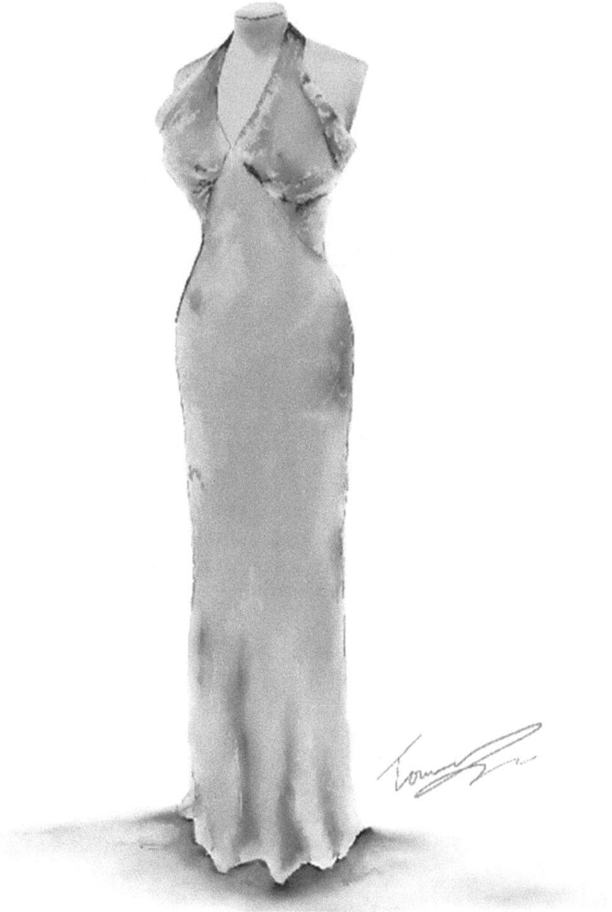

Figure 3.2 Charles James Evening Dress About 1934 V&A Museum no. T.272-1974

Historically, in the 1930s and 1940s, fashion designer Elsa Schiaparelli had collaborated with Salvador Dalí. Moreover, her alliance with surrealist artists such as Man Ray and Cocteau is noted as having an artistic influence on her art works.[79] This can be seen in her fashion designs. For example, the lobster was a feature by both Dalí and Schiaparelli; for Dalí, in his paintings, and by collaboration with Schiaparelli for her dress design, the lobster dress.[80] The dress was

79 Francesco Pastore, 'Elsa and the Artists' (*Sotheby's*, 1 March 2023) https://www.sothebys.com/en/articles/elsa-schiaparelli-and-the-artists accessed 10 March 2025

80 Laird Borrelli-persson, 'Lobsters in Fashion: A Timeline of Crustacean Chic' (*Vogue*, July 6, 2022) <https://www.vogue.com/article/lobsters-in-fashion-a-timeline-of-crustacean-chic> accessed 12 February 2023

Figure 3.3 Charles James 1937 La Sylphide Dress V&A Museum no. T.226.1 to 3–1993

designed for Wallis Simpson, the Duchess of Windsor, which she had worn to announce her engagement to Edward III in *Vogue* in 1937.[81] The dress not only is regarded as a conceptual work of art but is also a statement piece. The statement being the annunciation of the royal engagement but more pertinent to this study, being regarded as a function of the dress, the functionality of the art – to *speak* for the wearer.

81 Hattie Brett, 'Schiaparelli Recreates Wallis Simpson's Famous Lobster Dress' (*Viva*, 24 January, 2017) <https://www.viva.co.nz/article/fashion/wallis-simpson-schiaparelli/> accessed 27 June 2022 and Susan Devaney, 'Walis Simpson's Most Iconic Style Moments' (*Vogue*, 7 April 2020) <https://www.vogue.co.uk/gallery/wallis-simpson-style-file> accessed 27 June 2022

3.3.1 Couture as a Conceptual Work of Art

To understand the notion of Couture as art, we turn to the late Dame Vivienne Westwood, a world-renowned British fashion designer. In relation to her endeavours in fashion creation, Westwood stated:

> [M]y duty is to understand. To understand the world . . . from people who have lived before us we can rediscover different visions of the world through art – this is the true meaning of culture – and by comparison, we form our own ideas of a world better than the one we are in, the one that we've made a mess of. We can change our future.[82]

As part of a career that has spanned eight decades,[83] Westwood's creations are referenced as 'art.'[84] She expresses that 'picture galleries' which exhibit still-life and landscapes in addition to costume influence her fashion ideas.[85] In this concept, it is noticeable how creativity preserves art through the process of expression. In other words, art lives on through new creations, and through subsequently developed expressions, and this same process is reflected in Couture. The couturiers perpetually re-create innovative and influential works for generations of couturiers to come. In consideration of fashion as a conceptual art form, the earlier quote from Vivienne Westwood is particularly pertinent to the idea of art being one that is derived from historical culture(s) and used as a tool to understand our history and perhaps create our future. For example, the late Dame Vivienne Westwood's creations can be described as iconic, cultural, and conceptual art practice. When, therefore, the elements of culture and conceptual art are brought together, the result appears to produce an ostentatious effect which naturally occurs in Couture pieces.

Haute Couture has been referenced as a '[f]usion of fashion and costume, the consummate arts of dressmaking, tailoring and constituent crafts to apparel and accessories.'[86] The quote specifically expresses haute Couture as being the 'consummate arts of dressmaking,'[87] a description which not only acknowledges art within Couture, but Couture *as* art; the use of the word costume would imply a utilitarian notion. The nature of haute Couture is that it incorporates hand embroidery and stitching techniques into the design, which can be illustrated by the evening dress by Antonio Castillo, for Lanvin whereby a Lesage embroidery technique was used, pertinent to the French embroidery firm. The dress is made of white silk

82 Vivienne Westwood and Ian Kelly, *Vivienne Westwood* (Pan Macmillan 2014) 4

83 Ian Kelly and Viviennne Westwood, *Vivienne Westwood* (Picador 2014) 49

84 Ian Kelly and Viviennne Westwood, *Vivienne Westwood* (Picador 2014) 327

85 Richard Jonathan, *Vivienne Westwood: Vision and Craft Selected Excerpts From Claire Wilcox, Vivienne Westwood* (V&A Publications 2004)' (*Marammriettacom*, 2022) <https://www.maramarietta.com/the-arts/fashion/vivienne-westwood/> accessed 11 July 2022

86 Tim Jackson and David Shaw, *The Fashion Handbook* (Routledge 2006) 30, quoting Martin and Koda 1995:21

87 Tim Jackson and David Shaw, *The Fashion Handbook* (Routledge 2006) 30, quoting Martin and Koda 1995:21

zibeline, and the embroidery incorporates chenille and diamante elements.[88] We hereby see a fusion of art in fashion, and arguably Couture as art.

Conversely, the idea of fashion as art is not a new concept and shall now be evaluated through the work of historic British couturiers for the purposes of understanding Couture today, and whether copyright law can offer adequate protection to current and future works. To begin, explored is the work of Charles James, a U.S. fashion designer who began his career as a milliner.[89] During the 1930s, London was where he founded his fashion design business and his creations were very much influenced by architecture, sculpture, and geometry.[90] Experimental with various concepts such as spirals, James is referenced as a 'conceptual designer.'[91] James is said to have been influenced by the 'folds of an envelope,' experimenting with various fabrics such as silk-satin for an evening dress, which he expressed in 1950 as a 'sculpture of folds.'[92] James was known to have used one idea to influence an entire collection or fashion trend.[93] For instance, Long states that the quilted evening jacket (c.1937), made of satin-acetate, was considered 'a soft sculpture' by Salvador Dalí; this admiration from a world-renowned artist enhanced the concept of fashion as art.[94] In this chapter are two illustrations of Charles James Couture.

Following from the idea of fashion as art, another example is John Cavanah who was of Irish heritage, and was recognised for effecting Parisian style in London.[95] He is also noted for his Couture creations being heavily influenced by art, and is noted for being experimental.[96] During the 1950s, his work was said to be mirroring the abstract-expressionist movement.[97] Additionally, the 'Tachisme'[98] technique was introduced into his work, and it is noted for being influenced by American artists Jackson Pollock and Sam Francis using splashing and dripping techniques within their work.[99] The relationship between *art* and *Couture*, and the creative process for each being almost identical in how ideas are developed and expressed in tangible form for each, may support Couture as art, whereby the U.K.

88 Antonio Castillo, 'Evening Dress' (*V&A*, 2007) <https://collections.vam.ac.uk./item/O138937/evening-dress-castillo-antonio/> accessed 18 October 2021

89 Timothy A Long, *London Couture 1923–1975* (V&A Publishing 2019) 73

90 Timothy A Long, *London Couture 1923–1975* (V&A Publishing 2019) 73

91 Timothy A Long, *London Couture 1923–1975* (V&A Publishing 2019) 74

92 Timothy A Long, *London Couture 1923–1975* (V&A Publishing 2019) 74

93 Timothy A Long, *London Couture 1923–1975* (V&A Publishing 2019) 75

94 Timothy A Long, *London Couture 1923–1975* (V&A Publishing 2019) 83 please see 82 for image of jacket

95 Carly Eck, *London Couture 1923–1975* (V&A Publishing 2019) 183

96 Carly Eck, *London Couture 1923–1975* (V&A Publishing 2019) 185

97 Carly Eck, *London Couture 1923–1975* (V&A Publishing 2019) 185

98 Derived from the French word *tache*, meaning bolt, drip, or stain please see Carly Eck, *London Couture 1923–1975* (V&A Publishing) 185. The technique is also described as a style of painting that was popular in the 1940s–1950s. Although it is mainly pertinent to European art, it does comprise of American abstract expressionism. The French critic Michel Tapié describes these works as gestural methods. Please see: Tate, 'Art Term Art Informel' (*Tate*, 2023) <https://www.tate.org.uk/art/art-terms/a/art-informel> accessed 23 June 2023

99 Carly Eck, *London Couture 1923–1975* (V&A Publishing 2019) 185

copyright legislation must widen the criterion of 'artistic works' to include Couture garments.

The practice of fashion creation for Couture, particularly Couture as conceptual art found through the application of Tolstoy's definition of art, as a false view of life, seems to attest that the creation of Couture is the creation of art (as a false view of life). Considering how art is produced, that is, through the influence of other art, cultural trends, societal concerns, use of colours and textures, the same developmental process can be used for Couture creation. To elaborate, the creation of Couture using fabrics, embroideries, and sculpting techniques is mirrored through fine art developmental concepts. This is evident by James being influenced by sculptures, Westwood creating fashion as a tool by which she aims to understand and publicly portray a desire to improve society, and Cavanah taking inspiration from the abstract expressionist movement through the implementation of spirals in his works. We see how couturiers are influenced by many different elements within their environment; just like an artist they transfer these influences onto their innovative fashion practice, whereby the consumer's experience of the garment is of paramount importance to the success of the brand.

Whilst this section has focused on the parallels between 'fine art' and 'Couture practice,' the next section is aimed at understanding the relationship between art and copyright. If it is to be accepted and recognised that Couture is art, and therefore protecting it as a valuable commodity, what must be understood are the protections available and the challenges of limitations to art by copyright. Currently, Couture is not featured within the closed list of works under s.4 of the CDPA 1988.

3.4 The Relationship Between Art and Copyright

Today, copyright is understood to protect both artists and users of copyright.[100] Further, the French concept of *Droit D'auteur* is discussed later. Currently, the protection of artworks by copyright law is noted as being 'liberating' and not for the purposes of being 'limiting.'[101] Although ideas are not protected by copyright, the expression of ideas in a tangible form is, and further acknowledged is that copyright is not for the purposes of protecting the new idea for the creation, but to specifically protect the new work created by the artist.[102] The question that arises for this chapter is, what are the implications for Couture as a conceptual work of art?

3.4.1 Copyright – The Implications of Creation Records *on Couture*

In the case of *Creation Records*, it is the scene for the pop group Oasis' album cover 'Be Here Now,' which was devoid of the relevant criteria necessary to be

100 Emily Gould, 'Art and Copyright: What Can We Learn From the Past?' (Institute of Art and Law, 29 October 2018) <https://ial.uk.com/art-and-copyright-what-can-we-learn-from-the-past/> accessed 18 July 2022

101 John Geiger and Howard Suber, *Creativity and Copyright* (University of California Press 2019) 4

102 *Creation Records Ltd v News Group Newspapers Ltd* [1997] E.M.L.R. 444 and John Geiger and Howard Suber, *Creativity and Copyright* (University of California Press 2019) 12

accepted as a dramatic work. Featuring a white Rolls Royce in a hotel swimming pool, the scene arranged by Noel Galagher, was not regarded by the court as a dramatic work, as it was fundamentally static and absent of movement, a storyline or action.[103] Further as the scene did not possess the necessary requirements for an artistic work, it was not capable of being regarded as an artistic work, in law.

Although the photo shoot and purpose were expected to be confidential, the defendant had commissioned another photographer to take photographs of the scene, whereby those photographs were featured in the *Sun* newspaper.[104] Whilst the court did rule that there had been a breach of confidence by *The Sun* newspaper, the unauthorised photograph was not regarded by the court as a copy of the original photograph and therefore not an infringement.[105] Additionally, Noel Gallagher was considered not to own the copyright in the unauthorised photograph, since he had *organised the scene* for the album cover.[106] The copyright claim failed.[107]

Here it is apparent that the scene does not fit into a specific 'type' of artistic work as defined by s.4 of the CDPA 1988, as a work protected by copyright. If Couture is to be accepted as a conceptual work of art, it is not the concept (the idea) of the Couture work which may be subject to copyright protection, but the end-product derived from the expression, ultimately brought into existence from the initial concept. A conceptual work of art is noted as being founded on the notion of 'new ideas' rather 'than new expression,' and therefore argued as not being suitable to copyright protection.[108] This argument is *not* supported from the perspective of this thesis as it is the final tangible expression of the idea which *is* subject to assessment in law for copyright protection, and not the idea itself.[109]

Whilst conceptual works of art are founded on the principle of an idea, they ultimately produce the expression, the form of art. The discussion at this point leads to considerations for Couture as a conceptual work of art. Couture is based on the evolution of 'new ideas,' and ideas for fashion ultimately are derived through various influences.[110] The 'new' is not necessarily so, as ideas are essentially processed through art disciplines (mood boards, design drawings, illustrations, and the creation of toiles) and presented within a tangible form. Couture works may attract copyright protection, provided they fit into one of the closed list categories of works within s.4 of the CDPA 1988. It is this point which is at the heart of this

103 *Creation Records Ltd v News Group Newspapers Ltd* [1997] E.M.L.R. 444 and John Geiger and Howard Suber, *Creativity and Copyright* (University of California Press 2019) 12
104 *Creation Records Ltd v News Group Newspapers Ltd* [1997] E.M.L.R. 444
105 *Creation Records Ltd v News Group Newspapers Ltd* [1997] E.M.L.R. 444 and John Geiger and Howard Suber, *Creativity and Copyright* (University of California Press 2019) 12
106 *Creation Records Ltd v News Group Newspapers Ltd* [1997] E.M.L.R. 444 and John Geiger and Howard Suber, *Creativity and Copyright* (University of California Press 2019) 12
107 *Creation Records Ltd v News Group Newspapers Ltd* [1997] E.M.L.R. 444 and John Geiger and Howard Suber, *Creativity and Copyright* (University of California Press 2019) 12
108 Lori Petruzzelli, 'Copyright Problems in Post-Modern Art' (1995) 5(1) DePaul Journal of Art, Technology & Intellectual Property Law
109 CDPA 1988, s.1
110 Lori Petruzzelli, 'Copyright Problems in Post-Modern Art' (1995) 5(1) DePaul Journal of Art, Technology & Intellectual Property Law

study, and the subject matter which essentially tests the thesis question in relation to whether there is merit in widening the closed list for artistic works, to include Couture for copyright within s.4 of the CDPA 1988.

Mysoor raises an imperative consideration regarding the open nature of each category within section 4. The New Zealand case of *Green v Broadcasting* regarding a TV gameshow called Opportunity Knocks illustrates the difficulty of a creative work fitting into a category within a closed list. The format of the show could not be established as a dramatic work for the purposes of copyright.[111] Lord Bridge expressed that the word 'format' was stretched to metaphorical notion in relation to the features.[112] Firstly, this illustrates the difficulty in defining a creative work as a category of a prescribed closed list. Secondly, the case highlights the disparity between the law and what is defined as creative innovation. A closed list does not provide the opportunity for the development of creative innovation and therefore may always require the need to identify and prove through the courts by rigorous assessments that the intellectual creative expression meets with the originality requirements for the grant of copyright. This point is significant because whilst the closed list exists, it does not necessarily exclude all creative works outside of it. However, essentially the closed list is fixed and until such time that the list is updated, thus the law is changed, the courts shall no doubt see arguments for and against creative works not listed when deliberating over the grant of copyright.

The thesis raises another key argument in relation to artistic craftmanship, and this is that Couture is comprised of artistic craftmanship. This is significant as the CDPA categorises artistic works under section 4, 'works of artistic craftmanship.' This thesis argues that Couture is exceptional in that artistic craftmanship is an *inclusive part* of the artistic work for Couture. This is important as traditionally copyright has been concerned with categorising artistic works as those which are works of artistic craftsmanship and those which are artistic works. This was seen in the case of *Hensher Ltd v Restawile* where the claimants had failed to determine the sofa suite as 'artistic craftmanship.'[113] The decision fundamentally rested on how the terms 'artistic' and 'craftmanship' are defined legally, and additionally the utilitarian character of the sofa suite was contrary to the artistic quality of the work.[114] Later decisions have recognised fashion works as works of artistic craftmanship, such as the prototype garment in *Radley Gowns*[115] and the jacquard fabric

111 Poorna Mysoor, 'Does U.K. Really Have a "closed" List of Works Protected by Copyright?' (2019) 41(8) EIPR 474–79 and *Green v Broadcasting Corp, of New Zealand* [1989] [1989] R.P.C. 700 Privy Council New Zealand

112 Poorna Mysoor, 'Does U.K. Really Have a "closed" List of Works Protected by Copyright?' (2019) 41(8) EIPR 474–79 and *Green v Broadcasting Corp, of New Zealand* [1989] [1989] R.P.C. 700 Privy Council New Zealand

113 *George Hensher v Restawile Upholstery* [1976] A.C. 64

114 Swarb, 'George Hensher Ltd v Restawile Upholstery (Lancs) Ltd: HL 1975' (*Swarbco.uk*, 2021) <https://swarb.co.uk./george-hensher-ltd-v-restawile-upholstery-lancs-ltd-hl-1975/> accessed 31 December 2021

115 *Radley Gowns v Costas Syprou [1975] F.S.R. 455 at (2) and George Hensher Ltd v Restawhile [1976] A.C. 64*

in *Response Clothing*.[116] This thesis would argue that Couture works, as artistic works, should not be confined to deliberations of artistic craftmanship which essentially correspond to the ornamental features of works which are comprised within the whole work, but must look to artistic craftmanship as *contributing* to the artistic work in its entirety.

What remains to be considered is, to what extent should the sub-types of works from the various categories listed be extended? Mysoor asks a pertinent question as to 'how open-ended each category is, before a conclusion on its exhaustive nature can be drawn?'[117] Mysoor discusses *Abraham Moon* in relation to the tickets being described as graphic works, so the clear visual image therefore is seen to be of 'visual significance.'[118] Further, the case of *Norowzian v Arks Ltd* in relation to a dramatic work, provides for the expansion and a wider inclusion of works that can be included within the definition of a dramatic work. Nourse LJ described a dramatic work as 'a work of action, with or without words or music, which is capable of being performed before an audience.'[119] On this basis, the definition of dramatic a work is wide, and a cartoon is acknowledged as a dramatic work.[120] In consideration of these notions, the categories can be regarded as widening with the innovative development of existing categories of works, as discussed earlier, a ticket as a graphic work or a cartoon as a dramatic work. In application to Couture, not being listed within s.4 as an artistic work means that the position for the grant of copyright for Couture will most likely be the author arguing and proving the various elements of copyright for the grant of protection.

Currently, it seems obscure that Couture must try to fit in with the categories within the closed list in s.4 of the CDPA, when this provision could be widened to include Couture. On this point, the language used within the construction of legislation should reflect and accurately align with industry definitions and objectives and therefore a closer dialogue between law makers and the fashion industry is necessary to ensure the law accurately protects Couture.[121] In contrast, E.U. law decisions have required open-ended categorisations applied to subject matter in copyright. This is seen in the case of *Infopaq International*,[122] whereby the grant of copyright rests on the 'authors own intellectual creation,' and the same is said for

116 *Response Clothing Ltd v Edinburgh Woollen Mill Ltd* [2020] E.W.H.C. 148 (IPEC)

117 Poorna Mysoor, 'Does U.K. Really Have a "Closed" List of Works Protected by Copyright?' (2019) 41(8) EIPR 474–79

118 Poorna Mysoor, 'Does U.K. Really Have a "Closed" List of Works Protected by Copyright?' (2019) 41(8) EIPR 474–79 and *Abraham Moon v Thornber* [2012] F.S.R. 17 at [102–[103]

119 Poorna Mysoor, 'Does U.K. Really Have a "Closed" List of Works Protected by Copyright?' (2019) 41(8) EIPR 474–79 and *Norowzian v Arks Ltd (No:2)* [2000] F.S.R. 363 at 366–67

120 Poorna Mysoor, 'Does U.K. Really Have a "Closed" List of Works Protected by Copyright?' (2019) 41(8) EIPR 474–79 and *Norowzian v Arks* [2000] F.S.R. 363 at 366–67

121 Heilpern, 'Dialects of Art: A Corpus-Based Approach to Technical Term of Art Determinations in Statutes' (2022) 58(4) Jurimetrics 377–410 also referring to Stefan Th Gries and Brian G Slocum, 'Ordinary Meaning & Corpus Linguistics' (2017) 6 BYU Law Review 1417, 1471

122 Case C-5/08 *Infopaq International A/S v Danske Dagblades Forening* para 35

the cases of *BSA*,[123] *Football Premier League*,[124] *Painer*,[125] and the case of *SAS*.[126] These cases shall be discussed within the next two chapters. The next section looks specifically to the French system of *Droit D'Auteur* which considers the exclusive incorporeal right in the work which is set aside for the author.

3.4.2 The Concept of **Droit D'Auteur** *in Consideration of Copyright*

Copyright systems have been noted as being different specifically regarding the variations between the French, and to an extent, the German and Swiss regimes in contrast to the Anglo-Saxon approach.[127] Identified is the approach to copyright which is different, the Anglo-Saxon approach regarding the work as an object, or product.[128] Monta identified the wording of the 1956 Act as effectively describing the work as property, and as something which can be transferred without restriction, limitation, or reservation.[129] However, on the contrary, the French legislation appears to confer a 'pecuniary . . . droit moral' right which essentially is 'attached' to the author and cannot be 'transferred, disposed or waived.'[130] Monta highlights the wording of the French legislation as:

> The author of the work of the mind (intellectual work) shall by the mere fact of its creation enjoy an exclusive incorporeal right in the work effective against all persons . . . this right includes attributes of an intellectual and moral nature as well as attributes of an economic nature.[131]

123 Case C-393/09 *Bezpečnostní softwarová asociace – Svaz softwarové ochrany v Ministerstvo Kultury* at paras 45–46

124 C-403/08 and C-429/08 Football Association Premier League Ltd Net Med Hellas SA, Multichoice Hellas SA para 97

125 Case C-145/10 *Eva-Maria Painer v Standard Verlags GmbH and Others* at para 87

126 C-406/10 *SAS Institute Inc. v World Programming Ltd* at para 27

127 Monta Rudolf, 'The Concept of Copyright Versus Droit D'auteur' (1958–1959) 32 Southern California Law Review 177

128 Monta Rudolf, 'The Concept of Copyright Versus Droit D'auteur' (1958–1959) 32 Southern California Law Review 177

129 Monta Rudolf, 'The Concept of Copyright Versus Droit D'auteur' (1958–1959) 32 Southern California Law Review 177

130 Monta Rudolf, 'The Concept of Copyright Versus Droit D'auteur' (1958–1959) 32 Southern California Law Review 177

131 Monta Rudolf, 'The Concept of Copyright Versus Droit D'auteur' (1958–1959) 32 Southern California Law Review 177 – In contrasting the French and U.K. regimes, s.77 of the CDPA 1988 is the right to be identified as author or director and s.78 is concerned with moral rights; it is hereby acknowledged that this echoes the French system to some degree. The wording is relatively more refined in nature than the French legislation and appears to be effective for the mechanism of copyright to be exercised rather than specifically concerned with the 'incorporeal' right of an intellectual and moral nature. The French system effectively addresses the significant existence of the ethereal relationship between the author and the work whereas the U.K. legislation looks specifically to the work itself for copyright and does not address the relationship on an ethereal level between the author and the creation

Based on the preceding discussion, questions considered regarding the absence of Couture from s.4 of the CDPA 1988 relate to the value of Couture as a conceptual work of art. If Couture is essentially defined as a work of art, would the exclusion from the closed list of the s.4 of the CDPA therefore confer a lower value to Couture than those artistic works listed? Further, as a derivative question, what are the implications for copyright legislation widening the criterion of 'artistic works,' to include Couture garments?[132]

3.4.3 Artistic Craftmanship

Lord Simon of Glaisdale: '[F]rom those who are either themselves acknowledged artist-craftsmen or concerned with the training of artistic-craftsmen.'[133]

Lord Morris of Borth-Y-Gest: [I]f it is asked whether there is artistry if there is an appeal to the eye I would say that something more is needed.[134]

It is necessary to understand how the concept of artistic works, most pertinently 'a work of artistic craftmanship,' to ascertain the legal definition of these terms, to perhaps explain the exclusion of Couture from the CDPA closed list. To evaluate the concept of artistic craftmanship, it is necessary to ask whether the designer is an *artist* and whether the Couture garment is *art*? The definition of 'artistic'[135] is someone 'good at drawing or painting or arranging things in a beautiful way.'[136] Additionally expressed is the definition of artistic as 'relating to art and artists.'[137]

Significant is the extent of value given to the couturier as an artist, and whether this is overlooked in law. To explore this concept, the case of *Hensher* is examined. This case concerned claims in the copyright of a sofa suite in prototype form, designed and made by George Hensher.[138] The main legislation considered in the case was the Copyright Act 1956. The sofa suites were mass produced and commercially given names as 'Florida,' 'Bronx,' whereby 'Bronx' had a derivative suite called 'Atlantic' and 'Continental.'[139] Lord Reid in the case defined a work of

132 S.4 Copyright Designs and Patents Act 1988 (CDPA 1988)

133 *George Hensher v Restawile Upholstery* [1976] A.C. 64

134 *George Hensher v Restawile Upholstery* [1976] A.C. 64

135 Iona Silverman, 'Copyright and Fashion: A U.K. Perspective' (*WIPO*, June 2014) <https://www.WIPO.int/WIPO_magazine/en/2014/03/article_0007.html> accessed 31 May 2021

136 Collinsdictionary.com, 'Artistic' (2019) <https://www.collinsdictionary.com/dictionary/english/artistic>, accessed 9 January 2020

137 Collinsdictionary.com, 'Artistic' (2019) <https://www.collinsdictionary.com/dictionary/english/artistic>, accessed 9 January 2020 and Tomruk Űstűnkaya, 'The Functionality Doctrine: The Challenges to Fashion Copyright' (2020) 42(3) EIPR 156

138 Copyright Act 1956 s.3(1) and Swarb, 'George Hensher Ltd v Restawile Upholstery (Lancs) Ltd: HL 1975' (*Swarbco.uk*, 2021) <https://swarb.co.uk./george-hensher-ltd-v-restawile-upholstery-lancs-ltd-hl-1975/> accessed 31 December 2021 and Centre for intellectual property and information law, 'Hensher v Restawile [1976] A.C. 64' (*University of Cambridge*, 2023) <https://www.cipil.law.cam.ac.uk./virtual-museum/hensher-v-restawile-1976-ac-64> accessed 27 July 2023

139 Centre foe intellectual property and information law, 'Hensher v Restawile [1976] AC 64' (*University of Cambridge*, 2023) <https://www.cipil.law.cam.ac.uk./virtual-museum/hensher-v-restawile-1976-ac-64> accessed 27 July 2023

'craftsmanship' as 'a durable useful handmade object,' and considered 'a work of artistic craftsmanship . . . whether of practical utility or not, which its owner values because of its artistic character.'[140] Lord Glaisdale asked '[i]t is more pertinent to ask, is this the work of one who was in this respect an artist-craftsman?'[141] Certainly, the judge was concerned with the role of the creator (artist-craftsman) and the significance of this distinction. Lord Glaisdale further considers

> [w]hether the subject matter is or is not a work of artistic craftsmanship is a matter of evidence; and the most cogent evidence is likely to be from those who are either themselves acknowledged artist-craftsmen or concerned with the training of artistic-craftsmen in other words, expert evidence.[142]

To elaborate on this point, Lord Kilbrandon referred to the craftsman intention as being the principal test

> [t]he conscious intention of the craftsman will be the primary test of whether his product is artistic or not; the fact that many of us like looking at a piece of honest work, especially in the traditional trades, is not enough to make it a work of art.[143]

The statement is essentially denying the notion of the work being art, irrespective of the work being created through the artistic process, and therefore comprising of artistic features. The claimants failed to establish 'artistic-craftmanship.'[144]

This perspective was supported to some extent in *Guild v Eskandar* where the garments Mrs Guild had displayed in the V&A Museum were viewed by the court as being exhibited because they were regarded as new developments in fashion, and not because the garments were artistic.[145] It is necessary here to emphasise that this view was the view of the court, and curious is the aspect of the garments being exhibited at a major U.K. *art* institution, and not being regarded as artistic. A different set of circumstances existed in the case of *Radley Gowns*,[146] where a garment was considered a work of 'artistic craftmanship.'[147] The case concerned the defendant arguing that a prototype was not a work of artistic craftmanship due to the elements of artistic and craftmanship being pertinent to different authors, although the only evidence presented pertained to manufactured garments, as the

140 *George Hensher Ltd. v Restawile Upholstery* [1976] A.C. 64

141 *George Hensher v Restawile Upholstery* [1976] A.C. 64

142 *George Hensher Ltd v Restawhile* [1976] A.C. 64

143 Swarb, 'George Hensher Ltd v Restawile Upholstery (Lancs) Ltd: HL 1975' (*swarb.co.uk*, 2021) <https://swarb.co.uk/george-hensher-ltd-v-restawile-upholstery-lancs-ltd-hl-1975/> accessed 31 December 2021

144 *George Hensher Ltd v Restawhile* [1976] A.C. 64 at 94

145 *Guild v Eskandar* [2001] (38) F.S.R. 645 and please see: Tomruk Űstűnkaya, 'The Functionality Doctrine: The Challenges to Fashion Copyright' (2020) 42(3) EIPR 156

146 *Radley Gowns v Costas Syprou* [1975] F.S.R. 455

147 Copyright Act 1956 s.3(1)(a), (b), (c),9(8),20(1),48(1)

original prototype was no longer available. Further, the defendant claimed that the patterns were functional in nature and that the design sketches were absent in originality as they were based on dresses produced at an earlier time, and finally, it was argued that 'a version of an artistic work could not be a reproduction of an artistic work unless it was itself an artistic work, which the production garments were not.'[148] It is noticeable that the aspect of *art* in fashion is challenged by the defendant as an argument to support a defence for breach of copyright. Therefore, from the perspective of this study, the main issue to be adduced from the judgement is the correlation between the view of the court, particularly as it relates to whether copyright has been infringed, and the artistic merit of the garments at the centre of the contention. Considering *Hensher* in relation to the prototype garment, the court held that 'it was at least arguable that in this case the prototype garment was a work of artistic craftsmanship.'[149] Regarding the submission of the defendant's argument, that artistry and craftmanship were not united in one author, the court asserted that this was not supported by any 'conclusive authority.'[150] Additionally, the design drawings were regarded by Oliver J as consisting of sufficient originality to be capable of copyright protection, since the sketches were distinct from the garment.[151] Significantly, 'the prototype garment was a work of artistic craftsmanship.'[152] Therefore, both, the garment and the drawings were separately protected in their own right.

The main difference in the evaluation by the judges in *Radley Gowns*[153] and *Hensher*[154] regarding determining the existence of artistic craftmanship is that in *Hensher*,[155] the ruling concerned the 'arrangement of the wording'[156] of the Copyright Act 1956.[157] For this reason, the thesis argues that the method of evaluation appears to be disconnected from the significant aspect of design, that being the visual impression, whereas, in *Radley Gowns*, the design drawings were considered when specifically making a comparison to the garment. In addition to this, the prototype was examined in addition to the legislation, and therefore the court's evaluation did not solely rely on the wording of legislative provisions.[158] It is hereby asserted that *Radley Gowns*[159] is a significant case for fashion as it demonstrates

148 *Radley Gowns v Costas Syprou* [1975] F.S.R. 455

149 *Radley Gowns v Costas Syprou* [1975] F.S.R. 455 at (2) and *George Hensher Ltd v Restawhile* [1976] A.C. 64

150 *Radley Gowns v Costas Syprou* [1975] F.S.R. 455 at (3), *Burke & Margot Burke Ltd. v Spicers Dress Designs Ltd.* [1936] Ch.D. 400; [1941] A.C. 417, considered

151 *Radley Gowns v Costas Syprou* [1975] F.S.R. 455 at (5)

152 *Radley Gowns v Costas Syprou* [1975] F.S.R. 455 at (2)

153 *Radley Gowns v Costas Syprou [1975] F.S.R. 455 at (2)*

154 *George Hensher Ltd v Restawile [1976] A.C. 64*

155 *George Hensher Ltd v Restawile* [1976] A.C. 64

156 Tomruk Űstűnkaya, 'The Functionality Doctrine: The Challenges to Fashion Copyright' (2020) 42(3) EIPR 156

157 Copyright Act 1956 s.3(1)(a)

158 *Radley Gowns v Costas Syprou* [1975] F.S.R. 455

159 *Radley Gowns v Costas Syprou [1975] F.S.R. 455*

the objectives of the law, aligning the exact meaning of artistic to a product in its entirety, based on the visual impression.

Conversely, questioned is whether the recent case of *Response Clothing*[160] demonstrates a development in how U.K. copyright is assessed for fashion.[161] Response clothing is a fashion brand that designs, creates, and markets clothes.[162] Response clothing provided women's apparel to the defendant, Edinburgh Woollen Mill. In the instant case, the contentious issue surrounded women's tops constructed using a fabric which was described as a jacquard, and the design referred to as the 'wave arrangement.'[163] The jacquard fabric[164] was assessed for how it will be protected for copyright, e.g. graphic work as defined under s.4(2) CDPA 1988, which is inclusive of:

(a) any painting, drawing, diagram, map, chart, or plan, and
(b) any engraving, etching, lithograph, woodcut, or similar work

The decision of the court was that a fabric can be protected as a work of artistic craftmanship, but not as a graphic work.[165] Further, the work was established to qualify as an original work pursuant to 'art.2 of EC Directive 2001/29 on the harmonisation of certain aspects of copyright and related rights in the information society.'[166]

In law therefore, considerations must extend to not only the subject matter, but to the method of creation and construction, particularly when considering the notion of artistic craftmanship.[167] For example, Iris Van Herpen designed a Couture vegan dress using bio-plastic materials; the dress further incorporates organza fabric, copper-coated embellishments, and 3D printed cocoa-husks.[168] It is hereby observed that in relation to the closed list system of the s.4(1) CDPA 1988, the criterion of 'artistic works' places further limitations for Couture garments in meeting the definition in law. This is because (as stated earlier), Couture, as art, comprises of artistic craftmanship, and it is not in its entirety, a work of artistic craftmanship.

160 *Response Clothing Ltd v Edinburgh Woollen Mill Ltd [2020] E.W.H.C. 148 (IPEC)*
161 Simon Clark, Sara Sefton and Marc Linsner, 'A Fabric Design Has Been Found to be a Work of Artistic Craftsmanship: Will Response Clothing Cause a Shift in How U.K. Copyright is Assessed?' (2020) 42(9) EIPR 612
162 Simon Clark, Sara Sefton and Marc Linsner, 'A Fabric Design Has Been Found to be a Work of Artistic Craftsmanship: Will Response Clothing Cause a Shift in How U.K. Copyright is Assessed?' (2020) 42(9) EIPR 612
163 Simon Clark, Sara Sefton and Marc Linsner, 'A Fabric Design Has Been Found to be a Work of Artistic Craftsmanship: Will Response Clothing Cause a Shift in How U.K. Copyright is Assessed?' (2020) 42(9) EIPR 612
164 *Response Clothing Ltd v Edinburgh Woollen Mill Ltd* [2020] E.W.H.C. 148 (IPEC)
165 *Response Clothing Ltd v Edinburgh Woollen Mill Ltd* [2020] E.W.H.C. 148 (IPEC)
166 *Response Clothing Ltd v Edinburgh Woollen Mill Ltd* [2020] E.W.H.C. 148 (IPEC)
167 S.4(1)(c) CDPA 1988
168 Phillip Keane, 'World's First Printed Haute Couture Vegan Dress Debuts' (*3D printing-com*, 6 July 2022) <https://3dprinting.com/news/worlds-first-printed-haute-Couture-vegan-dress-debuts/> accessed 25 July 2022

3.5 Aesthetics and Commercial Viability

Aesthetics in art have been defined as the element which holds the observer's attention. In understanding the degree to which Couture is art, the notion of aesthetics, most associated with art, is analysed here once again. As mentioned earlier, Bence identifies 'attention' as the component which can make a work of art a success or a failure.[169] When we apply this notion to Couture in consideration of Couture as a conceptual work of art, the bi-annual fashion shows are peak opportunities to market and generate interest in the works. With that said, the attention given to the shows is indicative of the aesthetic component within art. An example of this is Alexandre Vauthier's Autumn/Winter 2022 collection using silver metallic fabrics and Zuhair Murad's incorporation of silver embroideries.[170] These considerations extend to the economic and social value of Couture as art being *intrinsically* linked. On this basis, it appears that the societal value of Couture derives from the concept of Couture being an artistic work, which in turn fuels economic interests. Below statistics on Couture illustrate the economical scale of Couture as an artistic concept.

3.5.1 Couture Statistics

It is estimated that the global haute Couture market will grow at the rate of 5.4% between 2021 and 2028, owing to various elements relating to technological advancements in textiles and an increase of emerging designers.[171] These figures are based on the following haute Couture houses: Dior, Chanel, Giorgio Armani Prive, Atelier Versace, Jean Paul Gaultier, Elie Saab, Zuhair Murad, Ralph & Russo, Givenchy, Julien Fournie, Saint Laurent, Valentino, Stephane, Schiaparelli, Viktor & Rolf, Giambattista Valli, Guo Pei, Iris Van Herpen, Yuima Nakazato, and Georges Hobeika.[172] The report identifies the regions and expresses that Canada and the U.S. are the main markets for haute Couture in the North American region.[173] Brazil is a significant market for Latin America based on the numerous Couture

169 Nanay Bence, *Aesthetics: A Very Short Introduction* (Oxford University Press 2019) 28

170 Wwd Staff, 'Couture Fall 2022 Trend: Metal Mining' (*Womens Wear Daily (WWD)*, 25 July 2022) <https://wwd.com/fashion-news/fashion-trends/metal-metallic-trend-Couture-paris-1235260615/> accessed 25 July 2022

171 Data Intelo, 'Global Haute Couture Market by Type (Jackets & Coating, Vests, Pants and Bibs, Boots, Others), By Application (Catwalk, Daily Wearing) and By Region (North America, Latin America, Europe, Asia Pacific and Middle East & Africa), Forecast From 2022 To 2030' (*Data Intelo*, 2022) <https://dataintelo.com/report/haute-Couture-market/> accessed 30 December 2022

172 Data Intelo, 'Global Haute Couture Market by Type (Jackets & Coating, Vests, Pants and Bibs, Boots, Others), By Application (Catwalk, Daily Wearing) and By Region (North America, Latin America, Europe, Asia Pacific and Middle East & Africa), Forecast From 2022 To 2030' (*Data Intelo*, 2022) <https://dataintelo.com/report/haute-Couture-market/> accessed 30 December 2022

173 Data Intelo, 'Global Haute Couture Market by Type (Jackets & Coating, Vests, Pants and Bibs, Boots, Others), By Application (Catwalk, Daily Wearing) and By Region (North America, Latin America, Europe, Asia Pacific and Middle East & Africa), Forecast From 2022 To 2030' (*Data Intelo*, 2022) <https://dataintelo.com/report/haute-Couture-market/> accessed 30 December 2022

designers.[174] Europe sees France being the market leader for haute Couture owing to its historical establishment of the art, and being host to notable fashion houses such as Dior and Chanel.[175] Japan is noted as the key market leader for the Asia Pacific region, and the United Arab Emirates leads in the Middle Eastern market.[176] The predicted growth is said to be determined by key factors such as the increase of online shopping amongst consumers, events such as catwalk shows generating the demand for Couture, and the implementation of stringent regulations for the textile industries.[177] The most prominent haute Couture houses globally are noted as being 'Chanel, Dior, Armani, Givenchy' with only four making up 43% of the market:[178] Europe is reported to account for 34% of the consumer market for haute Couture, and 64% of the total consumer market attributed to womenswear.[179] In terms of economic value, global Couture is currently valued at USD 11460 million, and by the end of 2027, this figure is expected to grow to USD 13450 million, a growth rate of CAGR 2.3% between 2021 and 2027.[180]

3.5.2 Statistics Analysis

The statistics demonstrate an upward trend in growth for Couture, which relates to the global economic value and market growth. The growth would suggest the demand for Couture by consumers is increasing and furthermore the economic

174 Data Intelo, 'Global Haute Couture Market by Type (Jackets & Coating, Vests, Pants and Bibs, Boots, Others), By Application (Catwalk, Daily Wearing) and By Region (North America, Latin America, Europe, Asia Pacific and Middle East & Africa), Forecast From 2022 To 2030' (*Data Intelo*, 2022) <https://dataintelo.com/report/haute-Couture-market/> accessed 30 December 2022

175 Data Intelo, 'Global Haute Couture Market by Type (Jackets & Coating, Vests, Pants and Bibs, Boots, Others), By Application (Catwalk, Daily Wearing) and By Region (North America, Latin America, Europe, Asia Pacific and Middle East & Africa), Forecast From 2022 To 2030' (*Data Intelo*, 2022) <https://dataintelo.com/report/haute-Couture-market/> accessed 30 December 2022

176 Data Intelo, 'Global Haute Couture Market by Type (Jackets & Coating, Vests, Pants and Bibs, Boots, Others), By Application (Catwalk, Daily Wearing) and By Region (North America, Latin America, Europe, Asia Pacific and Middle East & Africa), Forecast From 2022 To 2030' (*Data Intelo*, 2022) <https://dataintelo.com/report/haute-Couture-market/> accessed 30 December 2022

177 Data Intelo, 'Global Haute Couture Market by Type (Jackets & Coating, Vests, Pants and Bibs, Boots, Others), By Application (Catwalk, Daily Wearing) and By Region (North America, Latin America, Europe, Asia Pacific and Middle East & Africa), Forecast From 2022 To 2030' (*Data Intelo*, 2022) <https://dataintelo.com/report/haute-Couture-market/> accessed 30 December 2022

178 MarketWatch News Department, 'Haute Couture Market Analysis Report 2023 Along With Statistics Figures, Forecasts Till 2028' (*Market Watch*, 26 November 2022) <https://www.marketwatch.com/press-release/haute-Couture-market-analysis-report-2023-along-with-statistics-figures-forecasts-till-2028-2022-11-26> accessed 30 December 2022

179 MarketWatch News Department, 'Haute Couture Market Analysis Report 2023 Along With Statistics Figures, Forecasts Till 2028' (*Market Watch*, 26 November 2022) <https://www.marketwatch.com/press-release/haute-Couture-market-analysis-report-2023-along-with-statistics-figures-forecasts-till-2028-2022-11-26> accessed 30 December 2022

180 MarketWatch News Department, 'Haute Couture Market Analysis Report 2023 Along With Statistics Figures, Forecasts Till 2028' (*Market Watch*, 26 November 2022) <https://www.marketwatch.com/press-release/haute-Couture-market-analysis-report-2023-along-with-statistics-figures-forecasts-till-2028-2022-11-26> accessed 30 December 2022

value supports appreciation by consumers for the Couture garment. The global market share of 43% for Couture is dominated by major Couture houses of Chanel, Dior, Armani, and Givenchy. This figure would suggest the marketing power of the major Couture houses is formidable and therefore, may indicate a monopoly over newer or financially weaker brands, without the capacity to promote the collections to the extent of the major global players. In terms of the E.U. position, with haute Couture holding 34% of the consumer market, the appreciation by consumers for haute Couture is very strong.[181] This would further suggest that consumers in Europe appreciate the concept of haute Couture pieces. However, whilst the statistics demonstrate the economic value in respect to market share and market growth, they do not indicate whether consumers appreciate Couture as an artistic concept or rather appreciate the goodwill in the brand.

3.6 Couture as Art: The Purpose

What is the purpose of Couture? This question brings forward the necessity to distinguish between the useful practical part of Couture from the artistic elements. In 1964, the late Paco Rabanne showcased his first Couture collection titled Twelve Unwearable Dresses.[182] An example from the collection is the 'sculptural micro-mini dress,' characterised by 'rectangular aluminium plates joined with metal rings.'[183] The dress was innovative for this period and appeared to be of space-age in theme. In analysis of the dress, pertaining to the materials in terms of providing a malleable comfort to the wearer, the dress would not be wearable for that reason, although as an artistic concept (space theme, metallic, and unwearable) and as a work of art, the dress fulfils the brief as a piece of Couture, a work of art.

The notion of unwearable Couture has been examined by Lenzholzer in 'Conceptualizing Urban Places as a "Fourth Skin".'[184] Lenzholzer examines Couture from the viewpoint of the garment being utilised to express the 'status' and identity of the wearer, and furthermore identifies this as a 'mere display and overt self- expression' whereby the parameters of wearing a garment for protection is expanded.[185] The notion of self-expression feeds into any artist's objective of creative expression, however, within the context of fashion this concept has two limbs. The first is that the couturier engages in creative expression through the creative process of the garment, and the second limb extends to the wearer of the Couture garment and the degree of creative self-expression engaged with *when* wearing the

181 Market Watch News Department, 'Haute Couture Market Analysis Report 2023 Along With Statistics Figures, Forecasts Till 2028' (*Market Watch*, 26 November 2022) <https://www.marketwatch.com/press-release/haute-Couture-market-analysis-report-2023-along-with-statistics-figures-forecasts-till-2028-2022-11-26> accessed 30 December 2022

182 The Met, 'Dress Designer Paco Rabanne' (*The Met*, 2000) <https://www.metmuseum.org/art/collection/search/145899> accessed 12 February 2023

183 The Met, 'Dress Designer Paco Rabanne' (*The Met*, 2000) <https://www.metmuseum.org/art/collection/search/145899> accessed 12 February 2023

184 Sanda Lenzholzer, 'Conceptualizing Urban Places as a "Fourth Skin"' (2006)

185 Sanda Lenzholzer, 'Conceptualizing Urban Places as a "Fourth Skin"' (2006)

garment. On this basis, unlike other types of fashion, Couture fulfils the creative expression of both the wearer and the designer as does an abstract piece of art. It is not essential for the marks on the canvas to be identified as anything in particular; for example, consider Jackson Pollock's work *Autumn Rhythm*.[186] In consideration of the discussion thus far, with emphasis on *the art in Couture, and Couture as art*, this book aims to provide for a closer alignment of industry and legal definitions.

Interim Conclusion

The relationship between art, Couture, copyright, and economic considerations in relation to commercial viability are presented within the interim conclusion. One of the challenges of this chapter was to find a single definition for art. In addition, the connection between art and beauty was a theme which was a consistent notion within the material researched for this study. For this reason, the most pertinent aspects of art relate to understanding what it is, beauty, and aesthetics. Pertinently, all three of these concepts are integral to Couture.

Tolstoy recognised that art does not necessarily have to be beautiful; instead Tolstoy noted the emotive response to art by the observer.[187] Tolstoy's notion of art was it being a 'false view of life.'[188] This concept was instrumental to the thesis direction when applied to Couture, because to adorn the body as a part of cultural practice extends beyond clothing being a need, but acknowledges *adornment* provided by Couture as a cultural paradigm.[189] For this reason, the study appreciates Tolstoy's views on art as being comfortably applicable to contemporary notions of art. In contrast, Rand's view of art does not include works such as 'conceptual incendiary or pop.'[190] In consideration of these views, the perspective of this thesis is that Couture would fall outside of Rand's definition of art.[191]

In terms of understanding the aesthetic component within art, Bence identified that the 'attention' given to a work determines the aesthetic component, particularly in whether the work will be successful or not.[192] In application to Couture, the aesthetic component provides for the commercial success of the garment and moreover supports Couture being art.

Art creation in consideration of couturiers and the analysis of their methods for the creation of Couture is fundamentally valuable to the thesis. Vivienne Westwood, John Cavanagh, and Charles James are all noted as creating through, not only the influence of art, but in addition, using the process of art creation in the

186 Jackson-pollockorg/the-flamejsp, 'The Flame' (*Jackson pollockorg*, 2023) <https://www.jackson-pollock.org/the-flame.jsp> accessed 12 February 2023

187 Leo Tolstoy, *What Is Art* (True Sign Publishing 1 March 2021) 172

188 Leo Tolstoy, *What Is Art* (True Sign Publishing 1 March 2021) 33

189 Please see chapter 2

190 Louis Torres and Michelle Kamhi, *What Art Is the Esthetic Theory of Ayn Rand* (Open Court 2000) 7593

191 Louis Torres and Michelle Kamhi, *What Art Is the Esthetic Theory of Ayn Rand* (Open Court 2000) 7593

192 Nanay Bence, *Aesthetics: A Very Short Introduction* (Oxford University Press 2019) 28

Figure 3.4 Autum/Winter 1932 Patrimonies de CHANEL, Paris HC.AH.1932.3 (V&A Chanel 2023 Exhibition)

development of Couture. Conspicuously, Charles James in his exploration of geometry and spirals was known as a conceptual designer, whereby one of his designs was understood as a sculpture.[193] We can also see parallels with the method of creation, knowledge, skill, and craftmanship an artist uses, and that of which a couturier chooses to employ. In consideration of the findings thus far, Couture appears to be art, particularly in consideration of art practice methods and creations by couturiers. However, the chapter sought to understand whether artistic works were understood in law in the same way as in the creative industries. This was a key aspect of the research, because if Couture is identified as art within the fashion

193 Timothy A Long, *London Couture 1923–1975* (V&A Publishing 2019) 74

industry, it does not necessarily mean that this is equally translates or is understood and therefore accepted within law. This part of the research necessitated an exploration of relevant case law to determine whether the law was in alignment with the creative industries in relation to the definition of art.

The concept of artistic craftmanship was considered through examining the case of *Hensher Ltd v Restawile*, where the claimants had failed to establish 'artistic craftmanship' through the evaluation of expert evidence.[194] The decision in *Hensher* essentially presented a conflict between the two terms of *artistic* and *craftmanship* and further the utilitarian nature of the work appeared to negate the artistic quality, in law. However, regarding identifying artistry, for this book, the words of Lord Morris of Borth-Y-Gest hold much weight '[I] would say that something more is needed.'[195]

However, in *Radley Gowns*, the prototype garment was arguably regarded as a work of artistic craftmanship.[196] Further, the design drawings were considered as having sufficient originality.[197] More recently, the jacquard fabric design in *Response Clothing* was held to be a work of artistic craftmanship.[198]

This book argues that in legal disputes where an assessment in copyright must be made in relation to a work of art, a visual analysis of the work is of paramount importance and should supersede any interpretation made by legal text. This would be for the purposes of honouring the visual and artistic nature of the work as it relates to the aesthetic, form, shape, texture, and composition.

In consideration of the market response to Couture, whilst the statistics indicate growth for Couture, it is not clear as to whether the demand by consumers is based on a demand for Couture as an art, specifically. However, the findings indicate that the demand implies an appreciation for Couture, as a concept. Whilst the chapter has established the parallels between fine art and Couture, the next necessary step is to evaluate whether the value of Couture is reflected in copyright law, and whether Couture can be considered a conceptual work of art in law.

194 *George Hensher v Restawile Upholstery* [1976] A.C. 64

195 *George Hensher v Restawile Upholstery* [1976] A.C. 64

196 *Radley Gowns v Costas Syprou* [1975] F.S.R. 455 at (2) and *George Hensher Ltd v Restawhile* [1976] A.C. 64

197 *Radley Gowns v Costas Syprou* [1975] F.S.R. 455 at (5)

198 *Response Clothing Ltd v Edinburgh Woollen Mill Ltd* [2020] E.W.H.C. 148 (IPEC)

4 Copyright for Couture

Introduction

This chapter examines the relationship between Couture and copyright. To ascertain the position of originality for Couture, case law is examined through the case of *BSA*.[1] The discussion leads to considerations for Couture as *art* and considers the case of *Lucasfilm* where the concept of utilitarian was noted as part of the ruling.[2] The artistic craftmanship analysis begins with asking whether Couture is accepted as an artistic work, in law. Further, in considering Couture as art, copyright law is examined to evaluate the concept of fixation as a requirement and the implications for Couture. The section on substantiality considers the industry practice for Couture creation, which leads to the analysis on intention in Couture and whether intention of the creator is relevant. The conclusion provides analysis on the arguments and issues raised and attempts to suggest considerations for reform to support Couture copyright protection. The chapter shall attempt to answer the secondary research question B: Are the limitations in copyright justified in Couture, as for other subject matter, in consideration of the exclusion of Couture from s.4 of the CDPA 1988?

4.1 Treaties

The provisions under Part II, section 1 of the TRIPS agreement is imposed by the WTO on all members and signatories to TRIPS. In relation to the Berne Convention, TRIPS states, 'Copyright protection shall extend to expressions and not to ideas, procedures, methods of operation or mathematical concepts as such.'[3]

The Berne Convention was 'adopted' in 1886 (as soft law) for the protection of creative works and the rights of their authors.[4] As it relates to Couture, various provisions of the Berne Convention are of interest, Articles 2 (1) literary and artistic works, (2) possible requirement of fixation, (3) derivative works, (7) works of

1 *Bezpečnostni softwarová asociace*, Case C-393/09 [2011] ECR I-13,971 [49]

2 *Lucasfilm v Ainsworth* [2009] E.W.C.A. Civ 1328; [2010] Ch. 503

3 TRIPS, section I Part II Article 9(2)

4 World Intellectual Property Organisation, 'Berne Convention for the Protection of Literary and Artistic Works' (*WIPO*, 2022) <https://www.WIPO.int/treaties/en/ip/berne/> accessed 16 February 2022

DOI: 10.4324/9781003599456-4

applied art and industrial designs. Each of these provisions are echoed in the U.K. legislative provisions. The Convention refers to artistic works, and consequently the thesis argument and discussion is that the concept of Couture being recognised as art (and for the art within Couture) is crucial to ascertain whether Couture can be protected as an artistic work pursuant to the Convention.[5]

The couturier must combine their intellectual creative abilities with their technical skills for the purposes of Couture design.[6] The creative process is inherently rooted in art, and it has been said: '[g]reat design is first and foremost art.'[7] The relationship between Couture and the requirements provided for by the Convention such as: 'originality fixation, derivative works,'[8] and works of applied art and industrial designs are to be examined below.[9]

4.2 Originality

This section on originality shall explore this specific requirement of copyright law, firstly beginning with a generic analysis on what *originality* means and then looking at the individual aspects that are required to fulfil the originality criteria, such as the requirement for the work to be non-functional. Since 1911, originality is a usual statutory requirement of copyright law.[10] Bently et al express that the meaning of *originality* is not precise and the historic requirement was a necessary requirement of the work being created and derived through a consequence of 'labour, skill and judgement.' This traditional British test of originality has uncertainties, and one specific 'civil law' approach has not been established.[11]

Originality is a necessary requirement for copyright protection, within the context of s.1(1)(a) of the CDPA, and refers to the work not being copied from another work, and therefore being the author's own creation.[12] It is the expression of originality and the 'form' that is necessary to attain copyright.[13] Specifically, the content or an idea is not a requisite.[14] Copyright is associated with specific categories

5 The Berne Convention for the Protection of Literary and Artistic Works, 1886, Article 2 (1)
6 See 1.5.1
7 Miklos Philips, 'Art vs Design: A Timeless Debate' (*Toptalcom*, 2021) <https://www.toptal.com/designers/creative-direction/art-vs-design#:~:text=Design%20is%20an%20art%20form%2C%20a%20method%20of,but%20there%20is%20no%20guarantee%20that%20it%20will> accessed 19 February 2022
8 The Berne Convention for the Protection of Literary and Artistic Works, 1886 Article 2 (3)
9 The Berne Convention for the Protection of Literary and Artistic Works, 1886, Article 2 (7)
10 L Bentley and others, *Intellectual Property Law* (6th edn, Oxford University Press 2022) 93 stating that '. . . the requirement was introduced for paintings, drawings, and photographs by the Fine Art Copyright Act 1862.'
11 L Bentley and others, *Intellectual Property Law* (6th edn, Oxford University Press 2022) 93 referring to E Judge and D Gervais, 'Of Silos and Constellations: Comparing Notions of Originality in Copyright Intellectual Creation'
12 Judith Embley, Keir Bamford and Nick Hancock, *Commercial and Intellectual Property Law and Practice* (CLP 2021) 642
13 Judith Embley, Keir Bamford and Nick Hancock, *Commercial and Intellectual Property Law and Practice* (CLP 2021) 642
14 Judith Embley, Keir Bamford and Nick Hancock, *Commercial and Intellectual Property Law and Practice* (CLP 2021) 642

of works,[15] and the U.K. refers to 'literary, dramatic, musical, and artistic works' (LDMA).[16] The list of artistic works under s.4(1) of the CDPA are:

(a) a graphic work, photograph, sculpture or collage, irrespective of artistic quality,
(b) a work of architecture being a building or a model for a building, or
(c) a work of artistic craftsmanship.

The traditional approach to originality in copyright is said to have been most focused on the connection between the creator of the work to the work, assessed by the 'labour, skill, or effort' exerted for the creation of the work.[17]

The Italian Supreme Court ruled in the case of *Casucci Spa v Unipol Sai Assicurazione*, that a technical regulation drafted by a lawyer was 'in principle' capable of copyright protection.[18] The question regarding the originality of the work pertained to the 'standard legal text for technical-professional use.'[19] However, through developments in intellectual property law, specifically in the case of *Cofemel*, of which the Italian Supreme Court referenced in this case, 'that the subject matter reflects the personality of its author, as an expression of his free and creative choices.'[20] The court therefore did not disregard the fact that copyright could in fact protect a technical work, although the free and creative choices exercised by the author must extend further than the parameters of the technical concerns and regulations.[21] The decision of the court was that the work effectively did not demonstrate the personality of its author pertaining to the organisation of the legal

15 Judith Embley, Keir Bamford and Nick Hancock, *Commercial and Intellectual Property Law and Practice* (CLP 2021) 640
16 L Bentley and others, *Intellectual Property Law* (6th edn, Oxford University Press 2022) 91
17 L Bentley and others, *Intellectual Property Law* (6th edn, Oxford University Press 2022) 93 referring to *Ladbroke v William Hill* [1964] 1 All E.R. 465, 469 (Lord Reid)
18 Eleonora Rosati, 'Italian Supreme Court Rules That Technical Regulation (Drafted by an IP Lawyer) May Be *In Principle* Protected by Copyright' (*IP Kat*, 21 June 2020) <https://ipkitten.blogspot.com/search/label/decision%2010300%2F2020%20Casucci%20v%20Unipol%20Assicurazioni%20S.p.A.%20and%20Others> accessed 19 February 2022
19 Eleonora Rosati, 'Italian Supreme Court Rules That Technical Regulation (Drafted by an IP Lawyer) May Be *In Principle* Protected by Copyright' (*IP Kat*, 21 June 2020) <https://ipkitten.blogspot.com/search/label/decision%2010300%2F2020%20Casucci%20v%20Unipol%20Assicurazioni%20S.p.A.%20and%20Others> accessed 19 February 2022 Please note: whereas, in the 2016 hearing, the court held judgement for the defendants due to originality not being evident
20 Eleonora Rosati, 'Italian Supreme Court Rules That Technical Regulation (Drafted by an IP Lawyer) May Be *In Principle* Protected by Copyright' (*IP Kat*, 21 June 2020) <https://ipkitten.blogspot.com/2020/06/italian-supreme-court-rules-that.html> accessed 1 July 2023 <https://ipkitten.blogspot.com/search/label/decision%2010300%2F2020%20Casucci%20v%20Unipol%20Assicurazioni%20S.p.A.%20and%20Others> accessed 19 February 2022 referring to *Cofemel v G-Star Raw CV* (C-683/17) at para 30
21 Eleonora Rosati, 'Italian Supreme Court Rules That Technical Regulation (Drafted by an IP Lawyer) May Be *In Principle* Protected by Copyright' (*IP Kat*, 21 June 2020) <https://ipkitten.blogspot.com/2020/06/italian-supreme-court-rules-that.html> accessed 1 July 2023 <https://ipkitten.blogspot.com/search/label/decision%2010300%2F2020%20Casucci%20v%20Unipol%20Assicurazioni%20S.p.A.%20and%20Others> accessed 19 February 2022 referring to *Cofemel v G-Star Raw CV* (C-683/17) at para 30

principles, and the author's own experience within the arrangement and contextualisation of the draft.[22]

However, recent E.U. case law demonstrates a shift in focus and development for originality, in that, the work must demonstrate the author's free and creative choices.[23] In satisfying the criterion for originality, the work should not be functional.[24]

4.2.1 Non-Functional

This issue was deliberated in the E.U. case of *BSA*, the point of contention vested in the issue of the 'graphic user interface' regarding the technical workings.[25] This rationale was also supported in the copyright infringement proceedings in the case of *SAS Institute v World Programming* regarding computer software.[26] Pertinently, recent case law in the cases of *Cofemel*[27] and *Brompton*[28] are discussed later in subsequent chapters. In consideration of the case law discussed,[29] the main argument put forward by this study is whether the extent of originality is relevant across different industries as it pertains to procedural practice and creative techniques. Functionality is discussed in depth in chapter 5. In the pursuit of ascertaining the position of Couture in copyright, the next section examines the relationship between originality and substantiality.

4.2.2 Substantiality

The issue of substantiality is significant to the discussion for Couture because it is necessary to evaluate the relationship between originality and substantiality in consideration of Couture, for the purposes of a grant of copyright protection. Substantiality, so it seems, is of significance because it appears to only exacerbate the existing challenges for Couture in obtaining copyright protection due to the requirement of the non-functional criterion to establish originality.[30]

The correlation of substantiality to Couture is established through the process of Couture creation, specifically as it relates to the trend forecasting system. The purpose

22 Eleonora Rosati, 'Italian Supreme Court Rules That Technical Regulation (Drafted by an IP Lawyer) May be *in Principle* Protected by Copyright' (*IP Kat*, 21 June 2020) <https://ipkitten.blogspot.com/2020/06/italian-supreme-court-rules-that.html> accessed 1 July 2023 <https://ipkitten.blogspot.com/search/label/decision%2010300%2F2020%20Casucci%20v%20Unipol%20Assicurazioni%20S.p.A.%20and%20Others> accessed 19 February 2022 referring to *Cofemel v G-Star Raw CV* (C-683/17) at para 30

23 Please see: *Cofemel v G-Star Raw* CV (C-683/17) and *Casucci spa v Unipol Sai Assicurazione* unreported 29 May 2020 (It Cass (I))

24 L Bentley and others, *Intellectual Property Law* (6th edn, Oxford University Press 2022) 100

25 *Bezpečnostni softwarová asociace*, Case C-393/09 [2011] ECR I-13,971, [49]

26 *SAS Institute Inc v World Programming Ltd*, Case C-406/10 [2012] 3 C|MLR (4) 55,68, [AG44] (AG Bot)

27 *Cofemel v G-Star Raw CV (C-683/17)*

28 *Brompton Bicycle Ltd v Chedech/Get2Get (C-833/18)*

29 *Bezpečnostni softwarová asociace*, Case C-393/09 [2011] ECR I-13,971, [49] *and SAS Institute Inc v World Programming Ltd*, Case C-406/10 [2012] 3 C|MLR (4) 55,68, [AG44] (AG Bot)

30 CDPA 1988 s.1(2)

of the trend forecasting system is to ascertain the most prevalent trends.[31] Therefore, the use of trend forecasts as an industry practice mechanism places limitations on designers to produce designs in line with trend expectations and popular styles. The analysis has observed the extent of originality, and 'copying' permitted by the courts, whereby the significant question raised is whether the copying is substantial, and to what extent does this affect originality? Although, in analysing the trend forecasting system, it is argued that the practice appears from the perspective of this study to be an *influence* for designers as an industry practice tool, and *not* a copying mechanism. However, in deliberation of the previous question, the necessary question to ask is, at what point does an *influence* stop and *copying* begin? Additionally, does the law recognise the concept of influence, or is influence copying in law? These questions are based on measurable notions for copying. For this reason, it is desirable to establish these quantities as they relate to the quality in legal definition form, specifically relating to the concept of substantial. This is significant for the purposes of establishing copyright mechanisms that are appropriate to Couture, specifically.

Furthermore, 'substantial copying' shall be evaluated through an analysis of the *Designers Guild* case.[32] Designers Guild brought proceedings against Russel Williams for copying a fabric design. The judge considered the design as a whole and established that the defendant had engaged in 'substantial' copying.[33] The assessment for 'substantial' appears to have been made according to the comparison of the *quality* between the two works. The defendant appealed against the finding of 'substantial' copying;[34] the 'judge noted the similarities between both designs, and made a correlation between artistic copyright and the absence of subsistence that is most likely to be reduced when the design is simple and abstract.'[35] The inspection of the fabric consisted of a very close examination of the details in contrast of both fabric designs, and the aspects analysed were: the stripes as it related to the width and flower design, the brushstroke technique in the design, the vertical brush strokes in relation to the background, the brushstrokes as they relate to the petals, the transparent nature of the petals over the stripes otherwise known as 'the resist effect,' the mark at the centre of the flowers, the green colour of the leaves, and the brush stroke and arrangement over the design.[36] On the aspect of visual comparison, Morritt L J stated that '[t]hey just do not look sufficiently similar.'[37] Further on the issue of brushwork and the resist effect was referred to by Moritt L J.[38] It was

31 Gwyneth Holland and Rae Jones, *Couture Trend Forecasting* (Laurence King Publishing 2017) 22

32 *Designers Guild Ltd v Russel Williams (Textiles) Ltd* [1998] F.S.R. 803

33 *Designers Guild Ltd v Russel Williams (Textiles) Ltd* [1998] F.S.R. 803

34 *Designers Guild Ltd. v Russell Williams (Textiles) Ltd.(trading as Washington D.C.).* [2000] 1 W.L.R. 2416

35 *Designers Guild Ltd. v Russell Williams (Textiles) Ltd.(trading as Washington D.C.).* [2000] 1 W.L.R. 2416

36 *Designers Guild Ltd. v Russell Williams (Textiles) Ltd.(trading as Washington D.C.).* [2000] 1 W.L.R. 2416 at 2

37 *Designers Guild Ltd. v Russell Williams (Textiles) Ltd.(trading as Washington D.C.).* [2000] 1 W.L.R. 2416 at 2(para. 30). Clarke L.J. agreed

38 *Designers Guild Ltd. v Russell Williams (Textiles) Ltd.(trading as Washington D.C.).* [2000] 1 W.L.R. 2416 at 2

recognised that whilst both designs had stripes and flowers, they were different, and it was specifically pointed out that the flowers were not copies. The resist effect exercised throughout the design established a different result and therefore, the properties of the design which appeared to be the same, could not amount to substantial copying.[39] Originality was noted to be found in the 'author's skill and labour.'[40] Further, it is argued that this concept could be applied to Couture when distinguishing between designs of different brands which follow the same trends to identify 'originality' of a product.[41] Certainly, the detailed inspection carried out in *Designers Guild* could benefit the Couture industry as it relates to copyright protection by providing an indicator for the measurement of *substantiality* in Couture design.[42]

In considering the nature of creative works and coincidental similarities and the implications for originality, the recent case of a copyright infringement claim for the song by Rudimental called 'Waiting All Night' was put to the court.[43] The case concerned the composer Kelly-Marie Smith of the song 'Can You Tell Me?' The allegation was that the melody and chorus of 'Waiting All Night' were copied from her song.[44] The songs were considered in light of whether the copy had occurred knowingly or unknowingly, and thus, Zacaroli J considered the genre of music and agreed that the lyrics were accompanied by comparable melodies.[45] It was held that no copying had taken place and whilst similarities existed, differences were also present. The voice note taken by James Newman (who was the fourth defendant and the only person against whom the infringement claim was made by the end of the trial) demonstrated 'spontaneously and independently . . . in the course of trying out various ideas.'[46] The implications of this case for Couture as it relates to originality are that the nature and realisation of Couture design is impacted heavily by many industry directions, and thus, it is observed that this is similar to the case of *Smith v Dryden*, which focused on the accompanying melody to the lyrics being influenced from the genre of music. Couture design is influenced by various trends and cultural influences for specific seasons, and therefore, based on this case, it would appear quite possible that designs by different designers can be created "spontaneously and independently . . . in the course of trying out various ideas," without being perceived as copying or lacking originality in law.[47] The next section on artistic craftmanship explores these concepts further.

39 *Designers Guild Ltd. v Russell Williams (Textiles) Ltd.(trading as Washington D.C.).* [2000] 1 W.L.R. 2416 at 2

40 *Designers Guild Ltd. v Russell Williams (Textiles) Ltd.(trading as Washington D.C.).* [2000] 1 W.L.R. 2416

41 Tomruk Űstűnkaya, 'The Functionality Doctrine: The Challenges to Couture Copyright' (2020) 42(3) EIPR 156

42 *Designers Guild Ltd. v Russell Williams (Textiles) Ltd.(trading as Washington D.C.).* [2000] 1 W.L.R. 2416

43 *Smith v Dryden & Ors* [2021] E.W.H.C. 2277 (IPEC)

44 *Smith v Dryden & Ors* [2021] E.W.H.C. 2277 (IPEC)

45 *Smith v Dryden & Ors* [2021] E.W.H.C. 2277 (IPEC)

46 *Smith v Dryden & Ors* [2021] E.W.H.C. 2277 (IPEC)

47 *Smith v Dryden & Ors* [2021] E.W.H.C. 2277 (IPEC)

4.2.3 Intention

The preceding discussion on substantiality in relation to quality raises further issues as they relate to the intention of the couturier. To what extent has the couturier relating to the quality of the work been influenced by a previous work. Anecdotally, the notion of inspiration is the very first seed of an idea which derives from engaging with an experience. For example a sunset, a couturier may decide they wish to use the colours of the said, and experienced sunset for the next collection. Influence will be the next concept, whereby the couturier will look for past works (not necessarily artistic or fashion) to influence the direction of the collection. These two concepts will naturally raise questions relating to whether by drawing inspiration and influence, to what extent it is the couturier's intention to copy existing works. The law therefore must be clarified specifically as to the degree of a similar quality between works and the intention of the couturier when faced with industry practice limitations. This can be attributed to the matter of trend forecasts and influences on design, or alternatively arguable is that the trend forecasting guides may therefore be limited in application to exercise creative freedom and expression. With this freedom limited, the couturier shall be producing Couture that should ultimately meet market demand; therefore, a pertinent question is whether the 'copying' is intentional, and to what extent does this matter, in law?

As argued earlier, following trend forecast guidelines may be perceived as acquiring influence for the purposes of meeting market trend demands. For this reason, substantiality and intention are very closely connected because depending on the intention of the designer as it relates to the creative objective, the effect, and properties of the work, will determine whether the copying is substantial as discussed in *Designers Guild*.[48] Would the effect and quality of the design being different from a similar work make the intention of copying irrelevant? If so, would this amount to a copyright infringement, and should it be considered as an infringement for the purposes of Couture in consideration of the limitations placed on couturiers?

The matter of *intention* was examined through the case of *Temple Island*.[49] Before the discussion progresses further, it is necessary to mention at this point that *intention* is only a consideration in law for secondary infringement and not primary.[50] In this case a photograph of Westminster Bridge, London, in black and white with only the bus shown in the colour red was reproduced.[51] The issue of infringement could be decided by considering two specific factors:

1. Identification of the original elements in the claimant's work.
2. Contrasting the claimant's 2005 work with the defendant's image printed on a tea bag tin.[52] Although originality was considered by the court, the intention of New

48 Please see: *Designers Guild Ltd. v Russell Williams (Textiles) Ltd.(trading as Washington D.C.)*. [2000] 1 W.L.R. 2416 at 2

49 *Temple Island Collection v New English Teas Ltd [2011] E.W.P.C.C. 19; [2012] F.S.R.*

50 Inbrief, 'Copyright Infringement: Remedies & Defences' (*Inbrief*, 2020) <https://www.inbrief.co.uk./intellectual-property/copyright-infringement/?msclkid=75d2aef7b31811ec9e479df9733f7c40> accessed 26 March 2022

51 *Temple Island Collections Ltd v New English Teas Ltd*, 2012 WL 14602 (2012)

52 *Temple Island Collections Ltd v New English Teas Ltd*, 2012 WL 14602 (2012) at 37

English Teas was to produce a *new* image to avoid the occurrence of 'substantial reproduction.'[53] The court held that the intention was 'irrelevant' and further that the defendant was aware of the claimant's work.[54] A significant part of Couture is the awareness of market trends and intention as part of the design process.

4.2.4 Derivative Works

One key question in consideration of originality is whether derivative works are original. The thesis question specifically addresses Couture in consideration of widening the copyright legislation to include *and* define Couture as an artistic work. To support this, the expression of the ideas derives from art and artistic concepts in Couture.[55] Conversely, Couture works are considered here as being perpetually derivative. Derivative creative works are based on or are derived from existing works, and it is irrelevant whether the existing works they are based upon are protected by copyright.[56] The requirement for copyright protection for a derivative work is that it must meet the criterion of being an original, as a work in its own right. This point is significant due to Couture being regarded (from the perspective of this thesis) as being *perpetually derivative*. For example, the design process incorporates influences from key trends or artefacts, a work of cultural or historical interest.[57] Further in the merchandising process, it is commonplace to see more updated versions of successful designs, in other words different versions of derivative works.

The derivative work was considered in *Interlego v Tyco industries*,[58] where Lord Oliver expressed that an aspect of 'material alteration or embellishment' must be present to identify the work as original.[59] Therefore, copyright can be infringed by derivative works, irrespective of the derivative work being original; this is established when the original work is clearly identified within the derivative.[60] Bently et al regard this as a curious perspective as they state 'good reproductions are denied copyright, but poor ones have sufficiently visually significant variation.' This view is supported by Tappin and Others in *The Modern Law of Copyright.*[61]

53 *Temple Island Collection v New English Teas Ltd* [2011] E.W.P.C.C. 19; [2012] F.S.R.

54 Tomruk Űstűnkaya, 'The Functionality Doctrine: The Challenges to Fashion Copyright' (2020) 42(3) EIPR 156 referring to *Temple Island Collection v New English Teas Ltd* [2011] E.W.P.C.C. 19; [2012] F.S.R.

55 Alex Kessler, 'Art And Couture Collided At the Couture Shows' (*Vogue*, 28 January 2022) <https://www.vogue.co.uk/Couture/gallery/best-artistic-looks-Couture-ss22?msclkid=abdc77f3b31c11ec97282a3139722379> accessed 26 March 2022

56 L Bentley and others, *Intellectual Property Law* (6th edn, Oxford University Press 2022) 93

57 Cambridge, 'Artefact' (*Cambridge Dictionary Online*, 2022) <https://dictionary.cambridge.org/dictionary/english/artefact?msclkid=28de3876b31f11eca3de67abb0015c8a> accessed 26 March 2022

58 *Interlego v Tyco Industries* [1989] A.C. 217, 268

59 *Interlego v Tyco Industries* [1989] A.C. 217, 268 and L Bently and others, *Intellectual Property Law* (5th edn, Oxford University Press 2018) 114

60 L Bentley and others, *Intellectual Property Law* (6th edn, Oxford University Press 2022) 94 referring to *Redwood Music v Chappell* [1982] R.P.C. 109, 120; *ZYX Music GmbH v King*

61 *L Bentley and others, Intellectual Property Law (6th edn, Oxford University Press 2022) 114 referring to Interlego v Tyco Industries [1989] A.C. 217, 268 and Tappin MQC and others, Laddie, Prescott and Victoria, The Modern Law of Copyright (5th edn, Lexis Nexis Butterworths 2018)*

The argument further considers that a copy is not the same as a derivative work and additionally, a derivative work is not intended in Couture to be a copy of something else. A derivative work in Couture is based on developing an existing idea to produce a different work, expressing the designers' individual creative freedom. Therefore, a derivative work runs the risk of being conflated with a 'poor' copy. Establishing originality in Couture is perceived as being difficult should derivative works be regarded as copies in law, due to assessments of substantiality being considered. It is therefore imperative that the law provides clarification for the absolute difference between *copies* and *derivatives*, as the nature and natural process of Couture design is inspiration taken from *something* in existence, which is then developed for the purposes of Couture.[62] This is also important in consideration of establishing originality in derivative works.

4.3 Fixation

Fixation is a requirement of copyright law. The Berne Convention stipulates that signatories are prescriptive when legislating for specific categories of works, in that for the purposes of granting copyright protection, works are required to be fixed in 'material form.'[63] Declayre identified a notable and significant detail in this analysis in that works of artistic craftmanship do not necessitate a static position, rather that they must subsist of a static component.[64] She argues that although fixation is not a requirement for artistic works which is set up by the CDPA 1988, notable is that a work will only attract copyright protection when it is recorded tangibly or visually.[65] To understand this concept further, the case of *Merchandising Corporation of America Inc* illustrates that the make-up of the pop star Adam Ant was not protectable by copyright as it was not tangibly fixed.[66] In *Komesaroff*,[67] an art work consisting of a glass panel containing coloured sand, liquid and air bubbles was not considered a work of artistic craftmanship. Significant here is the aspect of movement for the 'painting' which could be achieved by the user reversing the painting. The judge acknowledged the 'kinetic' aspect of the 'painting' and stated, '[as] no sand landscape is a static feature for any length of time, such landscapes cannot be taken into account as part of a "work of artistic craftsmanship".'[68]

In consideration of the aforementioned points as it relates to Couture and the aspect of fixation, the intrinsic movement within a garment exists by virtue of the functional elements such as a shoulder strap tie, a tie belt, buttons on cuffs, etc.

62 'Something' being any 'thing' that inspires the designer, whether this be an object, nature, or Couture itself

63 Article 2 (2) The Berne Convention for the Protection of Literary and Artistic Works, 1886

64 Dr. Estelle Derclaye, 'Debunking Some of U.K. Copyright Law's Longstanding Myths and Misunderstandings' (2013) 1 IPQ 1

65 Dr. Estelle Derclaye, 'Debunking Some of U.K. Copyright Law's Longstanding Myths and Misunderstandings' (2013) 1 IPQ 1 referring to Macqueen and others, *Contemporary Intellectual Property* (2010) 51

66 *Merchandising Corporation of America Inc v Harpbond Ltd* [1983] F.S.R. 32. Tangibly fixed means that the work must be fixed in a tangible medium, for example an oil painting on a canvas

67 *Komesoroff* [1988] R.P.C. 204

68 Komesoroff [1988] R.P.C. 204 at 210

Although, considerations extend further to the natural movement of the body to enable movement within the fabric, and moreover technological advances such as Lycra make it possible for the fabric to move, and expand with the body.[69] This consideration is crucial, as a Couture garment is not a 'static feature for any length of time.'[70] Declayre's analysis of the issue of fixation identifies works of artistic craftmanship as not being expected to be static, but must comprise a static component to be regarded as a work of artistic craftmanship.[71] This effectively means that Couture articles could be recorded in some way. In the case of *Abraham Moon* (as mentioned earlier in 4.3.1), it was held acceptable that the design of the plaid fabric was recorded in a weaving ticket.[72] On this basis, it is necessary to outline that a static artwork can be considered as a work of artistic craftmanship without being recorded,[73] and further that an oral verification as evidence pertaining to an artwork shall suffice in the event of the artwork being destroyed.[74]

4.4 Subject Matter

The case of *Interlego*[75] is noted as making a distinction between artistic works and those of literary creations. The judge had recognised that 'small variations' necessitate 'skill, labour and judgement.'[76] The reason this appears to be significant for copyright as it applies to Couture, is due to the application of copyright law being applied to many different types of works in a *generic* and general manner. The distinction on subject matter made in *Interlego*[77] is absent in *Infopaq*.[78] The implications here are that, although copyright law did see a development specifically distinguishing between different types of subject matter in *Interlego*, the latter *Infopaq* decision reverted to the generic application of copyright law across different types works. Converseley, the *Infopaq* decision was one of the first decisions of its kind for the E.U. significant for the harmonisation of laws across the Union.[79] In addition, the absence of distinguishing between subject matter can add to the challenges in copyright for Couture.

69 Lycra, 'Lycra Redefining Comfort and Fit Since 1958' (*Lycracom*, 2021) <https://www.lycra.com/en> accessed 31 December 2021

70 Komesoroff [1988] R.P.C. 204 at 210

71 Please see: Dr. Estelle Derclaye, 'Debunking Some of U.K. Copyright Law's Longstanding Myths and Misunderstandings' (2013) 1 IPQ 7

72 *Abraham Moon and Sons v Thornber* [2012] E.W.P.C.C. 37

73 Dr. Estelle Derclaye, 'Debunking Some of U.K. Copyright Law's Longstanding Myths and Misunderstandings' (2013) 1 IPQ 1–17

74 Dr. Estelle Derclaye, 'Debunking Some of U.K. Copyright Law's Longstanding Myths and Misunderstandings' (2013) 1 IPQ 1–17 referring to Bently and Sherman, Intellectual Property Law (2009) 92

75 *Interlego v Tyco Industries [1987] F.S.R. 409*

76 *Interlego v Tyco Industries* [1987] F.S.R. 409

77 *Interlego v Tyco Industries [1987] F.S.R. 409*

78 *Infopaq International A/S v Danske Dagblades Forening* (C-5/08) E.U:C:2009:465; [1987] F.S.R.

79 *Infopaq International A/S v Danske Dagblades Forening* (C-5/08) E.U:C:2009:465; [1987] F.S.R.

Couture does not align neatly with any subject matter within s.4 of the CDPA, and in addition to the decision of *Infopaq*,[80] it is considered from the perspective of this thesis, that the prospect of developing laws which consider subject matter beyond the existing categories is currently challenging. Introduced here is the prospect of initiating a new category of subject matter for Couture specifically, within the CDPA 1988, which considers the art, aesthetics, and function comprised within Couture. If there is no recognition of the significance of each category of subject matter in preference of applying a generic copyright legislation, in the current form, copyright protection for Couture appears to be inevitably strained.

In *Painer*,[81] a photograph was at the centre of the legal contention as to whether 'the standard of originality to be applied to photographs – whether portrait photos are afforded inferior copyright protection or no copyright protection – whether art.5(3)(d) of Directive 2001/29 allows quotation if author is not attributed.'[82] The court considered the scope of the right of reproduction and the protection provided by art.17, Directive 98/71 on designs and art.96(2), Regulation 6/2002 which is the community design right[83] in consideration of artistic character, and qualified the criterion of originality by stating that it is the maximum requirement expected from Member States for the purposes of benefiting from copyright.[84] The court noted that there was an absence within the regulation 'to suggest that the extent of such protection depends on any differences in the possibility of artistic creation, when producing the various categories of works . . . and cannot consider that such protection is completely excluded on that basis.'[85] In answering the question put to the court which was:

> Are Article 1(1) of Directive 2001/29 in conjunction with Article 5(5) thereof and Article 12 of the Berne Convention . . ., particularly in the light of Article 1 of the First Additional Protocol to the European Convention for the Protection of Human Rights and Fundamental Freedoms [signed at Rome on 4 November 1950] and Article 17 of the Charter of Fundamental Rights of the E.U., to be interpreted as meaning that photographic works and/or photographs, particularly portrait photos, are afforded "weaker" copyright protection or no copyright protection at all against adaptations because, in view of their "realistic image," the degree of formative freedom is too minor?

It was stated by the court that the case of *Painer*[86] made clear, 'the protection conferred by art 2(a) of Directive 2001/29 cannot be inferior to that enjoyed by other works.'[87]

80 *Infopaq International A/S v Danske Dagblades Forening* (C-5/08) E.U:C:2009:465; [1987] F.S.R.
81 *Painer v Standard Verlags GmbH* E.U:C:2011:798; [2012] E.C.D.R. 6
82 *Painer v Standard Verlags GmbH* E.U:C:2011:798; [2012] E.C.D.R. 6 at H1
83 art.17, Directive 98/71 on designs and art.96(2), Regulation 6/2002
84 *Cofemel v G-Star Raw CV* (C-683/17) at para 31
85 *Cofemel v G-Star Raw CV* (C-683/17) at para 31
86 *Painer v Standard Verlags GmbH E.U:C:2011:798; [2012] E.C.D.R. 6*
87 *Cofemel v G-Star Raw CV* (C-683/17)

4.5 The Limitations of S.4 CDPA 1988: *Lucasfilm*

Between 1974 and 1976, the 'stormtroopers' characters were conceived by George Lucas for the Star Wars film *A New Hope* and were 'given visual expression in drawings and paintings by Mr Ralph McQuarrie, and three-dimensional form by Mr Nick Pemberton . . . and Mr Andrew Ainsworth.'[88] Mr Ainsworth had produced 50 helmets for the film and had later sold some of the props he had made for the film for between USD 8,000 and USD 30,000. On this basis, Mr Ainsworth was sued by Lucasfilm in 2005, and had obtained a default judgement for damages pursuant to the Lanham Act in the United States District Court, Central District of California.[89] Mann J held that Mr Ainsworth had made 'substantial reproductions' of the work by Mr McQuarrie and other persons, although copyright claims in English law failed as the helmet could not be established as a work of sculpture.[90] On this basis, the U.S. judgement was unenforceable in the U.K. over Mr Ainsworth and his company. In the U.K., the point for the court to establish was whether the helmet was a protected artistic work as a 'sculpture' under ss 51 and 52 of the CDPA 1988 or a work of artistic craftmanship.[91]

In consideration of whether the helmet was 'a work of artistic craftmanship'[92] the court turned to the decision in the case of *Hensher.*[93] It was established in *Lucasfilm* that s.4(1)(c) of the CDPA 1988 intends for articles whose primary purpose is utilitarian, in that its purpose was functional as a costume prop, could not be regarded as sculpture.[94] The court recognised '[t]he relative significance of the *functional* and the artistic is central to this appeal.'[95] [emphasis added]

In relation to the notion of final products being sculptures, the court considered the New Zealand case of *Wham-O*, regarding Frisbees, whereby it was held that the final products were not sculptures. It was recognised that the relevant parts of the Copyright Act 1962 were similar but not identical to the 1988 Act, which is relevant because *Lucasfilm* was relying on the CDPA 1988.[96] Although in the court of first instance, it was held that the wooden models were considered as sculptures

88 *Lucasfilm Limited and others (Appellants) v Ainsworth and another (Respondents),* [2011] U.K.SC 39

89 *Lucasfilm Limited and others (Appellants) v Ainsworth and another (Respondents),* [2011] U.K.SC 39 at para 4

90 *Lucasfilm Limited and others (Appellants) v Ainsworth and another (Respondents),* [2011] U.K.SC 39 at para 5

91 *Lucasfilm Limited and others (Appellants) v Ainsworth and another (Respondents),* [2011] U.K.SC 39 at para 7

92 *Lucasfilm Limited and others (Appellants) v Ainsworth and another (Respondents),* [2011] U.K.SC 39 at para 7

93 *Retawaile v Hensher [1976] A.C. 64*

94 *Lucasfilm Limited and others (Appellants) v Ainsworth and another (Respondents),* [2011] U.K.SC 39 at para 29

95 *Lucasfilm Limited and others (Appellants) v Ainsworth and another (Respondents),* [2011] U.K.SC 39 at para 29

96 *Lucasfilm Limited and others (Appellants) v Ainsworth and another (Respondents),* [2011] U.K.SC 39 at para 30

and protected by copyright, the final product was subsequently identified by the Court of Appeal as not being a sculpture, as they were produced industrially.[97] The rationale for the decision is significant because it identified 'inappropriate to regard utilitarian objects . . . as items of sculpture for the purposes of the Copyright Act.'[98] Observed is a pattern emerging amongst the copyright cases in that the definitions in law do not necessarily adequately furnish the true description of the creative piece. In other words, to bring a claim in court, the parties must define the 'work' they are contending as fitting into one of the listed categories, and it therefore becomes a futile exercise of trying to fit 'a round peg into a square hole.' The words used within s.4 of the CDPA 1988 may facilitate a challenge for creative works not adhering to the description or definition therein. The reason for this is because firstly, judges refer to the list when making a judicial decision, and secondly because the list describes the work.

The *Lucasfilm* judgement expresses that the helmet was:

i. Utilitarian in its primary function.[99]
ii. The artistic component was to fulfil the utilitarian objective.[100]
iii. The artistic expression contained within the work did not constitute the work to be regarded as a sculpture, only that it contributed to the artistic element of the film.[101]

Guidelines were put forward by Mann J in para 118 of his judgement.[102] Firstly, an artistic work must be approached within the context of the 'normal use.' Bearing this in mind, at times it may go beyond an individual's expectation of art, and what might be displayed in art galleries, although Mann J added that it would be 'inappropriate' to drift too far away from the usual expectation of sculpture. It was also held that 'not every 3-dimensional concept can be regarded as sculpture,' and Mann J recognised that a sculpture may comprise of 'visual appeal' as part of its purpose. Further, if a work does have another purpose, this would not automatically exclude it from being a sculpture, although it would require the 'intrinsic quality' of being enjoyed visually. Lastly, Mann J expressed that he could not see why an object that is purely functional (and not decorative) should be regarded as sculpture. Applying these guidelines to Couture, to potentially establish Couture as an artistic work, pursuant to s.4 of the CDPA 1988, questioned is whether Couture

97 *Lucasfilm Limited and others (Appellants) v Ainsworth and another (Respondents)*, [2011] U.K.SC 39 at para 30
98 *Lucasfilm Limited and others (Appellants) v Ainsworth and another (Respondents)*, [2011] U.K.SC 39 at para 30
99 *Lucasfilm Limited and others (Appellants) v Ainsworth and another (Respondents)*, [2011] U.K.SC 39 On appeal from: [2009] E.W.C.A. Civ 1328 at para 40
100 *Lucasfilm Limited and others (Appellants) v Ainsworth and another (Respondents)*, [2011] U.K.SC 39 On appeal from: [2009] E.W.C.A. Civ 1328 at para 32
101 *Lucasfilm Limited and others (Appellants) v Ainsworth and another (Respondents)*, [2011] U.K.SC 39 On appeal from: [2009] E.W.C.A. Civ 1328 at para 32
102 These guidelines were also stated in full in the Court of Appeal case [2010] Ch 503, para [54]

may be perceived as going beyond the usual parameters of what an individual may expect to see in a gallery as art. The next question that would naturally follow is whether Couture would be perceived as straying too far from what one would identify as an artistic work.

Mann J also considered 'visual appeal,' which could be translated as the aesthetic appeal of art and recognised that this would be intrinsic to its purpose. In consideration of haute Couture works, it must be questioned whether the aesthetic appeal is an intrinsic requirement of the garment. Finally, Couture is not purely functional,[103] as it is observed to carry artistic qualities, one of which may be aesthetic (although a subjective notion, not all artistic works may be considered as holding aesthetic appeal).[104] The preceding discussion addresses the current approach taken by the law regarding copyright, and the challenging relationship between Couture and copyright is discussed next.

4.6 The Relationship Between Couture and Copyright

First and foremost, pursuant to the CDPA 1988, a Couture work has the *potential* to be protected by copyright, however, as the study has thus far illustrated, challenges exist. The challenges observed by this thesis are considerations related to the limitations of the closed list system in s.4 of the CDPA 1988, which does not include Couture (or Couture as a subject matter). Another challenge is the aspect of functionality which shall be discussed in chapter 5. Each of these challenges are considered next in relation to the thesis question.

The perceived problem with the closed list is that to attempt to attain copyright protection, Couture will be required to fit into one of the current listed categories. The focus of this study is the end-product, the garment, a work of art with the potential to be protected by copyright. The difficulty in defining Couture as an artistic work is apparent. Legal arguments could attempt to position Couture as a sculpture, but in reality, a garment is not a sculpture. In applying the case of *Lucasfilm* whereby a costume prop, specifically a stormtrooper helmet, was the subject of copyright proceedings, whereby the helmet was not a work of *artistic* craftmanship pursuant to s.4 CDPA 1988.[105] The criterion of *artistic* in copyright is significant, for the thesis objective of defining of Couture as an artistic work, and in the pursuit of it being included within the list of protected works under s.4 of the CDPA 1988. An official definition of Couture in law has not been established, though scholarly commentary and industry opinion that has been presented thus far supports Couture being regarded as an artistic work. What must be addressed is the concept of artistic craftmanship, which, from the perspective of this thesis,

103 As analysed in chapter 2 onwards

104 These concepts are considered in chapter 4, when questioning whether Couture is art

105 *Lucasfilm Limited and others (Appellants) v Ainsworth and another (Respondents),* [2011] U.K.SC 39

Couture is comprised of, and which contributes to the end-product.[106] This is an important distinction to make, particularly to meet the objective of this thesis for Couture to be identified as an artistic work, and not as a work of artistic craftmanship entirely.[107]

One notable recognition on the black-letter of law is that legal definitions in a statute are not necessarily wide enough to be inclusive of specific subject matter, such as Couture. [To elaborate on this point, Heilpern expresses the complications in attempting to define art whereby the courts 'determining a statutory phrase as a technical term of art.'[108]] This argument is crucial to the pursuit of aligning legal definitions of artistic works with industry definitions. If alignment is achieved, it may potentially result in the subject matter being protected by the statute.

4.7 Copyright: Assessment of Artistic Works

In consideration of the preceding discussion, particularly considering the judgement in *Lucasfilm* whereby the helmet was not regarded as a work of artistic craftmanship,[109] and the case of *Response Clothing* which deliberated over the threshold for copyright regarding the design of the fabric, it was held that aesthetic appeal was not a necessary consideration for copyright protection.[110] These cases are analysed further next.

4.7.1 Response Clothing

In the case of *Response Clothing*, the fabric was deliberated upon by HHJ Hacon in consideration of the claim made by Response clothing that as the work was created on a loom, it should be categorised as:

a. A graphic work, or
b. A work of artistic craftmanship.

It was held that the work did not qualify as a graphic work because s.4(1)(a) could not be extended to include fabric.

In ascertaining whether the fabric could be established as a work of artistic craftmanship, the case of *New Zealand of Bonz Group (Pty) Ltd v Cooke* was a

106 Iona Silverman, 'Copyright and Couture: A U.K. Perspective' (*WIPO*, June 2014) <https://www.WIPO.int/WIPO_magazine/en/2014/03/article_0007.html> accessed 31 May 2021

107 S.4 CDPA 1988

108 Heilpern, 'Dialects of Art: A Corpus-Based Approach to Technical Term of Art Determinations in Statutes' (2022) 58(4) Jurimetrics 377–410

109 *Lucasfilm Limited and others (Appellants) v Ainsworth and another (Respondents),* [2011] U.K.SC 39

110 *Response Clothing Ltd v Edinburgh Woollen Mill Ltd* [2020] E.W.H.C. 148 (IPE.Z.L.RC)

major consideration.[111] HHJ Hacon considered the judgement of the case, particularly the decision of Tipping J where he identified that the work was a combination between the 'artistry of the designer and craftmanship of the knitters,' which had created an aesthetically pleasing fabric. On this point, *Response Clothing* had come to the conclusion that the fabric was aesthetically pleasing due to the commercial success. HHJ Hacon further went on to consider the decision in *Cofemel*, and in alignment with that decision, held that the Response clothing fabric was capable of copyright protection and the additional requirement of aesthetic appeal was not a necessary consideration. Further HHJ Hacon asserted that a work is not prevented from copyright protection due to multiple copies of the work being made and sold.

This case is regarded as a positive decision for the fashion industry as it relates to 'artistic craftmanship,' as it heralds the clarification of aesthetic appeal not being a necessary requirement for copyright protection for fashion works. However, in analysis and in relation to the objective of this study, the case is significant. This is because the *Response Clothing* case identifies the fabric as a work of artistic craftmanship; therefore, the fabric is capable of copyright protection based on being created by the designers' free and creative choices. From the perspective of this study, this decision only enhances support for the assertion that artistic craftmanship is a *part* of Couture. The various elements of Couture comprise elements of artistic craftmanship, for example, embroidery, specific assembly techniques pertaining to the stitching, form, and shape of the garment. Copyright, therefore, in consideration of Couture is a wider consideration, and this study identifies that the garment as a complete work must be legally determined as a work of art without the necessity to consider individual aspects which are comprised within the work. Nevertheless, the study wholly supports copyright protection for the components capable of copyright protection which are comprised within the work, although the ultimate work must be valued, entirely.

Could the fragmentation in the assessment of an artistic work to determine copyright cause devaluation? The nature of the copyright regime is that only some parts of the creation are capable of copyright protection, whilst other components cannot attract copyright due to not meeting the relevant criteria. On this basis, to what extent does this give way to notions of worthiness and value for the work? Further, would the value of the work be fragmented, i.e. the parts of the work which can attract copyright are valuable, whilst the elements that have not attained copyright are deemed worthless or less held as lesser valued features? In application to Couture, did the couturier intend for their work not to have artistic value as a complete work? Why would a copyright protective mechanism, that applies to only a part of the garment, be adequate or satisfactory protection? Afterall, would a fine art oil painting (an artistic work) be scrutinised in the same way? Would only parts of the painting attract copyright protection? The answer would most likely be more than likely not, as the painting would be regarded as an artistic work in its entirety. Therefore, why is it acceptable for a Couture creation only to be

111 *New Zealand of Bonz Group (Pty) Ltd v Cooke* [1994] 3 N

capable of being granted copyright for some components, i.e. embroidery, fabric, or graphic work?

Interim Conclusion

The implications of divergent approaches to copyright are apparent within this chapter. Arguments are put forward next to encourage a more robust framework for the legal protection of Couture pertaining to:

1. An alignment of industry and legal terms. These must be clarified in law, between the designer's practice of deriving *influence* and the perception of *copying* in law, specifically in substantiality cases.
2. For the courts to always exercise an intricate visual analysis of creative works as in *Designers Guild*,[112] and not a reliance solely based on words as in *Hensher.*[113]

The preceding points explicitly address the interplay between art and copyright law. From the perspective of this thesis, the case of *Designers Guild* demonstrates a measured approach to the issue of copying to establish originality, which was found to be in the author's skill and labour.[114] On appeal the court conducted a meticulous visual assessment between the two contested designs, and it is this which is of significance to Couture. It is the visual basis for assessment which must be considered, and not a reliance on the words of the law only. This is to ensure a comprehensive assessment for works which are visually operational in nature. This is a development in the standard for copyright of the originality criteria.

The concept of influence links with the aspect of whether derivative works are original. A derivative work runs the risk of being confused with a 'poor' copy and suggested previously is that absolute clarification is required between derivatives and copies.[115] One suggestion here is that the concept of influence is included within the assessment and as mentioned earlier, the influenced work which is argued within this study to be a derivative, must be understood as such; Couture is naturally perpetually derivative. It is asserted once more that a derivative work, an influenced work, is an expression of the designer's creative freedom, an expression that operates within the parameters of market demands and the natural and essential elements of Couture.

The considerations regarding the aspect of fixation for the purposes of qualifying for copyright protection were analysed through the case of *Komesaroff*[116] and more recently *Abraham Moon.*[117] For this reason, elements of Couture garments

112 *Designers Guild Ltd v Russel Williams (Textiles) Ltd* [1998] F.S.R. 803

113 *George Hensher Ltd v Restawile [1976] A.C. 64*

114 *Designers Guild Ltd. v Russell Williams (Textiles) Ltd.(trading as Washington D.C.).* [2000] 1 W.L.R. 2416

115 L Bentley and others, *Intellectual Property Law* (6th edn, Oxford University Press 2022) 114 referring to *Interlego v Tyco Industries* [1989] A.C. 217, 268 and Tappin MQC and others, *Laddie, Prescott and Victoria, The Modern Law of Copyright* (5th edn, Lexis Nexis Butterworths 2018) 228–30

116 *Komesoroff [1988] R.P.C. 204*

117 *Abraham Moon and Sons v Thornber* [2012] E.W.P.C.C. 37

Figure 4.1 Valentino Evening Dress 1969 V&A Museum no. T.443-1974

such as embroidery, the fabric design or graphic, or other features which amount to artistic craftmanship, can be recorded and fulfil the fixation criteria.[118] However, it appears that the disconnect between copyright and Couture exists in that Couture as a complete artistic work necessitates a fragmented assessment of various 'artistic' elements to attain copyright protection for those only.

The development in *Response Clothing* established that the fabric was a work of artistic craftmanship.[119] The case of *Response Clothing* appears to be the most significant case supporting the arguments put forward for this study for Couture to be

118 *Abraham Moon and Sons v Thornber* [2012] E.W.P.C.C. 37
119 *Response Clothing Ltd v Edinburgh Woollen Mill Ltd* [2020] E.W.H.C. 148 (IPEC)

recognised, and to attain copyright protection in its own right as a whole garment, an artistic work.[120] Response clothing attained copyright for the fabric, as a work of artistic craftmanship, as it was regarded as being created by the designers' free and creative choices. [*Cofemel* applied.] This point only emphasises that the copyright system only facilitates copyrightable *features* which are *comprised* within the Couture garment. Instead, should the optimum position not be that the Couture garment is an artistic work in its entirety? Therefore, it should not be necessary to fragment the Couture garment to make an assessment as to which features are copyrightable.

Further, if features within the garment are regarded as works of artistic craftmanship, essentially the effect of this in law is that the work of artistic craftmanship is sitting as an isolated feature. In fact, the feature is not separate from the whole creative work, and has been created as *part of* and to *complete* the *art*.

As stated previously, due to the current copyright regime and process for assessment, whilst the study wholly supports features capable of copyright protection which are comprised within the work to attain copyright protection, the desired position is that a Couture work be capable of copyright protection in its entirety. This would not only provide the value to the couturier's artistic efforts and skill, but also it may add value to copyright by recognising the vast and wider potential of application.

Upon reflection for the thesis question, this chapter has specifically considered copyright legislation in relation to widening the criterion of 'artistic works' to include 'Couture fashion garments' specifically. The limitations of copyright must be regulated to prevent impacting protection for creative elements which are intrinsically technical. The most notable observation of this chapter is the requirement for the law and the creative industries to be more closely aligned when defining artistic works and the impact of creative processes, in law. The chapter intended to provide a rationale for the significance, in only protecting works of Couture within the fashion framework. The reason for this is because it is these works which influence the wider fashion marketplace (clothing made for mass manufacture for industrial purposes).[121] Couture works are made through the artistic processes and by the couturiers' free and intellectual creative choices, which comprises of, but are not exclusive to, highly skilled artistic craftsmanship elements.[122]

120 *Response Clothing Ltd v Edinburgh Woollen Mill Ltd* [2020] E.W.H.C. 148 (IPE.Z.L.RC)

121 Divya Bala, 'About the Inner Workings of Haute Couture' (*Vogue*, 6 July 2020) <https://www.vogue.co.uk/Couture/article/behind-the-scenes-at-haute-Couture> accessed 5 March 2022

122 *Radley Gowns v Costas Syprou* [1975] F.S.R. 455 at (2) and *George Hensher Ltd v Restawhile* [1976] A.C. 64

5 The Functionality Doctrine Rationale

Introduction

The focus of this chapter is to determine whether the limitations of copyright to technical features must be prevented from encroaching upon the artistic components of Couture. The relationship between technicality and copyright, whereby technical features generally cannot be granted copyright protection (through the functionality doctrine), is examined. Through previous chapters, the analysis of the thesis has brought forward the concept of an intrinsic existence of technicality which enables functionality within fashion.

The copyright exclusion specifically relates to the work being non-functional, as this will impact the originality requirement for copyright.[1] The parallels across the wider framework shall be acknowledged throughout this chapter to decipher the implications for copyright, if any. The conclusion attempts to assemble the findings of the chapter to ascertain an understanding of copyright, and the adequacy of copyright law in relation to the application of the functionality doctrine to Couture.

5.1 Defining the Functionality Doctrine

A legal 'doctrine' has been defined as a 'rule, principle, theory, or tenet of the law.'[2] It is understood as establishing the legal provisions for future resolution of specific issues, and therefore, the law is set by judicial opinion.[3] A doctrine is defined as:

> [sometimes the doctrine is stated explicitly in a judicial legal opinion.] Sometimes, the doctrine has to be constructed by the reader out of the raw materials of the judicial opinion itself – the recitation of facts together with the issue and holding, and perhaps even the rationale and the procedural posture of the case.[4]

1 L Bentley and others, *Intellectual Property Law* (6th edn, Oxford University Press 2022) 108

2 Pierre Schlag and Amy J Griffin, *How to Do Things With Legal Doctrine* (University Chicago Press 2020) 10 referring to Black's Law dictionary

3 Emerson H Tiller and Frank B Cross, *What is Legal Doctrine?* (16 May 2005) <https://ssrn.com/abstract=730284 or http://dx.doi.org/10.2139/ssrn.730284>

4 Pierre Schlag and Amy J Griffin, *How to Do Things With Legal Doctrine* (University Chicago Press 2020) 10

DOI: 10.4324/9781003599456-5

Decisions of the courts develop, define, and implement such legal doctrines. Therefore, it is perceived that doctrines essentially develop through their malleable existence based on judicial opinion. In terms of perceiving the doctrine from the perspective of doctrinal scholarship, the comprehension of the process arises through the 'the doctrinalist' placing 'himself inside the legal system.'[5] The significance of this approach forms the foundation in the method that shall be adopted to understand the functionality doctrine. Firstly, operating in its current form, with a view to application specifically to Couture fashion. This method is defined by the legal process as being the substantive focus of the analysis and in addition, underpins the structure for the research in this area.[6]

The functionality doctrine in the U.K. is enacted through legislative provisions and judicial opinion. The reference to the doctrine in copyright law is recognised from the perspective of this thesis as indirect. This is due to most judicial decisions, and commentary, not being reliant on a single document containing 'the' doctrine.[7]

For the purposes of obtaining copyright protection, are we to address and accept Couture as a hybrid product intrinsically containing both the functional and non-functional features? Or should we be separating the functional features from the non-functional features? In the U.S. the latter has demonstrated that in separating these components, it is possible to afford copyright to the non-functional elements within a garment, which was seen with the graphics on cheerleading uniforms.[8] The following section aims to demonstrate that the functional, creative, and artistic elements of Couture exist in unison, holistically.

5.2 Functionality in Couture

Couture is differentiated from other fashion works in that it is of a very high quality and comprises of exalted artistry, both during the creative process and as an artistic work in its own right. The study will now examine the functional aspect of Couture and the extent to which function impacts attaining copyright. Functionality for Couture is examined through two new notions; developed specifically for this study by the author, these are referred to as *tangible* and *intangible* functionality.

5 Jan M Smits, *What is Legal Doctrine? On the Aims and Methods of Legal-Dogmatic Research* (1 September 2015). Rob van Gestel, Hans-W Micklitz and Edward L Rubin (eds.), *Rethinking Legal Scholarship: A Transatlantic Dialogue* (Cambridge University Press 2017) 207–28, Maastricht European Private Law Institute Working Paper No. 2015/06 <https://ssrn.com/abstract=2644088 or <http://dx.doi.org/10.2139/ssrn.2644088>

6 Jan M Smits, *What is Legal Doctrine? On the Aims and Methods of Legal-Dogmatic Research* (1 September 2015). Rob van Gestel, Hans-W Micklitz and Edward L Rubin (eds.), *Rethinking Legal Scholarship: A Transatlantic Dialogue* (Cambridge University Press 2017) 207–28, Maastricht European Private Law Institute Working Paper No. 2015/06 <https://ssrn.com/abstract=2644088 or http://dx.doi.org/10.2139/ssrn.2644088>

7 The doctrine operates through deliberations of the court on matters of utilitarian, functional, or technical aspects of works

8 Please see, *Star Athletica v Varsity Brands Inc* 799 F.3d 468 (2015) (6th Cir (US)) and more recently *Warm v Innermost Ltd.*, CV 21-4402-MWF(SHKx) (C.D. Cal. November 5, 2024)

5.2.1 Tangible Functionality

Apparel was originally for the purposes of 'shelter and protection,'[9] and it is noted that development has led to the shift in focus considering attainment of the required body form through dress.[10] This can be seen in the Victorian era of 1860–1880s where women's apparel was designed to incorporate supportive elements using boning for corsets,[11] skirts incorporated a layering of petticoats and a hoop for the wide hem midi length, and a bustle.[12] The following illustrations show historical technical shaping undergarments.

Today, materials incorporated for the purposes of supporting fashion are items such as:

> 'Canvas, fusible and non-fusible tape, iron-on interlining/fusing, rigid interlining for extreme support, tailor's front supporting piece with canvas and wadding, tailored shoulder pads, shoulder roll, Crinoline, Boning, plastic and metal with plastic coating, wadding, raglan shoulder pads.[13]

The incorporation of the support materials into the apparel is a consideration for the designer, not only in terms of enhancing the function of the apparel but also to enhance the aesthetic appeal. It is evident that the couturier must take into consideration the technicality of the garment within the artistic work. The combination of both therefore demonstrates the creative pursuits being employed throughout both processes. The creative thought must be extended to achieving the objective of the apparel in terms of performance in tandem with achieving a pleasing aesthetic. [For instance, the incorporation of nano technology illustrates the use of technology within fabric for the purposes of performance, therefore the fabrics technicality.] Sportswear incorporates aspects of functional features for enhanced performance and to meet the objectives of keeping the sportsperson comfortable. Sports bras are designed to minimise pain caused by movement during exercise,[14] and 'Dri-fit' is a textile product designed to draw perspiration away from the sportsperson.[15] Further, Speedo developed the LZR racer swimsuit, and the fabric was developed

9 Annette Fischer and Kiran Gobin, *Construction for Fashion Design* (2nd edn, Bloomsbury 2017) 142
10 Annette Fischer and Kiran Gobin, *Construction for Fashion Design* (2nd edn, Bloomsbury 2017) 142
11 Annette Fischer and Kiran Gobin, *Construction for Fashion Design* (2nd edn, Bloomsbury 2017) 142
12 Annette Fischer and Kiran Gobin, *Construction for Fashion Design* (2nd edn, Bloomsbury 2017) 142
13 Annette Fischer and Kiran Gobin, *Construction for Fashion Design* (2nd edn, Bloomsbury 2017) 145
14 Australian Fitness Academy, 'Technology in Sports Clothing: Do We Really Need It?' (*Australian Fitness Academy*, 26 October 2016) <https://www.fitnesseducation.edu.au/blog/industry-trends/technology-in-sports-clothing-do-we-really-need-it/> accessed 6 July 2021
15 Australian Fitness Academy, 'Technology in Sports Clothing: Do We Really Need It?' (*Australian Fitness Academy*, 26 October 2016) <https://www.fitnesseducation.edu.au/blog/industry-trends/technology-in-sports-clothing-do-we-really-need-it/> accessed 6 July 2021

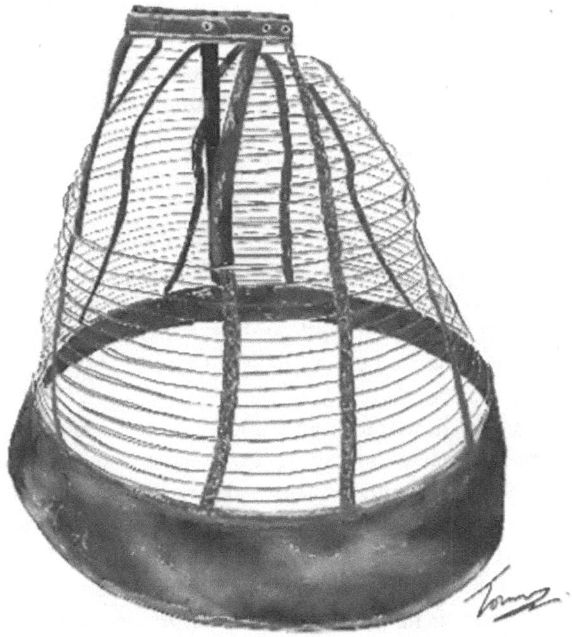

Figure 5.1 Crinoline 1860–1865 V&A Museum no. T.150-1986

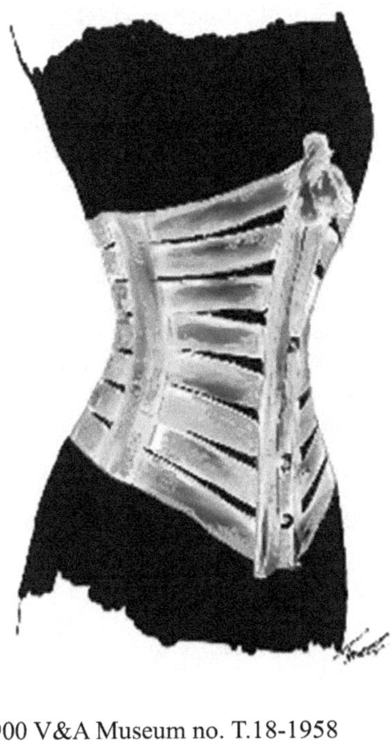

Figure 5.2 Corset 1900 V&A Museum no. T.18-1958

with 'fluid software technology'[16] which is noted for the ability to enhance performance.[17]

The term that has been developed by this thesis, through the analysis of fashion in the first few chapters,[18] is the notion of *tangible functionality*. This concept is developed through considerations relating to the functional aspects of fashion, which is considered as technical and therefore fundamentally useful. These aspects could be regarded as the technicality, which is derived from the whole garment, for example wearing a raincoat to shield from the weather. It could also relate to the aspects of fashion that are integrated features of a garment such as zips, buttons, ties, and belts. When considering the significance of tangible functionality to fashion, it is regarded as an integral part[19] and further the technical aspects of a design can be enhanced by the designer as a design feature. Therefore, functional aspects embody an element of creativity.

It is observed that function is an imperative consideration for the technicality of a garment and relates to problem solving by the designer.[20] The designer is observed to 'move between two forms of thinking: divergent (spreading out to explore a wide range of ideas and information) and convergent (narrowing in or focus attention on the most pertinent ideas and concepts).'[21] Therefore, the designer takes into consideration both the wider and more focused necessary considerations when designing, and it is noted that both *rational*[22] and *imaginative*[23] methods are employed, although the designer is said to alternate between both during the design process. We can hereby see that functionality is an integral part of Couture; it is not a separate component that sits outside of the garment, but one that is intertwined with the article through technical components. [The study will examine the approach of copyright law towards the two themes of fashion as it relates to creativity and function, and further whether the approach of the law is similar through all other IP rights outside of copyright.] With the tangible aspects of function examined, next an analysis of the notion of *intangible functionality* is provided.

16 Australian Fitness Academy, 'Technology in Sports Clothing: Do We Really Need It?' (*Australian Fitness Academy*, 26 October 2016) <https://www.fitnesseducation.edu.au/blog/industry-trends/technology-in-sports-clothing-do-we-really-need-it/> accessed 6 July 2021

17 Harvard University, 'The Rocket Swimsuit: Speedo's LZR Racer' (*Harvard University*, 15 September 2008) <https://sitn.hms.harvard.edu/flash/2008/issue47-2/> accessed 6 July 2021

18 Tomruk Űstűnkaya, 'The Functionality Doctrine: The Challenges to Fashion Copyright' (2020) 42(3) EIPR 156

19 Tomruk Űstűnkaya, 'The Functionality Doctrine: The Challenges to Fashion Copyright' (2020) 42(3) EIPR 156

20 Susan Watkins and Lucy Dunne, *Functional Clothing Design: From Sportswear to Spacesuits* (Bloomsbury 2015) 2

21 Susan Watkins and Lucy Dunne, *Functional Clothing Design: From Sportswear to Spacesuits* (Bloomsbury 2015) 2

22 *Susan Watkins and Lucy Dunne, Functional Clothing Design: From Sportswear to Spacesuits,(Bloomsbury 2015) 2*

23 *Susan Watkins and Lucy Dunne, Functional Clothing Design: From Sportswear to Spacesuits (Bloomsbury 2015) 2*

5.2.2 Intangible Functionality

Historically, the concept of fashion has been a tool in consideration of the functional element of the necessity of clothing, and it has also been culturally significant in how an individual can speak through their apparel. The idea of reading clothing[24] has been established as not being as easy as reading text, although cultural notions have been noted historically through art.[25] These relate to ideas such as beauty,[26] gender,[27] morality,[28] and power.[29]

Aesthetics were examined in chapter 3, particularly in relation to the concept of beauty.[30] As a recap, chapter 3 identified Rybczynski acknowledging fashion as a 'task of mating utility with beauty.'[31] This concept speaks to the notion of eye-appeal that fashion deploys, which is something that is considered in trade mark and design law.[32] However, whilst the notion of beauty is regarded as a matter of taste, the aesthetic appeal which is borne through the communicative aspect of Couture is a greater consideration as it relates to the intangible functionality of Couture. For example, chapter 3 evaluated the Dior show which appeared to communicate sociological and cultural changes; therefore the beauty (subjective notion) of the clothes contributed to the aesthetic impression provided which ultimately was rooted in the communicative significance of the Autumn/Winter 2022 collection.[33] These considerations lead to providing context for the study, particularly in this that Couture is utilised as means of expression for the purposes of communication. This also demonstrates a functional purpose; however, unlike the *tangible functionality* concept, the *intangible functionality* notion is also developed by this thesis and regarded as being set within an incorporeal context. The reason for this is because an intangible function is not necessarily something that can be held but one which exists through the utilisation of the garment for any other purpose other than the basic need for it. This is particularly significant for Couture, as Couture is not a concept derived from need as with other fashion/apparel articles. Is Couture being sold not only for its aesthetic appeal, but also for the value entrusted in Couture pertaining to the *intangible function*, such as communication?

Fashion is recognised as being a 'visual language,' although Barnard questions whether in fact 'emotions' and 'moods' which are stirred avoid explicit

24 Ingrid E Mida, *Reading Fashion in Art* (Bloomsbury 2020)

25 Ingrid E Mida, *Reading Fashion in Art* (Bloomsbury 2020)

26 Ingrid E Mida, *Reading Fashion in Art* (Bloomsbury 2020)

27 Ingrid E Mida, *Reading Fashion in Art* (Bloomsbury 2020)

28 Ingrid E Mida, *Reading Fashion in Art* (Bloomsbury 2020)

29 Ingrid E Mida, *Reading Fashion in Art* (Bloomsbury 2020)

30 Nanay Bence, *Aesthetics: A Very Short Introduction* (Oxford University Press 2019) 5

31 Louis Torres and Michelle Kamhi, *What Art Is the Esthetic Theory of Ayn Rand* (Open Court 2000) 294 Referring to Witold Rybczynski, "Gentlemen, Here Is the Winner," Review of Architectural Competitions, by Cees de Jong and Erik Mattie, Times Literary Supplement, 11 August 1995, 19

32 This concept is based in the consumer response to the product, which is essential for a successful design or trade mark which shall be distinctive

33 Ellecom, 'Dior's Couture Collection Wants to Bring Beauty to An Ugly World' (*Elle*, 4 July 2022) <https://www.elle.com/fashion/a40500543/dior-Couture-collection-fall-2022/> access ed 9 July 2022

interpretations.[34] Barnard expresses that the clothes worn are statements, although he goes further to analyse the 'nature' of the statements made through clothes. Considerations are also given to the clarity of purpose clothes provide, and the suggestive attributes of communication.[35] In the same line, Sapir identifies semiotics as playing a role in understanding fashion due to the 'unconscious symbolisms attaching to forms, colours, textures, postures, and other expressive elements of a given culture.'[36]

Upon analysis, clothes are part of communication, that may or may not be intended to be understood. On this basis, the purpose of the intangible function is fulfilled, although does this matter? Fashion is very much an extension of one's personality and malleable presence, and we change our perceptions and our attitudes as these may evolve over time. These changes are not only reflected upon through time, but in how we express ourselves through our clothing at any given period.

To explore this notion further we must consider historical works of art to understand what Couture is communicating, and the evolution of social attitudes as a response to fashion. For instance, Elisabeth Vigée Le Brun's portrait of Marie Antoinette in 1783 was the subject of controversy regarding the clothing adorning the Queen, due to being perceived as indecent.[37] In the portrait, the Queen was dressed in chemise *á la reine*, 'a loose- fitting chemise style gown,'[38] which she favoured for its 'comfort'[39] and 'simplicity.' The Queen's subjective view of her attire, we can assume, was more than likely quite far removed from how it was regarded by the public at that time. If we look at the portrait today, with today's social values, it may or may not still be regarded as indecent depending on a variety of subjective cultural influences and expectations.[40]

Likewise, in the late 1980s Jean Paul Gaultier was propelled into the limelight for his design of the corset worn by Madonna on her Blond Ambition tour. In 1987, the corset was initially presented on the catwalk[41] and adapted for Madonna's concert series in 1990, and later exhibited at the Barbican exhibition titled: From Sidewalk to Catwalk in 2014.[42] An extraordinary creative piece, gold in colour with a satin finish, the bust comprises of cones and a zip down the front centre, a tangible

34 Malcom Barnard and A Reader, *Fashion Theory* (2nd edn, Routledge 2020) 225

35 Malcom Barnard and A Reader, *Fashion Theory* (2nd edn, Routledge 2020) 226

36 Malcom Barnard and A Reader, *Fashion Theory* (2nd edn, Routledge 2020) 226

37 Ingrid E Mida, *Reading Fashion in Art* (Bloomsbury 2020)

38 Ingrid E Mida, *Reading Fashion in Art* (Bloomsbury 2020)

39 Ingrid E Mida, *Reading Fashion in Art* (Bloomsbury 2020)

40 For example, in western cultures today, most attire is acceptable, although there are appropriate forms of dress expected when visiting places of worship. In eastern cultures, the dress etiquette is much more restricted as it relates to showing skin

41 Liam Hess, 'The Story Behind Madonna's Iconic Jean Paul Gaultier Cone Bra' (*Vogue*, 18 April 2020) https://www.vogue.com/article/madonna-blonde-ambition-jean-paul-gaultier-cone-bra accessed 31 May 2021

42 Barbican, 'The Fashion World of Jean Paul Gaultier: From the Sidewalk to the Catwalk' (*barbican.org.uk*, 2014) <https://www.barbican.org.uk./whats-on/2014/event/the-fashion-world-of-jean-paul-gaultier> accessed 31 May 2021

functional purpose for ease of wearing. On the contrary, the belt can be considered as a decorative element, not necessarily for the tangible functionality such as the usual conventional use to assist in the fit of garments such as trousers, skirts, or dresses. Finally, the suspenders complete the garment,[43] although they were not in use for the conventional purpose of holding up stockings but left hanging. Therefore, the belt and suspenders served an intangible functional purpose. The costume has been described as iconic[44] and as 'one of the defining fashion statements of the decade,'[45] although shocking.[46] The costumes created for the tour were noted as fusing the connection between Couture and pop costumes.[47]

Upon deeper investigation and as documented here, it is apparent that the purpose of the function was one of communication, and this does not seem to be an inadvertent consequence of the creation, but a deliberate strategy for the corset to be a conduit to facilitate a dialogue with the audience, and communicate with the wider public at large. Although, if we are to analyse the expressive element of the clothing as communication, there are three elements we must evaluate. The first is, what was the intention of the designer as it relates to what he wanted to communicate? The second is, what did the artist/singer Madonna want to express? Lastly, how does the public view this iconic piece, and is it possible that the interpretation by the audience would differ when viewed at a different time? To address the designers' intention, the corset encapsulated a dual purpose, both femininity and masculinity, further that a woman can be viewed as seductive but also strong.[48] This was a successful collaboration between the artist Madonna and the designer, Gaultier. Gaultier expressed, 'She knew what she wanted. . . . Madonna likes my clothes because they combine the masculine and the feminine.'[49] In terms of addressing the public sentiment, as mentioned earlier, fashion is very much subject to the changes in society and is used as a vessel to communicate. We can therefore draw parallels

43 Liam Hess, 'The Story Behind Madonna's Iconic Jean Paul Gaultier Cone Bra' (*Vogue*, 18 April 2020) https://www.vogue.com/article/madonna-blonde-ambition-jean-paul-gaultier-cone-bra accessed 31 May 2021

44 Sam Rogers, 'Madonna's Most Sensational Stage Costumes' (*Vogue*, 3 May 2019) <https://www.vogue.co.uk/gallery/madonna-tour-outfits> accessed 6 July 2021

45 Michel Linssen Redferns, 'How Madonna's Blond Ambition Tour Changed Pop Concerts Forever' (*Madonna Underground*, 17 April 2020) <https://madonnaunderground.com/how-madonnas-blond-ambition-tour-changed-pop-concerts-forever/> accessed 6 July 2021

46 Lauren Alexis Fisher, '40 Times Madonna Shocked Us All With Her Outfit' (*Harpers Bazaar*, 5 August 2019) <https://www.harpersbazaar.com/celebrity/red-carpet-dresses/g7709/madonna-most-shocking-outfits/> accessed 6 July 2021

47 Drew Mackie, '25 Reasons Madonna's Blond Ambition Tour Still Rules, 25 Years Later' (*People*, 13 April 2015) <https://people.com/celebrity/madonnas-blond-ambition-tour-25-years-later/> accessed 6 July 2021

48 Boy Culture, 'Jean Paul Gaultier on His Use of Corsets: Madonna, Masculinity, Femininity' (*YouTube*, 25 October 2013) <https://m.youtube.com/watch?v=4yJgt8aBo8o> accessed 27 May 2021

49 Liam Hess, 'The Story Behind Madonna's Iconic Jean Paul Gaultier Cone Bra' (*Vogue*, 18 April 2020) https://www.vogue.com/article/madonna-blonde-ambition-jean-paul-gaultier-cone-bra accessed 31 May 2021

between the 1783 Elisabeth Vigée Le Brun painting of Marie Antoinette and the Madonna corset (in relation to the shocking nature of the images, at the time of publication).[50]

The tangible and intangible function of apparel appears to be an integral and significant part of fashion. These observations therefore form the basis and build on the argument of both tangible and intangible functionality as being an integral part of fashion and an inseparable vital element.[51] On this basis, it is clear to see how the concept of Couture sits somewhere in between the practical considerations and creative pursuits.

5.3 Functionality: Considerations of Technical Components for Couture

Functionality of fashion is observed to be derived from technical elements. For example, this could be the front opening panel of a blouse embellished with fastenings such as buttons, a zip, or ties. By creating the opening panel, the creative and artistic components of the garment must work in unison to fulfil both requirements. This is the main concern of this thesis as this inherent functionality of the design seems to exclude the work from obtaining copyright. To elaborate, are the technical components inclusive of, and adding to, the artistic quality of the work? The matter is addressed because the functional components may not necessarily be used within the garment for their original purpose, such as pockets to hold items and buttons for fastenings, but these so-called functional components may in fact only be a design feature. A further question would be, what if the functional component of the garment whilst serving its function has a dual purpose as a design feature, such as the mechanisms of corsetry? The 'white cotton camisole corset cover with a cross-boned front creating a monobosom silhouette . . . cotton over a wire framework' by Spirella is an example of technical components (the boning, designed and set within the garment in such a way as to provide structure and form) being entwined with the artistic element of fashion (the creative design process).[52] Equally, another example is the *La Ligne Sinueuse* dress by Christian Dior. The dress 'is assembled with a municipality of buttons and tiny snap fasteners,' consequently, the fastenings and buttons form and contribute to the design of the dress, and are not entirely and primarily functional in nature.[53] These elements of entwinement cannot be separated conceptually within a fashion garment and therefore, to separate them in law appears contradictory to the nature of fashion.

50 Ingrid E Mida, *Reading Fashion in Art* (Bloomsbury 2020)

51 Tomruk Űstűnkaya, 'The Functionality Doctrine: The Challenges to Fashion Copyright' (2020) 42(3) EIPR 156

52 Spirella, 'Corset Cover' (*V&A*, 21 November 2007) <https://collections.vam.ac.uk./item/O140747/corset-cover-spirella/> accessed 22 May 2022

53 Christian Dior, 'La Ligne Sinueuse' (*V&A*, 2007) <https://collections.vam.ac.uk./item/O120852/la-ligne-sinueuse-day-dress-christian-dior/> accessed 22 May 2022

5.4 Copyright

Chapter 4 discusses the aspect of the originality criteria, and we can see the doctrine of functionality in copyright is exercised through E.U. case law in *BSA*[54] and *SAS Institute v World Programming*. Further developments in E.U. law are considered in chapter 6.[55] However, for now, the discussion on copyright continues by considering copyright in relation to the technical components of Couture, beginning with an analysis of the case *Interlego v Tyco Industries*, in the following section.

5.4.1 Interlego v Tyco Industries

Technicality which dictates function is a major consideration in copyright law, as seen in the significant deliberation of the Privy Council in the case of *Interlego*. *Interlego*, a toy manufacturer of interlocking building blocks, brought an infringement claim against Tyco who also started to manufacture interlocking blocks. The blocks created by Interlego, were a larger version (produced for younger children) of the original Lego bricks. The drawings produced in 1973 were created from earlier drawings and the design drawings, facilitated the manufacture of both of the building block types. The manufacture by the defendants, of the indirect copied blocks led to Interlego seeking an injunction against the defendants to restrict the infringement of their copyright in Hong Kong. Although the injunction was granted, the defendants were allowed a partial appeal[56] Interlego was capable of design registration protection prior to 1973 under section 10 of the CDPA 1956. Lord Oliver stated that 'only certain kinds of skill, labour and judgment confer originality.'[57] Further, Lord Oliver expressed that 'copying . . . however much skill or labour may be devoted to the process, cannot make a work original.'[58] The Privy Council held that the alterations were acknowledged as being 'technically' important, however the alterations were not found to be visually substantial and therefore the drawings were not held to be original.[59] A significant observation by Bentley et al is that the decisions relating to the technical alterations could not have been deemed as creative due to functionality dictating the intellectual choices of

54 *Bezpečnostni softwarová asociace, Case C-393/09 [2011] ECR I-13,971, [49]*

55 *SAS Institute Inc v World Programming Ltd, Case C-406/10 [2012] 3 C|MLR (4) 55,68, [AG44] (AG Bot). In recent developments, the case of Cofemel may have inadvertently softened the application through a shift in legal perspective when assessing copyright works in relation to exercising the concept of the author's own intellectual creative expression, a key consideration at the forefront of any copyright evaluations (please see chapter 6)*

56 *Interlego v Tyco Industries* [1987] F.S.R. 409 and L Bentley and others, *Intellectual Property Law* (6th edn, Oxford University Press 2022) 115

57 *Interlego v Tyco Industries* [1987] F.S.R. 409 and L Bentley and others, *Intellectual Property Law* (6th edn, Oxford University Press 2022) 105

58 *Interlego v Tyco Industries* [1987] F.S.R. 409 and L Bentley and others, *Intellectual Property Law* (6th edn, Oxford University Press 2022) 105

59 *Interlego v Tyco Industries* [1987] F.S.R. 409 and L Bentley and others, *Intellectual Property Law* (6th edn, Oxford University Press 2022) 115

the designer, and thus curbing creative freedom.[60] When applied to Couture, the discussion is significant as to satisfy originality requirements and to attain the grant of copyright protection, the work must be original, however, in *Interlego* the law appears to have not provided any scope for the constraints of essential functionality requirements necessary to achieve the desired result, a functional work.

5.4.2 Separability and Unity

The separability doctrine of the U.S. is explored through the scholarly work of Keyes, discussed later in this section.[61] Separability is a U.S. doctrine that interlinks both industrial design and applied art, and on the other hand interlinks fashion design, as it applies to many products concerning the daily life of individuals.[62] Separability operates in copyright to distinguish the functional part of a work from the aesthetic.[63] Correspondingly, the concept of *unity* of art is explained by Guven as taking 'different forms' when distinguishing between fine arts and applied arts.[64] This notion specifically addresses the approach Germany takes towards the arts as one being focused on industry, unlike the French perspective which aims to preserve the craft custom rooted in the medieval era.[65]

Significant is that the *Werkbund*[66] is noted as being related to Germany's attempts to promote, standardise, and establish primacy over the international design sphere.[67] Further, the most notable point is that it appears that Germany was concerned with design, and this is identified in Germany's preference for a modernist style that turned away from an intricate ornamental character of works.[68] On the contrary, the French approach was clearly from the perspective of categorising *art*, as until 18th century, France had not differentiated between art and craft. This distinction only transpired following the founding of art institutions.[69] The

60 *Interlego v Tyco Industries* [1987] F.S.R. 409 and L Bentley and others, *Intellectual Property Law* (6th edn, Oxford University Press 2022) 115

61 Barton Keyes, 'Alive and Well: The (Still) Ongoing Debate Surrounding Conceptual Separability in American Copyright Law' (2008) Ohio State Journal

62 Barton Keyes, 'Alive and Well: The (Still) Ongoing Debate Surrounding Conceptual Separability in American Copyright Law' (2008) Ohio State Journal referring to Mark A LoBello, 'The Dichotomy Between Artistic Expression and Industrial Design: To Protect or Not to Protect' (1992) 13 Whittier Law Review 107; Jennifer Mencken, 'A Design for the Copyright of Fashion' (1997) Intellectual Property and Technology Law Section 121291

63 *Star Athletica v Varsity Brands Inc* 799 F.3d 468 (2015) (6th Cir (US))

64 Koray Gűven, 'Unities of Art: Reconciling Function and Copyright' (2021) 52(9) IIC 1161–89

65 Koray Gűven, 'Unities of Art: Reconciling Function and Copyright' (2021) 52(9) IIC 1161–89

66 *A German art movement where the purpose was to integrate design and craftmanship into manufactured objects*

67 Koray Gűven, 'Unities of Art: Reconciling Function and Copyright' (2021) 52(9) IIC 1161–89 referring to Sparke (2013) 60 and Muthesius and Van de Velde (2010) 101

68 Koray Gűven, 'Unities of Art: Reconciling Function and Copyright' (2021) 52(9) IIC 1161–89 referring to Maciuika (2011) 98–101

69 Koray Gűven, 'Unities of Art: Reconciling Function and Copyright' (2021) 52(9) IIC 1161–89 referring to Shiner (2001) 5, 34–42, 90–97; Barnard (1998) 59–64

French approach at the turn of the 19th century was steeped in decorative style.[70] These observations clarify the perspective of Germany as being one concerned with design and France's position effectively connected to art. The notion of unity appears to have been borne through the acknowledgement of the artistic value in industrial products. In deeper analysis, the principal objective of the unity concept appears to be rooted in art and not industry, as the art verifies the industrial object by dictating the purpose of the industrial object.

To apply the unity concept to Couture, it is necessary to ascertain the extent to which Couture is industrial in nature and further, the extent to which this issue matters. Chapter 3, the heart of this thesis, attempts to provide a rationale in defining Couture as a conceptual work of art in law. For this reason, the study is more aligned with the French concept of unity of art which has a focus on craft, instead of the German perspective focusing on industry.[71] The theory of unity[72] identifies and establishes that the functional component may provide part of the appearance, and therefore part of the aesthetic.[73]

The aspect of function being a fundamental characteristic of the German approach is significant.[74] This viewpoint has been termed as the 'holistic' approach, which considers the contribution of non-functional components and suggests that this should be introduced into the copyright standard to replace the current prevention of copyright protection for works whereby function occupies part of the appearance.[75] In consideration of the *unity* concept, an inference can be drawn that art, function, and industry are inseparable. However, in line with the nuanced approach, the thesis would argue that the extent and perspective of how creativity is engaged with is significant. This provides for the character of the work and further assists in categorising industrial works as art or design. To gain perspective on the objectives of this thesis, and to appreciate Couture, it is important to distinguish Couture as art. This is quite divergent from a design work, which is most concerned with the functional attributes of the work, and whereby functionality aligns more closely with market and industrial concerns, most akin to the perspective unity Germany takes.

Keyes references a significant quote by Judge Oakes from the case of *Bandir International*, which describes separability as 'alive and well.'[76] In this case, it was held that where functional and aesthetic factors exist in unison, the artistic components were not deemed as being 'conceptually separable from the

70 Koray Gűven, 'Unities of Art: Reconciling Function and Copyright' (2021) 52(9) IIC 1161–89 referring to Sparke (2013) 61, 62

71 Koray Gűven, 'Unities of Art: Reconciling Function and Copyright' (2021) 52(9) IIC 1161–89

72 Koray Gűven, 'Unities of Art: Reconciling Function and Copyright' (2021) 52(9) IIC 1161–89

73 Koray Gűven, 'Unities of Art: Reconciling Function and Copyright' (2021) 52(9) IIC 1161–89

74 Koray Gűven, 'Unities of Art: Reconciling Function and Copyright' (2021) 52(9) IIC 1161–89

75 Koray Gűven, 'Unities of Art: Reconciling Function and Copyright' (2021) 52(9) IIC 1161–89

76 Barton Keyes, 'Alive and Well: The (Still) Ongoing Debate Surrounding Conceptual Separability in American Copyright Law' (2008*) Ohio State Journal and Brandir Int'l, Inc. v Cascade Pacific Lumber Co.*, 834 F.2d 1142, 1144 (2d Cir. 1987) (noting that conceptual separability is "alive and well" in the Second Circuit)

utilitarian elements.'[77] However, in the case of *Varsity Brands v Star Athletica*, separability exists where the designer's artistry is executed independently of technical considerations.[78]

Keyes, however, identifies an inadequacy of the varying application of the conceptual separability test.[79] Keyes refers to the decision in *Bandir International* and suggests: firstly, the test should identify the extent to which the designer is influenced by aesthetics compared with functional considerations; and secondly, it is necessary to recognise the degree to which utilitarian function is directed by the design. The rationale for the test Keyes proposes concerns engaging the subjective and objective principles to establish separability considerations.[80] Keyes also analyses the test adopted in *Galiano*, *Pivot Point*, *Kieselstein-Cord*, and *Goldstein*. By doing so, Keyes identifies the expansion of the test for the purpose of granting protection to works that comprise separable components by making copyright more predictable.[81] On this basis, Keyes suggests that the test therefore establishes the equilibrium essential to encouraging designers to create useful products driven by aesthetic impetus. Finally, Keyes expresses that this model will be beneficial to the public as it relates to the designs and makes available a more expansive choice in useful products.[82]

5.5 Considering the Wider IP Framework in Relation to the Implications of Technical Function for Copyright

This section of the study examines the wider IP framework in relation to the functionality doctrine specifically. The analysis will evaluate the extent to which functionality is a feature of the various IP rights, namely: Patents, trade marks, and design rights and whether it plays or should play a role in copyright.

5.5.1 Patents

Patents unify 'technical, commercial, and legal documents.'[83] It is the aspect of a patent being 'technical' which is significant to the analysis, as a patent is functional. Therefore, the functionality doctrine to be used as a form of protection does

77 Barton Keyes, 'Alive and Well: The (Still) Ongoing Debate Surrounding Conceptual Separability in American Copyright Law' (2008) Ohio State Journal

78 Barton Keyes, 'Alive and Well: The (Still) Ongoing Debate Surrounding Conceptual Separability in American Copyright Law' (2008) Ohio State Journal

79 Barton Keyes, 'Alive and Well: The (Still) Ongoing Debate Surrounding Conceptual Separability in American Copyright Law' (2008) Ohio State Journal

80 Barton Keyes, 'Alive and Well: The (Still) Ongoing Debate Surrounding Conceptual Separability in American Copyright Law' (2008) Ohio State Journal

81 Barton Keyes, 'Alive and Well: The (Still) Ongoing Debate Surrounding Conceptual Separability in American Copyright Law' (2008) Ohio State Journal
Referring to Galiano, 416 F.3d and Pivot Point, 372 F.3d and *Kieselstein-Cord v Accessories by Pearl, Inc.*, 632 F.2d 989 (2d Cir. 1980) and Paul Goldstein, Copyright: Principles, Law and Practice 99 (1989)

82 Barton Keyes, 'Alive and Well: The (Still) Ongoing Debate Surrounding Conceptual Separability in American Copyright Law' (2008) Ohio State Journal

83 L Bentley and others, *Intellectual Property Law* (6th edn, Oxford University Press 2022) 390

not apply to patents. The Patents Act 1977 s.1(2) explicitly states the exclusion of artistic works. Couture articles have previously been considered as artistic works which can influence the industrially mass-produced market.[84]

Additionally, artistry is argued as being an essential element of the product development process for fashion.[85] It is this point that is significant to this study based on the aforementioned developments in copyright law.[86] The reason this is significant to patents is because, if copyright law can practically develop the extent of application of the functionality doctrine to be expanded and applied to creative objects of technical character, why would patents not do the same for artistic works?

5.5.2 Trade Marks

The functionality doctrine is apparent in the Trade Marks Act 1994 s.3(2)(b) which states 'A sign shall not be registered as a trade mark if it consists exclusively of (b) the shape (or another characteristic) of goods which is necessary to obtain a technical result.'[87] The rationale for the trade marks technicality exclusion from the E.U. law perspective can be understood through the English case of *Philips*.[88] This case was for infringement proceedings regarding the three-headed rotary shaver whereby Philips had registered a trade mark for the appliance pursuant to the Trade Marks Act 1938.[89] In the first proceedings, the mark was held to be invalid due to not being regarded as distinguished (Article 3(1)(a)) and, was not regarded as having distinctive character (Article 3(1)(b)), and in addition consisted of a shape relevant to obtaining a technical result (Article 3(1)(e)) pursuant to the Council Directive 89/104/EC.[90] Questions were referred by the Court of Appeal to the E.U. court (CJEU) regarding the interpretation of various provisions under Article 3(1). The E.U. interpretation is:

1. There is no category of marks which is not excluded from registration by Article 3(1)(b), (c) and (d) and Article 3(3) of First Council Directive 89/104/EEC of 21 December 1988.
2. For the purposes of establishing a distinguishing article for the purposes of Article 2, the sign is not required to have 'embellishment which has no functional purpose.'

84 Tomruk Űstűnkaya, 'Fashion Law: The Limitation Conundrum of the Patents Act 1977' (2020) 42(10) EIPR 621

85 Tomruk Űstűnkaya, 'Fashion Law: The Limitation Conundrum of the Patents Act 1977' (2020) 42(10) EIPR 621

86 Please see: *Cofemel v G-Star Raw CV* (C-683/17) AG3 and *Brompton Bicycle Ltd v Chedech/Get-2Get* (C-833/18), Opinion of Advocate General M. Campos Sánchez-Bordona, E.U:C:2020:79

87 The Trade Marks Act 1994 s.3(2)(b)

88 *Philips v Remington* [2002] ECR Case C-299/99 and Antoon Quaedvlieg, *Shapes with a technical function: an ever-expanding exclusion?(2016) ERA*

89 *Philips v Remington* [2002] ECR Case C-299/99

90 *Philips v Remington* [2002] ECR Case C-299/99

3. Where a sign has been in extensive use, by a trader who is the only supplier of those goods, whereby the sign comprises of shape, distinctive character can be established for the purposes of Article 3(3) of Directive 89/104. It is for the national courts to determine the circumstances for which the requirement is satisfied.
4. Where a sign comprises wholly of the shape, it will be unregistrable by virtue of Article 3(1)(e).

The U.K. Supreme Court ruled that justifications for the technicality exclusion should essentially be linked to an 'anti-monopoly rationale . . . to be interpreted as one allowing freedom of choice for competitors.'[91] The court expressed that limitations on choice for 'technical solutions' are noted to be an encumbrance for competitors and therefore the extent of Article 3(1)(e) is understood to be for the purposes of preventing protection available by going beyond the scope of signs in distinguishing between competitive brands.[92] This point was established through the application of *Windsurfing*[93] which essentially makes a point in the public interest regarding a sign consisting of a shape 'whose essential characteristics perform a technical function and were chosen to fulfil that function may be freely used by all.'[94] This point is significant as the judgement makes the distinct statement outlining the *intention* of Article 3(1)(e), in relation to a bar on competition, therefore, a monopoly consideration for 'technical solutions.'[95] However, is this point regarding the *intention* dependent on the interpretation of the provision? This is considered here due to developments in trade mark law, as discussed in the following.

Recent developments would suggest that the application of a trade mark to shape *exclusively* has been challenged in the landmark case of *Louboutin.*[96] *Louboutin* provides for a pivotal shift in how E.U. law approaches the issue of technicality in whereby it was established that a sign consisting of a colour (comprised of shape) was capable of registration as a trade mark. This was founded due to the instrumental use of the word *exclusively* within the interpretation by the CJEU of Article 3(1)(e)(iii) of Directive 2008/95.[97] Here it was determined that the colour of the sole of the shoe did not consist exclusively of a shape,[98] which is further noted as bypassing the limitation of the functionality doctrine, as essentially, the question the court focused on was the registration of a colour mark and not the shape.[99] The word *exclusively* is viewed as having substance as it relates to

91 Antoon Quaedvlieg, 'Shapes With a Technical Function: An Ever-Expanding Exclusion?' (2016) ERA

92 *Philips v Remington* [2002] ECR Case C-299/99 and Antoon Quaedvlieg, 'Shapes With a Technical Function: An Ever-Expanding Exclusion?' (2016) ERA

93 *Windsurfing v Chiemsee [1999] ECR at para 25 Cases 108/97*

94 *Philips v Remington* [2002] ECR at para 80 Case C-299/99

95 *Philips v Remington* [2002] ECR at para 80 Case C-299/99

96 *Louboutin v Van Haren Schoenen BV Case C-163/16*

97 *Louboutin v Van Haren Schoenen* BV Case C-163/16

98 *Louboutin v Van Haren Schoenen* BV Case C-163/16

99 Lavinia Brancusi, 'Trade marks "Functionality" in E.U. Law: Expected New Trends After the Louboutin Case' (2019) 41(2) EIPR 98 and Ilanah Fhima, 'Technical Functionality in European Trade Mark Law' (2021) 137 LQR 113

the test on functionality, and it is observed that the trade mark circumvented the functionality exclusions owing to the description and registration of the mark not pertaining to shape.[100] Fhima argues that the word *exclusively* enables hybrid signs to bypass the technical functionality exclusion, thus, to therefore be capable of registration.[101] In consideration of trade mark law, Fhima further argues that the use of the word *exclusively* would 'undermine' the 'channelling' policy for the purposes of exclusion. On this basis, the notion of the word *exclusively* as it relates to fashion and the functional component could theoretically come under some criticism when considering Fhima's argument as it relates to trade mark law, which may in pragmatic terms enable fashion to circumvent the technicality exclusions based on functionality.

The CJEU stated:

> [t]he shape of the product or of a part of the product plays a role in creating an outline for the colour, it cannot, however, be held that a sign consists of that shape in the case where the registration of the mark did not seek to protect that shape but sought solely to protect the application of a colour to a specific part of that product. . . . Article 3(1)(e)(iii) of Directive 2008/95 must be interpreted as meaning that a sign consisting of a colour applied to the sole of a high-heeled shoe . . . does not consist exclusively of a 'shape,' within the meaning of that provision.[102]

The concept of 'characteristic' as understood by the Advocate General is 'part or an element of the goods.'[103] Deliberated is whether graphics or words attached to the shape can be recognised as a component of the product, and the scope of functional exclusions as being limited in relation to the graphical representations.[104] In consideration of both two-dimensional and three-dimensional marks, trade marks facilitate a strong brand identity within the marketplace for Couture (as seen with the red sole in the *Louboutin* case) and can therefore provide a protective mechanism for Couture through the branding concept.[105]

The developments in law relating to the approach to 'technicality,' and therefore the intention of law makers placing a bar for technical components on products, are understood to be rooted in the public interest. However, it is apparent that the shape of a product is dependent on the interpretation by the law as to whether it will be regarded as a shape performing a technical function. This is significant for fashion designers as it essentially enables innovative creativity to be engaged with by the designer for the purposes of enhancing a particular feature, which incorporates the technical element but is not exclusive of it.

100 Lavinia Brancusi, 'Trade Marks "Functionality" in E.U. Law: Expected New Trends After the Louboutin Case' (2019) 41(2) EIPR 98

101 Ilanah Fhima, 'Technical Functionality in European Trade Mark Law' (2021) 137 LQR 113

102 *Louboutin v Van Haren Schoenen BV* Case C-163/16

103 Opinion of AG Maciej Szpunar in *Louboutin v Van Haren* E.U:C:2018:64 at [23], [30]

104 Dr Lavinia Brancusi, 'Trade Marks "Functionality" in European Law: Expected New Trends After the Louboutin Case' (2019) 41(2) EIPR 98

105 *Louboutin v Van Haren Schoenen BV* Case C-163/16

For the purposes of ascertaining a deeper understanding of copyright law and the implications on Couture, it is necessary to observe developments in trade mark law, particularly seen in recent developments between the *Windsurfing* and the *Phillips* cases, in comparison to the recent *Louboutin* decision. These developments are observed from the perspective of this thesis as recognising the limiting nature of the technicality exclusions in trade mark law. To extend this notion further, the limitation is perceived as an unnecessary blanket restriction when applied to fashion Couture. This is on the basis that Couture is regarded as employing particularly creative endeavours, however the risk of innovative designs being perceived as incorporating standard technical components is that they could still potentially (unless the approach of the court is that reminiscent of the *Louboutin* decision) be regarded as being unable to acquire trade mark protection, should the *Windsurfing* or *Phillips* cases be applied.[106]

5.5.3 Design Rights

Design rights are concerned with the appearance and shape of manufactured products.[107] Exclusions to a registered design right are implemented on the basis of: 'A right in a registered design shall not subsist in features of appearance of a product which are solely dictated by the product's *technical* function' [emphasis added].[108]

The definition of design is limited by the RDA 1949 when:

> A right in a registered design shall not subsist in features of appearance of a product which are solely dictated by the product's technical function.[109]

In relation to the Community Design Right, Article 8(1) of the Community Design Right states:

> A Community design shall not subsist in features of appearance of a product which are solely dictated by its *technical* function. [emphasis added][110]

Analysis on Article 8(1) reflects on the provision as necessitating an independent approach, specifically as it relates to 'the possibility of conferring protection on designs deprived of any "aesthetic quality," as is expressly set out in *Recital 10(2) CDR*.'[111] The *Lindner* case outlines that a design which is purely aesthetic would conflict with this provision and conveyed that the purpose of the test is establishing the character of the functional features and additionally reflected on the aspect

106 *Philips v Remington* [2002] ECR at para 78 Case C-299/99, *Windsurfing v Chiemsee* [1999] ECR Cases 108/97 at para 25 and *Louboutin v Van Haren Schoenen* BV Case C-163/16

107 Judith Embley, Keir Bamford and Nick Hancock, *Commercial and Intellectual Property Law and Practice* (CLP 2021) 702

108 Registered Designs Act 1949, s 1(c)(1)

109 Registered Designs Act 1949, s 1(c)(1)

110 Art 8(1) CDR

111 Dr Lavinia Brancusi, 'Designs Determined by the Product's Technical Function: Arguments for an Autonomous Test' (2016) 38(1) EIPR 23

of 'anything other than purely functional.'[112] The decision in *Austretherm v Termo Organika*[113] aligns with the decision in *Lindner*[114] in consideration of the extent to which Article 8(1) applies was expressed as 'the design will be only invalid as a whole, if all of the essential features of the appearance of the product were solely dictated by its technical function.'[115] Here, the decision appears to indirectly recognise other attributes as an inclusive part of design as it relates to the 'appearance.'[116]

The technical attributes of a design have been perceived as establishing a legal argument due to the risk of providing a monopoly right over functional design features.[117] It is noted that before the E.U. legislation was in place, a large body of case law placed a bar on design rights conferred over functional features, similar to the approach of trade mark law. The purpose of the E.U. approach was to harmonise the distinction as it relates to aesthetic and utilitarian designs.[118] The harmonised approach was tested in relation to technical functionality pursuant to Article 8(1) by the German Court of Appeal in the case of *DOCERAM*, explained as follows.

The case of *DOCERAM* concerned a dispute relating to pins for welding, for three differing geometric forms.[119] The case was between DOCERAM GmbH (claimant) and Ceram Tec (defendant), who is the manufacturer of 'ceramic centring pins' in identical variants.[120] The court of first instance referred the case to the Court of Appeal of Dusseldorf. The main issue for the court was whether technical functionality established the product design. The issues for consideration were whether the design is completely dictated by its technical function pursuant to Article 8(1). Additionally, on the basis that it is, if the product is chosen regarding functionality, whether an 'objective observer' is needed and how would the 'objective observer' be determined.

112 Dr Lavinia Brancusi, 'Designs Determined by the Product's Technical Function: Arguments for an Autonomous Test' (2016) 38(1) EIPR 23 *and Lindner* (R-690/2007-3), 22 October 2009 at [42]

113 *Austretherm v Termo Organika, Case R 998/2013-3*

114 *Lindner (R-690/2007-3), 22 October 2009 at [42]*

115 *Austretherm v Termo Organika*, Case R 998/2013-3

116 *Austretherm v Termo Organika*, Case R 998/2013-3

117 Please see: *Austretherm v Termo Organika*, Case R 998/2013-3 and Lavinia Brancusi, 'Designs Determined by the Product's Technical Function: Arguments for an Autonomous Test' (2016) 38(1) EIPR 23

118 Lavinia Brancusi, 'Designs Determined by the Product's Technical Function: Arguments for an Autonomous Test' (2016) 38(1) EIPR 23 referring G Hasselblatt (ed.), *Community Design Regulation: A Commentary* (C.H. Beck 2015), art.1, para. 19, 11 and art. 3, para. 30, 35; M Franzosi, 'Commentary' in M Franzosi (ed), *European Union Design Protection: Commentary to the Directive and Regulation Proposals* (Springer 1995) 39–45

119 Meyer-Dulheuer MD Legal Patentanwalte Partg MB, 'Technical Function Determines the Design: Exclusion From IP rights?' (*Patent-Und Rechtsanwaltskanzlei*, 8 March 2018) <https://legal-patent.com/design-law-en/technical-function-determines-design-exclusion-ip-rights/> accessed 14 June 2022

120 Meyer-Dulheuer MD Legal Patentanwalte Partg MB, 'Technical Function Determines the Design: Exclusion From IP Rights?' (*Patent-Und Rechtsanwaltskanzlei*, 8 March 2018) <https://legal-patent.com/design-law-en/technical-function-determines-design-exclusion-ip-rights/> accessed 14 June 2022

The CJEU focused on the approach of the German courts to determine the extent to which the design was impacted by its technical features.[121] The usual approach applied by Germany in determining whether the design is dictated by its technical features was the 'multiplicity of forms' test. This establishes that should a different design be capable of the same function, the design is not completely dictated by its technical function. In this instance, the CJEU applied the 'no-aesthetic test.' In applying the test, the court must consider whether only technical features provided the design for the product or whether the design was realised through other aesthetic contributions, which would determine whether the design was/was not wholly dictated by its technical function.

When applied to Couture fashion, to ascertain whether the characteristics related to the appearance of the garment are solely dictated by the technical function, it is necessary to establish that the design of the garment is founded on those technical characteristics alone.[122] This may cause some disruption to Couture, the reason being that the subject of technical characteristics which enable function is at times the subject of the garment. For example, earlier the white cotton camisole corset by Spirella was highlighted to illustrate the unison of technicality and artistic components, however, the garment highlights the difficulty of the *DOCERAM* ruling in that the whole garment is dictated by its technical function. We can also see the same in the Portrait Corset, in the Spring/Summer collection from Vivienne Westwood.[123] The purpose of the garment is to enhance the torso shape; therefore, the garment design is dictated by its technical function, the appearance of the garment is founded solely on the technical characteristics. Without the technical characteristics, the garment could not be defined as a corset. The artistry of Couture must, therefore, be working in conjunction with technicality, as whilst a Couture creation is ultimately an artistic work, it cannot exist without the implementation of technical aspects.

Church et al[124] present an empirical analysis of the design case law of the E.U. Member States, as it relates to the Design Directive and Design Regulation.[125] The purpose of the analysis was to investigate the litigation and provide an analysis of

121 Bird and Bird, 'The CJEU DOCERAM Case: When is a Product Feature Solely Dictated by Its Technical Functionality Such That It Cannot Be Protected as a Community Design?' (*Bird and Bird*, 8 March 2018) <https://www.twobirds.com/en/insights/2018/U.K./CJEU-Doceram-case> accessed 14 June 2022

122 Referring to Bird and Bird, 'The CJEU DOCERAM Case: When is a Product Feature Solely Dictated by Its Technical Functionality Such That It Cannot Be Protected as a Community Design?' (*Bird and Bird*, 8 March 2018) <https://www.twobirds.com/en/insights/2018/U.K./CJEU-Doceram-case > accessed 14 June 2022

123 Vivienne Westwood, 'Portrait Corset' (*Vivienne Westwood*, 2022) <https://www.viviennewestwood.com/en/women/clothing/corsets/portrait-corset-multicoloured-15030001W003VO207.html> accessed 14 June 2022

124 Oliver Church, Estelle Derclaye and Gilles Stupfler, 'An Empirical Analysis of the Design Case Law of the E.U. Member States'(2019) 50(6) IIC 685

125 Directive 98/71/EC of 13 October 1998 on the legal protection of designs, OJ L289/28, 28 October 1998; Regulation 6/2002 of 12 December 2001 on Community designs, OJ L3/1, 5 January 2002

the decisions, taking specifically into consideration the differences in interpretation pertaining to different factors such as 'country, specialisation of the judge, and level of court.'[126] The paper presents findings pertaining to case law for 2D and 3D designs in respect of registered and unregistered designs and distinguishes between the prevalence for litigation between each. The paper goes further and extends the trajectory of design case law, specifically as it relates to infringement and invalidity.[127] It could not be confirmed that 3D designs would be found invalid more than 2D designs due to the functional component. The most likely reason for this is stated as designers/companies are careful to register only those designs they think are valid.'[128] This is significant as it indicates that the design rights legislation may in fact have the potential to 'control' the functional elements of designs to such an extent that designers/companies shall not even attempt to validate designs legally by registration due to the impact of the technical exclusions.

To elaborate on the discussion further, whilst *artistic craftmanship* is identified by this book as being comprised within Couture, the preceding discussion establishes that Couture is also comprised of a second element which is *design*. However, an artistic work is not determined by either one in isolation.

Interim Conclusion

The interim conclusions that follow specifically address the relationship between economic considerations and art and highlight the disconnect between the unity concept and the functionality doctrine.

Based on the definition of a doctrine,[129] the perspective of the thesis is that doctrines are flexible in nature and established on written and unwritten principles. The doctrine of functionality permeates through IP legislation and case law. In copyright, in consideration of originality, the functionality doctrine becomes challenging for Couture when the design of the garment incorporates and is essentially dictated by the technical characteristics.[130] In fact, from the perspective of this thesis, Couture could be defined by the functional characteristics in its entirety. Without the technical function, the garment would not operate and therefore could not be in existence. It is the creative component, the artistic attributes which entwine with the technical components – often skills deployed through the couturier's creative expression – which provide for the aesthetic appeal of the garment.

126 Oliver Church, Estelle Derclaye and Gilles Stupfler, 'An Empirical Analysis of the Design Case Law of the E.U. Member States' (2019) 50(6) IIC 685

127 Oliver Church, Estelle Derclaye and Gilles Stupfler, 'An Empirical Analysis of the Design Case Law of the E.U. Member States' (2019) 50(6) IIC 685

128 Oliver Church, Estelle Derclaye and Gilles Stupfler, 'An Empirical Analysis of the Design Case Law of the E.U. Member States' (2019) 50(6) IIC 685 as it relates to: Hypothesis 11 is confirmed: The proportion of designs found valid by courts does not depend on their dimension

129 Pierre Schlag and Amy J Griffin, *How to Do Things With Legal Doctrine* (University Chicago Press 2020) 10

130 L Bentley and others, *Intellectual Property Law* (6th edn, Oxford University Press 2022) 100

Figure 5.3 1925 Silk Satin Lace Silk Ribbon and Crystal Beads – Collection of Phoenix Art Museum – Chanel Exhibition V&A 2023

The recognition of the study regarding the notion of separation by law of the functional and artistic qualities of Couture leads to considerations of the concepts put forward by the U.S. author, Keyes, as it is recognised that developments in this area of IP law are seemingly reflective in the U.S., U.K., and E.U.[131] When considering the observations by Keyes and the decision in *Star Athletica*, the

131 Barton Keyes, 'Alive and Well: The (Still) Ongoing Debate Surrounding Conceptual Separability in American Copyright Law' (2008) Ohio State Journal referring to Mark A LoBello, 'The Dichotomy Between Artistic Expression and Industrial Design: To Protect or Not to Protect' (1992) 13 Whittier Law Review 107; Jennifer Mencken, 'A Design for the Copyright of Fashion' (1997) B.C. Intellectual Property and Technology F 121291

analysis of this study recognises that the separability doctrine remains as a mechanism of restraint for the technical function attributed to the design. On this basis, it is argued that the law does not go far enough to comprehend the relevance artistry. This may therefore lead to the generic view by law, that Couture is regarded as utilitarian in nature.

When considering the wider IP framework, patents are a significant consideration for functionality, as patents are required to be functional. The preceding findings have also indicated that all IP rights except for patents and GIs attempt to limit protection by controlling the functional features of designs/products. Therefore, observed is the emergence of a pattern in consideration of the scope of rights afforded to Couture, and the scope of limitations applied. This can be seen in trade marks, and design rights and patents. In trade marks, the word 'exclusively' in Article 3(1)(e)(iii) of Directive 2008/95 was stated as meaning that the colour applied to the sole of a shoe did not consist exclusively of a 'shape.'[132] The recent interpretation given to this provision in *Louboutin v Van Haren*[133] has widened the scope of rights but narrowed the scope for limitations as they apply to the technicality exclusions. However, in patent legislation artistic works are not considered for protection pursuant to the Patents Act 1977 s.1(2)(b), however recent copyright E.U. case law has developed to consider technicality. Copyright law is viewed within this analysis as stretching the parameters of copyright protection to consider functional subject matter, although the position for patents seems not to have developed to this extent.

Trade mark law appears to echo the pattern for the application of the functionality doctrine in that technical exclusions apply not only to shapes, but to marks, and would ultimately render them void of protection.[134]

The function of Couture is recognised as being led by aesthetic considerations. Aesthetics are dictated by the construction and decorative components. Technical characteristics are often included as design features, and at times can solely define the design in totality. Couture therefore is observed to be primarily concerned with the aesthetics of the garment; as its function of its natural wearability, the functional considerations are an integral part of the garment which must be accommodated for through artistry.

132 *Louboutin v Van Haren Schoenen BV* Case C-163/16
133 *Louboutin v Van Haren Schoenen BV Case C-163/16*
134 The Trade Marks Act 1994 s.3(2)(b) and *Philips v Remington* [2002] ECR Case C-299/99

6 Copyright Legal Systems

Global Appreciation

Introduction

The discussion extends to global appreciation for international copyright regimes outside of the U.K. These are the E.U., France, Tűrkiye, and the U.S. The reason for this is to understand the position in other jurisdictions through a comparative perspective and further, to consider whether there is any merit in implementing similar systems within the U.K. copyright framework. This chapter begins by examining landmark E.U. case law pertinent to the themes of this study, namely the cases of *Cofemel*[1] and *Brompton*.[2] The discussion moves to an exploration of the French legal system, specific to protecting fashion through the Code de la propriété intellectuelle.[3] Continuing the analysis, the Turkish legislation of the *Fikir ve Sanat Eserleri Kanunu 5486* is examined, whereby the language of the Legal provision in consideration of art appreciation is of specific interest. Finally, the U.S. legal regime is considered, particularly in relation to *separability* as seen in the case of *Varsity*.[4] The cases of *Baker v Seden*[5] and *Warm v Innermost*[6] are examined, before finally considering the merger doctrine through the scholarly work of Ghosh.[7]

6.1 The E.U

Although the U.K. has implemented Brexit, the U.K. retains much E.U. law pertaining to intellectual property. The main legislative provision pertaining to copyright is the Directive 2001/29/EC of the European Parliament and of the Council

1 *Cofemel v G-Star Raw CV (C-683/17)*
2 *Brompton Bicycle Ltd v Chedech/Get2Get* (C-833/18), Opinion of Advocate General M. Campos Sánchez-Bordona, E.U:C:2020:79
3 Article L112-2 - Code de la propriété intellectuelle
4 *Star Athletica v Varsity Brands Inc 799 F.3d 468 (2015) (6th Cir (US))*
5 *Baker v Selden, 101 U.S. 99, 102 (1879)*
6 *Corinna Warm and Studio Warm LLC v Innermost Ltd. and others, United States District Court Central District of California, Case No. CV 21–4402-MWF (SHKx) [2022] at 1011*
7 Shuba Ghosh, 'Legal Code and the Need for a Broader Functionality Doctrine in Copyright' (2000–2003) 71 Journal, Copyright Society of the USA

DOI: 10.4324/9781003599456-6

of 22 May 2001 on the harmonisation of certain aspects of copyright and related rights in the information society (Infosoc, aforementioned). The analysis to follow shall consider landmark case law, illustrating developing legal perspectives.

6.1.1 Cofemel

The case of *Cofemel v G-Star Raw CV*[8] concerned a Dutch fashion company issuing copyright infringement proceedings against a Portuguese company. Cofemel is a producer of jeans, t-shirts and sweatshirts, and G-Star Raw also produces jeans, sweatshirts, and t-shirts. G-Star brought an action requesting that Cofemel stopped infringing its copyright in addition to unfair competition associated with the business. The court held partially for G-Star, and Cofemel appealed on the grounds that clothing 'works' were not capable of copyright protection.[9]

The Advocate General looked to precedent to determine how copyright law is generally applied. He seemed to cast doubt in recognition of the general application of the law to protect fashion/textiles with copyright, specifically in consideration of industrially produced products. The Advocate General stated:

> The protection of designs by copyright law presents, in particular two types of danger: the inflation of protection by copyright law and the impediment to free economic competition. For this reason, many legal orders have developed provisions destined to reserve copyright protection for designs that present high artistic value[10]

The Advocate General is careful not to overstate copyright application and is cautious over copyright potentially being an obstacle to commercial competition. The Advocate General then identifies that the copyright provisions have effectively established that copyright is reserved for 'designs' that provide elevated artistic merit.[11] The approach to copyright protection is from the perspective of design and appears to be detached from the work as a whole concept. This deliberation, therefore, appears to specifically be focused on technical and restrictive aspects of design, which does not leave much scope for creative intellectual freedom.[12] Although the decision honours the rationale for how and when copyright can be applied, and equally the circumstances borne of the case provide for the decision

8 *Cofemel v G-Star Raw CV (C-683/17)*
9 *Cofemel v G-Star Raw* CV at H3
10 *Cofemel v G-Star Raw* CV at H3
11 *Cofemel v G-Star Raw* CV at H3
12 Simon Clark and Sarah Witton, 'Cofemel v G-Star Raw (C-683/17) and Its Effect on U.K. Copyright Law Before and After Brexit' (*Bristows*, 15 April 2020) <https://www.bristows.com/viewpoint/articles/cofemel-v-g-star-raw-c-683-17-and-its-effect-on-U.K.-copyright-law-before-and-afterbrexit/#:~:text=Cofemel%20argued%20the%20opposite%3B%20that%20the%20items%20of,profits.%20The%20Court%20of%20Appeal%20confirmed%20this%20decision> accessed 1 July 2023

to be suitable and adequate. However, the type of *design* matters and the decision may potentially not be adequate for a creative garment which goes beyond the parameters of technicality and function – *Couture.*

In *Cofemel*, the Advocate General Szpinar considered the 'utilitarian and functional character of applied arts objects.'[13] This phrase recognises the utilitarian and functional components of 'art objects' as part of their character.[14] Overall, the decision states that it is sufficient to 'literally' apply the 'author's own intellectual creation,' criterion and whilst this paragraph of the judgement continues to say 'it is not necessary to require utilitarian objects to have a particularly high artistic level compared to other categories of works,' it is important to note that whilst Couture cannot be described as a utilitarian object, only an artistic work which comprises of functional features.[15] The judgement in the case of *Cofemel* is noted as significant for this study, specifically Couture as provided the work is dependent on artistic creation, copyright protection cannot be entirely excluded for different types of subject matter (such as Couture).[16] Significantly, this thesis argues that Couture is a work of art in its entirety, and should not therefore be assessed for the grant of copyright along the same lines of a design work, whereby the risk of this happening appears high in application of *Cofemel* to Couture.

The decision as it relates to defining 'artistic' rests with law makers and appears to be a subjective notion. Moreover, in the same case, the Advocate General referred to *Painer,*[17] recognising the absence in Directive 2001/29 'or in any other applicable directive . . . the extent of protection depends on any differences in the possibilities of artistic creation, when producing the various categories of works,'[18] and added that for this reason protection could not be entirely excluded.[19] The authority of *Painer*[20] in consideration of the evaluation of photographic works is perceived by this thesis as significant for *Cofemel*[21] but further supports the viewpoint for Couture,[22] that works of Couture should be contrasted with works of Couture only, and not other types of artistic works such as a fine art painting, a photograph, or a sculpture.[23]

13 *Cofemel v G-Star Raw CV* (C-683/17) AG para 3

14 *Cofemel v G-Star Raw CV* (C-683/17) AG para 3

15 *Cofemel-Sociedade de Vestuário SA v G-Star Raw CV* [2019] E.C.D.R. 16 at AG57

16 *Cofemel-Sociedade de Vestuário SA v G-Star Raw CV* [2019] E.C.D.R. 16 at AG57

17 *Painer v Standard Verlags GmbH E.U:C:2011:798; [2012] E.C.D.R. 6*

18 *Cofemel v G-Star Raw CV* (C-683/17) AG31

19 *Cofemel v G-Star Raw CV* (C-683/17) AG31

20 *Painer v Standard Verlags GmbH E.U:C:2011:798; [2012] E.C.D.R. 6*

21 *Cofemel v G-Star Raw CV (C-683/17)*

22 Tomruk Űstűnkaya, 'The Functionality Doctrine: The Challenges to Fashion Copyright' (2020) 42(3) EIPR 156

23 Tomruk Űstűnkaya, 'The Functionality Doctrine: The Challenges to Fashion Copyright' (2020) 42(3) EIPR 156

Conversely, an E.U. sui generis right is provided for under Regulation No 6/2002 in relation to unregistered design rights. This right was discussed in the closing remarks in the opinion of Advocate General Szpunar:

> *Sui generis* protection of designs, such as that provided by Regulation No 6/2002, is well adapted to the specific characteristics of the protected subject matter, that is to say ordinary, practical and mass-produced goods which can nevertheless also possess original aesthetic characteristics worthy of protection . . . there is a risk that the copyright regime would supplant the *sui generis* regime intended to protect designs. This would have several negative effects: the devaluation of copyright, sought to protect everyday creations.[24]

This is a significant statement when applied to copyright in consideration of Couture for two reasons. The first relates to the study addressing the existing problems associated with attaining copyright protection for Couture, such as the doctrine of functionality. The second problem is identified through the statement, which is the 'devaluing' of copyright on the premise of using the sui generis right. The problematic aspect is identified in that copyright is sought to reflect the artistic value of the creation. The identification of copyright being devalued has further implications, as this may effectively devalue the creative work and not just the legal protective mechanism, copyright. The value of the art as artistic value, intellectual value, and economic value amounts to appreciation of the artwork, which would lead to the pursuit of copyright protection. In consideration of Couture, whilst a sui generis right does provide for an added or alternative legal protective mechanism, it may create an unwanted consequence of devaluing creative works. For this reason, the study would assert that specific copyright protection for Couture is desirable. The decision in *Cofemel* identifies that it is the 'author's own intellectual creation criterion' enabling the distinction to be made between subject matter capable of copyright protection and those that are not. Further, it is this standard which qualifies 'originality.'[25] Finally, significant for Couture is that in order for a work to be capable of copyright protection, it must comprise of features that are 'the expression of the author's own intellectual creation.'[26]

Overall, the *Cofemel* ruling appears to challenge the aspect of technicality further than the *BSA* decision, and to some extent further than the *Premiere League* case.[27] *Cofemel* places emphasis on *artistic creation*, and therefore Couture works would not necessarily be excluded from copyright protection.[28]

24 *Cofemel v G-Star Raw* CV (C-683/17)

25 *Cofemel-Sociedade de Vestuário SA v G-Star Raw CV* [2019] E.C.D.R. 16 at AG31

26 *Cofemel-Sociedade de Vestuário SA v G-Star Raw CV* [2019] E.C.D.R. 16 at AG62

27 *Football Association Premier League v QC Leisure and Karen Murphy v Media Protection Services*, Joined cases C-403/08 and C-429/08 [2011] ECR I-9083 (ECJ, Grand Chamber), [98]

28 *Cofemel v G-Star Raw CV* (C-683/17) AG3

6.1.2 Brompton Bicycle

The case of *Brompton Bicycle Ltd* considered the functionality doctrine as it relates to copyright and the extent to which this doctrine applies.[29] The implications of the functionality doctrine on the case were rooted in the defence raised by Get-2Get expressing that the Brompton bicycle could not attract copyright due to the appearance of the bicycle being dictated by the technical function.[30] In response, Brompton argued that copyright should not be barred as other shapes would also facilitate the folding of the bike into three positions. To add to this, Mr SI and Brompton Ltd argued that the choice of shape was not solely reliant upon functional considerations but included 'aesthetic' reasons.[31] The court considered the case of *DOCERAM*[32] which was about design right protection for weld centring pins, whereby the central issue was the exclusion for protection whereby the feature of the product was dictated by its technical function.[33]

The decision was based on establishing whether the technical function of the product governed the design.[34] Here we see the copyright and design intersection and additionally considering the same approach applied across both copyright and design rights whereby the creative expression must not be dictated by the technical features. To support this, the 'discrimination' towards industrial objects identified by Suthersanen appears to be evident in the qualitative considerations.[35] This point strongly brings forward the issue of creating objects, and in consideration of the subject for this study, Couture. Here it is seen that technicality which enables functionality is an integral part of the garment for which creation would be impossible without. The implementation of creative processes which incorporate technicality with creativity for the purposes of producing a viable product is crucial, i.e. it can be worn and allows for movement and all other functional purposes for the benefit of the client.

29 *Brompton Bicycle Ltd v Chedech/Get2Get* (C-833/18), Opinion of Advocate General M. Campos Sánchez-Bordona, E.U:C:2020:79

30 Ilanah Fhima, 'The CJEU Decision in Brompton Bicycle (Case C-833/18): An Original Take on Technical Functionality?' (2020) 42(11) EIPR 761–7

31 *Brompton Bicycle Ltd v Chedech/Get2Get* (C-833/18), Opinion of Advocate General M. Campos Sánchez-Bordona, E.U.:C:2020:79 at para 34

32 *DOCERAM (C-395/16, E.U:C:2017:779*

33 DOCERAM (C-395/16, E.U:C:2017:779 and Bird & Bird, 'The CJEU DOCERAM Case: When is a Product Feature Solely Dictated by Its Technical Functionality Such That It Cannot Be Protected as a Community Design?' (*Bird & Bird*, 15 March 2018) <https://www.twobirds.com/en/insights/2018/U.K./CJEU.-Doceram-case> accessed 26 March 2023

34 Bird and Bird, 'The CJEU DOCERAM Case: When is a Product Feature Solely Dictated By Its Technical Functionality Such That It Cannot Be Protected as a Community Design?' (*Bird & Bird*, 15 March 2018) <https://www.twobirds.com/en/insights/2018/U.K./CJEU-Doceram-case> accessed 26 March 2023

35 Uma Suthersanen, 'Copyright and Industrial Objects: Aesthetic Considerations and Policy Discriminations' in M David and D Halbert (eds), *SAGE Handbook of Intellectual Property* (21 January 2014, Forthcoming, Queen Mary School of Law Legal Studies Research Paper No. 168/2014) <https://ssrn.com/abstract=2382718>

6.2 France

As expressed previously, Article L.112–2.73 of the Code de la propriété intellectuelle protects fashion.[36] The principle of the unity of art does not make a distinction between 'pure art' and 'industrial art,'[37] and France regards fashion as an art creation. Pertinent to the concept of the unity of art, whereby artistic works are regarded equally irrespective of the type of work, an artistic work can be protected by both copyright and design law.[38] The protection by copyright is extended to all art forms, including those considered as possessing the qualities of 'industrial aesthetics' or applied art. When applied to Couture, both the idea of industrial aesthetics and 'pure art,' that is, if we are to consider the garment itself as an art form, Couture is art in its entirety, an art creation. In addition, Couture, in most cases, is likely to contain applied art; however, based on the founding principles of the 'unity of art,' the whole of Couture garment would be regarded as art and therefore, there is no need to make a fragmented analysis of the parts of the garment that can be protected by copyright and those which cannot.

To illustrate the position in France, discussed previously, in relation to Couture as art the work of Charles De Vilmorin is examined. Vilmorin was the artistic director for Rochas and launched his own brand in 2020.[39] The Spring/Summer collection for 2022 incorporates 'geometric colours and shapes.' Vilmorin's collection is an example of the unity of art principle in that the 'creation' is the Couture garment which cannot be dissected to distinguish the pure art from the industrial art.[40]

6.2.1 Specific Protection for Fashion

In addition to the E.U. legislation on copyright, French legislation has been specifically drafted to protect Couture. This is possible by Article L.112–2.73 of the Code de la propriété intellectuelle.[41] As with the U.K. and E.U. copyright legislation, originality is a key requirement for the grant of copyright protection under Article L.111–1 of the code.[42] The existence of copyright arises through the creation of the

36 Article L112-2 - Code de la propriété intellectuelle

37 G Finnis, 'The Theory of "Unity of Art" and the Protection of Designs and Models in French Law' (1964) XLVI (9) *Patent Office* <https://heinonline.org/HOL/LandingPage?handle=hein.journals/jpatos46&div=108&id=&page=> accessed 19 November 2022

38 Annabelle Gauberti, 'Fashion Law in France: A 2020 Overview' (*Crefovi*, 2020) <https://crefovi.com/articles/fashion-law-in-france/> accessed 19 November 2022

39 Kristen Bateman, 'Meet the New Guard of Haute Couture Designers Lending a Fresh Perspective to a Time-Honored Craft' (*Bazaar*, 29 January 2022) <https://www.harpersbazaar.com/fashion/fashion-week/a38915060/new-haute-Couture-designers/> accessed 19 November 2022

40 Kristen Bateman, 'Meet the New Guard of Haute Couture Designers Lending a Fresh Perspective to a Time-Honored Craft' (*Bazaar*, 29 January 2022) <https://www.harpersbazaar.com/fashion/fashion-week/a38915060/new-haute-Couture-designers/> accessed 19 November 2022 Please also see: Charles de Vilmorin, 'Charles de Vilmorin' (*Charles De Vilmorin*, 2022) <https://www.charlesdevilmorin.fr/> accessed 19 November 2022

41 Article L112-2 - Code de la propriété intellectuelle

42 Karina Dimdijian-Lecomte, Floriane codevelle, 'France' (*The Global Legal Post*, 2021) <https://www.globallegalpost.com/lawoverborders/Couture-law-2021-2116409480/france> accessed 31 December 2021

work.[43] The duration of copyright is the author's life plus 70 years pursuant to Article L.123-1IPC.[44] The code further provides 'the creations of the seasonal industries of dress and articles of protection' which arises automatically on the day of creation.[45] This is notable for two reasons. The first is that the code provides for Couture being regarded as a protected subject matter, and secondly, the notion of 'seasonal' is significant. It is stated that '[t]he creations of the seasonal industries of dress and articles of' are a protected subject matter, and 'uniform protection is given to original fashion designs automatically on the date of creation, regardless of registration, unlike different protection schemes given to registered and unregistered designs under the E.U. regulations.'[46] The code recognises the nature of Couture being seasonal, and therefore this is regarded as a notable recognition of the process for Couture creation, with design being an integral part of the process, and therefore implementing provisions to reflect the nature of Couture is significant. Article L.112–2 (14) of the Code de la propriété intellectuelle for fashion[47] specifies, 'The provisions of this Code protect author's rights on any work of mind, whatever its kind, form of expression, merit, or destination.'[48] This legislation refers to creations of the mind of which fashion belongs. The code specifically acknowledges the very nature of fashion in that it acknowledges the seasonal nature, the process whereby the renewal of shapes for the products, and specific acknowledgement for Couture is expressed within the legislation. Further, the code under L111-3 applies a protection to the incorporeal right distinct from the physical work.[49]

43 Karina Dimdijian-Lecomte, Floriane codevelle, 'France' (*The Global Legal Post*, 2021) <https://www.globallegalpost.com/lawoverborders/Couture-law-2021-2116409480/france> accessed 31 December 2021

44 Karina Dimdijian-Lecomte, Floriane codevelle, 'France' (*The Global Legal Post*, 2021) <https://www.globallegalpost.com/lawoverborders/Couture-law-2021-2116409480/france> accessed 31 December 2021

45 Francesca Montalvo witzburg, 'Protecting Fashion: A Comparative Analysis of Fashion Design Protection in the United States and Europe' (CARDOZOAELJ, 1st December 2016) <https://cardozoaelj.com/2016/12/01/protecting-fashion-comparative-analysis-fashion-design-protection-united-states-europe/#_ftn69> accessed 21 January 2025 referring to Intellectual Property Code, Article L-112-2

46 TFL, 'France: Legal Protections for Fashion' (*The Fashion Law*, 2023) https://www.thefashionlaw.com/resource-center/france-legal-protections-for-fashion/ accessed 20 July 2023

47 Article L112-2 - Code de la propriété intellectuelle

48 European Parliament, 'Copyright Law in the E.U: Salient Features of Copyright Law Across the E.U. Member States' (*European Parliament*, June 2018) <https://www.Europarl.Europa.E.U./RegData/etudes/STUD/2018/625126/EPRS_STU(2018)625126_EN.pdf> accessed 16 July 2023
Article L 112–1 CPI 'Les dispositions du présent code protègent les droits des auteurs sur toutes les œuvres de l'esprit, quels qu'en soient le genre, la forme d'expression, le mérite ou la destination.'

49 European Parliament, 'Copyright Law in the E.U: Salient Features of Copyright Law Across the E.U. Member States' (*European Parliament*, June 2018) <https://www.Europarl.Europa.E.U./RegData/etudes/STUD/2018/625126/EPRS_STU(2018)625126_EN.pdf> accessed 16 July 2023

6.2.2 Propriete Intellectuelle v ***Technical Exclusions***

The Code de la propriété intellectuelle appears to be absent in any provisions placing limitations on technical or functional features of creations of the mind, and therefore appears to accept the intrinsic nature of such works. The originality requirement is observed through the E.U. case law as a significant consideration for copyright in France.[50] It is the juncture of where the Code de la propriété intellectuelle and E.U. case law meets, which is significant. The reason for this is that the silence on exclusions on technical features that contribute to function relating to copyright, offers scope for E.U. case law to provide wider legal parameters. An advantage of this is that the E.U. case law can develop without cumbersome conflict with the national provisions of the Code de la propriété intellectuelle. However, the nature of the Code de la propriété intellectuelle protecting fashion as a creation of the mind, and whereby the legislation protects the incorporeal right separate to the physical object, is additionally advantageous, as E.U. case law provides direction for the physical work.[51]

6.3 Tűrkiye

The rationale for exploring Tűrkiye is to evaluate the Tűrkiye/Brexit nexus as it relates to the concept of Couture specifically in law. As the U.K. is no longer a part of the E.U. and as Tűrkiye also remains outside of the community, the independent approach to copyright is analysed in consideration of Couture as art for global appreciation purposes. Case law of Tűrkiye has not been used as the country follows an inquisitorial model, and is of a civil jurisdiction.[52]

Copyright provisions in Tűrkiye are provided for by the *Fikir ve Sanat Eserleri Kanunu 5486* (the code), translated as '*Code of Intellectual and Artistic Works 5846*.'[53] Works are categorised into four main classifications, which are: scientific, literary, computer programs and databases, fine art and musical.[54] In consideration of Couture, the code appears to provide protection for fashion design under section 4, *Fine Arts*.[55] This provision supports the approach of this study to Couture as an artistic work, whereby design is integral to the art of Couture, although it is

50 *Cofemel v G-Star Raw CV* (C-683/17) AG3

51 European Parliament, 'Copyright Law in the E.U: Salient Features of Copyright Law Across the E.U. Member States' (*European Parliament*, June 2018) <https://www.Europarl.Europa.E.U./RegData/etudes/STUD/2018/625126/EPRS_STU(2018)625126_EN.pdf> accessed 16 July 2023

52 Please see Dogan Cosgun and Kemal Tağa, 'Turkey: Overview of Turkish Litigation Practice – 2021' (*Mondaq*, 4 January 2022) https://www.mondaq.com/turkey/civil-law/1147264/overview-of-turkish-litigation-practice-2021 accessed 29 March 2024 and Fikir ve Sanat Eserleri Kanunu 5846

53 Gurulkan Çakir, 'Copyright Protection' (*Gurulkan Çakir*, 2021) <https://www.gurulkan.com/doing-business-in-Tűrkiye/copyright-protection> accessed 31 December 2021

54 Gurulkan Çakir, 'Copyright Protection' (*Gurulkan Çakir*, 2021) <https://www.gurulkan.com/doing-business-in-Tűrkiye/copyright-protection> accessed 31 December 2021

55 Fikir ve Sanat Eserleri Kanunu 5846 as amended 7.6.1995–4110/2 please note: the definition of *fine art* appears to be a translational enhancement in analysis of Mutlu Yildirim Köse, Hande Hançar

not the only definitive element. The design contributes to the end- product, Couture, the artistic work. Fine art works in section 4 of the code, require 'aesthetic value' for the purposes of copyright protection.[56]

6.3.1 Fashion Is Art

To consider the artistic process of Couture as it relates to Turkish design, the Zeynep Tosun's Spring/Summer 2021's collection is evaluated. This collection titled 'Apasas: City of the Mother Goddess' was debuted at the ruins within Efes, Tűrkiye.[57] Tosun expresses that the strong women who founded and constructed the city are depicted through the Couture garments, which are said to be an amalgamation of 'tradition and modernity.'[58] The collection incorporates the historical and mythological influences for the garments in a symbolic form[59] e.g., new beginnings are depicted by images of the sun rise and new moons.[60] The collection incorporated traditional Anatolian hand embroidery methods and reflects the structure of the city within the garment design.[61] Traditional craftmanship techniques from the Kastamonu region are entwined into the garments, specifically '[w]inding, wire breaking, knot and tassel processing.'[62] Textile art, innovation, traditional design, and construction methods are part of both the artistic craftmanship and overall creative design process.[63] There are two issues to analyse here: the first is the inclusion of fashion design within *the code*,[64] and the second is the considerations for Couture as *fine art*. Tűrkiye partially aligns with the 'unity of art' principle observed in France, and similarities exist with s.14 of Article L.112–2.73 of the French Code de la propriété intellectuelle.[65]

Çelik and Havva Yıldız, 'Tűrkiye: Insights as to Turkish Copyright Law' (*Mondaq*, 2020) Insights As To Turkish Copyright Law - Copyright - Turkey (mondaq.com)> accessed 20 July 2023

56 Mutlu Yildirim Köse, Hande Hançar Çelik and Havva Yıldız, 'Tűrkiye: Insights as to Turkish Copyright Law' (*Mondaq*, 2020) Insights As To Turkish Copyright Law - Copyright - Turkey (mondaq.com)> accessed 20 July 2023and Code of Intellectual and Artistic Works numbered 5846, s.4 which states: 'Güzel sanat eserleri, estetik değere sahip olan.'

57 DW for Minds, 'Turkish Haute Couture' (*DW for Minds*, 14 March 2022) <https://www.dw.com/en/turkish-haute-Couture/video-61121521> accessed 18 November 2022

58 DW for Minds, 'Turkish Haute Couture' (*DW for Minds*, 14 March 2022) <https://www.dw.com/en/turkish-haute-Couture/video-61121521> accessed 18 November 2022

59 Mythological symbols of serpents and snakes representing fertility, immortality and the colour white representing power

60 Fashion Week İstanbul, 'Zeynep Tosun' (*Fashion Week* İstanbul, 2021) <https://fashionweek.istanbul/press-release/zeynep-tosun> accessed 18 November 2022

61 DW for Minds, 'Turkish Haute Couture' (*DW for Minds*, 14 March 2022) <https://www.dw.com/en/turkish-haute-Couture/video-61121521> accessed 18 November 2022

62 Fashion Week İstanbul, 'Zeynep Tosun' (*Fashion Week İstanbul*, 2021) <https://fashionweek.istanbul/press-release/zeynep-tosun> accessed 18 November 2022

63 DW for Minds, 'Turkish Haute Couture' (*DW for Minds*, 14 March 2022) <https://www.dw.com/en/turkish-haute-Couture/video-61121521> accessed 18 November 2022

64 Fikir ve Sanat Eserleri Kanunu 5846, s.4

65 Hayrı Bozgeyik, 'Fikir ve Sanat Eserleri Kanununda Eser Çeşitleri: Karşılaştırmalı Bir Analiz' (2014) 15(1) Bilgi Dűnyası 125–58

The extent of the meaning of 'design' within the *code*[66] is significant, as it outlines whether the end-product, the garment, is regarded as a 'fine art' in addition to the design drawings.[67] Analysis of scholarly work suggests that 'design; (tasarım) extends beyond the design drawings. For example, in relation to fashion, when referring to fast fashion and alternative materials, the word 'tasarım' appears to equate to the garment and drawings as a whole concept.[68] This point on the distinction in language between English and Turkish for 'design' (tasarım) is significant, as when considering protections pursuant to the code.[69] This would therefore define fashion (moda) conceptually as a complete concept and therefore makes the protection very much akin to the French protections. This issue also highlights the point raised earlier relating to Heilpern encouraging the statute to be written as a 'technical term of art.'[70] The Turkish and French legislative provisions appear to be considering the language within the statute as a technical term of art. This is particularly notable by the wording of the statute being open to interpretation to define the subject matter as a technical industry definition, rather than considerations extending to whether the subject matter fits within the parameters of the legal definition.[71] Further, the meaning of aesthetic is relevant for works in s.4 of the code, as the code specifically states that these works must have aesthetic value, whereby the law can only make an objective assessment based on this point.[72] Generally, differentiated from the CDPA 1988, fashion *design* is included in the code[73] in Tűrkiye, and there is therefore a significant difference between the two legislative provisions.[74]

As the Turkish legislation defines 'fashion design' as *fine art* under s.4 of the code, the burden of proof for the work being *fine art* is not of the creator's concern, as it is already established.[75] Section 4 of the code provides copyright protection specifically for 'Handicrafts and minor works of art, miniatures and products of decorative art, and textile and fashion designs.'[76] Observed here is the potential for

66 *Fikir ve Sanat Eserleri Kanunu 5846, s.4*

67 Turkish translation: Tasarım

68 Nuray Bıyıklı and others, 'Tasarımda sürdürülebilirlik anlayışı ile bir değer yaratmak: Kültürel miras kavramı/Creating a Value With the Sustainability Approach in Design: Cultural Heritage Concept' (4 December 2021) 1(1) Sanat ve Tasarım Araştırmaları Dergisi 138–55 and Ezgi Hakan Verdu Martinez, 'Tasarımında sanatsal ifade önerisi olarak alternatif malzemeler: Seramik elbiseler/Allternative Materials in Fashion Design as a Proposal of Artistic Expression: Ceramic Dresses' (2012) 3(3) Sanat ve Tasarım Dergisi 162–81

69 Fikir ve Sanat Eserleri Kanunu 5846, s.4

70 Heilpern, 'Dialects of Art: A Corpus-Based Approach to Technical Term of Art Determinations in Statutes' (2022) 58(4) Jurimetrics 377–410

71 Heilpern, 'Dialects of Art: A Corpus-Based Approach to Technical Term of Art Determinations in Statutes' (2022) 58(4) Jurimetrics 377–410

72 Cahit Suluk, 'Güzel Sanat Eserleri ve Telif' (*Fikri Mülkiyet*, 2 January 2019) <https://fikrimulkiyet.com/guzel-sanat-eserleri-ve-telif/> accessed 18 November 2022 and Fikir ve Sanat Eserleri Kanunu 5846, s.4

73 Fikir ve Sanat Eserleri Kanunu 5846, s.4

74 Copyright Designs and Patents Act 1988, s.4

75 Moda tasarımları pursuant to Fikir ve Sanat Eserleri Kanunu 5846, s.4

76 Fikir ve Sanat Eserleri Kanunu 5846, s.4

Couture fashion to be protected in the design *and* as a product, as *fashion designs* are within the definition of fine art. The main difference between the U.K. and Turkish copyright provisions is that fashion design in the *code* is recognised as *fine art,* whereas it is unclear under the current U.K. copyright provisions, whether Couture/fashion is regarded as art, or even an artistic work. This therefore leads to considerations for Couture as a category of fashion, and the extent to which Couture is identified as art under the U.K. law.

6.3.2 Adaptation Works

Section 6 of the code[77] provides protection for '*Adaptations*' which is equivalent to derivative works in the U.K. copyright regime. In the Turkish code, Couture 'adaptation' works could potentially be protected under s.6(5) which states, 'Conversion of works of fine arts from one form into other forms,'[78] and s.6(6) expresses, 'the conversion of all works or works of the same kind of the owner of a work into a complete work.'[79] Therefore, s.6(5) would essentially protect an adaptation of an artwork made into a Couture fashion item and s.6(6) could potentially protect an adaptation of the author's own work of a different kind, made into a Couture fashion product. A notable absence within the Turkish copyright system is the functionality doctrine. Therefore, Couture works do not appear to be overly burdened by restrictions on their natural technical elements, as in the U.K.

6.3.3 Functionality

As with E.U. law, the perspective of the Supreme Court in Tűrkiye is that whilst it is a requirement to assess the extent to which the technical function dictates the appearance of the product, and whether creativity is impeded, the most significant point to deliberate is whether the product maintains originality.[80] The position of the Turkish Supreme Court, as it relates specifically to the component of the aesthetic assessment, is that products must be exclusive and extend beyond everyday use.[81]

In analysis of the Turkish position on copyright, a product which is industrial in nature can attain copyright protection under the law, provided the work is inherent in aesthetic quality. This would suggest that the extent of assessment of technicality

77 Fikir ve Sanat Eserleri Kanunu 5846, s.6

78 Fikir ve Sanat Eserleri Kanunu 5846, s.6(5)

79 Fikir ve Sanat Eserleri Kanunu 5846, s.6(6)

80 Gűn and Partners, 'Tűrkiye: Does Technical Function Impede Copyright?' (*Mondaq*, 28 April 2022) <https://www.mondaq.com/Tűrkiye/copyright/1187768/does-technical-function-impede-copyright-april-2022> accessed 18 June 2022

81 Gűn and Partners, 'Tűrkiye: Does Technical Function Impede Copyright?' (*Mondaq*, 28 April 2022) <https://www.mondaq.com/Tűrkiye/copyright/1187768/does-technical-function-impede-copyright-april-2022> accessed 18 June 2022

is weighed up in contrast to the degree of aesthetic quality. More significantly, the notion of a product extending beyond everyday use is a key factor. The analysis shall now consider the position in the U.S. relating to separability/entwinement of features pertinent to the doctrine of functionality.

6.4 The U.S. Approach to Copyright

The concept of Couture fashion as art in the U.S. will be explored from examining the notion of innovation.[82] The U.S. approach is founded in economic interests. Copyright protection for fashion has often been acknowledged within the U.S. Congress since 1914.[83] The argument to support the limited protection for fashion is maintained by the concept of a 'piracy paradox,' which purports that copying fosters 'innovation.'[84] The fact that the fashion industry is regarded as prospering reinforces this concept, as it does not compel a change in the law to protect fashion to a greater extent.[85] The U.S. places emphasis on innovation. The U.S. innovation policy expresses that 'the United States is the most innovative economy in the world. U.S. companies drive global innovation and the development of advanced and emerging technologies.'[86] The concept of innovation could ultimately be considered as the driving force behind *creation* and could be considered as far as fostering artistic development. The U.S. approach to copyright is founded in economic interests where the focus is on the utilitarian function, whereas the French system perspective is on the preservation of art and fostering creativity. The Turkish perspective appears to be more aligned with the French perspective, in that fashion design is regarded as fine art, in law.

The U.S. copyright legislation was developed from the Statute of Anne 1709, for the purposes of promoting 'the progress of science and useful arts.'[87] [Fourteen years was the initial duration of copyright granted, and this was capable of being renewed once.][88] Exact copying is said to be damaging to the industry, and that derivative works are the influence for the creation of Couture.[89]

82 Loni Schutte, Copyright For Couture (2011), Duke Law & Technology Review No. 011

83 Aleksandra M Spevacek, 'Couture Copyright: Copyright Protection Fitting for Fashion Design, the John Marshall Review of Intellectual Property Law' (2009) referring to 17 U.S.C. §§ 1301–1332 (2006)

84 Loni Schutte, 'Copyright For Couture' (2011) Duke Law & Technology Review No. 011

85 Loni Schutte, 'Copyright For Couture' (2011) Duke Law & Technology Review No. 011

86 U.S. Department of State, 'Innovation Policy' (*U.S. Department of State*, 2022) <https://www.state.gov/innovation-policy/> accessed 19 November 2022

87 Paul Goldstein and P Bernt Hugenholtz, *International Copyright Principles, Law, and Practice* (4th edn, Oxford 2019) 16

88 Paul Goldstein and P Bernt Hugenholtz, *International Copyright Principles, Law, and Practice* (4th edn, Oxford 2019) 16

89 Paul Goldstein and P Bernt Hugenholtz, *International Copyright Principles, Law, and Practice* (4th edn, Oxford 2019) 16

Today, the duration of U.S. copyright lasts for the duration of the author's life plus 70 years.[90] Subject matter is provided for under s.102 of the Act[91] as '(1) literary works: (2) musical works, including any accompanying words; (3) dramatic works, including any accompanying music; (4) pantomimes and choreographic works; (5) pictorial, graphic, and sculptural works; (6) motion pictures and other visual works; and (7) sound recordings.'[92]

Derivative works are protected under s.103 whereby only the author's original contribution is protected.[93] Copyright cannot protect a work whereby there is an unlawful use of the existing material.[94] The Act refers to the term 'useful article' which is defined as 'an article having an intrinsic utilitarian function that is not merely to portray the appearance of the article or to convey information. An article that is normally a part of a useful article is considered a useful article.'[95] To support this introduction to the U.S. copyright legislative provisions, U.S. case law shall be analysed in more detail in chapter 6 (in the discussion on functionality) to ascertain a deeper understanding of the position for Couture copyright. Although, identified here is that the Act, like the U.K. CDPA 1988, categorises subject matter for types of works, and further distinguishes between articles which are aesthetic (based on the appearance) and those which are utilitarian.[96] The aesthetic component would be protected, whereas the utilitarian would not (this is discussed further in chapter 6 in the case of *Star Athletica*).[97] This appears to raise complexity in the operation and application of the law in consideration of Couture, as the division between the two distinct aspects essentially compels lawyers to deliberate Couture as conceptually a two-part creation: 1. Utilitarian and 2. The aesthetic.

In terms of aligning the U.S. legislation with the E.U. legal developments, although attempts have been proposed to make amendments to the Copyright Act[98] for the purposes of introducing sui generis protection for fashion designs and to remove separability, the Bills were not passed by congress.[99]

90 US Copyright Office, 'What Is Copyright' (*US Copyright Office*, 2021) <https://www.copyright.gov/> accessed 31 December 2021
91 Copyright Act 1976, S.102 and Library of Congress Copyright Office, *Copyright Law of The United States*, [Ebook252] 3 May 2008, 7
92 Copyright Act 1976, S.102 and Library of Congress Copyright Office, *Copyright Law of The United States*, [Ebook252] 3 May 2008, 8 referring to Title 17, United States Code, Sections 101–810
93 Title 17, United States Code, Sections 103 (b)
94 Title 17, United States Code, Sections 103 (a)
95 Copyright Act 1976, S.102 and Library of Congress Copyright Office, *Copyright Law of The United States*, [Ebook252] 3 May 2008, 6
96 Copyright Act 1976
97 *Star Athletica v Varsity Brands Inc* 799 F.3d 468 (2015) (6th Cir (US))
98 Copyright Act 1976
99 John Zarocostas, 'The Role of IP rights in the Couture Business: A US Perspective' (*WIPO*, August 2018) <https://www.WIPO.int/WIPO_magazine/en/2018/04/article_0006.html#:~:text=Each%20bill%20proposed%20amendments%20to%20the%20US%20Copyright,creative%20elements%20of%20the%20design%20of%20their%20garment> accessed 3 April 2023

6.4.1 Star Athletica v Varsity Brands Inc

In *Star Athletica*, the court deliberated the extent of copyright protection over cheerleader uniforms. The decision of the court was that the graphics used for the uniforms was capable of copyright protection, as a separate component from the garment which was regarded as utilitarian.[100] Therefore, it is suggested that the art was extracted from the functional element of the uniform, and considerations for granting copyright protection were deliberated.[101] The decision in *Star Athletica* is viewed from the perspective of this study as making an assessment of the subjective design process as it relates to specific aesthetic motivation for the cheerleader uniforms. [The proposal put forward by Keyes is viewed as supporting the *Star Athletica* ruling.] Through analysis of the decision in *Star Athletica* together with Keyes' proposal, this thesis argues that the outcome is limited and therefore the application of the separability doctrine continues to impose restraints, (in not how a product is designed, the technical function attributed to it) in the view of subjectivity of the design method.

A criticism of the application of provisions such as the rulings in both the U.S. *Star Athletica*[102] and the E.U. *Brompton*[103] cases is that it would essentially subject fashion to fragmented copyright protection. To reflect on the case of *Star Athletica*,[104] applied art[105] is considered as to whether it can be regarded as being fixed and having permanence. In *Brompton*,[106] the folding nature of the bike, particularly as it relates to a requirement of copyright being fixed, is applied in consideration of fashion.[107]

Couture is dictated by technicality just as much as it is by the creative artistic elements. Although it is argued that the creativity in fashion is dictated by the technical aspects, and this is something that cannot be avoided due to the intrinsic nature of Couture being technical. Consequently, the design processes must accommodate both inherent features of technicality and artistry. The design of the functional components is a significant consideration when comparing similar fashion products from different fashion brands. The design will not only pertain to the technical components but in addition, it will relate to the style, fabrics used, and aesthetic appearance of the Couture item.

100 *Star Athletica v Varsity Brands Inc* 799 F.3d 468 (2015) (6th Cir (US))

101 Tomruk Űstűnkaya, 'The Functionality Doctrine: The Challenges to Fashion Copyright' (2020) 42(3) EIPR 156 referring to Deming Liu, 'Of Sculpture' (2014) 36 EIPR 229

102 *Star Athletica v Varsity Brands Inc 799 F.3d 468 (2015) (6th Cir (US))*

103 *Brompton Bicycle Ltd v Chedech/Get2Get (C-833/18), Opinion of Advocate General M. Campos Sánchez-Bordona, E.U:C:2020:79*

104 *Star Athletica v Varsity Brands Inc* 799 F.3d 468 (2015) (6th Cir (US))

105 'The application of art to a functional object' – Rosie Burbridge, *European Fashion Law* (Edward Elgar 2019) 64

106 *Brompton Bicycle Ltd v Chedech/Get2Get* (C-833/18), Opinion of Advocate General M. Campos Sánchez-Bordona, E.U:C:2020:79

107 Earlier in the thesis, it was established that movement is the intrinsic nature of fashion due to the functional characteristics, and on this basis technical function confers an absence of any permeance to the garment. To consider this in application to fashion in the U.K. is regarded as a positive measure but one that does not go far enough to address the limitations of the functionality doctrine

6.4.2 Warm v Innermost

The U.S. case of *Warm v Innermost* illustrates a significant point in the separability of design (the artistic component) and the technical elements. Corrina Warm designed lighting ranges in spun aluminium in a variety of colours and sizes. The case concerned a collection of lighting, 'Circus,' consisting of pendant lampshades and wall lights and the 'Glaze' which are pendant lampshades. The issue was whether copyright would be granted for the designs specifically considering the utilitarian function. The defendants put forward arguments that the lamps were not copyrightable as they were 'useful' articles and that the design could not be separated from the function. Although 'features' of the lighting were referenced by the claimants, the court could not establish these specifically or identify any separate elements.

In consideration of the decision of *Star Athletica* (discussed later), in relation to a sculptural work the court referenced a part of the judgement: '[T]he focus of the separability inquiry is on the extracted feature and not on any aspects of the useful article that remain after the imaginary extraction.'[108] Sculptural elements were not definitively identified in any of the lampshades. Further, the issue of conceptualising the lampshade separately from the lamp did arise in considering whether the lampshade could attain copyright protection had it been fixed in some 'tangible medium other than a useful article before being applied to a useful article.'[109] On this basis, the possibility of the lampshades being copyright protected as metal sculptures was a real potential.[110] However, the grant of copyright was denied on the basis that the defendants were unable to prove that the design was separable from utilitarian function.[111]

6.4.3 Scope of Copyright

It is established in the U.S. through Congress that the scope of copyright law only extends to 'expression and aesthetics' and the parameter of patents only encompasses 'utility and functionality.'[112]

The copyright requirement pursuant to the Copyright Act 1976 states that works must be original and fixed in a tangible form.[113] These are the same requirements in the U.K. and E.U. Member States copyright provisions as discussed earlier on. Couture fashion could disrupt the differentiation between patents and copyright. Whilst patents rely on function, copyright relies upon creativity, and Couture

108 *Star Athletica v Varsity Brands Inc* 799 F.3d 468 (2015) (6th Cir (US)) at 103

109 *Corinna Warm and Studio Warm LLC v Innermost Ltd. and others*, 'United States District Court Central District of California, Case No. CV 21–4402-MWF (SHKx) [2022] at 1011'

110 *Corinna Warm and Studio Warm LLC v Innermost Ltd. and others, 'United States District Court Central District of California*, Case No. CV 21–4402-MWF (SHKx) [2022] at 1011'

111 *Corinna Warm and Studio Warm LLC v Innermost Ltd. and others*, 'United States District Court Central District of California, Case No. CV 21–4402-MWF (SHKx) [2022]'

112 *Corinna Warm and Studio Warm LLC v Innermost Ltd. and others*, 'United States District Court Central District of California, Case No. CV 21–4402-MWF (SHKx) [2022]'

113 The Copyright Act 1976 (U.S.)

fashion may potentially be compelling a conceptual merging of the two IP rights due to the qualities required to acquire each IP right, which exist simultaneously within the same work. Conversely, the attempt to set apart each element is seen in the case of *Baker*, as follows.[114]

6.4.4 *Baker v Selden*

In this case, it was identified that not to examine the concept of novelty within the work would effectively be subjecting the public to fraud.[115] Further, a novel work of art and manufacture should be considered by the patent office for the purposes of establishing an exclusive right.[116] In this instance, the merger doctrine is engaged, which essentially means that the idea and expression have merged and therefore, it does not allow the grant of copyright when expression is restricted to one or a limited few methods.[117] This view in *Baker* attempts to ensure that functional components are kept within the realm of patents, and further asserts an authority of patents over functional attributes.[118]

To extend and consider this conception as applied to fashion Couture and specifically through the lens of the U.K. legislative provisions, would essentially mean that the technical aspect of fashion must be considered by the Patents Office and the aesthetic, artistic, or creative elements will be examined for the purposes of copyright. Therefore, whichever way we examine fashion, the current legal provisions oblige fashion to be separated and fragmented by law.

6.4.5 *U.S. – The Merger Doctrine*

The merger doctrine is noted as protecting the expression of ideas but not the ideas in isolation. In reference to the U.S. merger doctrine, Ghosh suggests that the decision in *Veeck*[119] is erroneous due to the focus on authorship.[120] This case was regarding an infringement proceeding against *Veeck* for posting Southern Building Code Congress Internationals' (SBCII) model codes online without authorisation.[121] SBCII had the potential to charge for the material which would be generated by the codes and of publishing them.[122] Ghosh suggests that the code should have been approached as 'a form of functional expression and deny copyright protection

114 *Baker v Selden*, 101 U.S. 99, 102 (1879)
115 *Baker v Selden*, 101 U.S. 99, 102 (1879)
116 *Baker v Selden*, 101 U.S. 99, 102 (1879)
117 Martin Luenendonk, 'Merger Doctrine' (*Cleverism*, 13 August 2016) <https://www.cleverism.com/lexicon/merger-doctrine/> accessed 9 June 2022
118 *Baker v Selden*, 101 U.S. 99, 102 (1879)
119 *Veeck v Southern Blg. Code Cong. Int'l, Inc. 293 F 3rd 791, 793 (5th Circuit 2002)*
120 Shuba Ghosh, 'Legal Code and the Need for a Broader Functionality Doctrine in Copyright' (2000–2003) 71 Journal, Copyright Society of the USA
121 *Veeck v Southern Blg. Code Cong. Int'l, Inc.* 293 F 3rd 791, 793 (5th Circuit 2002)
122 *Veeck v Southern Blg. Code Cong. Int'l, Inc.* 293 F 3rd 791, 793 (5th Circuit 2002)

on a more sophisticated and rigorous application of the merger doctrine.'[123] Ghosh identifies that when applied to the 'legal code' the functionality doctrine differs from when applied to a computer code, and identifies that the computer code concerns relate to 'interoperability, reverse engineering, and preventing bottlenecks' whereas the legal code is concerned with 'access and use.'[124] On this basis, we see the repeating pattern in copyright law whereby the application of rules surrounding functionality to different subject matter may not be ideal and is potentially producing a one size fits all outcome.[125] This notion forms the basis for considerations related to developing the law.

In consideration of the issues raised as they relate to copyright of Couture garments, the legal matter can be viewed as having two limbs. The first is the consideration of a more rigorous approach to the merger doctrine, and the second is the creativity exercised when drafting new law. The notion of a stricter approach to the merger doctrine is copyright should be denied based on functional expression.[126] Should fashion garments be inherently of 'functional expression,' it is argued that the concept would be extremely limiting and would extinguish any potential of copyright protection if adopted in a rigorous manner, as suggested by Ghosh.[127]

Interim Conclusion

The *Cofemel* judgement affirmed that when the work is shown to be determined by artistic creation, copyright protection cannot be totally omitted for different types of subject matter.[128] Similarly, *Brompton* highlighted that regardless of the functionality or 'technical result' of the fold-bike design, copyright protection was granted on the basis that the bike was regarded as an original work.[129]

So far, it is apparent that although the functionality doctrine is in existence, it is recognised to be balancing the competition concerns ignited by public policy

123 Shuba Ghosh, 'Legal Code and the Need for a Broader Functionality Doctrine in Copyright' (2000–2003) 71 Journal, Copyright Society of the USA

124 Shuba Ghosh, 'Legal Code and the Need for a Broader Functionality Doctrine in Copyright' (2000–2003) 71 Journal, Copyright Society of the USA

125 Please see Tomruk Űstűnkaya, 'The Functionality Doctrine: The Challenges to Fashion Copyright' (2020) 42(3) EIPR 156 for a discussion on the cases of *Painer v Standard Verlags GmbH* (C-145/10) E.U:C:2011:798; [2012] E.C.D.R. 6., *Infopaq v Danske Dagblades Forening* (C-5/08) E.U:C:2009:465; [2010] F.S.R. 20 and *Temple Island Collection v New English Teas* [2011] E.W.P.C.C. 19; [2012] F.S.R. 9 at [35]. 'in consideration of the decision in Infopaq, it appears from the perspective of this article, that the effect is of a "one size fits all" application. This is regarded as unfortunate from the perspective of this article, as creative works in fashion are subject to copyright case law whereby the "subject matter" is not necessarily a fashion article and furthermore limitations are placed by the functionality doctrine.'

126 Shuba Ghosh, 'Legal Code and the Need for a Broader Functionality Doctrine in Copyright' (2000–2003) 71 Journal, Copyright Society of the USA

127 Shuba Ghosh, 'Legal Code and the Need for a Broader Functionality Doctrine in Copyright' (2000–2003) 71 Journal, Copyright Society of the USA

128 *Cofemel v G-Star Raw CV* (C-683/17) AG3

129 *Cofemel v G-Star Raw CV* (C-683/17) AG3 at para 61

Figure 6.1 Madame Grés About 1950 Miniature Evening Dress V&A Museum no. T.20.1-2

considerations with those of the creators' need to protect their works. On this basis, the recent case law signals that Couture could potentially be accommodated by more expansive copyright provisions, either by express judicial legal opinion or as the thesis argues, to be explicitly added to the list within s.4 of the CDPA 1988.

To extend the implications for the unity concept, the thesis argues that when considering Couture, the approach to and understanding of the creation must be rooted in art, not function, as function is a by-product of Couture. Technical features are the main considerations for the application of the functionality doctrine, and therefore support industrial principles. The perspective from this thesis is that the unity notion is not aligned with the functionality doctrine, this is because the approach to industrial objects derives from and serves artistic significance.

The issue intensifies when the concept of unity is established; this as defined previously as the integration of art, function, and industry.[130] It is therefore necessary to consider the notion of artistry within a work and furthermore, that the creative and functional components may exist in unison. On this basis, the *Cofemel* ruling *effectively established that the work must be dependent on artistic creation*; on this basis, works which are functional are not necessarily excluded form copyright protection.[131] This is recognised as a significant development for Couture in that it establishes the ideal standard for fashion which is the recognition and acceptance of a creative work incorporating functional features. This essentially establishes that to identify Couture as artistic would not negate its functional, utilitarian qualities. The case of *Brompton* solidifies and supports this notion further as the ruling recognises the potential for creative works to acquire copyright protection.[132] As the focus of the case is to the shape, the analysis has unearthed that when applied to Couture, the ruling may effectively lead to Couture garments being separated by law, for the purposes of obtaining copyright protection, as the ruling specifically identified that not all parts of the bicycle are functional.[133]

Finally, Turkish copyright law would support the notion that Couture is primarily based on aesthetics pursuant to s.4 of the code, and therefore, the degree of technical function is to be assessed against the aesthetic attributes of the garment. As the functional components are seen as an essential and integral part of Couture which must be incorporated into the design, it is asserted that on this basis the limitations of copyright must be prevented from regulating technical works.

130 Koray Gűven, 'Unities of Art: Reconciling Function and Copyright' (2021) 52(9) IIC 1161–89

131 *Cofemel v G-Star Raw CV* (C-683/17) AG3

132 Rauer N, 'Law on copyright in shapes clarified in Brompton Bicycle case' (Pinsent Masons, 15thJune2020)<https://www.pinsentmasons.com/out-law/news/law-copyright-shapes-brompton> accessed 21 January 2025, referring to the case of Brompton Bicycle Ltd v Chedech/Get2Get (C-833/18), Opinion of Advocate General M. Campos Sánchez-Bordona, E.U:C:2020:79

133 Astrid Arnold, 'The Brompton Bicycle – The Collapsible Bike With a Collapsing Monopoly?' (*Stevens & Bolton LLP*, 17 June 2020) https://www.lexology.com/library/detail.aspx?g=9d517467-4630-49c6-81b5-574306d94106 accessed 29 May 2022

7 The Threshold for Copyright

Introduction

This chapter examines the standard expected for copyright protection and how this relates to Couture. The thesis question is tested within this chapter through the analysis of copyright legislation, and in the consideration of widening the criterion of 'artistic works' to include Couture fashion garments, based on the consideration of findings within the previous chapters. The chapter is the final within the study and aims to provide a birds-eye view of the issues discussed within the thesis in determining the criteria for copyright. The chapter brings together the findings of the study so far and considers whether the threshold for copyright and the extent to which the limitations identified impact Couture.

Subject matter is reconsidered in relation to the position for Couture as art, which comprises artistic craftmanship. In comparison, different types of artistic works and contemporary perspectives on copyright are addressed. The concepts of utilitarian and functional are considered as applied to Couture specifically, before the chapter progresses to ascertaining the threshold for copyright for Couture. The end of the chapter proposes draft legislation in consideration of the findings within the study to suggest reform for U.K. Couture.

7.1 Limitations of Copyright Law v Creative Innovation for Couture

Copyright has been described as a 'weak' legislative mechanism for protection.[1] The narrative surrounding this notion is due to copyright protecting the expression of the idea, and not the idea itself. The overall narrative breaking through the research for the study appears to maintain copyright as a monopoly. Whilst this may be regarded as having narrow parameters, copyright is a necessary part of commercial pursuits.[2] With this in mind, it is essential that Couture whilst an artistic pursuit, which is founded on deliberations of aesthetics, also contributes to commercial success through the attention afforded to a garment.[3]

1 Alan Beckley, 'Copyright Law: Monopoly or Monstrosity?' (1996) 146(6730) The New Law Journal
2 Alan Beckley, 'Copyright Law: Monopoly or Monstrosity?' (1996) 146(6730) The New Law Journal
3 Nanay Bence, *Aesthetics: A Very Short Introduction* (Oxford University Press 2019) 28

DOI: 10.4324/9781003599456-7

When looking at Couture, the construction and decorative methods are significant in consideration of the function. The sewing on Couture garments is described as having a dual objective as functional and ornamental.[4] Princess fitting seams (a seam with a reversed curve) are stated as functional and pockets are recognised as decorative and functional.[5] Chanel was known to be a significant influence on Couture; her pocket designs were at times functional and on other garments gave the illusion of a pocket, whereby the purpose was merely embellishment with the use of a flap.[6] The decorative aspects of sewing are also used in non-functional button holes, known as blind button holes.[7] The notable aspect of haute Couture therefore is the visual effect. What is regarded as a functional feature such as a pocket or buttonhole can be translated into a conceptually decorative and non-functional embellishment to the garment for the purposes of being a design feature.

7.1.1 Conceptual Art and Technical Considerations

The main purpose of haute Couture being conceptually visual is borne through notions of aesthetics which speak primarily to exclusivity. On this basis, can the application of the functionality doctrine be truly justified? To revisit the scholarly work of Keyes, the extent to which the designer engages in a subjective process is influenced by aesthetics, instead of functional notions.[8] Further, as stated earlier, Keyes suggests that products which are mainly utilitarian should not be afforded protection.[9] If we are to assess the degree that a product is regarded as being influenced by aesthetics and this is clearly shown to be the purpose and intention of the designer through the creative process, then Couture could be argued as being aesthetic only, and consequently the utilitarian notions should be negated from considerations relating to the grant of copyright for Couture. Afterall, trade marks and design rights provide technicality exclusions in consideration of the grant of either IP right, although in contrast, it seems unfair for the grant of copyright for artistic works to be deliberated on the grounds of the doctrine of functionality; specifically for creative works which incorporate technical features as an integral part of the creative work.

To extend the discussion further, a key issue to address is whether Couture is regarded as an industrial object. The proposed test put forward by Keyes portrays an awareness of the influence of functionality being essential for the pragmatism in industrial design. If we are to engage in this concept for Couture, the question to be asked is whether Couture must be pragmatic and moreover whether functionality therefore is essential.

4 Claire Schaeffer, *Couture Sewing Techniques* (Kindle edn, Taunton 2011) 1644

5 Claire Schaeffer, *Couture Sewing Techniques* (Kindle edn, Taunton 2011) 3341, 5692

6 Claire Schaeffer, *Couture Sewing Techniques* (Kindle edn, Taunton 2011) 3341, 5692

7 Claire Schaeffer, *Couture Sewing Techniques* (Kindle edn, Taunton 2011) 13747

8 Barton Keyes, 'Alive and Well: The (Still) Ongoing Debate Surrounding Conceptual Separability in American Copyright Law' (2008) Ohio State Journal

9 Barton Keyes, 'Alive and Well: The (Still) Ongoing Debate Surrounding Conceptual Separability in American Copyright Law' (2008) Ohio State Journal

Haute Couture utilises traditional handicraft methods of embellishment and construction practices; haute Couture designers are regarded as artisans.[10] Here, Couture is perceived as a incorporating artistic craftmanship in pursuit of creating the art. Whilst Dior is known for disrupting the older model of haute Couture after the Second World War as a pinnacle figure at the epicentre of international business, and is known for initiating more industrialised approaches, the handicraft methods are still used.[11]

With Couture being noted as founded on principles of aesthetics, the rationale for the application of the functionality doctrine may be difficult to comprehend. For example, the cocktail dress by Christian Dior in 1952 (Spring) demonstrates the application of embroidery as crafted to give the densest embellishment at the waist, with carefully considered spacing. The purpose of the embroidery is to provide a sense of dimension to the surface of the dress, creating patterns reminiscent of a 'meadow's variegation' and therefore to ultimately provide eye-appeal.[12] Another example would be the coral cotton lace evening gown by Hubert de Givenchy.[13] The dress is embellished with surface applique embroidery and re-embroidered with coral-coloured beads.[14] Whilst the shape of the A-line silhouette is described as minimalist, the overall aesthetic effect of the gown is the antithesis of simple.[15]

Ought creations of Couture be subjected to copyright limitations based on essential components such as zips and fastenings enabling wear, and which are intrinsic to the creative process, to be allowed to prevent or even fragment copyright protection (in consideration of separability), when much of the creation is hereby argued to be a work of art, comprising of artistic craftmanship? Are the limitations of copyright protection due to the comprising of the minority features, justified when Couture garments are created and apparently led by aesthetics? The next section shall examine the impact of sustainable innovation for Couture in relation to the creative techniques used and the impact on the originality requirement.

10 Fashinza, 'What is Haute Couture' (*Fashinza*, 2022) <https://fashinza.com/textile/fashion-industry/what-is-haute-Couture-and-why-does-it-matter/> accessed 12 June 2022 and The Business of Fashion (BOF), 'How Christian Dior Is Training Its Next Generation of Craftsmen' (*BOF*, 2023) <https://www.businessoffashion.com/videos/luxury/how-christian-dior-is-training-its-next-generation-of-craftsman/> accessed 1 June 2023

11 Veronique Poulliard, *Paris to New York, the Transatlantic Fashion Industry in the Twentieth Century* (Harvard University Press 2021) 145

12 Richard Martin and Harold Koda, 'Haute Couture' (1996) *The Metropolitan Museum of Art* 17, referring to Christian Dior, Cocktail Dress, Spring 1952

13 Richard Martin and Harold Koda, 'Haute Couture' (1996) *The Metropolitan Museum of Art* 211, referring to Hubert De Givenchy, Evening gown 1963

14 Richard Martin and Harold Koda, 'Haute Couture' (1996) *The Metropolitan Museum of Art* 211, referring to Hubert De Givenchy, Evening gown 1963

15 Richard Martin and Harold Koda, 'Haute Couture' (1996) *The Metropolitan Museum of Art* 211, referring to Hubert De Givenchy, Evening gown 1963

7.1.2 Sustainable Innovation and the Implications for Copyright

One issue which is of concern is the ethics behind a brand as it relates to sustainable innovation. E.U. policy is expected to consider environmental concerns when formulating policy, pursuant to TFEU. Articles 3(3) and 11.[16] These concerns are reflected in the general fashion industries, with sustainability being a vigorous consideration for brands in how they source, manufacture, and deliver their products. In the fashion industry, sustainability appears to have a two-purpose aim, that is to protect the employees in the manufacturing of the clothing whilst protecting the environment.[17] In short, sustainability is achieved through the reduction of CO_2 emissions, the reduction of waste, using textiles which are biodegradable, and good working conditions for employees pertaining to safety and fair wages.[18]

Couture, a branch of fashion, is suggested as being intrinsically more sustainable than mass-manufactured fast fashion. This is supported by Iris Van Herpen who has stated that couturiers are producing on demand, which is the opposite of producing in the *hope* to sell.[19] To illustrate the methods for implementing sustainability practice, Ronald van der Kemp has expressed that his Couture garments are created through the sourcing of textiles from 'vintage pieces.'[20] Other couturiers implementing sustainability strategies are Viktor & Rolf and Xuan.[21] Dior also uses methods in creating Couture through the use of textile recycling.'[22]

In consideration of copyright protection for Couture and the implications of sustainability, one matter which is highlighted is the originality requirement. It is evident from the preceding commentary that couturiers are being challenged by the sustainability issues to provide novel ways for production and business models. For this reason, the originality criteria pertaining to art could be assisted by sustainability considerations. For example, van der Kemp is using vintage textiles and Dior is recycling textiles; therefore, the methods used in the intellectual creation of the Couture garment only add to the originality. In consideration of the collateral effect of using novel sustainability methods in Couture, what may have

16 Max Oker-Blom, 'Some Thoughts on Sustainability and Upcycling From a Copyright and Trademark Law Point of View' (*IPR University Centre*, 6 September 2022) <https://iprinfo.fi/artikkeli/some-thoughts-on-sustainability-and-upcycling-from-a-copyright-and-trademark-law-point-of-view/> accessed 20 September 2023

17 Emily Chan, '16 Things Everyone Should Know About Sustainable Fashion' (*Vogue*, 18 April 2022) <https://www.vogue.co.uk/fashion/article/sustainable-fashion> accessed 20 September 2023

18 Emily Chan, '16 Things Everyone Should Know About Sustainable Fashion' (*Vogue*, 18 April 2022) <https://www.vogue.co.uk/fashion/article/sustainable-fashion> accessed 20 September 2023

19 Emily Chan, '16 Things Everyone Should Know About Sustainable Fashion' (*Vogue*, 18 April 2022) <https://www.vogue.co.uk/fashion/article/sustainable-fashion> accessed 20 September 2023

20 Emily Chan, 'Is Couture the Most Sustainable Fashion Week of All?' (*Vogue*, 2 July 2019) <https://www.vogue.fr/fashion/article/is-Couture-the-most-sustainable-fashion-week-of-all> accessed 20 September 2023

21 Emily Chan, 'Is Couture the Most Sustainable Fashion Week of All?' (*Vogue*, 2 July 2019) <https://www.vogue.fr/fashion/article/is-Couture-the-most-sustainable-fashion-week-of-all> accessed 20 September 2023

22 Dior, 'Dior Sustainability' (*Dior*, 2023) <https://www.dior.com/en_gb/fashion/news-fashion-shows/folder-news-and-events/dior-sustainability> accessed 20 September 2023

been previously overlooked by the courts may now be brought into focus. When assessing originality, the courts may find that the assessment will go beyond the visual as in historic copyright cases and extend to the sensory feel of the garment. To illustrate this further, one of the most intricate and careful examinations into an infringement claim is seen in the case of *Designer Guilds*, in which the judge looked at the brush strokes and varying differential effect of the two designs visually.[23] When assessing originality, sustainable innovation provides for novel creative methods, use of materials, and construction methods to be considered in the whole assessment. In doing so, the perspective from this thesis is that it would be unjust to only provide copyright protection for the drawings of those Couture garments, when it is the end-product which wholly and collectively comprises of the art. For example, when looking at a fine art painting or sculpture, the appreciation derives from the visual and the textural effect. This in essence provides for the experience of the observer of the art; to illustrate this, consider David Medalla's *Cloud Canyons*, the sculpture consisting of white foam, transparent tubes, and a circular pool to capture the movement.[24] The sculpture has more than a visual impact and provides the observer of the art with an extended sensory experience.

Furthermore, with sustainability at the heart of creative innovation, it is necessary to consider the opportunities presented for developing art. To further support for the grant of copyright for Couture as art, the issue of stifling creativity when not doing so arises. Suggested is that creativity drives innovation, and that in turn, innovation is essential for enhancing performance.[25] Additionally demonstrated is that when an individual hides knowledge, their creativity is affected negatively.[26] When this theory is applied to Couture creation, where the law is limited in the definition of artistic works as an apparent closed list, the law is effectively hiding the art. Where the art is not recognised, is there any incentive for further creativity by couturiers and further, when work is not recognised and therefore listed as art within s.4 of the CDPA 1988, the potential to develop upon existing creations by other creators may become limited and innovation, to a degree, stifled. With this expressed, originality in Couture can only be achieved through the cyclical process of creativity, driving innovation to influence further intellectual creations. To support this further, when considering a novel pattern cutting technique, subtraction cutting,[27] it is suggested that it is the 'aesthetic' that is copied, and not 'the technique or process developments.'[28] This is significant, as creating art rests upon the

23 *Designers Guild Ltd v Russel Williams (Textiles) Ltd* [1998] F.R. 803

24 Adrian Searle, 'Hepworth Sculpture Prize Review: A Brilliant Beginning' (*The Guardian*, 20 October 2016) <https://www.theguardian.com/artanddesign/2016/oct/20/hepworth-sculpture-prize-review-medalla-barlow-marten-claydon> accessed 20 September 2023

25 Matej Černe and others, 'What Goes Around Comes Around: Knowledge, Hiding, Perceived Motivational Climate and Creativity' (2014) 57(1) The Academy of Management Journal 172–92

26 Matej Černe and others, 'What Goes Around Comes Around: Knowledge, Hiding, Perceived Motivational Climate and Creativity' (2014) 57(1) The Academy of Management Journal 172–92

27 Subtraction method, please see key definitions

28 Holly Mcquillan Timo Rissanen Julian Roberts, 'The Cutting Circle: How Making Challenges Design' (2013) 17(1) RJTA Please see the key definitions on the subtraction technique in relation to pattern cutting

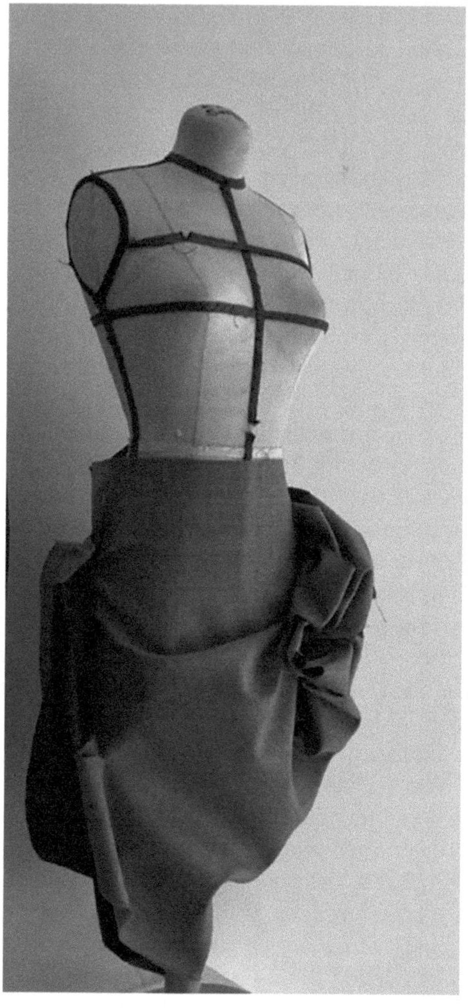

Figure 7.1 Skirt Toile Creation, Using the Subtraction Method. By Joshua Masih, Senior Lecturer, UAL, London College of Fashion

methods used to provide the effect to the final piece. The more innovative practices that are developed not only contribute to discovering new methods, but in turn form art. For this reason, the perspective of this thesis is that originality within art does not derive from the visual effect only, but it is in addition determined by the construction and practice methods. Sustainable innovation within the fashion sphere provides for the potential for exceptionally original innovative Couture creation.

Whilst drawings of Couture designs can be protected by copyright, when considering Couture as an artistic work, it potentially appears unjust not to protect the end-product, the *art*. Sustainable innovation practice for Couture provides for the expansion of contributing to the copyright requirement of originality. The appreciation of Couture as an artistic work originates from the entire practice of art creation to provide the wearer and observer with a multi-sensory experience, stemming from the texture and visual effect. Technical constraints shall be discussed later in this chapter.

7.2 The Concept of Utilitarian: Industrious v Creative Works

The preceding analysis draws upon a conceptual perception of Couture being whole when both artistic and functional elements exist together within one product. The rationale for industrially produced objects being withdrawn from copyright protection is said to be due to concern over monopolies, and it is further observed that the artist was regarded as an 'industrial worker.'[29] An industrial object is characterised by an object that is used within everyday life, which may range from 'simplest tools to automobiles.'[30] This question is identified as significant, as the answer may be dependent on the degree of industrial input as to whether a Couture garment is defined as an industrial object. The couturier could be identified as being an industrial worker. Therefore, are we to look at Couture as a utilitarian functional work, with added or derivative art? With the consumer in mind, art is usually utilised in product design to embellish industrially manufactured objects for the purposes of establishing commercial viability.[31] Copyright is examined here in consideration of what Couture is. Suthersanen refers to the issue of 'industrial objects,' which is defined as 'industrially manufactured objects expressed in three-dimensional form.'[32] This definition is now applied to Couture, to ascertain the extent to which Couture may be regarded as an industrial object. The rationale for the question is that the artistry within Couture utilises art to initiate viability within the marketplace; in other words, the art distinguishes Couture from other Couture products in terms of Couture being specifically skilfully crafted as opposed to mass produced, and attention to detail in the creative process for the garment, in consideration of the techniques for assembly and embellished features.[33] The creative process for Couture is of primary significance in consideration as an industrial object, as

29 Uma Suthersanen, 'Copyright and Industrial Objects: Aesthetic Considerations and Policy Discriminations' in Matthew David and Debora Halbert (eds), *SAGE Handbook of Intellectual Property* (Queen Mary School of Law Legal Studies Research Paper No. 168/2014, 21 January 2014) <https://ssrn.com/abstract=2382718>

30 Matt Fussell, 'Industrial Design: The Art of Objects' (*The Virtual Instructor*, 2022) <https://thevirtualinstructor.com/blog/industrial-design-the-art-of-objects-2> accessed 26 March 2023

31 Uma Suthersanen, 'Copyright and Industrial Objects: Aesthetic Considerations and Policy Discriminations' in Matthew David and Debora Halbert (eds), *SAGE Handbook of Intellectual Property* (Queen Mary School of Law Legal Studies Research Paper No. 168/2014, 21 January 2014) <https://ssrn.com/abstract=2382718>

32 Uma Suthersanen, 'Copyright and Industrial Objects: Aesthetic Considerations and Policy Discriminations' in Matthew David and Debora Halbert (eds), *SAGE Handbook of Intellectual Property* (Queen Mary School of Law Legal Studies Research Paper No. 168/2014, 21 January 2014) <https://ssrn.com/abstract=2382718>

33 Claire B Shaeffer, 'Couture Sewing: The Couture Cardigan Jacket, Sewing Secrets From a Chanel Collector' (*The Taunton Press Inc*, 2013) 347

it addresses the qualitative aspects such as 'merit, worthiness, functionality and aestheticism.'[34] Chapter 1 established the fact that the concept of Couture, whilst an independent notion, is inextricable from the garment.

This concept is a natural component of the product, whereby the couturier deploys autonomy pertaining to artistic craftmanship and innovation within the creative process, for the purpose of achieving a fashionable product. Suthersanen identifies a 'discrimination' towards industrial objects as it relates to qualitative considerations based on the 'nature of the substrate manifesting the form, or the purpose of the creator, or the value, or the final contextual use.'[35] In response to this point, this study raises concerns for Couture not being included within the closed list of protectable works within the CDPA 1988. In consideration of manufactured products and copyright exclusion, the position was clarified in the *Lucasfilm* judgement in that manufactured objects were not automatically excluded from copyright on this basis.

7.3 The Juncture: Originality and Subject Matter

With these considerations in mind for Couture, the following analysis attempts to ascertain the approach to originality and subject matter in copyright. This is in consideration of Couture and whether recent developments in the law are facilitating a move away from the generic application to different subject matter, and whether the implications of this are that a more specific application is necessitated, based on the quality and subject matter.

The main challenge which remains is that whilst subject matter can be differentiated in copyright as seen in *Interlego*, making legal provisions between different types of artistic works would be beneficial. This is because not all artistic works have technical elements and therefore, the standard of copyright between different types of artistic works must be established. Ultimately, not having the constraints as related to technicality would make attracting copyright protection more straightforward. Moreover, would this mean a lower standard for Couture (based on the technical attributes) or just different?

The idea within a creative work is an element that may significantly contribute to the creative expression within the context of the subject matter for which it has been formed. To elaborate, as mentioned previously, in the case of BSA, it was held that where the expression is dictated by the technical function, originality is

34 Uma Suthersanen, 'Copyright and Industrial Objects: Aesthetic Considerations and Policy Discriminations' in Matthew David and Debora Halbert (eds), *SAGE Handbook of Intellectual Property* (Queen Mary School of Law Legal Studies Research Paper No. 168/2014, 21 January 2014) <https://ssrn.com/abstract=2382718>

35 Uma Suthersanen, 'Copyright and Industrial Objects: Aesthetic Considerations and Policy Discriminations' in Matthew David and Debora Halbert (eds), *SAGE Handbook of Intellectual Property* (Queen Mary School of Law Legal Studies Research Paper No. 168/2014, 21 January 2014) <https://ssrn.com/abstract=2382718>

absent. Here the focus is on the 'idea' and expression of an idea, a significant point, specifically within the context of subject matter.

The decision reached in *Infopaq* does not distinguish between works of different subject matter, within the meaning of art.2(a) of Directive 2001/29.[36] On this basis, to what extent is it necessary to distinguish between varying subject matter. Bentley et al identify the advantages of having 'a generalised' test for originality.[37] The test would facilitate coherency, both horizontally and vertically. In a horizontal application of the regime, it would treat differing works according to one consistent standard; when applied vertically, the regime would create a rational link between the benchmark in infringement and subsistence.[38] However, significantly, a single standard is suggested to 'remove flexibility' relating to the different categories of artistic works.[39]

The *Cofemel* ruling appeared to place value on the 'free and creative choices' of the author as it appeared to not negate the possibility of copyright protection to technical works and furthermore reflected the subject matter.[40] The point on subject matter is an imperative one, as the standardisation for works 'ex ante' is identified as a challenge for artistic works.[41] This is particularly seen when the provisions in the legislation, namely s.4 CDPA 1988 operates a closed list. It seems burdensome to legally establish an artistic work outside of the given criteria of the closed list. Similarly identified by Rosati when referring to *Lucasfilm*, the storm trooper helmet could not be intended as a sculpture within the meaning of s.4 of the CDPA 1988.[42]

Although the *BSA* case was decided on a completely different subject matter, the originality decision related very strongly to the technical aspects of the 'graphic user interface.'[43] Here we see a constraint, a rule being implemented in that where 'the idea and the expression become indissociable' it becomes difficult to distinguish between the idea and the expression, the expression is dictated by the technical aspects and therefore originality cannot be identified in law.[44] The problem identified here is that the subject matter is significant: Should technicality in regard to Couture be assessed along the same lines as the technicality in computer

36 Please see: *Infopaq International A/S v Danske Dagblades Forening* (C-5/08) E.U:C:2009:465; [1987] F.S.R. 409 and Tomruk Űstűnkaya, 'The Functionality Doctrine: The Challenges to Fashion Copyright' (2020) 42(3) EIPR 156

37 L Bentley and others, *Intellectual Property Law* (6th edn, Oxford University Press 2022) 99

38 L Bentley and others, *Intellectual Property Law* (6th edn, Oxford University Press 2022) 99

39 L Bentley and others, *Intellectual Property Law* (6th edn, Oxford University Press 2022) 99

40 Eleonora Rosati, 'Italian Supreme Court Rules That Technical Regulation (Drafted by an IP Lawyer) May Be *In Principle* Protected by Copyright' (*IP Kat*, 21 June 2020) <https://ipkitten.blogspot.com/search/label/decision%2010300%2F2020%20Casucci%20v%20Unipol%20Assicurazioni%20S.p.A.%20and%20Others> accessed 19 February 2022 referring to *Cofemel v G-Star Raw CV* (C-683/17) at para 30

41 Please see: Eleanora Rosati, *Originality in E.U. Copyright* (Edward Elgar 2012) 125

42 Please see: Eleanora Rosati, *Originality in E.U. Copyright* (Edward Elgar 2012) 125

43 *Bezpečnostni softwarová asociace* Case C-393/09 [2011] ECR I-13971 [49]

44 Judgement of 22. 12. 2010 – CASE C-393/09 at para 49

programs (as in *BSA*, the graphic user interface)? Is the expression in computer programs the same as the expression conveyed in Couture, particularly as it relates to the incorporation of the technical aspects? This question is finite and nuanced, and this is the issue with copyright law. The derivative question is: To what extent should copyright law extend subject matter and, on this foundation, adapt the criteria for originality? Firstly, to consider the element of subject matter, this study is advocating that s.4 of the CDPA 1988 should include 'Couture' as an artistic work, although to elaborate, could the criteria therefore which applies to originality be amended to include exclusions?

A draft legislative provision is later in this chapter, based on the premise that Couture is included in s.4 of the CDPA 1988. S.1(1)(a) of the Act stipulates that the work must be 'original'; however, the 'rules' and constraints surrounding originality and its precise definition appear to have been developed (and to some extent is still developing by case law). On this point, the view put forward here is that perhaps the requirement for originality for copyright works, whilst necessary, was premature and therefore under-developed, when the legislation operates a generic application of copyright, without distinguishing between various subject matter (particularly as it pertains to the individual attributes for artistic works). It is evident through the decisions in both *Cofemel* and *Brompton* that it has been necessary to consider the aspect of technicality, specifically as a rule, as a constraint, and to rethink the parameters around the originality requirement in light of the previous case law, *BSA* and *SAS*.[45]

The implications of the developing narrative for originality rest on the notion that works are being assessed carefully on an individual basis and in addition that the originality criterion is being reconsidered as a natural part of the process. In turn, the generic application of copyright to different subject matter may have to be developed into a more specific application. In other words, there is an interconnection between originality and subject matter which must be addressed. Originality appears to be one of the most challenging factors in attaining copyright protection, as the work must be regarded as original in law. The non-functional requirement to establish originality was seen in the *BSA* case, when where the work is found to be dictated by its technical function, the work could not obtain copyright.[46] The originality requirement must be considered in conjunction with the subject matter and further facilitate a more specific application of copyright. Yes, it may very well be an onerous task and further, it is accepted that unless cases arise, problems are not necessarily recognised and cannot be legally acknowledged and resolved, until such a time. Although, developments have been such over the past few years as illustrated in this study that may indicate that reform is required in consideration of these issues.

45 *Bezpečnostni softwarová asociace* Case C-393/09 [2011] ECR I-13971 [49] and *SAS Institute Inc v World Programming Ltd*, Case C-406/10 [2012] 3 C|MLR (4) 55,68, [AG44] (AG Bot)

46 Eleanora Rosati, *Originality in E.U. Copyright* (Edward Elgar 2012) 124

7.4 The Standard for Couture

In terms of separability the use of the word 'indissociable' in the *BSA* case is significant as it addresses both the idea and the expression:

> As the Advocate General states in Points 75 and 76 of his Opinion, where the expression of those components is dictated by their technical function, the criterion of originality is not met, since the different methods of implementing an idea are so limited that the idea and the expression become indissociable.[47]

The *BSA* case raises issues pertaining to elements of creativity as it relates to the granting of copyright protection, the idea, expression, technical function. With this as a foundation in identifying the rationale for judicial decisions taken in *BSA* and thereafter, each element shall be analysed to understand whether each of these components can have different implications for the expression of an idea in conjunction with considerations for subject matter as follows:

7.4.1 The Idea

As seen in chapter 1, the various aspects involved in creating Couture rest within the research for the garment, particularly looking into future forecasts for trends.[48] The idea for the Couture garment must engage the constraints of functionality to facilitate performance and aesthetic objectives before it can be tangibly expressed.[49]

7.4.2 The Expression

The expression of the idea must accommodate both skill sets of 'creative'[50] and 'technical,' and it is here that industry and the legal definition of originality may conflict.[51] The ruling of *BSA* expresses that the expression is dictated by the technical function, and where the idea and expression become 'indissociable' confers that originality is absent.[52] The imperative question is: At which point can a Couture garment not be dictated by the technical function, therefore that the idea and the expression become separate components? As stated earlier on, without the technical function, the garment could not be worn. Would this therefore mean that all Couture garments are *not* original according to the ruling in *BSA*? The idea would be driven by the considerations for the expression, although the expression would

47 *Bezpečnostní softwarová asociace – Svaz softwarové ochrany v Ministerstvo kultury*, C-393/09 at para 49
48 Gwyneth Holland and Rae Jones, *Fashion Trend Forecasting* (Laurence King Publishing 2017) 73
49 Tim Jackson and David Shaw, *The Fashion Handbook* (Routledge 2006) 40
50 Tim Jackson and David Shaw, *The Fashion Handbook* (Routledge 2006) 40
51 Tim Jackson and David Shaw, *The Fashion Handbook* (Routledge 2006) 40
52 JUDGMENT OF 22. 12. 2010 – CASE C-393/09 at para 49

be dictated by the technical function. Essentially, the answer would be that based on *BSA* Couture works could not attract copyright protection.

7.4.3 Technical

Conversely, Bently et al address the case of the Football Association Premier League referring to the courts' reasoning that sporting events are absent in creative freedom due to the limitations of the rules of the game.[53] Bently et al evaluate the weight of this reasoning in consideration of the constraints as a consequence of the 'rules' in creative freedom and identify that 'the resulting work is unlikely to be original.'[54] Two points arise here which derive from the words 'constraint' and 'unlikely.' To establish originality, this notion should be considered further than in application to football events. Conversely, acknowledged previously is that the author of the work must exercise their creative freedom within the parameters of the constraints.[55] On this basis, the constraints may not necessarily be an impediment to copyright depending on the extent of the constraint, and further, this may be entirely dependent on the degree of implementation of the creativity into the *constraint* through the creative process. The argument put forward rests on the premise that the constraint is part of the intellectual creative process and therefore a contributing component to the artistic work. For example, we may consider the functional element of Couture, such as corsetry; as an integral part of the work, in consideration of the doctrine of functionality, the corsetry as it relates to the technical aspects is part of the art within the work as a whole.[56] Innovative implementation of the expression of creative ideas into artistic works may therefore enable the constraints to be overcome.

The *Brompton* case is identified by the study as having a significant impact on Couture as when considering the bicycle, the constraints for copyright pertaining to its technical and therefore functional aspects were regarded as being a part of the bicycle. In other words, there is more to consider for the purposes of copyright than the technical features as not all parts of the bicycle are functional. The attention of the court was drawn towards the creative expression and exercise of free and creative decisions of the author of the work.[57] Similarly to *Cofemel*, when applied to Couture, these decisions would affirm that a standard in copyright is emerging that is taking into consideration the various constraints (such as technicality) of

53 L Bentley and others, *Intellectual Property Law* (6th edn, Oxford University Press 2022) 100 referring to *Football Association Premier League v QC Leisure and Karen Murphy v Media Protection Services*, Joined cases C-403/08 and C-429/08 [2011] ECR I-9083 (ECJ, Grand Chamber), [98]

54 L Bentley and others, *Intellectual Property Law* (6th edn, Oxford University Press 2022) 100

55 Tomruk Űstűnkaya, 'The Functionality Doctrine: Is 3D Printing Challenging Rigidity in Fashion Law?' (2020) 42(5) EIPR 286

56 Please see: Tomruk Űstűnkaya, 'The Functionality Doctrine: Is 3D Printing Challenging Rigidity in Fashion Law?' (2020) 42(5) EIPR 286

57 Rauer N, 'Law on copyright in shapes clarified in Brompton Bicycle case' (Pinsent Masons, 15th June 2020) <https://www.pinsentmasons.com/out-law/news/law-copyright-shapes-brompton> accessed 21 January 2025, referring to the case of Brompton Bicycle Ltd v Chedech/Get2Get (C-833/18), Opinion of Advocate General M. Campos Sánchez-Bordona, E.U:C:2020:79

different subject matter rather than applying a blanket application of the 'rules' or 'constraints' of the doctrine of functionality.

The standard for copyright appears to be emerging as being reflective on specific characteristics of artistic works. Would this indicate that differentiating between subject matter in copyright will not be necessary? Moreover, that the copyright law is developing sufficiently enough to provide for the generic application for copyright law? An argument put forward from the perspective of this study is that in principle, whilst these developments are notable, when relying on case law, the risk of the law changing and reverting to the previous position in *BSA* is a possibility. This conclusion is reached due to the decision in *Interlego* where the distinction between artistic works and literary works was acknowledged in the decision, however, in *Infopaq* this recognition was absent.[58] This point supports implementation of and extension to s.4 of the CDPA 1988 for the inclusion of Couture as an artistic work, which specifically and additionally addresses the technical component of Couture as necessary.

Based on the rulings of *Cofemel* and *Brompton*, the development of copyright law must be to establish creative expression in consideration of technical elements and must derive from the viewpoint of assessing the artistic work (Couture) as being technicality dictated by creative expression. Should this be considered, the law would necessitate the approach to the functionality doctrine implementing exceptions for Couture works. Couture as an artistic work is supported throughout the thesis particularly in how Couture is realised, through artistic practices. On the basis that Couture is an artistic work, the approach of the courts should align in recognising Couture as an artistic practice and therefore implement legal provisions to reflect this significant point. Firstly, the courts could consider an approach akin to innominate terms in the law of contract, whereby the courts look to the effect of the breach on the agreement rather than whether the contract was breached or not.[59] However, in the case of Couture, to determine Couture as an artistic work, the courts would be looking to the extent the work is dictated by artistry and not *whether* the work is dictated by technical attributes or not. Secondly, this thesis would argue that when assessing Couture as an artistic work, the courts should be considering the extent to which the technical components deprive the garment of its artistic quality.

7.4.4 Two-Limb Test

Based on the preceding analysis, this study puts forward a two-limb test:

Step 1: To what extent is the work dictated by artistry? This must establish that the work was derived by and produced using artistic practice methods, derived

58 Tomruk Űstűnkaya, 'The Functionality Doctrine: The Challenges to Fashion Copyright' (2020) 42(3) EIPR 156. Please see: *Interlego v Tyco Industries* [1987] F.S.R. 409 at [50] and *Infopaq International v Danske Dagblades Forening* (C-5/08) E.U:C:2009:465; [1987] F.S.R. 409

59 Please see: *Hong Kong Fir Shipping Ltd v Kisen Kaisha Ltd* (1962) E.W.C.A. Civ 7

from the intellectual creative expression of ideas through various art mediums including digital.

a. Expression of ideas. This will be realised through the initial conception of the idea and rooted in research methods in trend forecasts and experimentation of colour palettes, shapes, form, and illustrations.
b. Product development stage which will include toile creation and final product.

Step 2: Assessment of the extent the technical components deprive the garment of artistic quality, if at all.

For step 1, all criteria must be satisfied and for step 2 the technical components must not be to the extent that the artistic quality is deprived. Where both of these elements are satisfied, the Couture garment must be considered as an artistic work in consideration of s.4 of the CDPA 1988.

7.5 Couture: Originality Standard?

It is reported that high street fashion stores are offering for sale 'versions' of Couture.[60] This leads to legal disputes between the couturiers and high street brands such as Chloe and Kookai, where Kookai was alleged to have copied Chloe's snakeskin Silvardo bag design.[61] Acknowledged is that in practice the difficulty for designers is rooted in the fact that fashion is derivative in nature irrespective of the distinction between copying and those creative works being inspired by the catwalk.[62]

Couture is observed to face more challenges in meeting the requirements of originality compared to other subject matter (such as a painting or photograph as these works are not technical in nature). This is due to the industry expectations in relation to the dictation of upcoming trends, in addition to the consideration of the non-functional requirement to establish originality (as related to the technical components). These issues lead to a two-limb contemplation regarding the standard for copyright. On the one hand it could be argued that the standard for Couture should be lowered to reflect these additional complications as other subject matter does not encounter both copyright and industry barriers to copyright. On the other hand, lowering the standard for Couture could be viewed as de-valuing a Couture creator's creation. Examined earlier was the standard for artistic craftmanship in *Hensher*, which may be argued as being too high; we therefore cannot expect the standard for Couture to be lowered either.[63] A conciliation between these two positions would necessitate reassessing the originality requirement in copyright

60 Catherine Baksi, 'Style Counsel' *Law Society Gazette* (15 September 2005) 32
61 Catherine Baksi, 'Style Counsel' *Law Society Gazette* (15 September 2005) 32
62 Catherine Baksi, 'Style Counsel' *Law Society Gazette* (15 September 2005) 32
63 *George Hensher Ltd v Restawile* [1976] A.C. 64

generally, as Couture has uncovered a disproportionate assessment of originality in consideration of the current requirements.

This complex outcome may be due to copyright law perceiving Couture as industrious. Rosati expresses that 'the very meaning of originality inevitably differs between works of imagination and those of industrious collection. . . . Yet, the legal test to be applied in order to determine whether a work is protected by copyright ought to be the same for both.'[64] This statement would very much support the concept at the centre of this thesis, and that is that Couture is both industrious and creative. Copyright law therefore appears to draw a distinction between the two concepts of creative and industrious, which essentially impacts copyright law application.

Defining a new standard for copyright in originality would necessitate looking closely at works to examine the artistic contribution to the work, but in addition, the distinction between a creative work and an industrious one would be absent.[65] This is imperative for Couture works because if copyright law protects artistic works, Couture must be observed closely enough by copyright law to enable the identification of the art contained therein and/or the whole work as a work of art.

Further, a close observation would require identifying and making a firm distinction between works which are *copied* and those which are *influenced*, which may essentially include derivative works. The distinction between copying and being influenced has been acknowledged in copyright law to some degree when Lord Bingham expressed that Designers Guild may have drawn inspiration from elsewhere as 'there is no new thing under the sun.' Conversely, this concept is found historically in other traditions such as in 17th century Chinese art, when artists were developing their own works.[66] At that time, some terms were suggested to promote this notion, such as the term *fang* which is said to be interpreted as 'copy' or 'imitate' although the natural intention of this term is 'to follow after' or 'be inspired by.'[67] Today, in contemporary practice, Bradley identifies the difference between influenced works and copied works, he expresses that copies are reproducing the work exactly as it is seen or heard, whilst to be inspired is to avoid copying. Bradley expresses that to avoid copying, the inspiration must be removed from the 'finished design' and suggests that inspiration is drawn from other industries and then applied to the new creative work.[68] When we apply this concept to copyright law, it could essentially mean that inspiration should be drawn from other

64 Eleanora Rosati, *Originality in E.U. Copyright Full Harmonisation Through Case Law* (Edward Elgar 2013) 59

65 This absence of a distinction between industrious and creative derives from the recognition Rosati expresses. Please see: Eleanora Rosati, *Originality in E.U. Copyright Full Harmonisation Through Case Law* (Edward Elgar 2013) 59

66 Katherine Persis Burnett, *Dimensions of Originality Essays on 17th Century Chinese Art Theory and Criticism* (Chinese University Press 2013) 19

67 Katherine Persis Burnett, *Dimensions of Originality Essays on 17th Century Chinese Art Theory and Criticism* (Chinese University Press 2013) 19

68 Steven Bradley, 'The Line Between Inspired By and Copied From And How to Stay on Its Right Side' (*Vaneso Design*, 13 May 2013) <https://vanseodesign.com/web-design/inspired-by-copied-from/> accessed 20 May 2022

subject matter. An example to illustrate this further could take the form of inspiration drawn from fine art in relation to colours and shape, then being incorporated to some degree into the Couture garments, either in the colour of the garment, the form, or textile print. The preceding commentary leads to establishing a criterion for the purposes of founding a standard in originality for copyright, which Couture would be inclusive of. The criterion is set out as follows:

1. Artistic works must be considered irrespective of being inclusive of either/or creative and industrious components.
2. The artistic contribution must be identified; and
   a. incorporated into the work as:
   b. colour, texture, image, applique, form, or shape.
3. Influence must be proved to be from a separate industry, other than the subject matter of which the work belongs to.

On this basis, draft legislation is suggested next to honour and echo the nature of the U.K. copyright protections whilst advancing and widening the subject matter to specifically include Couture.

7.6 Draft Legislation

CDPA 1988 s.4 to be widened to include/read:

S.4 (1) CDPA . . .
d) Couture
S.4 (2)
c) Couture is defined as a garment incorporating artistic characteristics which must be proved to exist throughout the work; and derived through the creative process in 2d design drawings and/or digital images.
(i) Developed by artistic craftmanship skill and labour.
(ii) Creative expression must dictate the function of technical components.

Interim Conclusion

In applying a standard for Couture, the originality criteria in copyright pertaining to subject matter is a significant consideration. The derivative question identified because of the study is to what extent should the law include Couture in s.4 of the CDPA 1988? The requirement for developing originality may be one that should be reconsidered as it pertains to Couture but also reassessed regularly for the purposes of legislative provisions remaining contemporary and responding to innovation adequately. Whilst drawings of Couture designs can be protected by copyright, when considering Couture as an artistic work, it would appear unjust *not* to protect the end-product, the art. Sustainable innovation practice for Couture provides for the expansion of contributing to the copyright requirement of originality. The appreciation of Couture as an artistic work originates from the entire practice of art creation, to provide the wearer and observer with a multi-sensory experience stemming from the texture and visual effect.

In consideration of the standard for copyright, the definition of a work of artistic craftmanship as considered in *Hensher* may potentially be too high, although a much lower standard for Couture would ultimately de-value the art.[69] Couture must be regarded as an artistic work based on the creative nature of the pursuit, and therefore the standard for all artistic works must establish a non-restrictive quality between creative works which is currently seen in the closed list within s.4 of the CDPA 1988. The current position for works included in s.4 of the CDPA may give the impression of superiority of artistic works (and this should be whether the artistic work is industrious in nature or not) between those which are listed and those which are not, and therefore may attribute to the arguments raised for the value afforded to Couture in law.

69 *George Hensher Ltd v Restawile* [1976] A.C. 64

Conclusion

The research for this thesis in determining whether copyright legislation must widen the criterion of 'artistic works,' to include Couture garments, was achieved by mainly considering the views of philosophers and scholars, and whether this is in alignment with the legal definition of an artistic work pursuant to s.4 of the CDPA 1988 and case law. The main findings of the thesis are as follows.

The most prominent points to take away from the study are that during the art creative process, influence is drawn from existing things and is integral to industry practice. For this reason, it is essential that the industry and legal definitions of 'copying' are closely aligned. Artistic craftmanship is an intrinsic element of Couture and therefore comprised within the artistic work. Similarly, design is equally a part of Couture, and similarly contributes to the artistic work. Finally, it is ultimately argued that Couture is an artistic work in its entirety which justifies copyright protection specifically under s.4 of the CDPA 1988.

As a category of fashion, Couture is known for the more experimental, creative expression and influential position it takes within the fashion industry. The study has developed to differentiate between a fashion designer and a couturier. The fashion designer designs for the mainstream market, whilst the couturier comprises their artistic skills, which also include fashion design, together with something more – *art.*[1] The couturier considers the incorporation of various artistic elements such as ornate features pertinent to creative expression, whilst also formulating the construction of an artistic work by merging technical components for the purposes of accomplishing the artistic work. Couture creation is regarded from the perspective of this thesis as being separate from designing clothes for the purposes of mass industrial manufacture only and forms the basis for the arguments raised in the study. By combining traditional hand crafting skills with those of artistic aptitude, a Couture garment is created as a work of art in its entirety. The purpose of this distinction is to acknowledge Couture as art and the couturier as an artist of fashion.

1 *Please see: Lord Morris of Borth-Y-Gest in George Hensher v Restawile Upholstery [1976] A.C. 64*

DOI: 10.4324/9781003599456-8

The process of Couture creation is very intricate and takes a considerable amount of time to create such as most artistic works.[2] The Couture garment may be conspicuous or subtle in style, although, what will be consistent is the artistic quality and impression it leaves upon its audience, as art does – *the expression.*

The most significant reason for the arguments raised is related to the acknowledgement of Couture as an artistic work and the couturier as the artist, creating the *art*. For this reason, the study has attempted to unearth how art is defined, the process of art creation, and the purpose of art. This was to ascertain whether Couture aligns with those tenets. The work of Tolstoy examined the idea of art being beautiful, whereby the notion of art and beauty was deliberated. Does art have to be beautiful? Tolstoy argues that it does not, but art has the ability to evoke emotions within the observer.[3] On this basis, Tolstoy's views on art would align with the more avant-garde concepts of art whereas Rand's conceptual ideas of art appear to be traditional in perspective. The contemporary notions of art such as 'conceptual incendiary or pop' do not appear to be included within Rand's appreciation.[4] This is a significant point, as the thesis question essentially is testing whether copyright legislation must widen the criterion of 'artistic works' in s.4 of the CDPA 1988 to include Couture, which may be defined as inherently technical and, as a conceptual work of art simultaneously.[5] This notion led the way for deliberations relating to asking, if Couture is art, how may it be defined in consideration of Tolstoy's and Rand's views, and whether Couture is a traditional or contemporary form of art? The study determined that Couture would most notably fall outside of Rand's idea of art and would be most akin to contemporary works.[6]

Tolstoy's notion of a false view of life provides a rationale for the interlink between this concept and Couture.[7] This is because Tolstoy expresses art as an extension of the creator in how they experience or view life. Tolstoy's views express that art may comprise of both positive and negative valuations. This is achieved by transferring the creator's feelings onto the observer of the art, which Tolstoy referred to as 'infection.'[8] The study applied these conceptual notions to Couture being a vehicle for expressing Tolstoy's notion of the false view of life, specifically relating to 'status, wealth, and exclusivity,' and that the adorning of the

2 Vogue, 'Couture By Numbers: What Does It Really Take to Make a Collection?' (*Vogue*, 5 July 2020) <https://www.vogue.co.uk./fashion/article/Couture-by-numbers> accessed 27 December 2022
3 Leo Tolstoy, *What Is Art* (True Sign Publishing 1 March 2021) 172
4 Louis Torres and Michelle Kamhi, *What Art Is the Esthetic Theory of Ayn Rand* (Open Court 2000) 7593
5 S.4 Copyright Designs and Patents Act 1988 (CDPA 1988)
6 Louis Torres and Michelle Kamhi, *What Art Is the Esthetic Theory of Ayn Rand* (Open Court 2000) 7593. Please see chapter 3
7 Leo Tolstoy, *What Is Art* (True Sign Publishing 1 March 2021) 171
8 Leo Tolstoy, *What Is Art* (True Sign Publishing 1 March 2021) 171

Table 8.1 Rationale for Couture as an Artistic Work

Rationale for Couture as an artistic work	**Application of Tolstoy**	**Application of Bence**
	Art does **not** have to be beautiful.	Aesthetics = attention
	Artist transfers feelings from the artist to the observer.	Attention = success
	Art can infect the observer.	
Argument: Couture is an artistic work, and commercial success is dependent on *attention* from the observer and wearer.		

body and decorative practices are secondary to characteristics of human nature.[9] For this reason, Couture, the artistic work, is derived from cultural practices and values through the expression of ideas and values realised through a tangible commodity, and would appear to align with Tolstoy's views on art.[10]

The connection between *attention* and *aesthetics* was established and supports the findings in establishing Couture as art. Bence argues that it is attention which establishes aesthetics, and the component which can determine the aesthetic experience as a success or failure.[11] With this unearthed, whilst the traditional view of Couture may be that of beauty, which is an arguable conceptualisation based on individual taste, it appears that the commercial success of Couture is dependant on the aesthetic.[12]

The following table summarises these key findings:

The study has further established differentiation between fashion design and Couture, and this would support the argument for Couture as an artistic work. Zhandra Rhodes expressed fashion as an art form and made comparisons to paintings or pottery,[13] although the design critic Alice Rawsthorn does not think fashion is art.[14] The two opposing views appear to be distinguishing between design and art. From the perspective of this thesis, design is concerned with the presentation of the practical and technical workings of the 'thing'; however, art is dependent on the expression of feelings through creativity and the feelings evoked within the observer of the art. Couture is noted for its 'creative thinking and a way to inspire.'[15] However, the study has concluded a fundamental significance of Couture, and this is that Couture is a unique form of art and *comprised* of design.

9 Please see chapter 3
10 Please see chapter 3
11 Please see chapter 3
12 Please see chapter 3
13 The Guardian, 'Is Fashion a True Art Form?' (*The Guardian*, 13 July 2003) <https://www.theguardian.com/artanddesign/2003/jul/13/art.artsfeatures1> accessed 23 June 2023
14 The Guardian, 'Is Fashion a True Art Form?' (*The Guardian*, 13 July 2003) <https://www.theguardian.com/artanddesign/2003/jul/13/art.artsfeatures1> accessed 23 June 2023
15 Issiah Lawrence, 'Does the World of Haute Couture and Design Still Belong in Art?' (*Art Dealer Street*, 14 May 2021) <https://www.artdealerstreet.com/single-post/does-the-world-of-haute-Couture-and-design-still-belong-in-art#:~:text=Haute%20Couture%20is%20considered%20a,and%20a%20way%20to%20inspire> accessed 25 June 2022

Table 8.2 Design as a Part of Couture

Fashion design	*Couture as art*
Concerned with practicality and technicality realised through design drawings.	• Form of intellectual creative expression realised through artistry. • Design is the skeleton for Couture, therefore, to only protect the design would not protect the artistry and cannot protect the garment entirely as an artistic work.
Argument: • **Couture comprises of fashion design.** • **Design is the skeleton for Couture.** • **Couture is an artistic work.**	

Fashion design considerations contribute to achieving the artistic work in its entirety and contribute to realising Couture. Artistry is the work of the couturier (as the artist of Couture), the intellectual creation which requires much more than the initial design. Artistry is applied to create the artistic work, Couture. This thesis advocates that Couture as an *artistic work* is the most significant element requiring protection. Design rights therefore can only protect the design, not the artistry, nor Couture as an artistic work in its entirety.

The following table illustrates this concept:
The study has validated that the functionality doctrine infiltrates most of the IP framework except for patents. The thesis argues that without technical features effecting the functionality of the garments, Couture would not exist.[16] However, Couture is *more* than a technical work, deploying tangible functionality. Couture showcases the couturier's exceptional crafting skills, entwined within the design to establish the couturier's intellectual creative expression, as a contemporary art form. Furthermore, the couturier's creative skills contribute to the aesthetic appeal of the Couture garment. The findings of the study would suggest that Couture is an artistic work, *comprised* of artistic craftmanship as an inclusive element, illustrated as follows.

The thesis argues that the creator is dependent on visual aspects, that this forms the basis for art and that this is what differentiates Couture from high street fashion. On this basis, the decision in *Hensher* regarding the literal interpretation of legal text is inconsistent with industry standards.[17] The case of *Radley Gowns* however did not solely rely on the wording of the text. The court used a much more integrated visual assessment to arrive at the decision.[18] However, with this said, the more recent case, as mentioned earlier, of *Response Clothing* appears to be more aligned with industry conditions in respect of considerations given to the

16 L Bentley and others, *Intellectual Property Law* (6th edn, Oxford University Press 2022) 100
17 L Bentley and others, *Intellectual Property Law* (6th edn, Oxford University Press 2022) 100
18 *Radley Gowns v Costas Syprou* [1975] F.S.R. 455

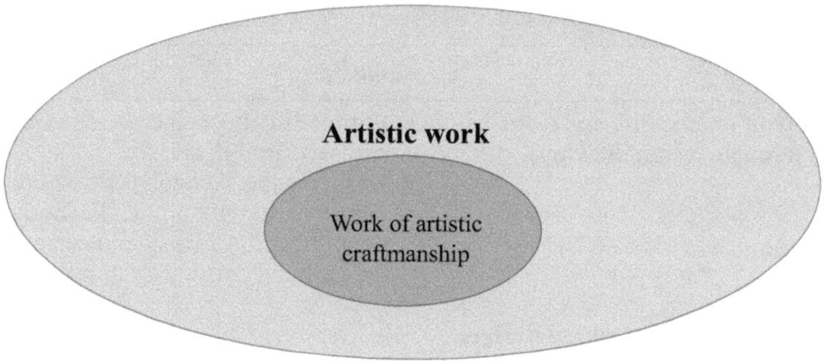

Figure 8.1 Artistic Craftmanship

commercial success being linked to the designers' artistry and the knitters' artistic craftmanship.[19]

Further, the thesis addressed considerations regarding the recognition of Couture as an artistic work and the extent of appreciation for Couture works, and the relevance of the extent of copyright for Couture as it *influences* the wider mass manufactured fashion industry.[20] The creation of Couture works relies upon being influenced by trends, other art, and fashion works.[21] On this point, it is conceivable that influence plays a very large part in producing Couture, and therefore a derivative work. However, derivative works have been referred to as a 'poor copy' and on this basis likely to attract copyright protection.[22] Although, the study outlines that the difference between the meanings of the words *copy* and *influence* must be addressed, as *influence* appears to be linked to a positive operative notion of industry practice, whereas the word *copy* carries a negative connotation. On this basis, the study would infer that this is likely to be detrimental, as it may stifle creative innovation for Couture (particularly in consideration of the creative process) when *copying* is confused with drawing *influence* by law makers.

The study evaluated the unity concept, whereby art forms are differentiated. This was specifically seen in the differing approaches by Germany and France.[23] Germany is focused on industry, while France focuses on preserving the craft tradition.[24] In consideration of the unity concept the study would suggest that the functionality doctrine would not support this notion. Whereas the unity concept

19 *Response Clothing Ltd v Edinburgh Woollen Mill Ltd* [2020] E.W.H.C. 148 (IPEC)

20 Divya Bala, 'About the Inner Workings of Haute Couture' (*Vogue*, 6 July 2020) <https://www.vogue.co.uk/Couture/article/behind-the-scenes-at-haute-Couture> accessed 5 March 2022

21 Gwyneth Holland and Rae Jones, *Fashion Trend Forecasting* (Laurence King Publishing 2017) 59

22 L Bentley and others, *Intellectual Property Law* (6th edn, Oxford University Press 2022) referring to *Interlego v Tyco Industries* [1989] A.C. 217, 268 and Tappin MQC and others, *Laddie, Prescott and Victoria: The Modern Law of Copyright* (5th edn, Lexis Nexis Butterworths 2018) 228–30

23 Koray Gűven, 'Unities of Art: Reconciling Function and Copyright' (2021) 52(9) IIC 1161–89

24 Koray Gűven, 'Unities of Art: Reconciling Function and Copyright' (2021) 52(9) IIC 1161–89

would support the study in relation to asserting the art and artistic components, this specifically can be seen in relation to the French perspective on the unity of art concept.[25]

In relation to functionality, the study considered the separation of functional components in the assessment of whether the work may be granted copyright protection. This was seen in *Brompton* whereby the ruling indicates an assessment based on separation of various components of a work.[26] The ruling indicates that an assessment based on separation of various components of a work would likely be the method of application of the case as precedent for Couture works, as the ruling acknowledged that not all parts of the bike were capable of copyright protection in relation to shape.[27] However, a pertinent point to note is the reference to the 'expression of creative ability in an original manner,' which denotes that the author must be able to create and express whilst executing an original work. Although, is it always possible for the author to make free and creative choices? The points identified here have implications for copyright of those artistic works which sit within an industrial sphere. This is because the decision is absent in recognition of challenges, particularly in relation to the scope of industrial practice limitations that may be an encumbrance to the author's free and creative choices.

Similarly, the doctrine of separability is applied in the U.S.[28] The case of *Star Athletica* established that whilst copyright was possible it was for the applique on the cheerleading uniforms only.[29] This thesis identifies that the separability doctrine is an instrument to exclude technical components from the grant of copyright. On this basis, the study argues that art within fashion is insufficiently accredited, which may result in a generic view of Couture being functional in nature and on this basis, copyright is limited.

The perspective of the book is that instead of the grant of copyright being based on whether a garment is dictated by its functional features, the approach of the courts should be dictated by the *extent of the effect of artistry on the work.*

25 Koray Güven, 'Unities of Art: Reconciling Function and Copyright' (2021) 52(9) IIC 1161–89

26 Astrid Arnold, 'The Brompton Bicycle: The Collapsible Bike With a Collapsing Monopoly?' (*Stevens & Bolton LLP*, 17 June 2020) https://www.lexology.com/library/detail.aspx?g=9d517467-4630-49c6-81b5-574306d94106 accessed 29 May 2022

27 Astrid Arnold, 'The Brompton Bicycle: The Collapsible Bike With a Collapsing Monopoly?' (*Stevens & Bolton LLP*, 17 June 2020) https://www.lexology.com/library/detail.aspx?g=9d517467-4630-49c6-81b5-574306d94106 accessed 29 May 2022

28 Barton Keyes, 'Alive and Well: The (Still) Ongoing Debate Surrounding Conceptual Separability in American Copyright Law' (2008) Ohio State Journal referring to Mark A LoBello, 'The Dichotomy Between Artistic Expression and Industrial Design: To Protect or Not to Protect' (1992) 13 Whittier Law Review 107; Jennifer Mencken, 'A Design for the Copyright of Fashion' (1997) B.C. Intellectual Property & Technology F 121291

29 *Star Athletica v Varsity Brands Inc* 799 F.3d 468 (2015) (6th Cir (US))

(Like an innominate term in the law of contract, the courts look to the effect of the breach, and whether this has deprived the claimant of the whole benefit of the agreement.[30]) With artistic works, *this thesis would argue that the courts should be looking at the extent to which the functional features deprive the work of the artistic quality*.

The case study evaluated the application of copyright in comparison to architecture which is listed as an artistic work in s.4 of the CDPA 1988. The case-study highlights a disparity in copyright as applied to art disciplines, particularly in consideration of the definition of an artistic work in law. Significantly, s.4 of the CDPA 1988 protects the building and only the architectural drawings. For Couture, currently it is possible to protect design drawings in copyright, and not the final product. However, the copyright protection of the drawings does not prevent an individual from reproducing a 3D version of the garment by virtue of s.51 of the CDPA 1988.

Although design drawings can be protected by copyright under the CDPA 1988, the view held from the thesis is that including Couture in the apparent closed list for protecting the end-product as an artistic work would be modernising copyright. This is because copyright could potentially be viewed as having an expansive definition of what *art* is, particularly relating to new techniques developed to provide for sustainable innovation practice for Couture. This in turn may provide for more diverse art, satisfying the originality requirement pertaining to the texture and visual effects.

Although Charles Frederick Worth is acknowledged to be the pioneer for the Couture movement, specifically the approach to the endeavour, the study has unearthed that France has developed the concept of haute Couture further and invested into protecting the *art* and works of haute Couture. Both the U.K. and France are quite distinct in the development of provisions for the art today.[31] The study has emphasised that the term 'haute Couture' can only be applied to a work in accordance with regulations set by governing bodies in France. On this basis, the U.K. refers to equivalent works produced here as 'Couture.' Another notable difference is that in France, the value placed on fashion is remarkable. France legally protects fashion under Article L.112–2.73 in the Code de la propriété intellectuelle, and notably Couture is further accounted for through the establishment of the Fédération de la Haute Couture et de la Mode.

A disparity exists between the U.K. and French legal approach to creative works. This is seen as rooted in the historical development of the two regimes with the U.K. implementing the notion of property that can be transferred, whereas the French system appreciates the value of the moral right being connected to the author. The French system determines an ethereal relationship between the author

30 Please see: *Hong Kong Fir Shipping Ltd v Kisen Kaisha Ltd* (1962) E.W.C.A. Civ 7

31 Elyssa Kostopoulos, 'The Mystique That is Haute Couture – Your Guide to Fashion's Exclusive World' (*RUSSH*, 25 February 2021) <https://www.russh.com/what-is-haute-Couture/> accessed 6 July 2021

and the creation whereas the U.K. appears to be concerned with the *work* and any words addressing the relationship between the author and creation are absent from the legislation, even in s.77 and s.78 of the CDPA 1988. This book addresses the cultural differences between the two regimes, more simplistically, may be a result of the taxonomic construct of the law. Further, the thesis asks whether works not listed within s.4 of the CDPA 1988 would be conferred a lower value, although this point could not be determined by this study.

The French, Turkish, and U.S. legal regimes all operate with the benefit of varying interests. The U.K. appears to have a distinct approach to copyright, which aims to balance the competing interests of the artistic work with that of economic concerns. Due to the common law system, the position for copyright appears to be developing with influential E.U. case law. This provides for a rich historical tapestry of rationale for decisions, although evident is that the E.U. (particularly seen in *Cofemel*) is increasingly demonstrating appreciation for creative intellectual expression, separate from function, and depending on the extent this is demonstrated within the work, a decision of the court would be applied accordingly.

Elements which cannot be separated from the intrinsic nature of Couture are 'fashion' as an independent concept and the technical attributes which are necessary to the function of the work.[32] Therefore, the couturier must comprise all of the necessary intrinsic features to create Couture, although the complexities of the law involved in the pursuit of protecting Couture in copyright provide for an analysis of Couture which is based on separating the inherent and fundamental elements of Couture. The consequences appear to compel creators of artistic works to seek separate IP rights for specific parts of the work, such as copyright, design rights, trade marks, patent protection, and possibly GIs.

From the perspective of this study, the case of *Magmatic* is instrumental to the copyright argument put forward, in consideration of the 'appreciation' for the whole Couture garment as an artistic work, embodying the *design*.[33] The *Louboutin v Van Haren* case could have implications for copyright law in the assessment pertaining to the method of assessment by the court, as this would rest on a nuanced approach to functionality in conjunction with the art.[34] The study has inferred that the case may be influential on copyright cases in respect of how the grant of copyright is assessed in relation to works with functional features.[35] Whilst policy justifications appear to provide the rationale for the limitations on technical features,

32 Yuniya Kawamura, *Fashion-ology* (2nd edn, Bloomsbury Academic 2017) 282

33 *Magmatic Ltd v PMS International Ltd* [2016] U.K.SC 12; [2016] 4 All E.R. 1027; [2016] 3 WLU.K. 280 (SC)

34 *Louboutin v Van Haren Schoenen BV* Case C-163/16

35 *Louboutin v Van Haren Schoenen BV* Case C-163/16

recent case law such as *Louboutinv Van Haren*,[36] *Brompton*,[37] and *Cofemel*[38] indicate that the scope of exclusions pertaining to the functionality doctrine is becoming narrower. These developments indicate a shift in the approach the courts take towards creative works with technical features and signal a move away from the traditional method of application of the functionality doctrine. Aside, passing-off reflects the goodwill of the brand pertaining to *intangible* qualities. For Couture this is important due to the art, which significantly contributes to the intrinsic value of a brand.[39] For these reasons it is considered as to whether Couture being specifically recognised as an artistic work in copyright would increase the value in the brand.[40]

Summary

The thesis completes the findings in consideration of the primary and secondary research questions, which are in summary as follows:

1. The law does not appear to clearly define Couture, or fashion in general, as an artistic work, however, the possibility of Couture being regarded as such is a real prospect provided the work demonstrates the intellectual creative expression of the author.
2. The limitations for Couture as it relates to other subject matter do not appear to be equal. This was demonstrated by the case study on architecture. Architecture is listed within the closed list under s.4 of the CDPA 1988, whilst Couture is not. With the absence of Couture from the closed list, case law must be relied upon heavily and with that, subject matter is not always of a similar product, i.e. a photograph in the case of *Painer*. With the legislative provision to protect Couture not being added to s.4, it appears that the position for Couture shall remain challenging, although to a lesser degree than before, mainly due to legal developments through the *Cofemel* and *Brompton* cases.[41]
3. From the perspective of this thesis, the limitations of copyright to technical features should be prevented from encroaching upon the artistic components of Couture. The reason for this is due to the integral nature of technicality within Couture for the purposes of enabling functionality. However, this may be achieved with the draft for s.4 of the CDPA 1988 at 7.6 and additionally, the thesis would recommend under s.4(2)(c)(ii) that:

   Creative expression must dictate the function of technical components.

36 *Louboutin v Van Haren Schoenen BV* Case C-163/16

37 *Brompton Bicycle Ltd v Chedech/Get2Get* (C-833/18), Opinion of Advocate General M. Campos Sánchez-Bordona, E.U:C:2020:79 at para 22

38 *Cofemel v G-Star Raw CV (C-683/17) AG para 3*

39 Tomruk Űstűnkaya, 'Fashion Law: Exploration Through Trademarks and Passing-Off' (2021) 43(3) EIPR 181

40 Catherine W Ng, 'The Law of Passing Off: Goodwill Beyond Goods' (2016) 47(7) IIC 817–42

41 *Cofemel v G-Star Raw CV* (C-683/17) AG3 and *Brompton Bicycle Ltd v Chedech/Get2Get* (C-833/18)

Figure 8.2 1935 Printed Silk Organza Patrimoine de CHANEL Paris HC.INC 1935.3 (V&A Chanel 2023 Exhibition)

4. The doctrine of functionality applies to Couture to a great extent; in this respect the position has not changed. However, the response to the doctrine appears to have developed since *Cofemel* and *Brompton* in considerations pertinent to intellectual creative expression of the author.[42] The apparent current position is

42 *Cofemel v G-Star Raw CV* (C-683/17) AG3 and *Brompton Bicycle Ltd v Chedech/Get2Get* (C-833/18)

that courts are demonstrating striking a balance between functional considerations and intellectual creative expression of the author.

Primarily, in consideration of the findings within this study, it is the perspective from this thesis that copyright legislation should widen the criterion of 'artistic works' in s.4 of the CDPA 1988 to include *Couture* fashion garments, which may be defined as inherently technical and as a conceptual work of art simultaneously.[43] Recommendations based on the findings of this study are as follows.

Recommendations

These recommendations are listed as informed by fashion industry practice considerations; art, copyright, and economic theory; and in response to the conclusions reached throughout the thesis.

1. When courts are assessing whether copyright subsists within a Couture garment, a visual assessment should be made based on the intellectual creative expression of the author.
2. Regarding visual consideration of the degree of influence from other works, assessment must be based on acceptable fashion industry practice.
3. The extent of the intellectual creative expression of the author must be addressed to reach an acceptable harmonised standard in copyright, which should be based on the noteworthy *intellectual creative expression of the author* in each of the following categories:

   A. Artistic merit.
   B. Craftmanship.
   C. Design.
   D. *Creative expression* must be seen to *dictate functional* components.

4. As the technical features of Couture are intrinsic, a new test must be established for determining the extent to which technical components deprive a Couture garment of its artistic value as set out in the suggested two-limb test in 7.4.4.
5. Draft legislation as set out in (or similar to) 7.6 is implemented into s.4 of the CDPA 1988.

43 S.4 Copyright Designs and Patents Act 1988 (CDPA 1988)

Bibliography

Legislation

Statutes and Statutory Instruments

Copyright Act 1911
Copyright Act 1956
Copyright Designs and Patents Act 1988
Patents Act 1977
Registered Designs Act 1949
Statute of Anne 1709
Trade Marks Act 1994

Scotland

Harris Tweed Act 1993
Scottish Register of Tartans Bill 2008

E.U.

Directive 98/71/EC of 13 October 1998 on the Legal Protection of Designs, OJ L289/28, 28 October 1998
Directive 2006/116/EC of the European Parliament and of the Council of 12 December 2006 on the Term of Protection of Copyright and Certain Related Rights
Regulation 6/2002 of 12 December 2001 on Community Designs, OJ L3/1, 5 January 2002

France

Code de la Propriété Intellectuelle

Tűrkiye

Fikir ve Sanat Eserleri Kanunu 5846

U.S.

Architectural Works Copyright Protection Act, Pub. L. No. 101–650, § 701–06, 104 Stat. 5133 (codified in scattered sections of 17 U.S.C.)
Copyright Act 1976, U.S.

Treaties and Conventions

Agreement on Trade-Related Aspects of Intellectual Property Rights 1994
The Berne Convention for the Protection of Literary and Artistic Works 1886

Books

Barnard M and A Reader, *Fashion Theory* (2nd edn, Routledge 2020) ISBN: 9781351583657
Bence N, *Aesthetics: A Very Short Introduction* (Oxford University Press 2019) ISBN: 9780198826613
Bentley L and others, *Intellectual Property Law* (6th edn, Oxford University Press 2022) ISBN: 9780198869917
Bersier N, C Bezemek and F Schauer, *Common Law: Civil Law the Great Divide?* (Springer 2022) ISBN: 978-3-030-87718-7
Burbridge R, *European Fashion Law* (Edward Elgar 2019) ISBN: 9781788113007
Calboli I and S Ragavan, *Diversity in Intellectual Property* (Cambridge University Press, 2015) ISBN: 9781107588479
Cerchia ER and B Pozzo, *The New Frontiers of Fashion Law* (MDPI 2020) ISBN 978-3039437078
Declayre E, *The Copyright/Design Interface* (Cambridge 2017) ISBN: 13978-1107198678
Embley J, K Bamford and N Hancock, *Commercial and Intellectual Property Law and Practice* (CLP 2021) ISBN: 978-1913226831
Findlay M, *The Value of Art* (Prestel Verlag 2014) ISBN: 978-3791349138
Finnis J, *Natural Law and Natural Rights* (Oxford University Press 1980) ISBN: 0199599130, 9780199599134
Fischer A and K Gobin, *Construction for Fashion Design* (2nd edn, Bloomsbury 2017) ISBN: 9781472538758
Geiger J and H Suber, *Creativity and Copyright* (University of California Press 2019) ISBN: 9780520303522
Gestel R, HW Micklitz and EL Rubin (eds), *Rethinking Legal Scholarship: A Transatlantic Dialogue* (Cambridge University Press 2017) ISBN: 9781107578722
Goldie P and E Shellekens, *Philosophy and Conceptual Art* (Oxford University Press 2007) ISBN: 9780199285556
Golding MP and WA Edmundson, *The Blackwell Guide to the Philosophy of Law and Legal Theory* (Wiley-Blackwell 2004) ISBN: 978-0631228318
Goldstein P and P Hugenholtz, *International Copyright Principles, Law, and Practice* (4th edn, Oxford 2019) ISBN: 978-0199737109
Holland G and R Jones, *Fashion Trend Forecasting* (Laurence King Publishing 2017) ISBN: 978-1786270580
Hudson E and A Kenyon, *Intellectual Property Law and Empirical Research From Part III: Across Disciplines* (Cambridge University Press 27 March 2020) ISBN: 9781108750066.022
Hudson Hick D, *Introducing Aesthetics and the Philosophy of Art* (Bloomsbury 2017) ISBN: 978-1350006904
Jackson T and D Shaw, *The Fashion Handbook* (Routledge 2006) ISBN: 9780415255806

Jenkyn SJ, *Fashion Design* (3rd edn, Laurence King 2002) ISBN: 9781856696197
Jones M, *London Couture and the Making of a Fashion Centre* (MIT 2022) ISBN: 9780262046572
Jones SJ, *Fashion Design* (3rd edn, Laurence King 2002) ISBN: 9781780675145
Kaplan B, *An Unhurried View of Copyright* (Columbia University Press 1967) ISBN: 9789780231878166
Kawamura Y, *Fashion-Ology* (2nd edn, Bloomsbury Academic 2017) ISBN: 9781350331860
Kelly I and V Westwood, *Vivienne Westwood* (Picador 2014) ISBN 13: 9781447254126
Kelsen H, *The Pure Theory of Law* (University of California Press 1967) ISBN: 9781584775782
Library of Congress Copyright Office, Copyright Law of the United States (3 May 2008)
Lock ST, *The Object of Copyright* (Routledge 2016) ISBN: 9781317804604
Locke J, *Second Treatise of Government* (Awnsham Churchill 1689) ISBN: 9780521069038
Long TA, *London Couture 1923–1975* (V&A Publishing 2019) ISBN: 9781851778508
Macqueen H and others, *Contemporary Intellectual Property* (Oxford University Press 2010) ISBN: 9780199575329
Marmor A, *Law in the Age of Pluralism* (Oxford University Press 2007) ISBN: 9780195338478
Martin R and H Koda, *Haute Couture, The Metropolitan Museum of Art* (Yale University Press 1996) ISBN: 9780300199918
McConville M and W Chui, *Research Methods for Law* (Edinburgh 2007) ISBN: 9781474404259
Mida IE, *Reading Fashion in Art* (Bloomsbury 2020) ISBN: 9781350032736
Persis Burnett K, *Dimensions of Originality Essays on Seventeenth-Century Chinese Art Theory and Criticism* (Chinese University Press 2013) ISBN: 9789629969141
Poulliard V, *Paris to New York: The Transatlantic Fashion Industry in the Twentieth Century* (Harvard University Press 2021) ISBN: 978-0674237407
Raz J, *The Authority of Law and Morality* (2nd edn, Oxford University Press 2009) ISBN: 9780199573561
Raz J, *Morality and Freedom* (Oxford University Press 1986) ISBN: 978-0198248071
Read G, *Introduction: The Play's the Thing Architecture as Performance Art* (Routledge 2013) 1 ISBN: 978-1409442356
Rosati E, *Originality in E.U. Copyright Full Harmonisation Through Case Law* (Edward Elgar 2013) ISBN: 9781782548935
Schlag P and AJ Griffin, *How to Do Things With Legal Doctrine* (University Chicago Press 2020) ISBN: 978-0226726106
Shaeffer C, *Couture Sewing: The Couture Cardigan Jacket, Sewing Secrets From a Chanel Collector* (The Taunton Press Inc 2013) ISBN: 978-1600859557
Shaeffer C, *Couture Tailoring* (Laurence King Student & Professional, 2021) ISBN: 9781786275752
Shapiro SJ, *Legality* (Harvard University Press 2016 [2011]) ISBN: 9780674267299
Speck A and others, *The Modern Law of Copyright* (5th edn, Lexis Nexis Butterworths 2018) ISBN: 9781474306898
Steiner R and A Lord, *Aristotle, Thomas Aquinas and Rudolph Art, Aesthetics and Colour* (Temple Lodge 2018) ISBN: 978-191223022
Steriacci F and J Arbuckle, *The A-Z of the Fashion Industry* (Scarecrow Press 2009) ISBN: 978-0810868830
Susen S, *The 'Postmodern Turn' in the Social Sciences* (Palgrave Macmillan 2015) ISBN: 9780230579293
Taylor K, *Vintage Fashion & Couture: From Poiret to McQueen* (1st edn, Mitchell Beazley 2017) ISBN: 9781845338565
Tolstoy L, *What Is Art* (True Sign Publishing 1 March 2021)
Torres L and M Kamhi, *What Art Is: The Esthetic Theory of Ayn Rand* (Open Court 2000) ISBN: 978-0812693737

Waddell G, *How Fashion Works: Couture, Ready-to-Wear and Mass Production* (Wiley 2004) ISBN: 978-0632057528
Watkins S and L Dunne, *Functional Clothing Design: From Sportswear to Spacesuits* (Bloomsbury 2015) ISBN: 9780857854674

Journal Articles

Alan B, 'Copyright Law: Monopoly or Monstrosity?'(1996) 146(6730) The New Law Journal
Andrew C, 'A Proposal for Simplifying United Kingdom Copyright Law' (2001) 23 EIPR 26, 28
Baksi C, 'Style Counsel' *Law Society Gazette* (15 September 2005) 32
Černe M and others, 'What Goes Around Comes Around: Knowledge, Hiding, Perceived Motivational Climate and Creativity' (2014) 57(1) The Academy of Management Journal 172–92
Christopher B and JC Fromer, 'Fashions Function in Intellectual Property Law' (2016) 93 Notre Dame Law Review 1
Church O, E Derclaye and G Stupfler, 'An Empirical Analysis of the Design Case Law of the E.U. Member States' (2019) 50(6) IIC 685
Clark S, S Sefton and M Linsner, 'A Fabric Design Has Been Found to Be a Work of Artistic Craftsmanship: Will Response Clothing Cause a Shift in How U.K. Copyright is Assessed?' (2020) 42(9) EIPR 612
Derclaye E, 'Debunking Some of U.K. Copyright Law's Longstanding Myths and Misunderstandings' (2013) 1 IPQ 7
Dixon M, 'A Doctrinal Approach to Property Law Scholarship: Who Cares and Why' (2014) 3 Researching Property Law 160
Edwards B, 'We Are Fatally Influenced by Goods Brought in Bond Street: London, Shopping and the Fashionable Geographies of 1930s Vogue' (2006) 10(1–2) Fashion Theory 73–96
Fhima I, 'The CJEU Decision in Brompton Bicycle (Case C-833/18): An Original Take on Technical Functionality?' (2020) 42(11) EIPR 761–67
Fhima I, 'Technical Functionality in European Trade Mark Law' (2021) 137 LQR 113
Ghosh S, 'Legal Code and the Need for a Broader Functionality Doctrine in Copyright' (2002) 50 Journal of the Copyright Society of the USA 71
Gray C and J Malins, 'Research Procedures/Methodology for Artists and Designers' (1993) *Aberdeen: Robert Gordon University*
Gries ST and BG Slocum, 'Ordinary Meaning and Corpus Linguistics' (*Brigham Young University Law Review*, 14 October 2017) <https://ssrn.com/abstract=3053146>
Gűven K, 'Unities of Art: Reconciling Function and Copyright' (2021) 52(9) IIC 1161–89
Hayrı B, 'Fikir ve Sanat Eserleri Kanununda Eser Çeşitleri: Karşılaştırmalı Bir Analiz' (2014) 15(1) Bilgi Dűnyası 125–58
Heilpern J, 'Dialects of Art: A Corpus-Based Approach to Technical Term of Art Determinations in Statutes' (2022) 58(4) Jurimetrics 377–410
Keyes B, 'Alive and Well: The (Still) Ongoing Debate Surrounding Conceptual Separability in American Copyright Law' (2008) 69 Ohio State Journal 109
Kharel A, 'Doctrinal Legal Research' 10.2139/ssrn.3130525
Khosravishakib M, 'The Contributions of Postmodernism Methodology as a Prevailing Practice on Ground of Humanities Sciences' (2012) 2(1) International Journal of Arts
Lavinia B, 'Designs Determined by the Product's Technical Function: Arguments for an Autonomous Test' (2016) 38(1) EIPR 23
LoBello MA, 'The Dichotomy Between Artistic Expression and Industrial Design: To Protect or Not to Protect' (1992) 13 Whittier Law Review 107
Malem W and others, 'High-End & Designer Manufacturing Report' (2015) Protecting Existing Resource and Encouraging Growth and Innovation – Commissioned by the British

Fashion Council, U.K. Fashion & Textile Association, Creative Skillset and Marks & Spencer Research by Oxford Economics and Glasgow Caledonian University

Martinez EVH, 'Tasarımında sanatsal ifade őnerisi olarak alternatif malzemeler: Seramik elbiseler/Allternative Materials in Fashion Design as a Proposal of Artistic Expression: Ceramic Dresses' (2012) 3(3) Sanat ve Tasarım Dergisi 162–81

McKenna MP, '(Dys)Functionality' (2011) 48 Houston Law Review 823

Mcquillan H, T Rissanen and J Roberts, 'The Cutting Circle: How Making Challenges Design' (2013) 17(1) RJTA

Mencken J, 'A Design for the Copyright of Fashion' [1997] B.C. Intell. Prop. & Tech. F. 121291

Molina-Azorin JF, 'Mixed Methods Research: An Opportunity to Improve Our Studies and Our Research Skills' (2016) 25(2) European Journal of Management and Business Economics 37–8

Monta R, 'The Concept of Copyright Versus Droit D'auteur' (1958–1959) 32 Southern California Law Review 177

Mysoor P, 'Does U.K. Really Have a "Closed" List of Works Protected by Copyright?' (2019) 41(8) EIPR 474–79

Ng CW, 'The Law of Passing Off: Goodwill Beyond Goods' (2016) 47(7) IIC 817–42

O'Leary C, 'Postmodernism as a Theoretical Framework for Learner Autonomy Research' (2018) 9(3) Studies in Self-Access Learning Journal 342–70

Pedroni M and P Volanté, 'Art Seen From Outside: Non-Artistic Legitimation Within the Field of Fashion Design' (2014) 43 Poetics 102–19

Petruzzelli L, 'Copyright Problems in Post-Modern Art' (1995) 5(1) DePaul Journal of Art, Technology & Intellectual Property Law

Quaedvlieg A, 'Shapes With a Technical Function: An Ever-Expanding Exclusion?' (2016) ERA

Russell F and H Hurdle, 'What is the Direct Product of a Patented Process?' (1995) 17(5) EIPR 249

Saatçıoğlu K, NE Bıyıklı and SE Sezgin, 'Tasarımda sürdürülebilirlik anlayışı ile bir değer yaratmak: Kültürel miras kavramı'/'Creating a Value With the Sustainability Approach in Design: Cultural Heritage Concept' (4 December 2021) 1(1) Sanat ve Tasarım Araştırmaları Dergisi 138–55

Schutte L, 'Copyright for Couture' (2011) Duke Law & Technology Review 011

Smits JM, 'What is Legal Doctrine? On the Aims and Methods of Legal-Dogmatic Research' (1 September 2015)

Spevacek A, 'Couture Copyright: Copyright Protection Fitting for Fashion Design' (2009) 602 The John Marshall Center for Intellectual Property

Suthersanen U, 'Copyright and Industrial Objects: Aesthetic Considerations and Policy Discriminations' in M David and D Halbert (eds), *SAGE Handbook of Intellectual Property* (Queen Mary School of Law Legal Studies Research Paper No. 168/2014 21 January 2014) <https://ssrn.com/abstract=2382718>

Tiller EH and FB Cross, 'What is Legal Doctrine?' 16 May 2005 < https://ssrn.com/abstract=730284; http://dx.doi.org/10.2139/ssrn.730284>

Űstűnkaya T, 'Fashion Law: Exploration Through Trademarks and Passing-Off' (2021) 43(3) EIPR 181

Űstűnkaya T, 'Fashion Law: The Limitation Conundrum of the Patents Act 1977' (2020) 42(10) EIPR 621

Űstűnkaya T, 'The Functionality Doctrine: Is 3D Printing Challenging Rigidity in Fashion Law?' (2020) 42(5) EIPR 286

Űstűnkaya T, 'The Functionality Doctrine: The Challenges to Fashion Copyright' (2020) 42(3) EIPR 156

Wibbelmann J, 'Protection of "Products Directly Obtained by Processes" According to Article 64(2) EPC' (1996) 18(3) EIPR 174–76

Websites

Adam G, 'Why Is Art So Expensive?' (*BBC*, 2 May 2013) <https://www.bbc.com/culture/article/20130417-why-is-art-so-expensive> accessed 26 March 2023

Alexander E, 'Hussein Chalayan' (*Vogue*, 22 August 2011) <https://www.vogue.co.UK/article/hussein-chalayan-biography> accessed 27 December 2022

Antonelli P and M Fisher, 'Announcing Items: Is Fashion Modern?' (*Inside Out*, 5 April 2016) <https://www.moma.org/explore/inside_out/2016/04/05/announcing-items-is-fashion-modern/> accessed 20 September 2023

Arnold A, 'The Brompton Bicycle: The Collapsible Bike With a Collapsing Monopoly?' (*Stevens & Bolton LLP*, 17 June 2020) https://www.lexology.com/library/detail.aspx?g=9d517467-4630-49c6-81b5-574306d94106 accessed 29 May 2022

Art in Context, 'Conceptual Art: An Exploration of the Conceptualist Art Movement' (*Art in Context*, 8 December 2021) <https://artincontext.org/conceptual-art/> accessed 9 July 2022

Australian Fitness Academy, 'Technology in Sports Clothing: Do We Really Need It?' (*Australian Fitness Academy*, 26 October 2016) <https://www.fitnesseducation.edu.au/blog/industry-trends/technology-in-sports-clothing-do-we-really-need-it/> accessed 6 July 2021

Bala D, 'About the Inner Workings of Haute Couture' (*British Vogue*, 6 July 2020) <https://www.vogue.co.uk/fashion/article/behind-the-scenes-at-haute-couture> accessed 5 March 2022

Bannerman SL, 'Why Are There No Haute Couture Houses in London?' (*Culture Trip*, 22 October 2017) <https://theculturetrip.com/Europe/united-kingdom/england/london/articles/why-are-there-no-haute-Couture-fashion-houses-in-london/> accessed 12 June 2022

Barbican, 'The Fashion World of Jean Paul Gaultier: From the Sidewalk to the Catwalk' (*Barbicanorg U.K.*, 2014) <https://www.barbican.org.uk/whats-on/2014/event/the-fashion-world-of-jean-paul-gaultier> accessed 31 May 2021

Bateman K, 'Meet the New Guard of Haute Couture Designers Lending a Fresh Perspective to a Time-Honored Craft' (*Bazaar*, 29 January 2022) <https://www.harpersbazaar.com/fashion/fashion-week/a38915060/new-haute-Couture-designers/> accessed 19 November 2022

Beverly Hills Design Institute, 'Industry/Haute Couture: What is Haute Couture' (*Beverly Hills Design Institute*, 2022) <https://www.bhdi.edu/industry/haute-Couture/what-is-haute-Couture/> accessed 12 June 2022

BFC, 'The BFC Has Incorporated All Its Charities to Form the BFC Foundation' (*British Fashion Council*, 2020) <https://www.britishfashioncouncil.co.uk/About> accessed 6 July 2021

Bird and Bird, 'The CJEU DOCERAM Case: When Is a Product Feature Solely Dictated by Its Technical Functionality Such That It Cannot Be Protected as a Community Design?' (*Bird and Bird*, 8 March 2018) <https://www.twobirds.com/en/insights/2018/uk/CJEU-Doceram-case> accessed 14 June 2022

Blue 17, 'Incredible Couturiers Alexander Mcqueen' (*Blue 17*, 6 March 2015) <https://www.blue17.co.uk/vintage-blog/incredible-couturiers-alexander-mcqueen/> accessed 6 July 2021

Boateng O, 'The Core Essence of Ozwald Boateng Tailoring' (*Ozwald Boateng*, 2022) <https://www.ozwaldboateng.co.uk/bespoke-couture> accessed 27 December 2022

Bobb B, 'In Celebration of the 100th Anniversary of the Harlem Renaissance, Ozwald Boateng Brought Fashion to the Apollo Theater' (*Vogue*, 6 May 2019) <https://www.vogue.com/article/ozwald-boateng-show-harlem-the-apollo> accessed 27 December 2022

Bowles H, 'Chanel Spring 2019 Couture' (*Vogue*, 22 January 2019) <https://www.vogue.com/fashion-shows/spring-2019-Couture/chanel> accessed 31 January 2023

Boy Culture, 'Jean Paul Gaultier on His Use of Corsets: Madonna, Masculinity, Femininity' (*Youtube*, 2014) <https://m.youtube.com/watch?v=4yJgt8aBo8o> accessed 21 January 2025

Boyes M, 'Vivienne Westwood' (*Vogue*, 22 April 2008) <https://www.vogue.co.uk/article/vivienne-westwood-biography> accessed 27 December 2022

Bradley S, 'The Line Between Inspired By and Copied From and How to Stay on Its Right Side' (*Vaneso Design*, 13 May 2013) <https://vanseodesign.com/web-design/inspired-by-copied-from/> accessed 20 May 2022

Brett H, 'Schiaparelli Recreates Wallis Simpson's Famous Lobster Dress' (*Viva*, 24 January, 2017) <https://www.viva.co.nz/article/fashion/wallis-simpson-schiaparelli/> accessed 27 June 2022

Britanica, 'Aesthetics Philosophy' (*Britanica*, 2022) <https://www.britannica.com/topic/aesthetics> accessed 12 July 2022

Britannica, 'Architecture' (*Britannica*, 17 August 2023) <https://www.britannica.com/topic/architecture> accessed 20 September 2023

British Copyright Council, 'Impact of Brexit on U.K. Copyright Law' (*British Copyright Council*, 2020) <https://www.britishcopyright.org/wp-content/uploads/Impact_of_Brexit_on_UK_copyright_law.pdf> accessed 19 February 2022

British Fashion Council, 'About' (*British Fashion Council*, 2022) <https://www.britishfashioncouncil.co.UK/About/BFC-Network> accessed 27 December 2022

British Fashion Council, 'The British Fashion Council Strengthens British Fashion in the Global Economy as a Leader in Creative, Responsible Businesses' (*British Fashion Council*, 2020) <https://www.britishfashioncouncil.co.U.K./home> accessed 6 July 2021

Business of Fashion. 'Professional' (*BOF*, 2021) <https://www.businessoffashion.com/> accessed 6 July 2021

The Business of Fashion (BOF), 'How Christian Dior Is Training Its Next Generation of Craftsmen' (*BOF*, 2023) <https://www.businessoffashion.com/videos/luxury/how-christian-dior-is-training-its-next-generation-of-craftsman/> accessed 1 June 2023

Cambridge, 'Artefact' (*Cambridge Dictionary Online*, 2022) <https://dictionary.cambridge.org/dictionary/english/artefact?msclkid=28de3876b31f11eca3de67abb0015c8a> accessed 26 March 2022

Carole Gray, ' Research Procedures / Methodology for Artists & Designers' (Carolegraynet, 1993) <http://www.carolegray.net/Papers%20PDFs/epgad.pdf> accessed 21 January 2025

Casa Batlló, 'History of Casa Batlló' (*Casa Batlló Gaudi Barcelona*, 2021) <https://www.casabatllo.es/en/antoni-gaudi/casa-batllo/history/> accessed 30 August 2021

Castillo A, 'Evening Dress' (*V&A*, 2007) <https://collections.vam.ac.uk/item/O138937/evening-dress-castillo-antonio/> accessed 18 October 2021

Centre for Intellectual Property and Information Law, 'Hensher v Restawile [1976] AC 64' (*University of Cambridge*, 2023) <https://www.cipil.law.cam.ac.U.K./virtual-museum/hensher-v-restawile-1976-ac-64> accessed 27 July 2023

Chan E, '16 Things Everyone Should Know About Sustainable Fashion' (*Vogue*, 18 April 2022) <https://www.vogue.co.uk/fashion/article/sustainable-fashion> accessed 20 September 2023

Chan E, 'Why Vivienne Westwood's Corsetry Remains Unparalleled' (*Vogue*, 7 October 2021) <https://www.vogue.co.uk/fashion/article/adele-vogue-vivienne-westwood-corset> accessed 27 December 2022

Chitrakorn K, 'What Makes a Popular Luxury Fashion Brand?' (*Vogue Business*, 5 June 2020) <https://www.voguebusiness.com/companies/what-makes-a-popular-luxury-fashion-brand> accessed 26 March 2022

Code of Intellectual and Artistic Works Numbered 5846 as Amended 7.6.1995–4110/2 Please Note: The Definition of *Fine Art* Appears to be a Translational Enhancement in Analysis of Mutlu Yildirim Köse, Hande Hançar Çelik and Havva Yıldız, 'Tűrkiye:

Insights as to Turkish Copyright Law' (*Mondaq*, 2020) <https://gun.av.tr/insights/articles/key-developments-and-predictions-for-copyright-law-in-turkey> accessed 20 July 2023

Collinsdictionary.com, 'Artistic' (2019) <https://www.collinsdictionary.com/dictionary/english/artistic> accessed 9 January 2020

Cooper M, 'Bruce Oldfield' (*Vogue*, 1 December 2010) <https://www.vogue.co.uk/article/bruce-oldfield-biography> accessed 27 December 2022

Copyright Act 1956 s.3(1) and Swarb, 'George Hensher Ltd v Restawile Upholstery (Lancs) Ltd: HL 1975' (*SwarbcoU.K.*, 2021) <https://swarb.co.uk/george-hensher-ltd-v-restawile-upholstery-lancs-ltd-hl-1975/> accessed 31 December 2021

Copyright Act 1976. (17 U.S.C. § 101) Please Also See: U.S. Copyright Office, 'Visual Arts' (*Copyrightgov*, 2022) <https://www.copyright.gov/registration/visual-arts/> accessed 19 November 2022

Cornell Law School, 'Functionality Doctrine (Trademark)' (*Legal Information Institute*, 2022) <https://www.law.cornell.edu/wex/functionality_doctrine_%28trademark%29> accessed 11 June 2022 and *Qualitex Co v Jacobson Products Co* 514 U.S.

'Couture' (*Vogue*, 2022) <https://www.vogue.com/fashion-shows/fall-2022-Couture/iris-van-herpen> accessed 12 February 2023

Creative Industries Council, 'Fashion: Why The U.K.?' (*CIC*, 14 January 2021 updated on 13 April 2021) <https://www.thecreativeindustries.co.uk/site-content/industries-fashion-fashion-why-the-uk> accessed 6 July

Crefovi, 'Fashion Law in France: A 2020 Overview' (*Crefovi*, 2020) <https://crefovi.com/articles/fashion-law-in-france/> accessed 21 January 2025

Data Intelo, 'Global Haute Couture Market by Type (Jackets & Coating, Vests, Pants and Bibs, Boots, Others), By Application (Catwalk, Daily Wearing) and By Region (North America, Latin America, Europe, Asia Pacific and Middle East & Africa), Forecast From 2022 To 2030' (*Data Intelo*, 2022) <https://dataintelo.com/report/haute-Couture-market/> accessed 30 December 2022

Di Boscio C, 'Why Is Couture So Expensive?' (*Eluxe Magazine*, 15 October 2020) <https://eluxemagazine.com/fashion/why-Couture-is-so-expensive-3-perspectives/> accessed 18 July 2022

Dior C, 'La Ligne Sinueuse' (*V&A*, 2007) <https://collections.vam.ac.uk/item/O120852/la-ligne-sinueuse-day-dress-christian-dior/> accessed 22 May 2022

Dior C, 'Dior Sustainability' (*Dior*, 2023) <https://www.dior.com/en_gb/fashion/news-fashion-shows/folder-news-and-events/dior-sustainability> accessed 20 September 2023

Drapers online, 'News' (*Drapers Online*, 2021) <https://www.drapersonline.com/> accessed 6 July 2021

Dulheuer M, MD Legal Patentanwalte and MB Partg, 'Technical Function Determines the Design: Exclusion From IP Rights?' (*Patent-Und Rechtsanwaltskanzlei*, 8 March 2018) <https://legal-patent.com/design-law-en/technical-function-determines-design-exclusion-ip-rights/> accessed 14 June 2022

DW for Minds, 'Turkish Haute Couture' (*DW for Minds*, 14 March 2022) <https://www.dw.com/en/turkish-haute-Couture/video-61121521> accessed 18 November 2022

Easter E, 'Performance Textiles: Institutional Products' (*Association for Linen Management*, September 2006) <https://cdn.ymaws.com/www.almnet.org/resource/resmgr/Certification/Contact_Hour_Articles/047_PerformanceTextiles.pdf> accessed 6 July 2021

Efor Patent, 'Turkish Industrial Property (IP) Law No 6769' (*EFOR PATENT*, 1999) <https://eforpatent.com.tr/en/turkish-industrial-property-law-no-6769/> accessed 21 January 2025

Elle.com, 'Dior's Couture Collection Wants to Bring Beauty to an Ugly World' (*Elle*, 4 July 2022) <https://www.elle.com/fashion/a40500543/dior-Couture-collection-fall-2022/> accessed 9 July 2022

Elyssa Kostopoulos, 'The Mystique That is Haute Couture: Your Guide to Fashion's Exclusive World' (*RUSSH*, 25 February 2021) <https://www.russh.com/what-is-haute-Couture/> accessed 6 July 2021

European Commission, 'Geographical Indications for Non-Agricultural Products' (*European Commission*, 2021) <https://ec.Europa.eu./growth/industry/policy/intellectual-property/geographical-indications/non-agricultural-products_en> accessed 30 August 2021

European Parliament, 'Copyright Law in the EU: Salient Features of Copyright Law Across the E.U. Member States' (*European Parliament*, June 2018) < https://www.europarl.europa.eu/RegData/etudes/STUD/2018/625126/EPRS_STU(2018)625126_EN.pdf > accessed 16 July 2023

Famous Fashion Designers Org, 'Ozwald Boateng' (*FamousFashionDesignersorg*, 2018) <https://www.famousfashiondesigners.org/ozwald-boateng> accessed 27 December 2022

Fashinza, 'What is Haute Couture' (*Fashinza*, 2022) <https://fashinza.com/textile/fashion-industry/what-is-haute-Couture-and-why-does-it-matter/> accessed 12 June 2022

Fashion ABC, 'Haute Couture Fashion Week' (*Fashion ABC Beta*, 2022) <https://www.fashionabc.org/wiki/haute-Couture-fashion-week/> accessed 27 December 2022

Fashion Addicted, 'Does Haute Couture Affect High Street Style?' (*Fashion Addicted*, 13 January 2014) <https://duncanozann.wordpress.com/2014/01/13/does-haute-Couture-affect-high-street-style/#:~:text=Haute%20Couture%20collections%20influence%20their%20pr%C3%AAt-%C3%A0-porter%20collections%20which,or%20normal%20Couture%20houses%2C%20then%20influence%20high-street%20fashion.?msclkid=119ddf55ace511eca1851d2e6122d036> accessed 26 March 2022

Fashion Week İstanbul, 'Zeynep Tosun' (*Fashion Week İstanbul*, 2021) <https://fashion-week.istanbul/press-release/zeynep-tosun> accessed 18 November 2022

Federation de la haute Couture et de la mode, 'Federation' (*Federation de la haute Couture et de la mode*, 2021) <https://fhcm.paris/en/#:~:text=La%20F%C3%A9d%C3%A9ration&text=The%20F%C3%A9d%C3%A9ration%20de%20la%20Haute,foster%20creation%20and%20international%20development.&text=It%20contributes%20to%20bolstering%20Paris,coordinating%20Paris%20Fashion%20Week%C2%AE> accessed 8 May 2021

Fédération de la haute Couture et de la mode, 'History' (*Fédération de la haute Couture et de la mode*, 2022) <https://fhcm.paris/en/the-federation/history/#:~:text=Founded%20in%201868%20and%20then%20known%20as%20the,de%20la%20Couture%20Parisienne%20on%20December%2014th%201910> accessed 23 December 2022

Ferguson K, 'U.K.: Common Law vs Civil Law: A Rough Guide For Your Business' (*Mondaq*, 1 June 2017) <https://www.mondaq.com/UK/contracts-and-commercial-law/598694/common-law-vs-civil-law-a-rough-guide-for-your-business> accessed 22 December 2022

Finnis G, 'The Theory of "Unity of Art" and the Protection of Designs and Models in French Law' (1964) XLVI(9) *Patent Office* <https://heinonline.org/HOL/LandingPage?handle=hein.journals/jpatos46&div=108&id=&page=> accessed 19 November 2022

Fisher AL, '40 Times Madonna Shocked Us All With Her Outfit' (*Harpers Bazaar*, 5 August 2019) <https://www.harpersbazaar.com/celebrity/red-carpet-dresses/g7709/madonna-most-shocking-outfits/> accessed 6 July 2021

Francesca Montalvo witzburg, 'Protecting Fashion: A Comparative Analysis of Fashion Design Protection in the United States and Europe' (CARDOZOAELJ, 1st December 2016) <https://cardozoaelj.com/2016/12/01/protecting-fashion-comparative-analysis-fashion-design-protection-united-states-europe/#_ftn69> accessed 21 January 2025 referring to Intellectual Property Code, Article L-112-2

FrenchBusinessLawcom, 'ArticleL111-1oftheFrenchIntellectualPropertyCode' (*FrenchBusiness LawCom*, 8 November 2023) <https://french-business-law.com/french-legislation-art/article-l111-1-of-the-french-intellectual-property-code/#:~:text=The%20existence%20or%20conclusion%20of%20a%20contract%20for,to%20the%20exceptions%20provided%20for%20by%20this%20Code> accessed 21 January 2025

Fury A, 'What Does "Couture" Actually Mean?' (*New York Times*, 27 January 2017)<https://www.nytimes.com/2017/01/27/t-magazine/fashion/what-does-couture-actually-mean-fashion-week.html> accessed 29 December 2022

Fussell M, 'Industrial Design-The Art of Objects' (*The Virtual Instructor*, 2022) <https://thevirtualinstructor.com/blog/industrial-design-the-art-of-objects-2> accessed 26 March 2023

Gauberti A, 'Fashion Law in France: A 2020 Overview' (*Crefovi*, 2020) <https://crefovi.com/articles/fashion-law-in-france/> accessed 19 November 2022

Gaylene M, 'Do You Toile?' (*CAFA*, 14 October 2020) <https://www.Couturearts.com.au/blog/do-you-toile#:~:text=Toile%20is%20a%20French%20word,translucent%20linen%20or%20cotton%20fabric> accessed 26 March 2020

Gould E, 'Art and Copyright: What Can We Learn From the Past?' (*Institute of Art and Law*, 29 October 2018) <https://ial.uk.com/art-and-copyright-what-can-we-learn-from-the-past/> accessed 18 July 2022

Gov.uk, 'Guidance, Trade Marks and Geographical Indications' (*Gov.uk*, 2021) <https://www.gov.uk/guidance/trade-marks-and-geographical-indications> accessed 30 August 2021

Gov.uk, 'Hague Agreement for the International Registration of Industrial Designs' (*Gov.uk*, 2018) <https://www.gov.uk/government/publications/hague-system-design-protection-for-applicants/hague-agreement-for-the-international-registration-of-industrial-designs> accessed 18 October 2021

Gov.uk, 'How Copyright Protects Your Work' (*Gov.uk*, 2020) <https://www.gov.uk/copyright> accessed 6 July 2021

Gov.uk, 'Intellectual Property After 1 January 2021' (*Gov.uk*, 28 October 2020) <https://www.gov.uk/government/news/intellectual-property-after-1-january-2021> accessed 19 February 2022

Gov.uk, 'Patenting Your Invention' (*Gov.uk*, 2021) <https://www.gov.uk/patent-your-invention> accessed 30 August 2021

The Guardian, 'Is Fashion a True Art Form?' (*The Guardian*, 13 July 2003) <https://www.theguardian.com/artanddesign/2003/jul/13/art.artsfeatures1> accessed 23 June 2023

Gűn + Partners, 'Does Technical Function Impede Copyright?' (*Gün + Partners*, 19 April 2022) <https://gun-ip.com/insights/articles/does-technical-function-impede-copyright> accessed 21 January 2025

Gurulkan C, 'Copyright Protection' (*Gurulkan Cakir*, 2021) <https://www.gurulkan.com/doing-business-in-Tűrkiye/copyright-protection> accessed 31 December 2021

Harper's Bazaar, 'The History of Haute Couture From Humble Beginnings to Present Day' (*Harper's Bazaar*, 19 January 2017) <https://www.harpersbazaar.com/uk/fashion/fashion-news/news/a31123/the-history-of-haute-Couture/> accessed 27 December 2022

Harvard University, 'The Rocket Swimsuit: Speedo's LZR Racer' (*Harvard University*, 15 September 2008) <https://sitn.hms.harvard.edu/flash/2008/issue47-2/> accessed 6 July 2021

Hess L, 'The Story Behind Madonna's Iconic Jean Paul Gaultier Cone Bra' (*Vogue*, 18 April 2020) <https://www.vogue.com/article/madonna-blonde-ambition-jean-paul-gaultier-cone-bra#:~:text=Designed%20by%20Jean%20Paul%20Gaultier,New%20York%20and%20Gaultier's%20ateliers> accessed 31 May 2021

Hurt H, 'Luxury, and How It Became Common' (*The New York Times*, 19 August 2007) <https://www.nytimes.com/2007/08/19/business/yourmoney/19shelf.html> accessed 26 March 2022

Inbrief, 'Copyright Infringement: Remedies & Defences' (*Inbrief*, 2020) <https://www.inbrief.co.uk/intellectual-property/copyright-infringement/?msclkid=75d2aef7b31811ec9e479df9733f7c40> accessed 26 March 2022

Jackson-pollockorg/the-flamejsp, 'The Flame' (*Jackson Pollockorg*, 2023) <https://www.jackson-pollock.org/the-flame.jsp> accessed 12 February 2023

Jeffrey B, 'Too Close for Comfort' (*Architect Magazine*, 2 November 2007) https://www.architectmagazine.com/practice/too-close-for-comfort_o accessed 19 September 2023 and Shine, 382 F. Supp. 2d

Kay R, 'Viscose Vs Modal Vs Lyocell- Difference?' (*Robert Owen Undershirts*, 30 April 2017) <https://www.undershirts.co.uk/blogs/research/viscose-vs-modal-vs-lyocell> accessed 3 October 2021

Keane P, 'World's First Printed Haute Couture Vegan Dress Debuts' (*3D printingcom*, 6 July 2022) <https://3dprinting.com/news/worlds-first-printed-haute-couture-vegan-dress-debuts/> accessed 25 July 2022

Kessler A, 'Art and Couture Collided at the Couture Shows' (*British Vogue*, 28 January 2022) <https://www.vogue.co.uk/fashion/gallery/best-artistic-looks-couture-ss22> accessed 21 January 2025

Kılıç M, 'Design Protection in Türkiye' (*Mondaq*, 25 February 2021) <https://www.mondaq.com/turkey/trademark/1037324/design-protection-in-turkey> accessed 21 January 2025

Köse MY, HH Çelik and H Yıldız, 'Türkiye: Insights as to Turkish Copyright Law' (*Mondaq*, 2020) <https://www.mondaq.com/turkey/copyright/906084/insights-as-to-turkish-copyright-law> accessed 20 July 2023

Kostopoulos E, 'The Mystique That is Haute Couture: Your Guide to Fashion's Exclusive World' (*RUSSH*, 25 February 2021) <https://www.russh.com/what-is-haute-Couture/> accessed 6 July 2021

Krick J, 'Charles Frederick Worth (1825–1895) and the House of Worth' (*The Met*, October 2004) <https://www.metmuseum.org/toah/hd/wrth/hd_wrth.htm> accessed 6 July 2021

Lawrence I, 'Does the World of Haute Couture and Design Still Belong in Art?' (*Art Dealer Street*, 14 May 2021) <https://www.artdealerstreet.com/single-post/does-the-world-of-haute-Couture-and-design-still-belong-in-art#:~:text=Haute%20Couture%20is%20considered%20a,and%20a%20way%20to%20inspire> accessed 25 June 2022

Linssen Redferns M, 'How Madonna's Blond Ambition Tour Changed Pop Concerts Forever' (*Madonna Underground*, 17 April 2020) <https://madonnaunderground.com/how-madonnas-blond-ambition-tour-changed-pop-concerts-forever/> accessed 6 July 2021

LK Bennett, 'Fashion' (*LK Bennett*, 2021) <https://www.lkbennett.com/> accessed 6 July 2021

Lependorf J, 'Law Creating NEA is a Work of Art in Itself' (*Blue Mountain Center*, 2022)

Luenendonk M, 'Merger Doctrine' (*Cleverism*, 13 August 2016) <https://www.cleverism.com/lexicon/merger-doctrine/> accessed 9 June 2022

Luxiders, 'Victoria Beckham' (*Luxiders*, 2022) <https://luxiders.com/sustainable-brands-victoria-beckham/> accessed 9 July 2022

Lycra, 'Lycra Redefining Comfort and Fit Since 1958' (*Lycracom*, 2021) <https://www.lycra.com/en> accessed 31 December 2021

M&S, 'M&S' (*Marks and Spencers*, 2022) <https://www.marksandspencer.com/?msclkid=c0eb86e7ad8a11ec9c056fb791e72995> accessed 26 March 2022

Mackie D, '25 Reasons Madonna's Blond Ambition Tour Still Rules, 25 Years Later' (*People*, 13 April 2015) <https://people.com/celebrity/madonnas-blond-ambition-tour-25-years-later/> accessed 6 July 2021

Management (September 2006) <https://cdn.ymaws.com/www.almnet.org/resource/resmgr/Certification/Contact_Hour_Articles/047_PerformanceTextiles.pdf> accessed 6 July 2021

Market Watch News Department, 'Haute Couture Market Analysis Report 2023 Along With Statistics Figures, Forecasts Till 2028' (*Market Watch*, 26 November 2022)

Martel Fashion, 'The Function of Couture Clothing' (*Martel Fashion*, 22 March 2022)

Matalan, 'Matalan' (*Matalan*, 2022) <https://www.matalan.co.uk/?msclkid=4133f4f3ad8b11ec8111c3aa3ccb7da1> accessed 26 March 2022

McCartney S, 'Our Commitments' (*Stella McCartney*, 2022) <https://www.stellamccartney.com/gb/en/sustainability/our-commitments.html> accessed 9 July 2022

The Met, 'Dress Designer Paco Rabanne' (*The Met*, 2000) <https://www.metmuseum.org/art/collection/search/145899> accessed 12 February 2023

Mima Studios, 'Stages of Architectural Design' (*Mima Studios*, 2022) <https://mim.archi/blog/architecture/stages-of-architectural-design/> accessed 20 September 2023

Mower S, 'Alexander McQueen' (*Vogue*, 7 October 2004) <https://www.vogue.com/fashion-shows/spring-2005-ready-to-wear/alexander-mcqueen> accessed 19 August 2023

Obelisk Art History LLC, 'The Value of Art Why Should We Care About Art?' (*Obelisk Art History*, 2022) <https://arthistoryproject.com/essays/the-value-of-art/> accessed 15 July 2022

Oijala L, 'What is Fast Fashion' (*Leaf*, 2022) <https://www.leaf.tv/articles/what-is-fast-fashion/> accessed 26 March 2022

Oker-Blom M, 'Some Thoughts on Sustainability and Upcycling From a Copyright and Trademark Law Point of View' (*IPR University Centre*, 6 September 2022) <https://iprinfo.fi/artikkeli/some-thoughts-on-sustainability-and-upcycling-from-a-copyright-and-trademark-law-point-of-view/> accessed 20 September 2023

Oldfield B, 'Bruce Oldfield Couture' (*Bruce Oldfield Couture*, 2022) <https://bruceoldfield-Couture.com/> accessed 29 December 2022

Olsen C, 'High Fashion Meets High-Tech Innovation at MFA's #techstyle' (*The Tufts Daily*, 9 March 2016) <https://tuftsdaily.com/arts/2016/03/09/high-fashion-meets-high-tech-innovation-at-mfa/> accessed 11 February 2023

Oxford Economics (OE) and Glasgow Caledonian University (GCU), 'The High-end & Designer Manufacturing Report' (*BFC*, 2015) <https://www.britishfashioncouncil.co.uk/pressreleases/The-High-end--Designer-Manufacturing-Report> accessed 21 January 2025Peacocks, 'Peacocks' (*Peacocks*, 2022) <https://www.peacocks.co.uk/?msclkid=2eb85589ad8a11ec85599828b97029cc> accessed 26 March 2022

Pastore F, 'Elsa and the Artists' (*Sotheby's*, 1 March 2023) https://www.sothebys.com/en/articles/elsa-schiaparelli-and-the-artists accessed 10 March 2025

Philips M, 'Art vs Design: A Timeless Debate' (*Toptalcom*, 2021) <https://www.toptal.com/designers/creative-direction/art-vs-design#:~:text=Design%20is%20an%20art%20form%2C%20a%20method%20of,but%20there%20is%20no%20guarantee%20that%20it%20will> accessed 19 February 2022

Premiere Vision, 'About' (*Premiere Vision*, 2021) <https://www.premierevision.com/en/about/?> accessed 6 July 2021

Rab S, Serle Court, 'Legal Systems in the U.K. (England and Wales): Overview' (*Practical Law*, March 2021) <https://uk.practicallaw.thomsonreuters.com/5-636-2498?transitionType=Default&contextData=(sc.Default)&firstPage=true> accessed 22 December 2022

Ralph & Russo, 'The Couture Process' (*Ralph & Russo*, 2022) <https://ralphandrusso.com/pages/Couture-process> accessed 27 December 2022

Rauer N, 'Law on copyright in shapes clarified in Brompton Bicycle case' (Pinsent Masons, 15th June 2020) <https://www.pinsentmasons.com/out-law/news/law-copyright-shapes-brompton> accessed 21 January 2025, referring to the case of Brompton Bicycle Ltd v Chedech/Get2Get (C-833/18), Opinion of Advocate General M. Campos Sánchez-Bordona, E.U:C:2020:79

Reiss, 'Fashion' (*Reiss*, 2021) <https://www.reiss.com/> accessed 6 July

Rendle A and L Popple, 'Important CJEU Ruling Could Mean Copyright Protection Is Available for All Original Designs' (*Taylor Wessing*, 9 January 2020) <https://www.taylorwessing.com/en/insights-and-events/insights/2020/01/important-cjeu-ruling-could-mean-copyright-protection-is-available-for-all-original-designs> accessed 21 January 2025

Richard J, 'Vivienne Westwood: Vision and Craft Selected Excerpts From Claire Wilcox, Vivienne Westwood (London: V&A Publications, 2004)' (*Marammriettacom*, 2022) <https://www.maramarietta.com/the-arts/fashion/vivienne-westwood/> accessed 11 July 2022

Rimmer M, 'Crystal Palaces: Copyright Law and Public Architecture' (2002) 14(2) Bond Law Review 320–46 <https://ssrn.com/abstract=600865>

Rogers S, 'Madonna's Most Sensational Stage Costumes' (*Vogue*, 3 May 2019) <https://www.vogue.co.uk/gallery/madonna-tour-outfits> accessed 6 July 2021

Rosati E, 'Italian Supreme Court Rules That Technical Regulation (Drafted by an IP Lawyer) May Be *In Principle* Protected by Copyright' (*IP Kat*, 21 June 2020) <https://

ipkitten.blogspot.com/search/label/decision%2010300%2F2020%20Casucci%20v%20 Unipol%20Assicurazioni%20S.p.A.%20and%20Others> accessed 19 February 2022

SAS Institute Inc v World Programming Ltd, Case C-406/10 [2012] 3 CMLR. (4) 55,68, [AG44] (AG Bot) and Swarb, 'SAS Institute Inc v World Programming Ltd: CA 21 Nov 2013' (*SwarbcoU.K.*, 2013) <https://swarb.co.uk/sas-institute-inc-v-world-programming-ltd-ca-21-nov-2013/> accessed 22 December 2021

Searle A, 'Hepworth Sculpture Prize Review: A Brilliant Beginning' (*The Guardian*, 20 October 2016) <https://www.theguardian.com/artanddesign/2016/oct/20/hepworth-sculpture-prize-review-medalla-barlow-marten-claydon> accessed 20 September 2023

Selfridges, 'Gucci' (*Selfridges*, 2023) <https://www.selfridges.com/GB/en/cat/gucci-double-g-leather-belt_141-77035800-400593AP00T/> accessed 16 July 2023

Sender T, '3 Strategies for U.K. Fashion to Adapt to the Pressures of COVID-19' (*Mintel Blog*, 4 May 2020) <https://www.mintel.com/blog/retail-market-news/covid-19-is-putting-huge-pressure-on-the-UK-fashion-sector> accessed 6 July 2021

Shahbandeh M, 'Export Value of Apparel and Clothing Accessories in the United Kingdom (U.K.) From 2008 to 2020' (*Statista*, 5 July 2021) <https://www.statista.com/statistics/293466/exports-of-apparel-and-clothing-accessoriesr-total-value-in-the-united-kingdom-uk./> accessed 6 July 2021

Shahbandeh M, 'Clothing and Accessories Import Value in the United Kingdom (U.K.) 2019' (*Statista*, 2021) <https://www.statista.com/statistics/294280/import-value-of-apparel-and-clothing-accessoriesr-by-continent-in-the-united-kingdom-uk/> accessed 6 July 2021

Shahbandeh M, 'Number of Clothing and Footwear Wholesalers in the U.K. 2020' (*Statista*, 2021) https://www.statista.com/statistics/467057/uk-enterprises-in-the-wholesale-of-clothing-and-footwear-turnover/ accessed 6 July 2021

Shahbandeh M, 'Number of Enterprises for the Manufacture of Wearing Apparel in the United Kingdom (U.K.) From 2008 to 2019' (*Statista*, 29 June 2021) <https://www.statista.com/statistics/290323/manufacture-of-wearing-apparel-clothing-number-of-enterprises-in-the-united-kingdom-uk> accessed 6 July 2021

Silverman I, 'Copyright and Couture: A U.K. Perspective' (*WIPO*, June 2014) <https://www.wipo.int/web/wipo-magazine/articles/copyright-and-fashion-a-uk-perspective-38881> accessed 31 May 2021

Simon C, S Sefton and M Linsner, 'A Fabric Design Has Been Found to be a Work of Artistic Craftsmanship: Will Response Clothing Cause a Shift in How U.K. Copyright is Assessed?'(2020) 42(9) EIPR 612

Sokanu Interactive Inc, 'What Does a Technical Artist Do?' (*Career explorercom*, 2023) <https://www.careerexplorer.com/careers/technical-artist/> accessed 11 February 2023

Spirella, 'Corset Cover' (*V&A*, 21 November 2007) <https://collections.vam.ac.uk/item/O140747/corset-cover-spirella/> accessed 22 May 2022

Statista Research Department, 'Economic Contribution of the High-End Fashion Manufacturing Sector in the United Kingdom (U.K.) in 2013 and 2018, by Turnover and GVA' (*Statista*, 10 March 2015) <https://www.statista.com/statistics/418622/fashion-designer-purchases-united-kingdom-uk-manufacturers/> accessed 6 July 2021

Suluk C, 'Güzel Sanat Eserleri ve Telif' (*Fikri Mülkiyet*, 2 January 2019) <https://fikrimulkiyet.com/guzel-sanat-eserleri-ve-telif/> accessed 18 November 2022

Susan Devaney, 'Walis Simpson's Most Iconic Style Moments' (*Vogue*, 7 April 2020) <https://www.vogue.co.uk/gallery/wallis-simpson-style-file> accessed 27 June 2022

Sutherland E, 'The Ongoing Reign of Alexander McQueen' (*Drapers Online*, 10 February 2020) <https://www.drapersonline.com/news/the-ongoing-reign-of-alexander-mcqueen> accessed 27 December 2022

Swarb, 'George Hensher Ltd v Restawile Upholstery (Lancs) Ltd: HL 1975' (*Swarbcouk*, 2021) <https://swarb.co.uk/george-hensher-ltd-v-restawile-upholstery-lancs-ltd-hl-1975/> accessed 31 December 2021

Swarb, 'Procter and Gamble Company v Reckitt Benckiser (U.K.) Ltd: ChD 13 Dec 2006' (*Swarbcouk*, 2006) <https://swarb.co.uk/procter-and-gamble-company-v-reckitt-benckiser-uk-ltd-chd-13-dec-2006/> accessed 30 August 2021

Swarb, 'SAS Institute Inc v World Programming Ltd: CA 21 Nov 2013' (*Swarbcouk*, 2013) <https://swarb.co.uk/sas-institute-inc-v-world-programming-ltd-ca-21-nov-2013/> accessed 22 December 2021

Tate, 'Art Term Art Informel' (*Tate*, 2023) <https://www.tate.org.uk/art/art-terms/a/art-informel> accessed 23 June 2023

Tate, 'Conceptual Art' (*Tate*, 2022) <https://www.tate.org.uk/art/art-terms/c/conceptual-art> accessed 9 July 2022

Teg, 'What is Couture? The Guide to High Fashion' (*The Evans Group*, 15 June 2021) <https://tegintl.com/what-is-Couture/> accessed 27 December 2022

Testex Textile, 'What is the Textile Fabric Testing, Test Method, Test Item Classification' (*Testex Textile*, 21 June 2019) <https://www.testextextile.com/what-is-the-textile-fabric-testing-test-method-test-item-classification/> accessed 6 July 2021

Textile Today, 'Brexit Impact in U.K. Fashion Industry' (*Textile Today*, 6 February 2021) <https://www.textiletoday.com.bd/brexit-impact-uk-fashion-industry/> accessed 6 July 2021

TFL, 'France: Legal Protections for Fashion' (*The Fashion Law*, 2023) https://www.thefashionlaw.com/resource-center/france-legal-protections-for-fashion/ accessed 20 July 2023

Thompson A, 'Creating One-Off Pieces' (*Amanda Thompson Courture*, 4 October 2018) <https://www.amandathompsoncouture.co.uk/> accessed 9 November 2022

Times Higher Education, 'University Rankings, University of the Arts' (*Times Higher Education*, 2021) <https://www.timeshighereducation.com/world-university-rankings/university-arts-london> accessed 25 October 2021

Tiwari S, 'Top British Luxury Brands' (*Luxury Abode*, 3 June 2020) <https://www.luxuryabode.com/blog/top-british-luxury-fashion-brands/artid123> accessed 31 March 2022

Tucker L, 'Top Fashion Schools Around the World' (*QS*, April 2021) <https://www.topuniversities.com/courses/art-design/top-fashion-schools-around-world> accessed 25 October 2021

University of East London, 'BA (Hons) Fine Art Technology' (*University of London*, 2023) <https://www.uel.ac.UK/undergraduate/courses/ba-hons-fine-art-technology> accessed 11 February 2023

U.S. Department of State, 'Innovation Policy' (*U.S. Department of State*, 2022) <https://www.state.gov/innovation-policy/> accessed 19 November 2022

US Copyright Office, 'What Is Copyright' (*US Copyright Office*, 2021) <https://www.copyright.gov/> accessed 31 December 2021

Vogue, 'Couture by Numbers: What Does It Really Take to Make a Collection?' (*British Vogue*, 21 January 2024) <https://www.vogue.co.uk/fashion/article/couture-by-numbers> accessed 21 January 2025

Weeraworawit C, 'Geographical Indications and the Textiles Industry in Developing Countries: The Case for Multilateral Protection' (*Fordham Institute*, April 2019) <https://fordhamipinstitute.com/wp-content/uploads/2019/04/Chomwan_Fordham-2019_GIs-and-multilateral-protection_reduced-size.pdf> accessed 30 August 2021

Westbrook D, 'When Fashion Changes Society: John Galliano and the Representation of the Homeless' (*World Stock Market*, 17 January 2022) <https://www.worldstockmarket.net/when-fashion-changes-society-john-galliano-and-the-representation-of-the-homeless/> accessed 21 January 2025

Westwood V, 'Celebrating the History of the Vivienne Westwood Catwalk Complete Collections' (*Vivienne Westwood*, 9 June 2021) <https://blog.viviennewestwood.com/celebrating-the-history-of-the-vivienne-westwood-catwalk-complete-collections/> accessed 6 July 2021

Westwood V, 'Portrait Corset' (*Vivienne Westwood*, 2022) <https://www.viviennewestwood.com/en/women/clothing/corsets/portrait-corset-multicoloured-15030001W003VO207.html> accessed 14 June 2022

WIPO, 'Frequently Asked Questions: Geographical Indications' (*WIPO*, 2023) <https://www.WIPO.int/geo_indications/en/faq_geographicalindications.html> accessed 17 January 2023

WIPO, 'Summary of the Geneva Act of the Lisbon Agreement' (*WIPO*, 2020) <https://www.WIPO.int/treaties/en/registration/lisbon/summary_lisbon-geneva.html> accessed 30 August 2021

WIPO, 'Tűrkiye: Law No 6769 of December 22, 2016, on Industrial Property' (*WIPO*, 2017) https://www.wipo.int/wipolex/en/legislation/details/16609 accessed 31 December 2021

WIPO, 'Law No 6769 on Industrial Property, Türkiye' (*WIPO*, 2020) <https://www.wipo.int/wipolex/en/legislation/details/22592> accessed 21 January 2025

World Intellectual Property Organisation, 'Berne Convention for the Protection of Literary and Artistic Works' (*WIPO*, 2022) <https://www.WIPO.int/treaties/en/ip/berne/> accessed 16 February 2022

WWD Staff, 'Couture Fall 2022 Trend: Metal Mining' (*Womens Wear Daily (WWD)*, 25 July 2022) <https://wwd.com/fashion-news/fashion-trends/metal-metallic-trend-Couture-paris-1235260615/> accessed 25 July 2022

Your Patent Team, 'What is the Difference Between Product and Process Patent in India?' (*Your Patent Team*, 2019) <https://yourpatentteam.com/hrf_faq/difference-between-product-and-process-patent/> accessed 18 October 2021

Zarocostas J, 'The Role of IP Rights in the Couture Business: A US Perspective' (*WIPO*, 3 August 2018) <https://www.wipo.int/web/wipo-magazine/articles/the-role-of-ip-rights-in-the-fashion-business-a-us-perspective-40479> accessed 21 January 2025

Index

Note: Page numbers in *italics* indicate figures, **bold** indicate tables in the text, and references following "n" refer notes.

Kolibri 360 GmbH
Ferdinand-Jühlke-Straße 7
99095 Erfurt, Deutschland
produktsicherheit@kolibri360.de